The Practice of Advertising

Edited by
Adrian R. Mackay

Fifth edition

ELSEVIER
BUTTERWORTH
HEINEMANN

AMSTERDAM • BOSTON • HEIDELBERG • LONDON • NEW YORK • OXFORD
PARIS • SAN DIEGO • SAN FRANCISCO • SINGAPORE • SYDNEY • TOKYO

Elsevier Butterworth-Heinemann
Linacre House, Jordan Hill, Oxford OX2 8DP
30 Corporate Drive, Burlington, MA 01803

First published 1978
Reprinted 1981
Second edition 1983
Reprinted 1984, 1985, 1986
Third edition 1990
Reprinted 1990, 1993
Fourth edition 1995
Reprinted 1996, 2001
Fifth edition 2005

British Library Cataloguing in Publication Data
A catalogue record for this book is available from the British Library

Library of Congress Cataloguing in Publication Data
A catalogue record for this book is available from the Library of Congress

ISBN 0 7506 6173 9

For information on all Elsevier Butterworth-Heinemann
publications visit our website at http://books.elsevier.com

Typeset by Newgen Imaging Systems (P) Ltd, Chennai, India
Printed and bound in Great Britain

Working together to grow
libraries in developing countries

www.elsevier.com | www.bookaid.org | www.sabre.org

ELSEVIER   BOOK AID
            International   Sabre Foundation

Contents

List of Contributors

Sarah Asprey

Sarah Asprey began her career in marketing and PR before moving into advertising 5 years ago. Sarah is now client services director of RAA Sprague Gibbons, one of the UK's leading independent recruitment advertising and communications agencies. Sarah began writing during her PR agency career, and has continued with it at RAA, producing marketing and editorial material for RAA, and client documents and papers. Sarah is committed to RAA Sprague Gibbons as one of the few truly independent recruitment advertising agencies in the UK, in a marketplace dominated by large plcs. Sarah's ideas have helped RAA to become the well-respected agency it is today, in particular with regard to shaping the client services function. Sarah believes that recruitment advertising needs to raise its profile to attract a better calibre of people into the industry, and become a more highly respected specialist service and profession. She considers that the existence of more educational text on the subject will help in this.

Marilyn Baxter

Marilyn Baxter is Chairman of Hall & Partners Europe, specialists in brand and communications research.

She has spent over 25 years in advertising and research in a number of agencies, most notably at Saatchi & Saatchi Advertising where she was Executive Planning Director and Vice Chairman for 12 years. During her time in advertising she was a Fellow and Member of the Council of the Institute of Practitioners in Advertising and Chairman of the IPA's Value of Advertising Committee. She is a Full Member of the Market Research Society and an Honorary Member of the Account Planning group.

She is also the Non-executive Director of the Government's Central Office of Information (COI).

Marilyn previously worked in a think tank (at IPC) and in public policy (at the National Economic Development Office).

She is a frequent writer and speaker on advertising, communications and related issues.

Peter Beaumont

Peter Beaumont is a director of Eclipse Creative Consultants Limited, a full service advertising and design agency based in Chester.

Peter began his career in advertising in 1985 joining Thompson Regional Newspapers (TRN) working in the tele-ad department for his local paper.

Progressing through both the classified and display advertisement departments, he left with colleagues in 1990 to set up his own agency.

Peter has regularly presented seminars and training sessions for both clients and newspaper groups and was also instrumental in helping Eclipse to become one of the first North West agencies to receive the coveted Investor in People Award.

Sangeet Kaur Chana

Sangeet Kaur Chana graduated with a Law degree from Leeds University before going on to qualify as a solicitor in 2000 having completed her legal training with Leeds firm, Gordons. After a period practising as a commercial litigator, Sangeet chose media law as her niche specialism leaving private practice to join Granada Media as an in-house lawyer in 2001. Sangeet is involved in most areas of Granada's business including advising production departments on legal compliance of programmes and intellectual property issues, negotiation and drafting of a wide range of commercial agreements, management and resolution of legal disputes and other non-contentious matters.

Ann Murray Chatterton

Ann Murray Chatterton is Director of Training and Development at the Institute of Practitioners in Advertising. The IPA is the trade body and professional institute for leading agencies in the UK's advertising, media and marketing communications industry and its role is to define, develop and help maintain the highest possible standards of professional practice within the business. Training and development is therefore an essential part of its service to the industry. Ann has spent 23 years on the practitioner side, starting out at the multi-national agency, Masius Wynne-Williams & D'Arcy MacManus (latterly known as D'Arcy) and subsequently running her own agency, Marshall Advertising. Ann joined the IPA in 1999 and, as well as overseeing the industry's growing training course portfolio, she launched the IPA's CPD accreditation standard in 2000 and the first in a new series of IPA professional qualifications in 2003. Ann read French Studies (BA Hons) at Portsmouth Polytechnic and The Science and Techniques of Audio Visual Communication at Bordeaux University. She is a member of WACL (Women in Advertising and Communications London) and the Marketing Society.

Leslie Claridge

Leslie Claridge is currently a principal lecturer in the School of Printing and Publishing at the London College of Communication. He is a printer by profession and in recent times has worked extensively in electronic imaging and desktop publishing. He is a training specialist responsible for vocational study in the specialised areas of printing, publishing and media studies. He is also a Fellow of the Institute of Administrative Management.

Martyn P. Davis

Martyn P. Davis, now an independent marketing communications consultant, has working experience with advertisers, agencies and media-owners, as well as academic institutions in this country and abroad. He attended the Harvard Business School and, on his return, was a founder and executive director of the Cambridge International Marketing Programme.

Martyn is the author of *The Effective Use of Advertising Media, Business-to-Business Marketing and Promotion* and *Successful Advertising: Key Alternative Approaches* as well as numerous articles.

A former member of the National Council of the Advertising Association, he was also a senior examiner for the Chartered Institute of Marketing and Moderator for the CAM Foundation examinations. Martyn was also a course director for the Chartered Institute of Marketing Interact International and for Popular Communication Courses, and has worldwide international experience.

Nigel Foster

Nigel Foster, Head of TV, J. Walter Thompson, originally started his career as a press production executive. Nigel moved to TV production from account management at Wasey-Campbell Ewald (as was) in 1980. He worked at FCB and KMP (Head of TV) before joining JWT, and over the years has worked on some of the UK's most prestigious clients, including British Airways, Dulux, Goodyear Tyres, Vauxhall Motors, British Telecom, Kellogg's and Esso.

Christopher Graham

Christopher Graham is Director General of the Advertising Standards Authority (ASA), the body that supervises the self-regulatory system of advertising controls in non-broadcast media. Christopher joined the ASA in April 2000 from the BBC, where he was Secretary to the Corporation – a role that had much to do with self-regulation, but nothing to do with advertising.

Christopher joined the BBC as a News Trainee and became a current affairs producer, first in radio and later in TV. Away from the BBC, Christopher was a producer on Channel 4's *A Week in Politics*.

Since April 2003, Christopher has been Chairman of the European Advertising Standards Alliance (EASA), the 'single authoritative voice of advertising self-regulation in Europe', which brings together the advertising self-regulatory systems of the 25 Member States of the European Union. Before becoming Chairman, he led the Self-Regulatory Committee of EASA.

Christopher has been closely involved in the discussions that led to the proposal by the new broadcasting and communications regulator Ofcom to contract out responsibility for complaints about TV and radio advertisements to a self-regulatory body 'under the banner of the ASA'.

He is a non-executive director of Electoral Reform Services Ltd, the not-for-profit balloting company.

David J. Hanger

David Hanger is a board director of The Economist Group. He is Publisher of The Economist Newspaper and director of economist.com.

He joined The Economist in 1968, and was appointed Worldwide Advertisement Director in 1979, adding Director with responsibility for group development in 1990, and Director of Specialist Magazines in 1994.

He holds a Diploma in Marketing and a Diploma in Management Studies, is a fellow of the Communications, Advertising and Marketing Foundation, a member of the Chartered Institute of Marketing, Immediate Past World President of the International Advertising Association, a board director of Creston plc, SITEL Inc and of the Advertising Standards Board of Finance, Master Elect of the Worshipful Company of Marketors and a Freeman of the City of London.

Richard Jeans

Richard Jeans was born in 1934. He went to school in Wales, read Classics at Oxford and was commissioned into the Intelligence Corps for National Service.

Primarily a writer, he spent 8 years with an engineering company, Dexion Ltd, ending up as Advertising Manager, responsible for all national and international advertising and sales promotion.

He left to join Roles & Parker (a pioneer business advertising agency) as Senior Writer.

Moved on to become a founder member of Primary Contact, where he was from time to time Creative Director, Deputy Managing Director and Chairman – sometimes all at once. It became Europe's largest business advertising agency, and was sold to Ogilvy.

Richard moved on to become founder member and Chairman of CHJS, which he left in 1995 to become a consultant.

He has worked on hundreds of business and quite a few consumer accounts, and has performed in most agency functional roles (but cannot do regression analysis). He has picked up all the awards you do pick up if you hang around long enough and let people enter the work.

Ian Linton

Ian Linton is a professional writer, specialising in business-to-business communications and management books. He has handled a wide range of integrated marketing communications for clients such as Barclays Bank, BP, Cisco, Ford, IBM, ICL, Shell Oils and Siemens, and is the author of more than 20 business books, mainly in the fields of customer service and marketing communications. He is co-author with Kevin Morley, founder of KMM, of *Integrated Marketing Communications*, also published by Butterworth-Heinemann.

Robert Love and Jackie Hewitt

Robert Love and Jackie Hewitt both work for Thomson Directories, as part of a Strategic Marketing group. Thomson Directories publish the Thomson Local and ThomsonLocal.com.

As Marketing Research Manager, Robert carries out research among directory users and advertisers to gain insights essential for strategic planning. With over 10 years' experience in marketing he has worked on both agency and client sides of market research.

Jackie has spent her whole career in marketing communications working for both b2c and b2b brands for over 11 years. She is a marketing communications manager and specialises in strategy, advertising and public relations.

Jackie is a full member of the Chartered Institute of Marketing.

Adrian R. Mackay

A Life-Science graduate, Adrian R. Mackay (Mac) gained significant marketing experience with Beecham and Nutricia, then worked in Home Counties advertising agencies before becoming Marketing Manager within Rhone Poulenc. He established Duncan Alexander & Wilmshurst in 1992 – Marketing and Training Consultants – and is Managing Partner.

Mac is a Faculty Member of the Chartered Institute of Marketing, a full Member and an examiner with the Chartered Management Institute. He has tutored on ISBA courses for advertiser companies and has an enviable reputation as a writer and speaker.

He holds a Diploma in Marketing and was one of the first in the UK to achieve a Master's Degree (MBA) in Strategic Marketing.

He co-authored *The Fundamentals of Advertising*, 2nd Ed. (1999) and *The Fundamentals and Practice of Marketing*, 4th Ed. (2002), both with John Wilmshurst and published by Butterworth Heinemann.

Mark Maguire

Mark Maguire started in the industry as an apprentice hand planner and platemaker (4-year indentured course) with the Mullis Morgan Group and moved on to digital pagemakeup systems where he was promoted to Production Director. In 2000 he joined TAG (The Adplates Group) and was subsequently appointed as Production Director of Tag@Comma, a newly formed joint venture with Comma (part of the Publicis Group), in March of that year. In September 2002 he set up Tag@Ogilvy and Tag@D'Arcy as in-house production facilities for the agencies Ogilvy & Mather and D'Arcy Masius Benton and Bowles, respectively. He currently sits on the executive committee of the APPA

(Advertising and Prepress Association) as Vice Chairman. The Association represents a group of companies, engaged in pre-press, digital production and allied businesses in response to an industry demand, to act as a standard bearer for quality and technology for the advertising, publishing and printing industries.

Richard Mayer

Richard Mayer, MA DIPM MCIM (Chartered Marketer), is Senior Lecturer in Marketing at the University of Derby where he is responsible for the management and teaching of CIM and Masters programmes.

Richard is also director of his own training company and has a wide range of experience in the running of marketing training programmes in both business to business and consumer marketing sectors. He has recently run courses for Heinz, Michelin, Scottish Widows and Ford in the UK and internationally with Bahrain Telecom and The Institute of Banking in Riyadh. He directs seminar programmes in Principles of Marketing, Business to Business marketing, Marketing Services and Strategic Marketing.

Richard has published in a number of marketing journals and is co-author of two marketing texts: *Internet Marketing* and *Introduction to Marketing*. He is also a contributory author for various marketing study guides.

Mike Monkman

Mike Monkman began his career in the research department of Odhams Press – part of the original IPC group. He then spent 15 years at Masius, first as a researcher and then as a media planning group head.

In 1983 he left Masius to set up his own consultancy. Since then he has received commissions from many media owners and media agencies. He is the technical consultant to the Institute of Practitioners in Advertising on television research, and is the co-editor with Colin McDonald of the *MRG's Guide to Media Research*, published in 1995.

Gareth Richards

Gareth Richards was born in 1958. Following a PhD in Plant Biochemistry at Kings College in London, he spent two years working for an American University before moving into advertising. He joined business-to-business agency CHJS as an Account Executive and spent 10 years with the agency managing integrated campaigns for a range of blue-chip clients – including Ericsson, Digital, and Sony.

He then spent two years on the client-side as Marketing Communications Manager for broadcast manufacturer Snell & Wilcox.

He joined Ogilvy Primary Contact in 1999 as a Business Director specialising in New Economy clients. He then ran a technology account group, before becoming Managing Director in January 2002.

Brenda Simonetti
Brenda Simonetti has worked in the promotional marketing industry for almost 30 years. She is a Past Chairman and Fellow of the Institute of Sales Promotion and, as sales promotions manager of Quaker Oats, served on the sales promotion sub-committees of the Advertising Standards Association, the Incorporated Society of British Advertisers and the FDF. She has also worked for a leading sales promotion agency, Clarke Hooper and a major supplier, Megaprint.

Her wide experience of all aspects of the industry is invaluable in her current position as Standards and Practices Consultant to the Institute of Sales Promotion.

Roger Stotesbury
Before setting up as Founding Director of the Milton Keynes-based advertising agency **infocus**, Roger worked with many of the top London agencies of the 1980s and 1990s. On the client-side at BT he helped establish the discipline of advertising-led integrated communications. He is a graduate of Imperial College and previously worked in the film industry. In 2003 he established the Milton Keynes Region Marketing Network.

Richard K. Warren
Richard K. Warren has worked in advertising for 15 years. During that time he has worked both in the UK and in the USA, on brands including: Asda, Pirelli, Midland Bank, First Direct, Boots, Cable & Wireless, Snapple and Charles Schwab.

In 2000 Richard was a founding partner in the management buyout of Delaney Lund Knox Warren. As Director of Strategy, he has strategic responsibility for the HBOS account, including Halifax, Bank of Scotland and Birmingham Midshires brands.

He is a regular speaker at conferences and has won both APG and IPA Effectiveness gold awards.

John Wilmshurst
John Wilmshurst ran his own marketing consultancy for 25 years with clients including Dun and Bradstreet, Shell International, Smith Kline Beecham, The Met Office, British Rail and the Open University. He conducted many training courses for his own clients and on behalf of the Chartered Institute of Marketing, of which he is a Fellow.

After selling his company (to form Duncan Alexander & Wilmshurst) he became a part-time director and chairman of Mustard Group in Kent.

He authored *Below-the-line Promotion* (1993) and co-authored *The Fundamentals of Advertising*, 2nd Ed. (1999) and *The Fundamentals and Practice of Marketing*, 4th Ed. (2002), both with Adrian 'Mac' Mackay and published by Butterworth Heinemann. He is a visiting lecturer at the University of Greenwich.

He is also Past-Master of his London Livery Company, the Worshipful Company of Carmen.

Preface

The Practice of Advertising, fifth edition has been completely revised and updated building on the original and much respected work of the late Editor, Norman Hart, who guided the text through the former four editions. Through his work, *The Practice of Advertising* gained its rightful place on the reading lists of many courses both in the UK and overseas. It has for many become a standard text.

This new edition has been thoroughly reviewed and updated to address crucial issues in today's advertising industry, presenting a thorough overview of its components.

This fifth edition has been revamped to feature the latest thinking with modern examples, thereby illustrating key points and supporting underlying principles. A wide spectrum of topics is covered, including:

- The roles of the advertiser and advertising agency
- Media
- Creativity
- Research
- Planning and budgeting
- Integrated Marketing Communications
- Business-to-business advertising
- Services advertising
- Directory advertising
- International advertising
- A career in advertising

New chapters in this edition feature: 'How advertising works' and 'Getting the best from advertising agencies and other outside suppliers'.

The specialist knowledge provided by the contributors – who are all top professionals in their own fields – offers a valuable insight for those wishing to gain a solid grounding in the subject. It is a valuable resource for students following CIM or CAM Certificate or Diploma courses or degrees in Business or Media Studies as well as for practitioners looking for a wider understanding.

Without the efforts of each and every contributor who have worked extremely hard to produce their manuscripts on time, this edition would not be in your hands today. I extend a personal thanks to them all on your behalf for making their specialist subject so engaging.

Final thanks must go to Jan Mackay, whose patience and tenacity working with the contributors and with the text has made this publication possible – I am so grateful that I am now married to the right woman!

Adrian R. Mackay

1 Marketing – and the Place of Advertising within It

Adrian R. Mackay

Learning outcomes

By the end of this chapter you will:

- Understand what marketing means.
- Have a clear idea of what is meant by the 'marketing concept'.
- Recognise the complex pattern of buying influences and that advertising is just one factor in the arena.
- Understand the place of marketing research and the information needs it can fulfil.
- See that the four Ps of marketing is out of date and explore the modern seven C model of the marketing mix.
- Explore how the marketing mix fits within strategic marketing planning and the place of marketing communications.

1.1   What does marketing mean?

Marketing is the management process responsible for identifying, anticipating and satisfying customer requirements profitably.

> Chartered Institute of Marketing Definition

Before going any further, look back at the definition above. What for you is the key word in the definition?

Is it *customer*? Indeed, marketing is about customers. The whole purpose of many an organisation has to do with meeting customer requirements and making a profit.

So is it *profitable*? Certainly, one needs to profit from the interaction between customers and the organisation and so much the better if both the customer and the organisation are satisfied by some sort of 'profit'.

So perhaps you feel that the key word is *satisfying*? Well, no business is going far without satisfying the needs of someone from those with a financial stake in the business, the creditors and the employees; and these are satisfied in the long term when customers continue to be satisfied. But how do we know what they need?

Then, does *identifying* needs seem paramount? Clearly this is going to be crucial, yet so will many other organisations be aiming to identify the same needs so there may be more than just satisfying identified needs alone.

Thus, *anticipating* needs suggests that if we can do this better than our competitors, we will keep ahead. So, perhaps that is the most fundamental. But without being able to satisfy the current need, the organisation may not survive long enough to deal with those anticipated needs!

All that is left is '*management process*'. If one takes a moment of reflection, how do any of the above happen without someone making sure that they do? How can an organisation identify, anticipate or satisfy any given customer requirement and make a profit without someone managing the process? Thus, the management process is the foundation for all successful marketing.

So, in the definition, it is the *management process* that is responsible for 'identifying, anticipating and satisfying customer requirements profitably' that enables everything else to happen. And it is the duty of all the people in an organisation whose activities make up all the processes that ultimately deliver what the customer needs. These are the marketing people and they are not just confined to the 'marketing' department.

However, the term 'marketing' is used in different ways by different people; so, let us disentangle these differences at the outset. Commonly, there are three ways in which people use the term:

1   As a description for some part of the organisation or in a person's function or job title, such as the 'marketing department' or the 'marketing director'.
2   To describe certain techniques used by the organisation. Such activities as advertising, market research and sometimes sales or product development, can be conveniently described by the collective term 'marketing' to distinguish them from other activities coming under the heading of 'production', 'finance' and similar main sub-divisions of an organisation. Some organisations feel that producing an advertisement or launching a web page is 'doing the marketing'.
3   To indicate a particular approach to business, or a management attitude, in relation to customers and their needs. This 'business philosophy' has become known as the 'marketing concept'.

It is in this third way that the term is mainly used here, and the meaning and implication of the marketing concept are discussed below.

1.2   The marketing concept

Many activities are particularly concerned with a company's relations with its customers – for example, market research, public relations, customer enquiries and advertising. Often these activities are grouped together under the collective term 'marketing'.

Since we all see advertising, buy products and services, or get direct mail through our letterboxes, we all 'consume' great volumes of 'marketing' and, therefore, become immediate experts. Since it appears so simple to the 'man (or woman) in the street' the role is often added to some poor hapless individual's task list with varying, and often poor, results.

However, marketing in its fullest sense must motivate the whole company from the managing director, through to keyboard operators, all must be concerned with marketing. To put the marketing label on some parts of the business might suggest that they and only they are concerned with marketing. This in turn would mean that they and only they are *concerned about the customers on which the business depends. The saying 'Marketing is too important an activity to be trusted to the marketing department'* contains a great deal of truth. A fairly common solution to the problem is to label these specialist departments 'Marketing Services'.

Be that as it may, we do commonly find within a company structure a marketing department set up something along the following lines.

Marketing is one of the three basic areas of activity in the typical industrial business. It begins by influencing the format of the product to secure maximum acceptance in the market. It also defines the prices at which and the quantities in which it should be offered in any given period to secure the maximum return to the business in the long term.

It normally includes:

1   An evaluation of the market and estimates of sales
2   Development of the marketing approach or policy
3   The planning and operation of the marketing function over all – internal and external – for maximising sales and for dealing with customers
4   All forms of promoting sales
5   Setting budgets for the marketing activity
6   The evaluation of results by reference to internal data and the results of market research.

This is a perfectly valid and worthwhile approach, provided it does not obscure the need for the whole company to be committed to the management process that 'identifies, anticipates and satisfies customer requirements efficiently and profitably'.

In its fullest sense, the marketing concept is a philosophy of business. Simply stated, it means that customers seeking satisfaction becomes the economic and social justification of a company's existence. So, all company activities in production, engineering, and finance, as well as in marketing, must be devoted first to determining what the customer's wants are and then to satisfying those wants while still making a reasonable profit.

1.2.1   Social marketing and the concept of value – a wider view of marketing

It is becoming increasingly recognised that the marketing concept is just as applicable in non-commercial situations, where profit at least in the strict sense is not one of the objectives, as in commercial situations. The term 'social marketing' is often used in this context. Government departments, the police, trade unions and trade associations, environmental groups and churches can all be said in a sense to have 'customers' and to be offering 'products' and 'services'.

However, all of these types of organisation have a problem to some degree with the term 'customer'. Yet, nonetheless, there is always some individual that is involved with the organisation and has some interest in the 'output' of what it is doing and will interact with that organisation to a varying degree. Since such 'customers' have a stake in what is going on, the term *stakeholder* has been used to help understand how the organisation may add value to the transactional relationship for the other party.

While any organisation that is legal has a right to exist, no organisation has a right to the support that is required if it is to exist. Therefore, do not be skilful in making a customer suit the interest of the business – be skilful in convincing and then making the business do what suits the interests of the customer. From this philosophy will come the concept of 'customer advocacy' – that is the support the organisation needs to prosper.

1.3   The marketing process

We can view marketing as a constant series of actions and reactions between customers and the marketing organisations trying to satisfy their needs. Customers make their needs and/or problems known while organisations make it their business to receive the information. They use their resources (money, materials, skills and ingenuity) to develop ways of satisfying the needs. Firms must then communicate the existence of the 'solutions' back to the customers, whose needs created the 'problems' (Figure 1.1). Customers will gladly pay for solutions to their problems or satisfaction of their needs.

1.4   The changing marketing environment

The object of marketing is to satisfy consumer needs. Those needs consist not merely of physiological urges (to eat, sleep and be warm) but such other needs

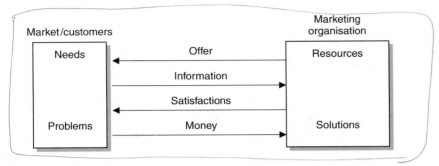

Figure 1.1   *The marketing process*

as to be loved and respected, to feel secure and not threatened and to develop one's personality to the fullest extent possible.

So, what shapes these needs and gives emphasis to one desire or another? Only by understanding these mechanisms can marketing ultimately be more than a mixture of carefully measured trial and error. ('If we sold the goods they must have been what the customers wanted').

At present the mechanisms are not wholly understood. The science of social studies (also called behavioural studies) carries out many research programmes, and the results of these investigations are gradually becoming available. They are still fragmentary, not always easy to relate to the marketing situation and too complex to do more than touch on here. But students of marketing should be aware of a pattern of knowledge that is beginning to take shape.

Figure 1.2 shows some of the many influences that go to shape a person's needs and responses; this has been modified in the light of recent thoughts on the influences on the individual – see Chapter 2.

There are a number of 'models' of the way buyer behaviour operates. The simplest is the 'economic model' that takes the view that people act in a purely rational way to optimise the satisfactions gained from their expenditure, balancing cost with value. This is probably true to some extent of industrial purchases (although how far it is true even there is disputed). But it is largely discounted by most marketing experts in the consumer field, especially for low-cost everyday purchases.

Much more favoured is the 'social–psychological model', which takes the view that human beings are social animals much influenced by the groups to which they belong – their family, workmates, their 'social class', etc. Friends, neighbours and other acquaintances, particularly those they would like to emulate and to whose life-style they aspire, are our 'reference groups' and have considerable influence on our behaviour ('Keeping up with the Joneses' is one everyday expression of this approach, 'peer group pressure' another). See Section 2.4.4 – How Advertising Works p31.

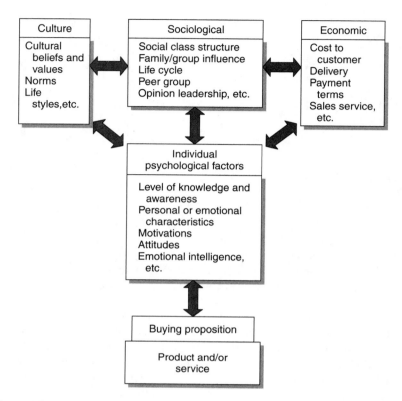

Figure 1.2   *The complex pattern of buying influences*[1]

It is known that some individuals set the pattern within their own circle of acquaintances. They are the 'opinion leaders', the trend-setters – the first to have a home sauna, a digital video camera or a third generation mobile telephone.

A person's purchasing behaviour changes as they move through their life cycle. One definition suggests the following stages:

1   Single.
2   Young married or cohabiting couples with no children.
3   People with young children.
4   Couples or single parents with older children.
5   Older people, children left home (the 'Empty Nesters').
6   Sole survivors.

Fairly obviously, the buying patterns of young married people setting up home for the first time (carpets, furniture, crockery, pictures) will be quite different from those with a young family (baby clothes, different foods, toys) and so on. Equally clearly, the cultural outlook of the community in which they live will influence what people spend their money on.

Figure 1.2 above takes all these ideas as having some relevance. It shows all the influences mentioned – cultural, sociological and economic – each having an influence on the individual's own psychological make-up, their attitudes and motivations.

1.4.1   Influencing consumer behaviour

Listed on Figure 1.2, under the heading 'Individual psychological factors', are three particularly important items: (1) level of knowledge and awareness, (2) motivations (which are closely related to the needs we discussed above) and (3) attitudes. This list suggests three very important ways in which we can influence consumer behaviour:

1   We can increase the level of knowledge and awareness. For example, we can tell people of the existence of a product they were previously unaware of, or we can tell them facts about its performance or the benefits it will bring them.
2   We can show people how our product will help to satisfy their needs. This is the basis of the 'emotional appeals' used in advertising.
3   We can change their attitudes. The view taken of mobile phones in the early 1980s was that most people saw them as unnecessary or even a rather expensive extravagance regarded as a gimmick. Today, they are largely taken for granted with an average of over 60 per cent penetration in Europe[2].

1.5   Customers and their behaviour

Since the customer is the focal point of all business activity, we must be clear about how customers behave. Because marketing is concerned with satisfying people's needs, we must understand what those needs are and the ways in which people go about getting them satisfied.

Any individual has a whole range of needs that they must or would like to satisfy, from the purely physical necessity of food and drink, through the emotional wish to be loved and appreciated to the desire to develop their personality – through education, a leisure activity or a fulfilling occupation. An American psychologist, A.L. Maslow, has expressed these varying levels of need in a way that is still useful today in the marketing context. He has written of the 'hierarchy of needs', the following five-stage progression[3]:

1   Basic physiological needs (food, sleep, warmth).
2   Safety needs (protection from danger).

3   The need for recognition (love, belonging).
4   Ego needs (self-esteem, respect from others).
5   Self-fulfilment (realisation of one's total being, creativity).

It is clear that, as we progress through these stages, we are dealing first with needs that all people at all times have to some extent or other and have to satisfy in order to live. At the other end of the scale we have needs that few will ever satisfy, mainly because the majority of people are preoccupied with the more pressing needs at the lower levels. On the other hand, once a pressing need is satisfied, it is no longer felt. This is why people with sufficient income to keep them well fed, safe and warm become more and more aware of other, less basic needs, such as egosatisfaction. 'Keeping up with the Joneses' may or may not be laudable but it does become a strong need for many people once they are fed, housed and clothed to a reasonable level.

Thus, individuals will vary widely in the needs that at present preoccupy them. Some will be mainly concerned with acquiring the bare necessities (you will fail to interest them in fancy furnishings), whereas others will be seeking exciting leisure pursuits (no good talking to them about buying their first television – they already have four!)

We also need to be aware of how people satisfy their needs. There is a multi-stage process, which can be expressed as follows:

1   *Need.* A need is felt. This may be a vague or general need (I am feeling jaded and need a bit of excitement) or specific (I want to go to the cinema today).
2   *Search.* Ways of satisfying the need are actively or passively sought. The newspapers and magazines may be scanned for offers that may satisfy the need (e.g. the lists of 'What's on' in entertainment); or one may merely keep ones' eyes and ears open and register more keenly than usual any possible solutions to their need.

In more complex situations the search process may be long and deliberate. The family seeking new kitchen equipment will read magazines, talk to friends, go to showrooms and exhibitions. The industrial buyer may ask for samples, demonstrations and competitive tenders or carry out extensive cost-benefit analysis.

3   *Decision.* When sufficient information has been gathered and suitable alternatives examined, a decision will be taken and the purchase made.
4   *Post-purchase feelings.* For the customer-oriented company the process does not end when the purchase is made. The customer's need is only satisfied if the product or service does perform in the expected fashion and does indeed meet their need, not only initially but, where appropriate, over

a longer period. It must perform in the expected way, and after-sales service must be adequate. Indeed, in some situations, advertising can be used to target existing customers to maintain their brand loyalty.

The precise way in which this process works needs to be understood. It will vary from one group of consumers to another, in particular in its time-scale: for a snack bought to satisfy a sudden pang of hunger the whole process may be over in a few minutes, but for a power station or a new military aircraft it will take many years. The domestic appliance industry in the UK wasted vast sums on advertising at one stage because it did not clearly appreciate that only when people are in the 'search' stage will they be receptive to advertising of this kind of product.

1.6   The need for marketing research

All business is conducted under conditions of risk and uncertainty – particularly about the future. Obviously, the future cannot be known totally, the uncertainty cannot be completely removed or the risks precisely calculated. However, it is asking for trouble not to use whatever information is available. Many facts can be known and unnecessary risk can thus be avoided.

For example, while a firm can very easily know how its own sales are progressing, this information is relatively meaningless without knowledge of the total size of the market and whether that is increasing or decreasing. Often, information on the total market is freely available – from government statistics, trade associations or similar sources. If it is not freely available in this way, market research techniques can be used to get it. But, as we shall see in Chapters 13 and 14, this is just one example of the vital necessity for information about the market situation.

The overwhelming reason for carrying out market research, however, is to keep open the channels of communication between customers and ourselves so that we can more effectively understand and then satisfy their needs.

1.6.1   Marketing information systems

In a well-ordered and sophisticated marketing-oriented organisation, marketing research will be part of a totally integrated marketing information system encompassing information derived from:

1   The internal accounting system, especially sales analysis.
2   Market intelligence, i.e. the capturing of information from many sources, including the media, industry reports, etc., regarding matters such as the economic situation and competitor activity.
3   Market research of all kinds.

The following sections highlight some fundamental marketing information needs:

1.6.1.1   Market research

1   What is the size of the market (in terms of volume and/or value) and is it decreasing or increasing?
2   What are the market shares of our competitors and ourselves and are these changing?
3   How are the size and trend of the market influenced by various factors (economic, social and seasonal)?
4   What is the composition of the market in terms of age groups, income groups, size of the company or geographical area?
5   What are the main distribution channels and how do they function?

1.6.1.2   Competitor research

1   What competitors are there and how do their product ranges, prices, etc., compare?
2   What are their marketing strategies?
3   How are their products distributed, advertised, packaged?
4   How does their sales force operate?
5   Are any new competitors likely to enter the market?

1.6.1.3   Product research

1   Who are our customers and what are their needs?
2   Which products do consumers prefer and why?
3   Are proposed new products acceptable?
4   Do consumers have complaints about products presently on the market that could indicate a possible new product opportunity?
5   What is the customer's reaction to new product concepts?

1.6.1.4   Advertising/marketing communications research

1   Who reads which publications; who watches/listens to which TV/radio channels?
2   Are existing or proposed advertising campaigns communicating effectively?
3   What are the motivations that activate consumers and is our advertising correctly interpreting them?
4   How do customers react to proposed advertising themes (copy-testing)?

1.6.2   How marketing research is organised

Marketing research is a specialised job. While in principle it can be carried out by anyone, there are serious potential pitfalls, as follows:

1 The necessary objective, unbiased approach needs to be acquired or 'trained into' people. Salesmen, for example, are usually not suitable for obtaining research information, because their training and instincts are such that they are enthusiasts for a particular point of view – partisan for their own product. If not, they might well be less effective as salesmen.
2 Some of the techniques employed demand skills and disciplines that have to be learned.

Usually, therefore, marketing research is a task for the specialist. These specialists are found in three main groups.

1.6.2.1   'In-company' departments

Many companies have their own marketing research departments. This has the advantage that the people concerned can specialise, and over the years acquire great knowledge of the fields in which they operate and the best techniques for gathering information for their particular purposes. It can thus be a very economic way of providing the necessary information. The disadvantages are a possible tendency to bias, which can, of course, be guarded against and resisted; and the fact that it may be difficult to give them a full workload at all times, so that the operation may become uneconomic. But they do provide additional security of information.

1.6.2.2   Advertising agencies

Advertising agencies need to prepare advertising campaigns within a total marketing plan and in the light of the fullest possible knowledge about markets. They also need much detailed information on readership and audiences, on motivation and on reactions to advertising themes. For these reasons many agencies employ their own marketing research specialists, who work for the agency and its clients. Indeed, the agencies had much to do with the whole development of market research in this country.

The trend over many years now has been for these market research units to be operated as quite distinct departments or completely separate companies. They work for a whole range of clients, in addition to those of the advertising agency, and normally charge for their services in the same way as a market research agency would (which is what they have in practice become).

1.6.2.3   *Market research agencies*

There are many individuals and companies offering their services as market research agencies. Some offer a very wide range of services, whereas others are highly specialised. The Market Research Society publishes a list of these with an indication of their capability in its annual Yearbook.

Among the specialist services available are (a) retail audits and panels, (b) motivation research, and (c) audience measurement. Some organisations specialise in one stage of the research process, such as interviewing or the processing and analysis of data.

1.7   The 'old' marketing mix

The 'marketing mix' is a term developed originally by Neil H. Borden to describe the appropriate combination, in a particular set of circumstances, of the four key elements that are at the heart of a company's marketing programme. They are commonly referred to as the 'four Ps'. It is easy to see why, if any one of these elements is wrong, the marketing programme will fail and the company will not profit from the operation, as it should. While an outmoded way of thinking, they are still in common use today. So, let us consider each component of the old 'four Ps' marketing mix in turn.

1.7.1   Product

If the product or service offered does not perform in the required way, customers will not buy a second time, and the word will get round to prospective customers so that they will not buy even once. A car with poor performance or excessive breakdowns, a 'tasty snack' that does not seem very tasty to its consumers, a magazine that does not interest its readers or a video rental shop that is never open when customers want to use it are all examples of faulty products. (Clearly, to some extent, other items in the marketing mix can act to compensate for shortcomings in this area. I may decide to accept more breakdowns in a car if it is cheap enough, or buy the snack I do not like too well if the shop I am in does not stock the one I prefer.)

1.7.2   Price

No matter how good the product, some people will be unable to pay more than a certain price. Others may be able to afford it but believe that another way of spending that sum of money would give them greater satisfaction. Conversely, as we have just seen, simply being cheap is not enough – the product must come up to some level of expected performance. In some situations (luxury goods, etc.) a high price may even make the product more desirable than a lower one. The likely response of demand to a change in price ('elasticity' in economic terms) will affect our decisions on pricing policy.

1.7.3 Place

We must not expect customers to shop around too much in order to find our particular product. It should be available at the place convenient to them. In some cases, their attachment (brand loyalty) to a particular manufacturer's product may be so strong that they will go miles to find it and refuse to accept alternatives; but this is unusual. If one type of beer is not available, many people will take another, or if one newspaper is sold out, will buy its rival. The biggest single factor in deciding which brand of petrol people buy is which garage is most convenient for them to stop at. Coca-Cola is the world's best-selling soft drink largely because it is readily available virtually everywhere. Sometimes the best way of making the product easily available is to give people easy access direct to the product (mail order, freephone ordering using credit cards, TV and Internet shopping, etc.).

The potentially negative factors must be avoided. For instance, not many people will 'shop around' to find a product that few stores have in stock. They will be reluctant to do business with a company whose telephones are not answered promptly, efficiently and courteously. Someone once defined marketing as 'making it easy for people to buy'. There is some truth in this observation, yet many organisations seem to go out of their way to make life difficult for their customers – complicated forms or administration, inadequate telecommunications systems and unhelpful staff are just some examples.

1.7.4 Promotion

The term is used here to include personal selling as well as all forms of advertising and sales promotion, packaging and display.

A well-presented product will score over one that is badly presented. Men would be unlikely to buy as a present for their partners a perfume, however good, which was offered in a cheap plastic bottle inside a grubby brown box. In the case of gifts, presentation can be all-important. Easter-egg packaging may well cost more than the chocolate it contains. The way some kinds of consumer product are spoken of by salesmen or in advertising may give them the aura customers seek, whereas an oil rig or a machine tool must above all else carry out its function, and its presentation is relatively unimportant. Note 'relatively' unimportant, because even in the extreme case it is likely that promotion will have some part to play.

So far we have established the point that a failure in any one of these four factors may damage the chances of success in the market place no matter how good the others are. The opposite point needs to be made also. Getting any one of them right adds to the total chances of success. Getting them all right will have a synergistic effect – the whole is greater than the sum of the parts.

There is, however, a complication: what we do to one element in the marketing mix can have an effect on one or more of the others, especially the price. Thus, if we want to improve the product's performance, we may have to build in features that will add to its price. On the other hand, the fact that the product performs better may make it more acceptable to more people; this in turn will lead to higher sales, bigger production runs and lower unit costs and prices.

Price and promotion are linked in this way also. Promotion can cost a great deal of money and, for example, heavy advertising expenditure can be justified only if either the advertising convinces customers that the higher price (necessary to cover advertising costs) is justified by the benefits the product offers them; or advertising leads to higher sales and therefore lower unit costs. The savings thus achieved pay for the advertising without an increase in price. Both these situations can apply at the same time, of course, so we may have an and/or rather than an either/or alternative here.

1.8   The modern marketing mix

Philip Kotler has suggested that satisfying customer needs through the four Ps does not go far enough (in an interview for *Marketing Business* Dec/Jan 1991/1992). We should, he says, be 'delighting customers' by using the 'four Cs'.

1   *Customer value.* In Kotler's view, the product, viewed from the customer's point of view, becomes the first 'C'. Customers go after what they value. So, identifying what customers' value will be paramount.
2   *Cost to the customer.* This may include time, effort, inconvenience, etc., as well as money to satisfy a need.
3   *Convenience.* Place, from the customer viewpoint, is convenience. Customers do not see channel management decisions, outlet selection or distribution strategy.
4   *Communication.* The fourth 'C' is crucial and better than promotion since it should be viewed as a two-way mechanism with customers rather than a one-way 'promotion'. Customers like to be heard, really listened to, rather than promoted to.

In the early part of this new century and beyond, success will be determined by the ability to go beyond the bare satisfaction of needs and on to the creation of 'delighted customers'. This approach ties in with the concept of Total Quality Management (TQM), which requires the commitment by everyone in the organisation to constant improvement in quality. (One major Japanese company includes in its quality precepts the statement 'perfection is not enough'.) Since quality is determined by customers' perceptions and preferences, it is only by working closely with customers that we can deliver the customer value that will make them 'delighted customers', in Kotler's phrase.

It has long been recognised that the four Cs were OK for product-based marketing operations but when one looks beyond the tangible products that people acquire, there is something missing: the service elements that have to do with the transactions occurring between the 'consumer' and the 'supplier'. For this reason Kotler added three other Ps that together form part of the 'mix' that marketers must address to complete the fulfilment of the needs, wants and desires of the customer. However, as we argue, the original thinking did not go far enough to meet the demands of today's market place.

5   *Competency*. We suggest that from the customer's viewpoint, when the customer interacts with a person delivering that service, it is the 'competency' of that person that is crucial. Not just people. (One of the original Ps). The customer experiences how capable the people are – competent not only in caring for the customer, but capable of making decisions that solve the customers' problems, find the product and deliver a personal – often individual – service. So, from an organisation's management approach, we see that a competency framework to personnel recruitment, job descriptions, performance appraisal, training and development will be better able to deliver exceptional service to customers, or 'best value' as defined for public service organisations.

6   *Customer relationship management*. It is not the process (another P) that is so important to the customer. Having purchased a product, the customer does not want to be told that there is a system – even if based on the quality standard ISO 2004 – that they must follow if they wish to complain. The concern with many of these processes is that they do not track customers' interaction with the organisation until they have the problem. That is not what the customer wants. More important, we suggest, is the way that the organisation manages *all* the customers' interactions, thus building a relationship over time. Rather than process, we suggest the focus should be on 'customer relationship management'.

7   *Context*. Finally, physical evidence (the final P) of the service delivery is today becoming less important. You may never see the 'one account' office in Norwich, or be particularly bothered by their bright yellow and red stationery, when you open a flexible mortgage with them. However, the way that they do business, how their interactions with you fit with your way of doing things is paramount. What are the values, meanings, associated surroundings or setting for the interactions? In what context are you considering your new financial arrangements? How does the account fit in your life style, job and recreational activities, your savings and plans for the future? In this situation, context is all-important.

Moreover, by considering the context of the customers needs, the total picture involving all the seven Cs is brought into play. It is this co-ordinated and holistic approach that delivers exceptional customer value, rather than a piecemeal approach.

Once we have made some decisions about the market, its customers and their needs, wants and desires, we need to pull together a route map of how we aim to satisfy them profitably. We need a plan!

1.9   Strategic marketing planning

The planning process can be usefully explored in detail with the help of Figure 1.3. Wilmshurst and Mackay[4] give a more complete discussion of the subject.

1.9.1   Corporate planning

Marketing plans are a detailed expression of 'how to get there' (how to make the future happen). But first there has to be a corporate vision of where 'there' is. Thus, top management must take a clear view of where the company as a whole is heading.

It is usual that the successful management of a business will depend on successful decisions at three levels:

1   strategic
2   administrative
3   operational.

Moreover, strategic decisions are primarily concerned with external, rather than internal, problems of the firm and specifically with selection of the product mix of the firm and the markets into which it will sell. Or, in other words, 'what business the firm is in and what kinds of business it will seek to enter'.

In the rapidly changing environment that the world now represents, decisions do have to be made. No company can simply drift along doing whatever comes next. There needs to be a clear idea of 'what business are we in?' Otherwise, the necessarily limited resources any company has to operate with will be dissipated rather than concentrated and hence, not totally effective. This need to be clear where the company is heading and what business it is in (sometimes referred to as a 'mission statement') is at the heart of the corporate planning aspect of top management's long-range decisions.

Once this general direction has been clarified (our business is in entertainment, or food and drink, or business systems) then specific product/market decisions can be taken. This involves balancing market opportunities on the one hand against the company's resources on the other.

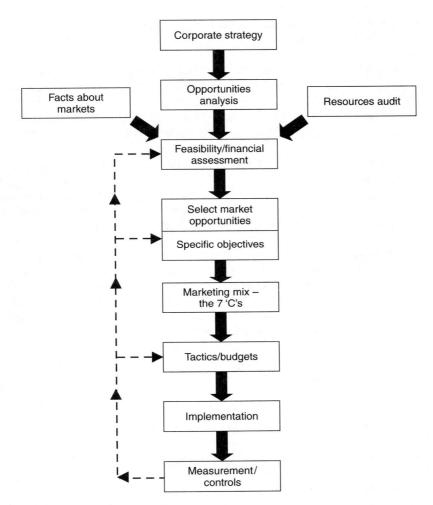

Figure 1.3 *The marketing planning process*

1.9.1.1 Resources audit

A key aspect of successful management is to ensure that on the one hand a company's resources are fully employed in profitable ventures. On the other hand, disaster can come if it takes on ventures that over-stretch its resources.

A careful review or audit of resources needs, therefore, to be carried out on a regular basis so that management is very clear what resources it does and does not have to operate with. It is convenient to carry out this audit under a number of headings:

1   *Production capability.* What experience/equipment/know-how do we have in providing particular products or services and in what other areas could these be relevant?
2   *Marketing capability.* Similarly, what is our experience in distributing and promoting to particular markets, what distribution channels and systems do we have available?
3   *Human resources.* What kind of people do we have, with what skills, experience and abilities?
4   *Financial resources.* Any new project is almost certain to need both capital investments to launch it and continuing finances to see it through the early stages of the life cycle and into a profitable state. 'Over-trading' – taking on more trade than a company can finance is still one of the commonest causes of bankruptcy – stock manufactured but not sold and goods delivered but not yet paid for can be voracious eaters of capital.
5   *Image.* Most companies have an 'image' of some sort – that is, their market sees them in a particular light and this can be a valuable asset. Therefore, new ventures should, when possible, reinforce this clear and favourable image – not conflict with it and thus confuse the customers.

The above concentrates on knowing positively which resources we have but it is, of course, also important to be clear what resources we do not have. A common experience of the authors and other consultants is to be asked to advise on marketing a new product only to find that the company can easily manufacture it but is in no way geared to market it (and is usually also short of finance for the long haul required to establish itself in a market that is totally new to it).

From this analysis companies often develop a list of their strengths and weaknesses, the first half of the 'SWOT' Analysis. However, there is a need to evaluate the usefulness of the strengths in terms of what the market demands and also to evaluate the weaknesses in terms of whether or not they will significantly compromise the business. (A classic mistake of many firms is to include a loyal customer base as a strength of the business – it is not. The business *reputation* or *brand name* may be a strength, the *database* would be a legitimate strength, but the customers themselves are external to a business and therefore represent an 'opportunity'.) From this position, priorities of activity can be developed.

1.9.1.2   Selecting marketing opportunities

Alongside the resources audit an analysis of market opportunities will be taking place. Similarly, there are likely to be identified a series of threats that come from other companies or changes in the marketplace. This is based on a constant review of 'facts about markets' provided by the company's marketing information system and review of the PEST analysis.[5] These findings are summarised under 'opportunities' and 'threats', the second part of the 'SWOT' analysis.

Out of these many opportunities a selection has to be made of those which are:

1 Feasible, given the company's resources. (For example, the fast food boom provides many market opportunities, but they may not be feasible for a company whose experience is in some totally different direction such as heavy engineering.)
2 Potentially profitable.

The latter needs to be established as early as possible and calculations will need refining at least once as the project progresses.

One common failing in this area is that many people only look at those opportunities that are obvious extensions of what they are already doing. There are often other more profitable opportunities that would be preferable if only someone had established that they existed. This is why 'facts about the market' must be gathered on a continuing basis and market opportunities compared one against another.

Once these decisions have been made, we can turn our attention to marketing mix variables, particularly marketing communications.

1.10   Marketing communications

This term is often used as convenient shorthand to embrace all the methods available for communicating with customers other than personal selling* and are normally 'across the board' communications to mass audiences carried out on a planned basis with a common message throughout.

The purpose of marketing communications is to help move a potential customer from a state of ignorance towards a position of decision and action. We use various methods to convey messages to help this process against opposing forces (Figure 2.1, p27).

For each situation, we have to choose which selection of communications methods will help us.

---

* Just to confuse the issue, marketing communications is occasionally used to include that also, but not often, and it is useful to be able to draw the distinction. We do make the distinction here mainly on the basis that personal selling is a highly individual ('one-to-one') affair transmitting slightly different messages at each encounter, depending on the recipient. While it can be planned to some extent, how he or she conducts each interview must be left to the individual judgement of the salesperson.

A very important (perhaps the most important) means of communication, which is easy to overlook, is 'word of mouth'. People looking for ways of satisfying a need do not merely talk to salesmen and read advertisements and sales literature. They read relevant newspaper and magazine articles, listen to the radio and watch TV, but, above all, they talk to each other. People contemplating buying a new car, or a new washing machine, talk to friends and relations and get their reactions. Neighbours compare notes on public services. People who buy a new product and like it recommend it to their friends. If they dislike it, they warn off their friends. On the Internet, this word-of-mouth technique is called 'viral marketing'.

In essence, viral marketing creates an incentive for others to communicate your marketing message through the Internet or email, via methods such as attachments or sign-up forms. Attachments allow one to add a degree of personality to a brand and encourage consumers to interact, as well as to find out more about you and your product or service. Just like their more dangerous cousins, viral marketing campaigns can spread across the entire Internet in a matter of days. No other method of marketing has been found that can generate such massive 'recommendation' marketing status with such a relatively small outlay.

Very frequently, however, we find ourselves using more 'structured' methods of communication, because they are faster and their effects are more predictable and controllable.

1.11   Choosing methods of communication

There is no 'best' way of communicating with customers. To discuss whether advertising is 'better' than public relations or personal selling is meaningless. Each method has advantages and disadvantages, and, depending on the circumstances, one may be more cost-effective than another. Every marketing situation calls for its own special marketing mix and its own unique promotional mix. Valid generalisations are few, but Table 1.1 gives a rough guide to the way some of the main methods of communicating with customers rate according to a few key criteria.

1.12   Summary

In this chapter:

- We have seen that marketing is a management process and is successful only as a result of the management of the interaction of an organisation and its customers through whatever communication channels are appropriate.
- The influences on consumer behaviour were explored and we saw that no one factor can work in isolation from others.

Table 1.1   *Promotional methods compared*

	Believable	Two-way	Fast	Cheap	Controllable	Action
Word of mouth	✓	✗	✗	✓	✗	✓
Personal selling	✗	✓	✗	✗	✓	✓
Seminars	✓	✓	✗	✗	✓	✓
Advertising	✗	✗	✓	✓	✓	✗
Sales promotion	✗	✗	✓	✓	✓	✓
Public relations	✓	✗	✗	✓	✗	✗

Notes:

1. In the table, a cross means 'No, rather than yes', a tick 'Yes, rather than no'. The judgements are subjective and simply illustrate the kinds of assessments that have to be made – based on facts if known or judgements if not.
2. The criteria used are:
   - *Believable* – do the receivers of the message tend to regard the source as believable?
   - *Two-Way* – is there good communication back to the company?
   - *Fast* – does the message travel quickly from source to destination?
   - *Cheap* – is the cost per message received relatively cheap?
   - *Controllable* – how much control does the company have over the message as received?
   - *Action* – is the message very likely to produce immediate action?
3. Seminars, in this context, are meetings to which prospective customers are invited to hear a technical presentation of new products or techniques. 'Hard sell' is kept to a minimum.

- The place of sound market research was established to help us understand the dynamics in the market and how our communications affect the behaviour of our various audiences.
- A modern marketing mix was established from the customers' perspective which enables us to drive our marketing from the customers' viewpoint: Customer value, Cost to the customer, Convenience, Communication, Competency, Customer relationship management and Context made the modern marketing mix.
- Finally, we reviewed strategic marketing planning and explored how to choose the appropriate method of marketing communication.

Notes

1   Adapted from Chisnall, P.M. *Marketing – a Behavioural Analysis*, McGraw-Hill, 1975.
2   AdStats, from World Advertising Research Centre, *AdMap*, 418, June 2001.

3   Maslow, A. *Motivation and Personality*, Harper & Row, 1954.
4   Wilmshurst, J. and Mackay, A. *The Fundamentals and Practice of Marketing*, 4th Ed., Butterworth Heinemann, 2002 – see Chapter 6 – The Strategic Operational Plan.
5   PEST = an acronym for political, economic, social and technological issues evaluated for their impact on an organisation and its markets.

2 How Advertising Works

John Wilmshurst

Learning outcomes

By the end of this chapter you will:

- Understand the key ingredients in effective advertising.
- Be aware of the main theories of how advertising works – and of their limitations.
- Appreciate different views on how individuals react to advertising.
- Understand the differences between attitudes, beliefs, cognitive dissonance and the effect of cigarette advertising on consumption.
- Have an appreciation of how the job that advertising is designed to do can affect research approaches.
- Explore current thinking on the effect of shifting advertising messages on the relationship people have with their existing view of the brand.

2.1 What is advertising?

Your dictionary will probably say of advertising that it is 'to give notice of; to give public information about merits claimed for; to draw attention to; to offer for sale by public notice, printed or broadcast; to inform or give notice....' Simply stated, it is about communication.

So, to be effective, it must be based on:

1 A precise definition of *to whom* we are trying to communicate
2 A clear idea of *what* we need to communicate
3 Some understanding of *what effect* we expect the communication to have
4 A clear understanding of *how* the communication process works.

While point 4 is much more difficult to achieve, if we can understand all elements and define what we expect to happen as a result of the advertising, then we can set out to measure whether it has been achieved or not.

Chapter 11 looks at planning and budgeting advertising so that what we are doing is more *likely* to work and Chapters 13 and 14 look at researching the media and the consumer to see whether the advertising is achieving the desired results. However, techniques can only be applied successfully if we have a clear idea of what the desired results are (points 3 and 4). While extremely difficult to arrive at, it does involve some understanding of some of the theories about what advertising does, to whom, and how it does it.

2.2   The role of advertising in 'selling'

Direct response advertising's objective is pretty clear – get people to place orders for what is on offer. However, much of advertising is not of this character. As we shall see in Section 2.6 the way that advertising works is on a scale of immediacy; direct response advertising being the most immediate while some campaigns reinforce attitudes and beliefs about the organisation or brand advertised.

Even in direct response advertising there are many factors at work beyond the advertised message: price, availability of offer and of alternatives, level of distribution, peer pressure, and competitive advertising all play a part. Moreover, for many products, such as beer and ice cream, weather plays a significant part. Advertising will frequently be only one influence among many on how consumers behave and what they buy. This is why it has proved to be so difficult to measure the effect of advertising alone among so many influences.

It was the recognition that advertising was only one factor in the total process of selling that led to the development of a series of advertising models. These are largely based on the idea that advertising can help move consumers through a series of steps that gradually build up the necessary conditions for a sale – the so-called 'hierarchy of effects' approach (such as DAGMAR – see Section 2.3.2)

2.3   A history of theories

Scientifically, the 'hierarchy of effects' approach is related to what is often referred to as 'learning theory'. The classic 'Pavlov's dogs' experiment is an example: he trained dogs to associate the arrival of food with the ringing of a bell, to the extent that eventually the sound of the bell alone would induce the salivation response.

Advertising was thus seen as a stimulus (like the bell) giving rise to a 'conditioned response' (salivation). A further development of learning theory gives rise to the so-called 'linea sequential' or 'hierarchy of effects' theories of advertising. All these theories have as their basis the notion that to be effective – and to achieve the desired behavioural response – any piece of persuasive communication must carry its audience through a series of stages, each stage being dependent on the success of the previous step. People must be routed to each stepping stone in turn to cross the river (the required effect) and the task of advertising or other piece of the communications mix is to encourage them to do so.

2.3.1   Starch

Daniel Starch in the early 1920s put forward the idea that in order to be effective, any advertising:

1   Must be *seen*
2   Must be *read**
3   Must be *believed*
4   Must be *remembered*
5   Must be *acted upon*

   This is a very useful rule of thumb or checklist against which to measure whether an advertisement seems likely to include the necessary ingredients. However, the model runs into difficulties when we examine each step in more detail. For example, does *read* mean scanned quickly or studied in detail? Similarly, does remembered mean remembered for a long time? If so, for how long and in what detail?
   An alternative, which is still often used as a quick check on whether the advertisement 'looks right' is the AIDA model, which suggests that an effective advertisement is one that:

1   Commands *Attention*
2   Leading to *Interest* in the product
3   And thence to *Desire* to own or use the product
4   And finally to *Action* (normally purchase or at least a step towards it, e.g. logging on-line for more information)

2.3.2   DAGMAR

In 1969 Russell Colley published a book entitled *Defining Advertising Goals for Measured Advertising Results* (DAGMAR for short). The main conclusions were expressed in the following quotation:

All commercial communications that weigh on the ultimate objective of a sale must carry a prospect through four levels of understanding:

1   The prospect must first be aware of the existence of a brand or company
2   He must have a comprehension of what the product is and what it will do for him

---

 * Note that this idea was put forward before broadcast media so advertising was presented only as the written word – hence an advertisement had to be *read*.

3   He must arrive at a mental suspicion or conviction to buy the product
4   Finally he must stir himself to action.

This is an improvement on the earlier models because it recognises the need to take account of the recipients' reactions and does not deal purely with the message as such yielding an automatic response. However, it still has some problems. For instance, is it always necessary to have a clear comprehension of what the product is before having a conviction to buy? The main objection is the underlying assumption that it is advertising that brings all this about and that the effects of advertising can be observed in isolation from the many other influences. (see Section 2.5).

Nonetheless, the DAGMAR model has one enormous value. It enables the main purpose of a particular advertising campaign to be defined as, for example, to increase awareness or to improve comprehension of the product. This lends itself to 'before and after' surveys that can measure what changes have taken place. Where sales may result at some distant time this can in some circumstances give a much more immediate measure of whether the advertising has been effective.

In relation to the *action* part of the DAGMAR hierarchy, it has been pointed out that a great deal of advertising is intended *not* to generate new users and thus calling for action, but rather to persuade existing users not to change to a competitive product. However, it can be argued that this apparent *inaction* is still in a sense creating a sale. This kind of consideration does highlight the fact that the model, while a useful one, is nowhere near as precise as it first appears.

In a broader sense, it is clear that the purpose of marketing communication is to help move a potential customer along a continuum from a state of ignorance towards a position of decision and action. We use marketing communications methods – and particularly advertising – to convey messages that will aid in this process in the teeth of the forces operating in the opposite direction (Figure 2.1). This is an enhancement on the DAGMAR model in that it identifies that there are opposing forces at work. Moreover, that the continuum has one further and important step – you may be convinced that the product might be right for you but do you *desire* it enough to want to go to take action?

It is clear that we would use a portfolio of marketing communication methods to take our potential customer from one end of the continuum to the other. While direct response advertising may take someone from being unaware right through to action in one 'hit', most other forms of advertising are just part of a wider communications mix. Chapter 1 shows the place of advertising within the marketing and communications mix and Chapter 3 stresses the importance of integrating all the variety of marketing communications so that a co-ordinated message is delivered.

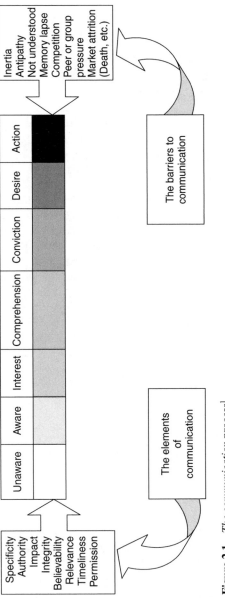

Figure 2.1 *The communication process*[1]

2.4   What acts on whom – individuals and herds

All these models tend to assume a passive audience being influenced by advertising messages aimed at it. One might argue that often the reverse viewpoint is relevant. An audience is actively seeking advertising messages because they are looking for the best answer to a well-defined problem such as 'which is the best computer in my price range?' or 'which digital camera will give me the sharpest pictures I need?' So, one might view the purchaser like some poor lottery ball being battered about by random forces and would prefer an alternative model that would recognise the purchaser as an active principal. The suggestion here is that people deliberately and purposefully select the messages that are of interest to them and 'filter out' those that are not.

One view might be that consumers are capable of defining their own goals and adapt to the restrictions imposed by their environment. This is why barriers to communication were identified in Figure 2.1.

In his book *How Advertising Works*, Colin McDonald[2] reviews in depth the arguments for and against the hierarchy of effects models such as DAGMAR and concludes that they are not so much theories of how advertising works, but rather *necessary conditions*. It is, for example, self-evident that people are unlikely to respond to advertising that has not caught their attention. It is this apparently obvious inherent truth in these models that accounts for their continuing to be strongly held by many. This is particularly the case since in some circumstances, such as direct response advertising, the 'hierarchy of effects' approach may still have relevance.

However, in most cases we have to look at the alternative approaches that have been put forward over the years. The following sections review some key ideas since DAGMAR.

2.4.1   Hedges

The realisation that many factors are involved has led to the relegation of the hierarchy of effects models to a far less dominant position than they once held, even though they persist strongly in some quarters and may still have relevance in a few circumstances.

Alan Hedges[3] points out, 'To the consumer, advertising is mainly just part of the background scene. Advertisements form part of the continual whirling mass of sense impressions that bombard the eye. Just as we cannot take all our consuming decisions in discrete rational steps, so we cannot stop to evaluate and classify all the pieces of sensory input we receive. This, too, has to be relegated to very low levels of consciousness for the most part.'

Hedges suggests that advertising can operate at a number of different levels:

1   Simply by creating a sense of familiarity one creates an awareness that the brand is 'around'. People are more likely to buy a brand that they

recognise, although that recognition may not consciously be associated with remembering the advertising.

2   Advertising may 'surround the brand with particular associations, with moods, feelings, emotional colours and so on'.

3   Advertising may convey information about price, functions, etc.

4   Sometimes rational arguments may be put forward. It is probably only at this level that the customers' conscious attention is likely to be engaged.

Advertising of everyday consumer products normally works over a period of time. Its effect is cumulative rather than instantaneous and may often be concerned with helping consumers to identify with a particular brand. Cases where advertising contributes to a 'once and for all' acceptance of a reasoned argument are likely to relate to occasionally purchased consumer durables, industrial capital goods, etc.

2.4.2   Longman

In order to select and transmit appropriate information in the most suitable manner to our target audience we must have some knowledge of what is involved for them in the buying process. What information do they work with in making their decisions? Is it an instant 'impulse' decision or carefully considered over a long period? Do they buy frequently and in doing so develop a habit of buying particular products and favourite brands or do they reconsider which one to buy this time? Do they actively seek out our product or service (as for example when they need a plumber because the tank is leaking) or must we first stimulate the interest of an initially passive audience?

Kenneth Longman[4] suggests three different models of the marketing and advertising situation, the one we use being determined by the following factors:

1   The purchase cycle – its length, regularity, and responsiveness to advertising.

2   The brand decision – whether it reflects conscious commitment, automatic choice, or something in between.

3   The purchase decision – how much deliberation and 'shopping around' it involves.

4   The relationship between time of purchase and time of use – on-premise consumption as compared with home inventory and regular or sporadic use at home.

5   The brand's competitive market position.

6   The functions assigned to other marketing activities for the brand.

Clearly answers to these questions can only come from a detailed study of the market place and how customers purchase and use the product.

Longman's suggested three models are:

1 *Brand switching model.* Here, the purpose of advertising is to encourage purchasers of a type of product used regularly (margarine or coffee for example) to 'switch' from one brand to another or alternatively to encourage continued purchase of their existing brand.
2 *Purchase cycle model.* Here, the purpose of advertising is to induce people who do not normally or regularly use the product to change their behaviour by using it. The irregularly used type of food product (e.g. some types of meat or dessert) is an example where advertising of the reminder type ('Why not give them *"Weetibangs"* for a change') could be appropriate. It could be said that the brand-switching model applies where there is a fixed purchase cycle, whereas here we are trying to influence the purchase cycle by encouraging more frequent or more regular usage.
3 *The attitude model.* Here, there may be no purchase at all unless we can encourage people to change their attitudes. New products in particular may involve the need to encourage people to accept change (video recorders, word processors). Existing attitudes may cause resistance to purchase (e.g. of exotic or unfamiliar foods). The attitude model will, of course, also apply to much of the public relations or 'corporate image' type of advertising.

2.4.3   Joyce

The 'brand switching' situation referred to above means that, as Timothy Joyce[5] puts it, 'much of the work of advertising consists of *preventing a decline in sales*'. He goes on to suggest that 'much advertising must be judged largely on its performance among present users, i.e. those who are already favourably disposed to the brand'.

Both Hedges and Joyce highlight the fact that much purchasing must of necessity be a matter of routine. As Joyce says '... a powerful determinant of consumer choice is habit or inertia. It suits the customer to treat much of her activity as a matter of routine. To indulge in a process of conscious deliberation at every purchase would take an enormous amount of time and mental effort that, not unnaturally, there is a strong drive to avoid'.

By '*her*' Joyce was presumably referring to 'the housewife' – a stereotype that was always questionable and has now been almost entirely discarded. However, much the same inertia will be found in any regular purchaser of any type of commodity. Even industrial buyers are reluctant to make the effort and take the risk of changing suppliers without strong reasons.

All of this comes down to the fact that a strong factor is the customers' relationship with and attitude towards products. A key function of advertising is to shape or reinforce those attitudes.

2.4.4 Earls

In a paper to the Market Research Society in 2003, Mark Earls[6] proposed that the word 'consumer' has not received as much attention as the word 'brand' in discussions about advertising and marketing research. He argued that so many theories of how advertising works misses one very fundamental point – that the most important characteristic if mankind is that of a herd-animal, not lone individuals. Despite arguments to the contrary (where so much effort has gone into understanding the mechanisms of the individual), he states that 'we are who we are and do what we do as a herd, not as individuals'.

While much of research on advertising focuses on the learning, recall, and awareness of individuals, many so-called 'framework models' (see Hall and Maclay[7]) that are used to explain how advertising might work can be explained in how individuals behave or think. They are concerned largely with how an individual processes and/or responds to new information or emotional inputs – see Section 2.5.

Individuals have been shown to be pretty unreliable, largely unaware of what they do (behaviours), why they do it (motivations), are easily influenced by others, capable of significant self-deception and so on. It may be that the individual decision-maker, reliable or otherwise, is not all there is to know about how individuals respond to advertising. It may be that thinking – conscious or otherwise – accurately reported or not – may best be understood in the group rather than at the level advertising researchers normally work – the individual.

It has been proposed that there is an important missing level of understanding human behaviour between the individual consumer and that of markets or segments (Figure 2.2). This has been called 'tribal' behaviour[8].

The idea presented here is that the individual, rather than being viewed as an independent self who is trying to collect ever more experiences driven by personal emotions, the consuming individual is a member of a tribe, where the

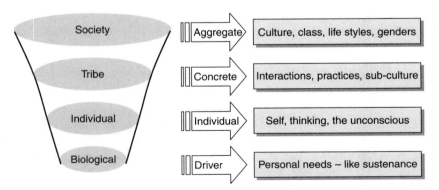

Figure 2.2 *Levels of consumption observed. Adapted from Cova and Cova (2002)*

brand symbol creates a universe for the tribe. It is this notion that has been used to describe the behaviour of VW Beetle owners or motorcyclists giving a knowing nod to drivers of similar vehicles. Examples are to be found in continental Europe from the Lomo tribe (based on the social usage of low-grade Russian cameras), inline skaters in Paris, and brands supporting tribes including Citroen supporting their enthusiasts, and Ricard supporting petangue players.

Earl suggests that many marketing people in the UK overlook this important area of human behaviour – it remains unconsidered and unexamined, with the notable exception of youth marketing.

'People are responding to an environment that consists of other people responding to their environment, which consists of people responding to an environment of other people's responses'. (See www.montyroberts.com for more ideas of herd behaviour influencing the individual – it is the herd not the horses that decides what the horses do.)

While the herd perspective is indeed useful to explain how things change rapidly and suddenly (certainly economists have used it for such things), can it tell us something about why some markets tend to be stable? For example, why do some big brands endure for 20 years or more, and why do smaller brands find it hard to make headway against the status quo? It has been argued that purchasing behaviour is force of habit rather than considered. An individual's next purchase is largely determined by his/her previous purchases – a self-determining individual agent model. However, suppose a large part of an individual's purchasing behaviour is determined by what other individuals do (or are thought to do), both now and in the past. What if my choice of Brand X is actually 'our' choice of Brand X? As if buying Brand X is something that 'we', our tribe, does!

Consider the classic Coke–Pepsi example where product preference (as indicated by blind taste tests) is overcome by either habit or the power of the brand. Earls argues that the herd is a better explanation for the strange phenomenon. 'We' buy Coke even though as individuals we prefer the taste of Pepsi, because buying Coke is something 'we' do.

For the moment, however, let us consider what is suggested about how individuals may react to advertising as much has been done to study the phenomenon.

2.5   Individuals' reaction to advertising

In a landmark paper by Judie Lannon and Peter Cooper,[9] they posed a question: What do people do with advertising? The authors explore the probability that the mechanistic theories of advertising such as DAGMAR concentrate too much on what the advertising does and pay too little attention to what has become known as the 'sophisticated consumer'. They suggest that we need to recognise 'the consumer as active participator in communication'. Lannon and Cooper go on to suggest that 'consumers endow the brands they buy and use with meanings, over and above their sheer functional value. It is the creative task to communicate these meanings in ways that motivate and reinforce;

research is (needed) to unlock them and make them available to the creative process. We are then making a clear distinction between the *ostensible* or face value aspects of brands and their latent or symbolic values.'

The authors suggest that it is the product as such and the symbolism associated with it that gives rise to a strong brand. The two aspects are illustrated in Figure 2.3

Neurological research has given rise to the belief that we all have two types of consciousness residing in the two hemispheres of the brain. The left hemisphere (which controls the right side of the body) is the practical side; the right hemisphere (controlling the left side of the body) is the symbolic side. Lannon and Cooper suggest that 'much advertising is essentially and increasingly "right hemisphere" communication, dealing in symbolic communication'. They picture the concerns of the left and right hemispheres as shown in Figure 2.4.

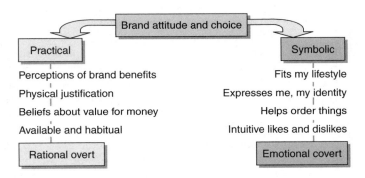

Figure 2.3   *Two views of brand symbolism – after Lannon and Cooper*

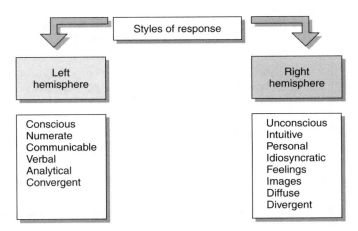

Figure 2.4   *Styles of response of the left and right sides of the brain*

Examples of symbolism frequently used in advertising are class (e.g. in After Eight chocolate mints advertising with its 'upper-class' overtones, and HOVIS bread with its 'working class' ones), youth, sex, indulgence, freedom.

Lannon and Cooper summarise the idea of the 'active consumer' in the following way.

Expectations of advertising – advertising is capable of entering language, daydreams, and intuition because of its independent existence. It does not simply do things to people in the sense of treating consumers as objects to manipulate, nor does it merely do things to products, like creating USPs, brand personalities. Rather, people *do* things to advertising, interact with it, and produce surprising outcomes.

Again, this notion is still presented only in terms of the individual consumer thinking and acting on his or her own whereas clearly, people interact with people, most of whom interact with advertising.

Two phenomena both point to advertising as something that sometimes at least works in the context of groups rather than individuals.

> *Word of mouth* is recognised as being very powerful and is considered to be a significant influence on an individual's purchasing behaviour – just think if a friend, whose opinion you value, recommends a new local restaurant you might like! Many advertising messages enter the culture themselves (Budweiser's 'Wazzzup?' or Walker's Crisps). These messages grow through the customer's relationship with other customers rather than the advertisers to the customer. This is not a new phenomenon as any reader old enough to remember 'Ahh ... Bisto' will testify. It is interesting to note that the message is rarely novel in itself nor is it particularly clever. Other elements get advertising talked about. Those factors seem to be the creative element (see Chapter 7) and not the finely tuned strategic elements.
>
> *Advertising as publicity* – this view, developed by Ehrinberg[10], suggests that advertising is rarely directly persuasive but merely something that draws attention to the brand and thus prevents the brand from being forgotten. Therefore, why bother to advertise Guinness in Ireland? This idea brings in the difference between 'talking points about the brand' (advertising as publicity model) and 'reasons to buy the brand' (advertising as persuasion model). As Earl questions, 'why have talking points if not to share with the rest of the group?'

At a time when mass marketing is on the decline, the herd-perspective provides a useful distinction between advertising and one-to-one communication: the first is with (and by) the herd, the other to individuals. Mass advertising communication is not a more expensive version of one-to-one communication. It is communication with and by the herd.

2.5.1   Active consumers

The Lannon and Cooper idea of an active, participating consumer, rather than a passive one that advertising 'does things to' is explored further by McDonald[2]. He states: 'those who receive advertising are *actively in control and pick and choose what they will attend to*'.

In other words, nobody is forced to pay attention to or respond to any advertising.

This approach has the following ingredients:

1   Habitual purchases for everyday use cannot be explained simply in terms of a sequence of (hierarchical) steps.
2   People can and do screen out advertising which has no relevance to them – most advertising is of no interest to most people most of the time.

We can distinguish between *passive* (non-intrusive) advertising that is there for us to refer to when we need it (jobs and other 'classifieds') and *active* (intrusive) advertising that tries to command our attention for items we would not go searching for.

Taking this view, suggests McDonald, puts a premium on the need to *target* advertising so that it is likely to 'find the right way to speak to those who are prone to be interested in what it has to say'.

In *How to Plan Advertising*[11] Jeremy Elliott suggests that 'The way advertising affects consumer choices, in totality, is not a neat, sequential and mechanistic system, but a largely muddled, often irrational and essentially *human* process'. If one takes the herd approach from Mark Earl we can see that an enhancement in the original Joyce's model of 1967 (see Figure 2.6) is still valid. We can see that different advertising campaigns, fulfilling different roles, will produce different kinds of effect (along the lines suggested in Section 2.8).

2.5.2   Attitudes and beliefs

The Chambers Dictionary defines an attitude as '... a personal viewpoint of or to a product or organisation'.

Psychologists define attitudes as 'a learned predisposition to respond in a consistently favourable or unfavourable direction towards a given attitude object', whereas a belief is 'any statement of any kind which connects the attitude object with some other object goal or value'. Psychologists arrive at a clear picture of attitudes by getting people to 'agree or disagree' with a series of statements. Sometimes asking people to rate a statement on a scale modifies this: for example 'Whisky is a strong drink ...'

* Strongly agree
* Slightly agree

- Neither agree nor disagree
- Slightly disagree
- Strongly disagree

By getting a number of people to respond in this way to a series of statements a picture of prevailing attitudes can be built up.

The idea, embraced in the psychologists' definition given above, that attitudes are *learned*, suggests that they can be modified and much advertising attempts to do this. For example, government advertising attempts to change people's attitudes to smoking, drinking and other behaviour which is seen as unhealthy or socially undesirable; a company seen as old-fashioned, conservative or antisocial may wish to encourage a different series of attitudes; a product seen as 'not for people like me' may need to be represented so as to become acceptable to 'people like me'. Again, we can see the idea of other people's influence on the individual in building their personal viewpoint.

Attitudes can be changed by the following means:

1   *Reasoned argument*, leading the audience to judge the suggested conclusion as 'true' or 'false' (an example is the use of health statistics to attempt to change people's attitude to smoking).
2   *Positive emotional appeals*, for example, 'Stop smoking and you will feel fitter and food will taste better'.
3   *Negative emotional appeals*, for example, 'If you don't stop smoking your lungs may end up looking like this'.

Some recent theories on customer behaviour have developed out of market research work on brand choice and related matters. A theory that has gained much support and certainly offering an elegant approach is that of Fishbein, encapsulated in the equation:

$$BI = A_{W1} \text{ act} + SN_{W2}$$

where BI is the Behavioural Intention, 'A act' the Attitude to the Act and SN the Subjective Norm; W1 and W2 are the weightings to be attached to the components 'A act' and SN.

Stated in words, the theory postulates that the way people intend to behave is influenced by two main factors, as follows:

1   Their attitude to the proposed act or behaviour (in terms of 'Do I like/ dislike, approve/ disapprove of this act').
2   The 'subjective norm', that is, the way they believe other people expect them to behave.

The first component 'A act' is in turn the summation of a set of beliefs about the act, that is, the connection a person perceives between the act and its possible/probable consequences. The beliefs included in the summation are those Fishbein calls 'salient beliefs', that is those that have the most influence. In practice, these are usually taken as being the first seven 'beliefs' the respondent lists in answer to an open-ended question such as 'Tell me what you think (about the act in question)'.

The subjective norm is an interesting phenomenon as it changes over time. For example, a decade or so ago, mobile phones were cumbersome and often derided as a 'yuppie' fad. To have one was not considered 'normal' in as much as few had them: 'Oh, they are for salesmen!' Today, however, the 'norm' is to have one (or more) and 'third generation' video phones are being advertised to overcome a similar slowness in the diffusion of the innovation.[12]

A problem of the whole attitudes and beliefs approach to influencing behaviour (including purchasing habits) is that the causal link between attitudes and behaviour is not proven, for example, studies on racial attitudes in the United States have shown that people's stated beliefs can be strongly at variance with their actual behaviour.

Favourable attitudes to products can often be shown to follow rather than precede purchase (a serious defect in the 'Hierarchy of Effects' models).

This will be explored further when we discuss incongruency and consistency in advertising.

2.5.3   Cognitive dissonance

It is a well-known fact that the way people see something depends on what they expect to see. Supporters of opposing football teams or political parties will react to a particular incident on the field or in a TV interview quite differently. L. Festinger[13] developed these findings into a body of theory labelled 'cognitive dissonance'. It argues that humans seek to maintain a state of mental 'consonance' or equilibrium. Anything that disturbs this causes 'dissonance' because it upsets the patterns of knowledge (cognitions) that the person has learned to find acceptable. In order to avoid dissonance, information, which is inconsistent with the existing pattern, will be rejected, while anything reinforcing it will be welcomed.

It works along the following lines in a marketing situation. Assume that somebody uses brand X and a marketing effort is made to convince him that brand Y is the 'best'. This information would be inconsistent with the existing mind-set and would, therefore, set up dissonance, which needs to be resolved. Because of this there will be a tendency to ignore the message; it will not form part of the psychological environment of brand X purchasers. Something very much like this would appear to happen to a great deal of advertising in the real world. However, if the message is too powerful to be ignored, it can be distorted. The recipient can convince himself that what is being said is not 'brand Y is best' but that 'brand Y is a good brand', which is acceptable information and would not cause dissonance. If, however, the message is so powerful that it can be neither ignored nor distorted, then dissonance results. The obvious way to resolve it is to buy brand Y. There are then two possibilities. Brand Y may be found not to be 'best' and, therefore, the purchaser goes back to buying brand X, convinced that brand Y's advertising and marketing is making false claims. Therefore, the purchaser does not experience dissonance. Or brand Y may indeed be found to be 'best', in which case a change of purchasing behaviour will result and as a consequence so will a change of attitudes and beliefs.

Much recent advertising on Skoda cars worked to change the cognitive dissonance in the market about their brand perceived as being poor when initially advertised as good cars.

2.5.4   Cigarette advertising

Considering individuals' reaction to advertising, it is interesting to reflect on the relationship between tobacco consumption and advertising. In a recent paper reviewing hundreds of studies on the economies of tobacco advertising, Kent and Alyse Lancaster[14] made some interesting observations on advertising spending, demand, and the effects of bans.

In 1962 the British government released the Royal College of Physicians Report that described the dangers of smoking. Studies examining the effect of this report have found that it had significant effects in lowering cigarette consumption. Similar results were found when the Royal College of Physicians released their second (1971) and third (1977) reports.

In 1992, the UK Department of Health published the 'Smee' Report named after the Department's Chief Economic Adviser. The report, on review by Luik,[15] found that:

1   There is no statistically significant relationship between tobacco advertising and tobacco consumption.
2   Advertising bans do not necessarily lower consumption.
3   Consumer recognition of tobacco advertising is not related to tobacco consumption.
4   Among young people, the primary factor that influences smoking is not advertising, but rather the smoking behaviour of parents and older siblings.

Their paper concluded that '... the evidence that full or partial bans on advertising are likely to have little of no effect on aggregate cigarette or tobacco demands because the banned advertising itself apparently has little or no effect on aggregate demand'.

Again, as we can see from point 4 above, the influence from social groups on adoption of smoking far outweighs the advertising message.

2.6　King's scale of immediacy

Stephen King[16] drew attention to the discrepancy between the various theories of advertising and the largely pragmatic ways of measuring effectiveness. He suggested that we should not try to produce advertisements or evaluate their effect without having some theory of how they are meant to work. At the same time he did not think that we will ever solve the 'how advertising works' problem.

He suggested a middle course – that advertising operates in a number of different ways according to his 'scale of immediacy'. (See Figure 2.5.)

It does seem to be able to cope with today's changing circumstances, changing consumer attitudes, different product types, different types of advertising, and different media values. The scale is a simple entity, yet it does not suggest that one single mechanism can explain everything.

King related the scale to the following kinds of advertising:

1　*Direct* ('selling off the page').
2　*Seek Information* (or 'tell me more' advertising).
3　*Relate to own needs, wants, desires* (the 'what a good idea' response).

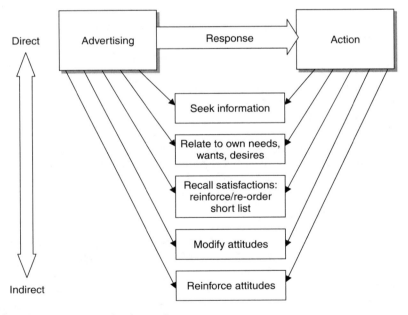

Figure 2.5　*King's scale of immediacy*

4   *Recall satisfactions; reinforce/re-order short list* (the 'that reminds me' response).
5   *Modify attitudes* (Skoda cars was one example).
6   *Reinforce attitudes* (common with established brand leader products such as Persil, Heinz soup, Kellogg's cornflakes).

The methods used to determine advertising effectiveness will then clearly depend on the part of the 'scale of immediacy' in which we believe a particular piece of advertising is operating.

2.7   Incongruency and consistency

In Section 2.5.3 we discussed how a message that the individual does not agree with may cause cognitive dissonance towards the advertisement. While recognising the value of advertising that reinforced a known attitude or belief (congruent brand communication), Henrik Sjödin and Fredrik Törn[17] suggested that moderate incongruency might offer important benefits. They suggested that this was because incongruency in advertising elicits higher message involvement and therefore revives interest in a mature brand and low-risk, frequently purchased products.

While they make the case for maintaining a consistent and cohesive image by means of a congruent brand image across all media – see Chapter 3 on Integrated Marketing Communications – they do recognise that incongruency does have important advantages such as improved brand attitude, higher message involvement, and better memory involvement.

However, they did discover that it all depends on the degree of preference that people have for consistency – a trait that is related to the 'tribe' or 'herd' to which people belong. Their findings suggest that people with a low preference for consistency rarely are dependent on ad-brand congruency in forming their attitude to an advertisement.

They concluded that practitioners could include preference for congruency (PFC) in advertising research since PFC may significantly influence the evaluation of advertising. They also suggested that PFC might be useful to segment audiences so that the advantage of incongruent advertising can be harnessed.

2.8   Towards a synthesis

All of the above theories and statements represent varying ways of looking at how advertising seems to work. None of them has really yet reached the status of a truly scientific approach. That is to say, it is rarely possible to use them as a means of predicting exactly what will happen as a result of a particular advertising approach. Some do not even stand up to Karl Popper's criterion of a scientific statement – is it capable of being disproved if it is untrue? What does

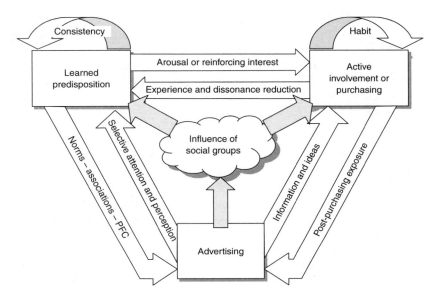

Figure 2.6   *How advertising may work*

seem to be the case is that the whole process, of which advertising forms a part, is a complex one. People's attitudes, social norms, existing purchasing and usage behaviour, as well as their reasoning power all have a part to play – as do other factors such as competition, the availability of alternatives, economic circumstances, and many other things. Figure 2.6 aims to attempt to illustrate this interrelationship diagrammatically, building on Joyce's work.

Hedges emphasised the importance of making it easy for people to identify easily with products. This means first that brands must have a clear identity which is a function not merely of advertising, but of all forms of promotion and also of the product itself, its name, packaging and so on. The notion of brand congruency and an individual's preference for congruency were seen to play a part.

The identity of the product has three parts, suggests Hedges:

1   The prominence or salience of the brand (the extent to which it springs readily to mind).
2   The clarity or distinctiveness of its identity (the extent to which it is seen to have clear and pronounced characteristics and properties).
3   The nature of its identity (the kinds of feeling, thought, and belief that people have about it).

All of this adds up to the fact that what matters is not just what people know about the product but how they feel about it and how they are able to relate it to their own personalities and lifestyles. The effect of advertising then becomes much more part of a continuing relationship with an individual and their peer group than a step-by-step sequential activity as envisaged in the earlier hierarchy of effects models (see Section 2.3). The right or creative/intuitive side of the brain will probably be more involved in purchasing decisions than the left or rational/logical side. Research and measurement techniques need to reflect this emphasis.

2.9 Summary

In this chapter:

- We have reviewed the key ingredients in effective advertising and explored the main theories of how advertising works – and of their limitations from the early days of Starch and DAGMAR through to Hedges, Longman, Joyce, and more recently Earls.
- There has been a description of views on how individuals react to advertising covering the practical/symbolic views of Lannon and Cooper and we have explored the differences between attitudes, beliefs, cognitive dissonance, and the effect of cigarette advertising on consumption.
- Through reviewing the work of King we have an appreciation of how the job that advertising is designed to do can affect approaches to advertising research.
- Recent research on the effect of shifting advertising messages on the relationship people have with their existing view of the brand was reviewed and we saw that moderate incongruency in advertising may elicit higher involvement from a target audience.
- Finally, a model of how advertising might work was put forward.

Notes

1 Wilmshurst, J. and Mackay, A. *The Fundamentals and Practice of Marketing* 4th Ed., Butterworth Heinemann 2002 – see Chapter 7 – The Message and the Medium.
2 McDonald, C. *How Advertising Works,* Advertising Association, 1992.
3 Hedges, A. *Testing to Destruction,* IPA, 1974.
4 Longman, K.A., *Advertising,* Harcourt Brace Jovanovich, 1971.
5 Joyce, T. *What Do We Know about How Advertising Works? (ESOMAR, 1976).*
6 Earls, M. Advertising to the Herd: How Understanding Our True Nature Challenges the Ways We Think about Advertising and Market Research, Research Conference Papers, 2003.
7 Hall, M. and Maclay, D. Science and Art; How Does Research Match Advertising Theory? MRS Conference Papers, 1991.

8   Cova, B. and Cova, V. Tribal Marketing – The Tribalisation of Society and its Impact on the Conduct of Marketing. *European Journal of Marketing*, **36** (5/6), 595–620, 2002.

9   Lannon, J. and Cooper, P. Humanistic Advertising. *International Journal of Advertising*, July September 1983.

10 Ehrenberg, A.S.C. How do Consumers Come to Buy a Brand? *Admap*, p. 20–24, March 1997.

11 Cowell, D. (Ed.), *How to Plan Advertising*, Cassell, 1989.

12 For further information on the diffusion of innovation, see Wilmshurst, J. and Mackay, A. *The Fundamentals and Practice of Marketing*, Butterworth Heinemann, 2002, p. 67.

13 Festinger, *L. A Theory of Cognitive Dissonance*, Rox, Peterson, 1957.

14 Lancaster, K. and Lancaster, A. The Economies of Advertising: Spending, Demand, and the Effects of Bans. *International Journal of Advertising*, **22**, 41–65, 2003.

15 Luik, J.C. 'The Smee Report as a Contribution to the Tobacco Advertising Debate'. In *Advertising and Markets*, Liuk, J.C. and Waterson, M.J. (eds), London: NTC, 1996.

16 King, S. Practical Progress from a Theory of Advertisements. *Admap*, October 1975.

17 Sjödin, H. and Törn, F. 'Ad-Brand Incongruency and The Role of Preference for Consistency'. EMAC Conference, May 2003.

3 Integrated Marketing Communications

Ian Linton

Learning outcomes

This chapter will give you

- An insight into the way advertising should be integrated with other forms of marketing communication to improve overall marketing effectiveness.
- An understanding of how you can use an integrated approach to reduce direct and indirect campaign costs and simplify campaign management.
- An understanding of the benefits of integration.

You will also be able to draw on

- Real-life examples so that you will be able to plan and develop your own integrated campaigns.

3.1 Introduction

Integrated marketing provides an opportunity to improve the precision and effectiveness of marketing programmes by handling all aspects of marketing through a single source. An integrated marketing solution uses the most appropriate media and communications techniques to achieve marketing objectives. There is no 'lead' technique, and the solution could include any of the following:

- Advertising
- Direct marketing
- Telemarketing
- Web marketing
- E-mail communications
- Public relations
- Internal communications

- Incentives
- Sales force communications
- Distributor communications
- Retail support
- Product and technical information
- Corporate identity and corporate communications
- Presentations and exhibitions
- Relationship marketing.

In traditional marketing, many of these activities would be handled by separate specialist agencies or suppliers. The marketing effort is fragmented and the results could be conflicting communications that confuse the customer. In integrated marketing, all communications are channelled through a central co-ordinator and handled by a single agency. The key benefits are:

- Creative integrity
- Consistency of messages
- Unbiased marketing recommendations
- Better use of all media
- Greater marketing precision
- Operational efficiency
- Cost savings.

In more complex business-to-business markets, integrated marketing is used to build effective relationships with the many different people involved in the purchase decision-making process. Although all communications use a consistent message, that message can be tailored to the interests and concerns of individual decision makers.

3.2   Integrated marketing communications in action

Before we look at the operation of integrated marketing, here are some examples of campaigns that are fictitious, but are based on real examples. The campaigns are:

(i)   Broadening the market for a hi-fi system
(ii) Increasing traffic for a regional business airline
(iii) Developing sales of a regional fast food chain.

3.2.1   Broadening the market for a hi-fi system

The manufacturer has an established reputation for quality hi-fi systems and holds a strong market share in a high-price sector. However, the manufacturer is aware that low-price competitors are opening up a wider market by making hi-fi more accessible and more affordable for consumers who might have only considered a basic audio system. The manufacturer wants to protect share and margins in the traditional market, but take advantage of the broader opportunities.

The strategy is to use the established reputation to brand the lower-price range, and also demystify hi-fi for the new generation of buyers. The new product range will be marketed initially through popular electrical retailers, leaving the established brands with traditional dealers. However, in the long term, the manufacturer aims to market the whole range through traditional dealers to encourage consumers to trade up to higher-price products.

3.2.1.1   Press advertising

National press advertising highlights the affordable hi-fi concept and stresses the brand heritage to reassure consumers that they will have a quality product. Consumers are invited to visit a website, call a freephone number to request a brochure and get the name of their nearest retailer.

3.2.1.2   Web marketing

Consumers who visit the website are able to download general information about hi-fi, product information and details of retailers. The website includes a page that allows consumers to enter their own hi-fi preferences and 'build' their own system. This helps to demystify hi-fi and also provides the company with valuable information on customer preferences.

3.2.1.3   Direct marketing follow-up

Respondents are mailed with the offer of taking part in a free prize draw to win a collection of compact discs, whether they buy a system or not. As part of the data-capture process, prospects are asked to provide details of their current audio systems and musical tastes. Future mailings can be highly targeted with offers of music or event promotions that reflect the consumer's tastes.

3.2.1.4   Retail sales development

To ensure that prospects get the right level of service when they visit a retail outlet, the manufacturer provides product training for retail staff. The training covers the main features and benefits of hi-fi systems, and tells sales staff how to explain them in non-technical terms that will not intimidate a prospect who just wants to listen to music. To encourage sales staff to sell the product, an incentive programme will operate, offering 20 successful staff the reward of a trip to a great musical location such as Vienna, New York or Sydney.

3.2.1.5 Retail support

Retailers are provided with point-of-sale material that reflects the consumer advertising themes of affordable hi-fi. Brochures on 'making the most of hi-fi' are available and a 'free CD' offer runs for selected periods. Retailers also have access to a central telemarketing service which can be used to follow up respondents to the initial advertising campaign. Participating retailers can run competitions offering prospects the chance to win free concert tickets if they request a demonstration of the hi-fi system.

3.2.1.6 Customer information

To maintain the theme of accessible hi-fi, customers receive instructions and product guides in a simple, easy-to-use form. Technical terms are out and the guides are designed to ensure that customers are fully satisfied with their systems. A 24-hour helpline is available to any customer who needs advice.

3.2.1.7 Summary

The integrated campaign ensures that hi-fi is presented as a straightforward accessible product from the outset across all media. The manufacturer ensures that prospects will not be blinded by science at the retail outlet, and provides help and guidance after the sale.

3.2.2 Increasing traffic for a regional business airline

The airline operates mainly domestic flights between most major cities, with a small number of short-haul European flights to popular business destinations in Germany, France and the Netherlands. The company competes with larger airlines on the European routes, but faces competition from alternative forms of transport such as rail or road on many of its domestic routes.

The airline adopts a policy of niche marketing, targeting businesses that could benefit from a convenient, rapid service between certain destinations. The oil industry, for example, would be a heavy user of flights between production centres at Aberdeen and headquarters in London. The marketing strategy is to concentrate on this type of business and develop loyalty among frequent users.

3.2.2.1 Research

A research programme is used to identify companies with regional offices near the airline's terminals and head offices near other terminals. The company targets business sectors where meetings are important and where executives and other workers are likely to spend a great deal of time on travel.

3.2.2.2   Specialist advertising

The airline runs advertisements in business publications read by its target market – oil, engineering, accountancy, for example – inviting readers to receive a free business travel audit. The audit looks at their annual domestic business travel expenditure and includes a proposal for a travel package that could reduce costs. The airline also uses advertisements in the business section of regional newspapers in the catchment area of its terminals to raise awareness of the service that is available.

3.2.2.3   Direct marketing

To back up the specialist advertising, the company mails information on its services direct to companies in the target market. The companies are offered the travel audit as well as corporate discounts on staff travel. The direct marketing explains the benefits of using the airline between key destinations, and also describes the levels of customer service available.

3.2.2.4   Building customer loyalty

The loyalty programme operates at two levels – corporate and individual traveller. The corporate programme includes a package of discounts, travel information, management reporting and added-value services such as car hire and hotel bookings, which help to reduce the customer's travel administration burden.

At a personal level, travellers are offered the benefits of 'frequent flyer' programmes, including a programme like 'Air Miles', which provides points against distance travelled, the use of exclusive departure lounges and preferential rates on travel-related services such as car hire and accommodation. Information from the 'frequent flyer' programme is fed back into the airline's database to fine-tune future direct marketing to individual or corporate travel patterns.

3.2.2.5   Personalised website

The company's website provides travellers with immediate access to a wide range of travel information, as well as online booking facilities, which increase customer convenience and loyalty even further. Regular travellers can create their own personal page where they enter their personal travel preferences. The airline uses the information to ensure that the traveller's package is tailored to individual needs. The information can also be used as the basis for highly targeted e-mail communications with individual customers.

3.2.2.6 Summary

This programme makes extensive use of research data to operate a highly targeted direct marketing programme. The airline avoids head-on confrontation with larger rivals by targeting niche markets and building individual and corporate loyalty.

3.2.3 Developing sales of a regional fast food chain

A chain of fast food restaurants is expanding its local network on a region-by-region basis. Customers are offered a quality product with free home delivery within set times and a guarantee of money back if they are not completely satisfied.

In each location, the new outlet will be competing with other types of branded fast food outlet and local suppliers. The outlets are franchised and, as part of the agreement, the franchise holder must adhere to the company's quality standards. Integrated marketing support is provided centrally to ensure consistency across the network.

3.2.3.1 Regional and local advertising

Regional press, local press and local commercial radio are the main media for raising consumer awareness of the new outlets. Radio commercials include a freephone number to supply details of the nearest branch and for callers to obtain introductory vouchers. The press advertisements include the name of all the branches in the area and also include coupons. Poster sites outside cinemas, clubs and other entertainment venues are used to attract customers for late-night specials.

3.2.3.2 Customer loyalty programmes

Data capture through the freephone number and through coupon information is used as the basis for mailing customers with money-off vouchers and special offers for regular customers. Telemarketing is used selectively to offer frequent buyers a complimentary meal. Customers are also given a hotline number to call in the event of a problem, and they are asked to complete occasional questionnaires on the quality of service.

3.2.3.3 Staff motivation programmes

To ensure that each branch delivers the right level of customer service, branches are measured on their performance. Information from the customer questionnaires and the hotline is used to assess branch performance against targets, and selected staff from the best-performing branches qualify for a trip to an international convention.

3.2.3.4 Summary

The campaign combines consumer awareness with high levels of customer service and loyalty building programmes that attract new prospects and retain them as regular customers.

3.3   The benefits of integration

3.3.1   Creative integrity

Integrated marketing offers strategic and creative integrity across all media. In practical terms, that means the theme and style of advertising are followed consistently through all media. A company that produces many different campaigns, publications and other marketing support material for a large, complex product range will be able to introduce consistent creative and visual standards. That will enable the company to present a strong, unified identity and support all its products and services with powerful branding.

When a consumer gets messages, they should be consistent. In just one campaign, a consumer might view a television commercial, read a press advertisement, visit the website, receive a direct mail shot, visit a retail outlet where there is point-of-sale material, pick up a product leaflet and participate in an incentive programme. At the same time, the consumer might talk to members of the sales force, visit an exhibition and receive a call from a telemarketing specialist.

What happens if the creative treatment of each of these is different? Confusion and lack of impact. Does the consumer think he is dealing with the same company? Each of these elements reinforces each other. While it is not essential for the visual and copy treatment to be exactly the same on each element of the campaign, they must be telling the same story. A consistent build-up like this reinforces the impact of the other elements of the programme and helps to move the consumer towards a decision.

In business-to-business marketing, the scenario can be multiplied by the number of people in the decision-making process: executive briefing for the senior management team, management guides for departmental managers who might use the product, capability presentations for the buying team, technical literature for technical specialists, product literature for the purchasing department, corporate advertisements and financial public relations aimed at the important influencers direct marketing to other members of the purchasing team, sales presentations, videos and product proposals. Add the information that distributors and other influencers need in the form of retail advertisements and mailers, point-of-sale material and distributor training, and the picture becomes very complex.

3.3.2   Consistency of messages

In integrated marketing, all copy is written or edited centrally. Although techni-cal information will vary by product or service, each publication, campaign or marketing communication will include 'positioning' messages that stress generic customer benefits such as quality of service, customer focus, corporate strength and other key factors. This consistency is impossible when copy is produced separately for advertisements, direct mail, product literature – all aimed at the same customer. Integrated marketing will ensure that every form of customer contact reinforces the customer's positive perception of the company.

Visual standards also help to reinforce the consistency of integrated commu-nications. By imposing corporate design standards on all promotional material and utilising key visual elements on advertisements and all other communica-tions material, a company can reinforce the visual identity. A corporate identity is a major investment for any company, but it pays for itself in increased recog-nition and stronger perceptions. Integrated marketing reinforces the benefits of a corporate identity programme by applying it to all media and ensuring that the company is immediately recognised. Different products, different campaigns, information from separate divisions can all be co-ordinated by introducing consistent messages.

3.3.3   Unbiased recommendations

In integrated marketing, one agency should handle all aspects of marketing and operate 'through-the-line'. An agency that works through-the-line has no bias towards any particular media; they are all treated with the same attention, because an integrated agency does not have to worry about earning commis-sion. This means that the agency is able to recommend the most appropriate strategy, which might include direct marketing, incentives or sales support for distributors and agents.

If you approached an advertising agency or public relations consultancy, you would probably be surprised if they did not recommend media advertising or a public relations campaign. If you briefed a design consultancy on your com-munication requirements, the chances are that you would be operating a print-based programme. The more specific the supplier, the more likely you are to get a predictable response. This is not a criticism because it is the role of a specialist to provide a specialised service.

In an integrated strategy, it is important to know that every element of the marketing mix is working hard and contributing to the success of the campaign. Advertisements alone, for example, may not reach all the key decision-makers for a product. Sales force contact may be vital to securing a major contract. An extended video could provide a vital live action demonstration of the product and give the direct sales force an important training tool. The success of a campaign may depend on effective local marketing by a distributor network.

An integrated marketing agency handles the full range of communication tasks and is in a unique position to offer unbiased advice on the solution that is best for the marketing task.

3.3.4   Better use of all media

In integrated marketing, different techniques and media are used to support each other to improve marketing effectiveness. For example:

- Direct marketing and telemarketing are used to support direct response advertising campaigns.
- Selected customer incentives are used to increase response to advertising or direct marketing campaigns.
- Relationship marketing programmes are used to increase customer retention.
- Sales training, targeted incentive programmes and direct marketing are used to improve direct sales performance.

Integrated marketing ensures that each medium is used to its best advantage. An exhibition specialist, for example, would be in the best position to produce a high-quality exhibition stand, but might not have the resources or the experience to supply all the back-up services that were needed to make the exhibition successful. For example, direct marketing of invitations to delegates and follow-up by telephone of all attendees can help to reinforce the work that was done on the stand. Incentives during the exhibition and suitable exhibition literature can all help to make the exhibition work much harder.

A seminar that is integrated with an executive briefing programme, and a direct marketing campaign that provides senior executives with useful product and service management guides ensure that clients get full benefit from the seminar programme and that the communications effect is much stronger. By integrating editorial publicity with advertising and using telemarketing to follow up all direct marketing campaigns, you increase the impact and effectiveness of every campaign.

3.3.5   Greater marketing precision

Integrated marketing contributes to greater marketing precision. In an integrated marketing programme, direct mail and other precision marketing tools are used extensively to achieve specific communication objectives. For example, a programme that requires consistent nationwide retail performance must include local marketing activities – product training for distributors, retail support programmes, local advertising and staff incentives to ensure commitment. Provided these activities are given professional support within an integrated marketing programme, they can be used to achieve specific, measurable objectives.

Integrated marketing makes extensive use of database marketing techniques; information from direct response advertising, direct marketing campaigns and telemarketing is used to build up a comprehensive picture of individual customers and prospects, so that future marketing programmes are focused with great precision.

The development of personalisation techniques means that marketing through a website can offer even higher levels of precision. Using information that customers supply when they register for an offer, companies can build personal web pages or plan regular e-mail campaigns that offer individual prospects tailored information.

A single medium strategy may be concentrated on a key part of the target audience, but it runs the risk of missing the important prospects and attempting to do everything. Integrated marketing allows you to concentrate on your mainstream marketing programmes while introducing niche market programmes and focusing on specific elements of the marketing mix to win key prospects.

3.3.6 Operational efficiency

Another major benefit of integrated marketing is operational efficiency. It takes less people to manage integrated marketing. There is a single point of contact with one agency, which ties up less management and administrative time. Because there is a single point of contact, there is no inter-agency conflict of interest. When differing departments or individuals are working with separate specialist agencies, there can be little co-ordination and a great deal of duplication of effort. Agency and supplier management costs are duplicated because each agency/client relationship requires separate estimating, ordering, invoicing and other control procedures.

Compare the simplicity of an integrated marketing relationship with the traditional structures of client, agencies and specialist suppliers. In a large consumer goods company, for example, you might find brand managers working with different advertising agencies, a marketing director working with another agency on corporate campaigns, incentives and promotion specialists using groups of suppliers. There could be a publication manager dealing with designers, writers, photographers, new media companies and printers to produce product literature and point-of-sale, training managers producing and marketing information for the sales force and national account managers producing programmes for individual retail outlets. Add public relations executives handling press and public relations activities through a consultancy, a design manager developing a new corporate identity and a direct mail specialist to produce consumer direct marketing campaigns.

Each department or individual will be selecting and monitoring suppliers operating to their own standards, raising purchase orders, checking invoices and creating payment authorisation. This is time-consuming and inefficient.

It takes up a great deal of management time and it can lead to duplication of costs and effort.

In integrated marketing, single agencies are appointed to handle and co-ordinate all marketing and communication activities. While they may not handle every type of work with their own resources, they also provide a management service to deal with specialist suppliers, selecting them, briefing them, evaluating their work and handling all administration on behalf of the client.

3.3.7 Cost savings

Integrated marketing can also save money. Apart from the reduction in administrative costs, consolidating all expenditure in a single agency should mean greater value for money. Key savings might include:

- Better media rates through centralised buying
- Rationalisation of product literature
- Elimination of duplication in areas such as photography
- Reduction in hidden internal administration costs
- Competitive centralised buying across all marketing activities.

The benefits of centralised media buying through media independents and full service agencies have already been well established. Integrated marketing takes it a stage further and ensures that all media are purchased centrally, so the client not only gets the benefit of efficient press, television and radio buying, but also benefits from volume buying of print, artwork and other specialist marketing services. Integrated marketing agencies are able to select the most efficient, cost-effective suppliers and work in long-term partnership with them. Partnership and continuity of work mean that the supplier can afford to offer more competitive prices and better value for money.

Many integrated marketing agencies utilise international quality standards to manage the quality of their suppliers and their internal processes. This not only improves quality, it can also help to reduce the cost of waste, and that can be a significant saving.

Integrated marketing reduces a great deal of duplication in the creative and production processes. To take a simple example, photography can be planned in advance to ensure maximum utilisation of location and material. Take a car manufacturer, for example. Photography would be required for press and television advertisements, videos, product literature, direct mail, point-of-sale, training material and distributor support programmes. If each of these specialist departments or agencies organised its own photography, there would be an enormous element of wastage, not to mention creative disparity. Integrated marketing ensures that creative resources like this can be utilised in the most cost-effective way.

The development of creative treatment could yield further cost savings; as the first section showed, creative integrity is an essential element of integrated marketing. This means that the creative themes are developed centrally and then fine-tuned to the specific needs of each medium. Depending on the method of agency remuneration, this can represent a significant saving on production costs over a complete campaign and reduce the potential duplication of work.

3.4   Evaluating the benefits of integrated marketing communications

Integrated marketing offers important creative and cost benefits, but it must be carefully evaluated before a company makes a commitment to a single agency solution. These are some of the indicators that demonstrate the need for an integrated approach:

- Customers receive communications material from different sources in the same company.
- Different company departments commission their own marketing materials.
- Visual and copy standards vary between departments.
- The company is losing the opportunity to cross-sell and build long-term relationships with customers.
- The company uses many different suppliers to produce marketing support material and there is little co-ordination between suppliers.
- Visual standards do not result in consistency.
- The company uses many different sales channels to market its products, and channel performance varies considerably.
- The cost of marketing administration is high because of the number of different suppliers.
- Staff currently spending time on producing marketing support material could be better utilised on more productive customer-focused tasks.

3.5   Introducing an integrated marketing programme

These are the main stages in introducing integrated marketing into an organisation:

(i)   Establish the right internal structure.
(ii)   Select a suitable agency to handle integrated marketing.
(iii)   Select pilot projects or campaigns to evaluate the potential for integrated marketing.

3.5.1   Internal structure for integrated marketing

The client can simplify the structure of the marketing department. There should be one co-ordinator or co-ordinating group working with one contact within the agency, thus ensuring that the agency is briefed clearly on every aspect of the communications programme. The marketing director is likely to be the key person in the briefing process. It is his or her responsibility to determine the strategy and to co-ordinate the requirements of functional specialists.

3.5.2   Selecting an agency

Integrated marketing means that one agency handles all creative work and co-ordinates the work of other marketing specialists. These are the key factors in selecting an integrated marketing agency:

- The agency employs high-calibre staff in all the key marketing disciplines.
- The agency has quality-controlled suppliers to maintain consistent standards across all media.
- The agency has the financial stability to maintain a presence for the long term.
- The agency can demonstrate a successful track record in each of the key media.
- The agency can measure the marketing and financial performance of their campaigns.

Within the agency, the core team is:

- Account planner
- Creative director
- Account director.

These three have access to a range of specialists in each of the marketing disciplines. The account directors are the key players, because they liaise with the client marketing director and interpret the client brief to the rest of the team. The agency is used to working with a wide variety of suppliers, so is in a position to select the most appropriate for the project.

The client is likely to have a more limited choice. Specialist suppliers work on a partnership basis with the agency, meeting their quality requirements and operating within a consistent strategic brief. International quality standards have a useful role to play in maintaining an effective relationship between supplier and agency.

This close working relationship helps to maintain consistent quality visual standards. Suppliers are managed at a creative and strategic level, while the detailed project implementation is carried out by specialists who understand the practicalities of print, direct mail or events. By working closely with an agency, a supplier builds a better understanding of the project and quality requirements. This ensures a continuity of service.

3.5.2.1   The client /agency relationship

This needs to be a long-term relationship so that the agency gets to know the client's business thoroughly and the client adjusts to dealing with a single source of supply. Over a period of time, the client and the agency get to understand the other variables in the success of a marketing programme. The client retains the key role in developing marketing strategy, but can spend less time in managing supplier relationships and can concentrate on more important strategic tasks.

3.5.3   Selecting pilot projects or campaigns

Selecting pilot projects or campaigns to evaluate the potential for integrated marketing can highlight both benefits and risks. A small regional campaign, a campaign for a lower profile brand or product or a campaign targeted at a small part of the total market can indicate whether the integrated approach will work on a larger scale. Use this to test a number of factors:

- Does the agency really understand integrated marketing?
- Does the campaign include the right balance of media?
- Has the campaign produced measurable results?
- Does a different balance produce better results?
- Are costs and savings from integration in line with budgets?

3.6   Summary

In this chapter:

- We have seen how integrated marketing provides many important business benefits, including creative integrity, consistency of messages, unbiased marketing recommendations, better use of communications media, greater marketing precision, improved operational efficiency and cost savings.
- However, we have seen that introducing integrated marketing represents a considerable risk, and it is important to review its potential and implications through a pilot project or test campaign before committing to a single source solution.
- We saw that looking closely at internal structures and selecting the right agency are important stages in a successful transition to integrated marketing.

Further reading

Linton, I. and Morley, K. *Integrated Marketing Communications*, Butterworth-Heinemann, 1995.

Fill, C. CIM Coursebook 03/04, *Integrated Marketing Communications*, Butterworth-Heinemann, 2003.

Integrated Marketing Communications. Pickton, D. and Broderick, A. (eds), FT Prentice Hall, 2000.

Belch, G. and Belch, M. *Advertising and Promotion: An Integrated Marketing Communications Perspective*, McGraw Hill Education, 2003.

Smith, P.R. and Taylor, J. *Marketing Communications – An Integrated Approach*, Kogan Page, 2001.

Clow, K.E. and Baack, D. *Integrated Advertising, Promotion and Marketing Communications*, Prentice Hall, 2003.

4 The Advertiser

Peter Beaumont

Learning outcomes

By the end of this chapter you will:

- Review the different types of advertiser client.
- Gain a perspective on how they view advertising.
- How they go about buying advertising.
- Gain an introduction to how they might go about selecting an advertising agency and what their responsibilities are to the agency.

4.1 Who or what is 'the advertiser'?

In brief, the advertiser is an individual or company who wants to talk to a specific group of people and, most importantly, make that group of people want to do something!

Exactly what action or reaction an advertiser wants to achieve is, of course, dictated very much by the sales message; it could be that the advertiser wants to sell a specific product, influence public opinion, inform us of changes to a store, encourage visits to a website or even to buy from the trade or public (watches and jewellery wanted, cash paid for bric-a-brac, etc).

Let us examine the role of one advertiser from the advertising agency's point of view. What kinds of advertiser exist, how can an agency help them, and what type of relationship can the two expect to enjoy?

Advertisers are, of course, everywhere.

The market stallholder carefully arranging his display of fruit and vegetables, the corporate giant thrusting its logo forward in a blaze of pyrotechnics at seminars or sporting events, the cheap yet highly effective display from prostitutes advertising their talents in the windows of a red light district. There is nothing new about the phenomenon that is advertising yet one of the issues that still surprises me is how little thought is given to its importance by some of the advertisers (or 'clients' as we prefer to call them!) I meet.

By this, I mean that people running businesses (successful or otherwise) are often key decision makers across a wide spectrum of retail or commercial operations.

The day-to-day activities that a store owner or company MD undertakes can range from securing multi-million pound business deals to ensuring an adequate supply of toilet rolls for the washrooms!

Frequently, such multi-tasking dilutes the ability to focus on advertising and marketing activities, particularly if the business already enjoys relatively successful sales; a retail clothing outlet in a busy High Street for example might attract a high level of sales primarily because of its position. While it will still advertise its products through window displays and other points of sale, its manager may not have to consider other promotional avenues until its success is challenged by other market influences. The opening of a rival store selling cheaper products, parking limitations or a shift in consumer tastes may suddenly force that manager to re-evaluate its stance on advertising and seek professional advice to combat falling sales.

And that's where the agency comes in.

Advertiser attitudes to an advertising agency vary enormously. The sometimes vulgar excesses of the larger agencies in the heady days of the 1980s have, perhaps, left advertisers with a residue of suspicion and doubts about whether they get real value for money when securing the services of the so-called 'professionals'. It is often the case that advertisers 'need' to use agencies rather than 'want to' use them. The client is often aware that they have reached the limits of their own marketing knowledge or the creative well has run dry; rather like the avid DIY enthusiast who has been more than capable of some excellent decoration, maybe even laid a decent patio – but the extension on the back of the house is 'a brick too far'. So it's a phone call to 'Extensions R Us' or in the case of the inexperienced advertiser, 'Adverts R Us'.

Such reservations were very prevalent during the time I was repping for my local newspaper many years ago. It was easy to persuade potential advertisers as to the many benefits of why they should advertise (examples of which are no doubt highlighted by contributors elsewhere in this book) but the advertiser only gets one perspective on advertising medium when presented to by an agent for a local newspaper, radio station, web developer or direct mail house.

It is, of course, often a combination of the marketing mix that will best serve the needs of the advertiser, and the agency is, therefore, able to offer more pragmatic 'independent' advice in this regard. Indeed, when I personally made the transition from newspaper advertising salesperson to agency account handler, I was pleasantly surprised that advertisers I had previously dealt with welcomed my new found impartiality and listened to what I had to say with a more relaxed attitude. It is the 'independence' factor that would, to use the DIY analogy, put the advertising agency in the category of 'structural adviser' for the home extension, sourcing most reputable builders, bricklayers and joiners for the job.

Categorising types of advertiser (or clients) is a difficult and (in my opinion) rather futile exercise. It often serves only to highlight the individual nuances of clients so, as an agency, we tend to categorise advertisers by business types, that is, motors, property, retail, education, local authority, etc. There are, however, distinct categories of individuals with decision-making authority within these sectors, representing the advertising and marketing interests of their own particular business.

4.1.1 The sole trader

He or she is typically self-employed and will operate either alone or with a relatively small team.

Plumbers, electricians, builders, childminders, gardeners, roofing specialists, shopkeepers, etc. would generally fall into this category. The sole trader is primarily a 'classified' advertiser, utilising the service classification system found within the local or regional press, phone books and directories, etc. Home service-based websites also allow this type of advertiser a larger window of opportunity.

The sole trader, while rarely having the need or budget to employ agency services, is an excellent example of a business that recognises the value of advertising in all its guises, often from its inception.

Consider the leaflets from such advertisers that will regularly appear through your letterbox. Small businesses of this kind appreciate the need to remind their customers of their existence. Such advertisers also face the disadvantages of their classified marketplace; essentially, their sales message is on show with that of all their competitors! There is often a belief of 'the bigger the advert, the better the company' – at least from the end user's point of view.

In my experience of advising this type of advertiser, the greatest obstacle to overcome is changing attitudes based on a 'collective acceptance' of what classified adverts should look like.

Advertisers are often nervous about breaking what they perceive as being the standardised mould of advert content and as such end up with dull, non-persuasive messages that do not promote their businesses' unique selling points or excite their potential customers.

A glance through any Directory (Yellow or otherwise!) will provide countless examples of 'tombstone' advertisements where the advertiser boldly proclaims his name at the top of the advert as if that alone will tempt the reader to believe that his or her product or service is best.

There has been a slight shift in attitudes more recently that has seen sole trader advertising become more creative, informative and visually attractive. A lot of this has been influenced by advances in the art department services offered by newspapers and directories or the enhanced production values provided by local radio stations.

The sole trader may never set the benchmark for award-winning advertising campaigns, but he or she does at least have an appreciation of the power of advertising. Such advertisers may not have a shop front or corporate office from which to display their capabilities and so advertising is essential to the generation of new business as well as for helping to retain existing customers.

4.1.2   The owner/manager

Typically, in many small- to medium-sized businesses, control of an advertising budget will fall to the owner/manager. In addition to the responsibilities of the day-to-day running of the business, they will also have to consider sales forecasts and what marketing activities, if deemed necessary, will support their sales operation to achieve such forecasts.

Working for an advertising agency, I deal with this type of advertiser on a very regular basis. From the agency perspective there are a number of advantages to the relationship.

More often than not, this type of advertiser is happy to leave aspects of media planning, media buying, creative work and other marketing activities to the agency. The advertiser appreciates the need to advertise and also the advice and experience the agency has to offer across a wide spectrum of advertising activities. Owner/managers are busy people who are skilled at multi-tasking. They tend to have a good basic understanding of advertising and the reasons why their specific business should advertise.

Conversely, it is the fact that they often find their skills diluted across several operational areas that can also have drawbacks from the agency's perspective. The client may not always be able to brief agencies in a meaningful manner because of time constraints or other distractions. This can result in the agency producing work that does not adequately reflect the aims of the client nor, on occasions, correctly address the target market.

The hourly charges for work like design and photography can also be hard to digest for an individual with little knowledge of the way an agency and its team works and so the agency is often constantly seeking to justify its charges to clients used to keeping a tight hold of the purse strings.

However, the agency enjoys the benefit of working with a decision-maker with a sense of commercial responsibility so projects do not get bogged down or crushed beneath the wheels of bureaucracy!

4.1.3   The committee

Oh, the dreaded 'C-word'!

At the risk of being controversial here, I am not a big fan of the decision by committee. I also accept that there is a degree of hypocrisy in my view as I am a staunch advocate of creative 'brain-storming' with a team of designers (and with clients!) but I just have a bit of a problem with advertisers who make most of their marketing decisions in a democratic (but bureaucratic) environment.

Such committees tend to exist at the highest boardroom level or, more frequently, in local authority, education or other public sector situations.

And of course there is good reason for their existence. Public funds are not to be spent lightly, nor shareholders interests go unrecognised.

The collective decision-making process can also be a bit of a cop out as well! Mini power struggles and point-scoring between committee members can result in the overall dilution of many advertising campaigns; everyone wants their say! As the old saying goes 'A camel is a horse designed by committee'!

My belief is that with individual decision-making processes there automatically comes a greater degree of responsibility and thus the advertising objectives, strategies and results of a business tend to be more clearly focused. My concerns with some (certainly not all) advertising committees (or steering groups/project teams/whatever the current trend!) is that broadly shared responsibility, while protecting individuals from accusations of mismanagement, also fragments some of the bolder aspects of advertising and marketing campaigns. Great campaigns are not just the brainchild of the agency. Often they are a shared vision of both advertiser and agency based on a relationship of understanding and experience.

However, to redress the balance, because of the nature of these grouped decision-making processes, what often happens is that an agenda becomes the basis for an advertising brief – that Holy Grail for an agency. Advertisers are forced to at least agree on goals/funds/time scales/information available for marketing projects and this is a valuable starting point for both client and agency.

4.1.4   The sales and marketing manager

Many companies and businesses recognise the value that the marketing mix brings to their organisations. They see the correlation between advertising (above, below and through-the-line) and sales and take steps to harness the potential in a structured manner. Often, this results in the appointment of a sales and/or marketing manager – an individual, often from a sales background, with an understanding of the target market and responsibility for sales and marketing budgeting and forecasts.

In large corporations it is common to find brand managers who will work alongside sales and marketing operations to ensure that they dovetail with the development of the brand.

Marketing managers or brand managers will often have come from a marketing background; perhaps graduates or having had experience within other organisations. They are the most informed type of advertiser in that, as well as having an in-depth understanding of their own business and its customers, they will also have an appreciation of the range of marketing activities that they can utilise to maximise sales and profits for their business.

Often, these advertisers will work autonomously, buying their own media, developing their own creative strategies and, with the assistance of in-house design teams, producing artwork to a pre-press stage. Some of the large banks or catalogue companies are examples of organisations who, to a large extent, have become self-sufficient in many aspects of their advertising and marketing. Agencies are often contracted, along with media houses, to undertake just the creative and media buying aspects of a campaign, leaving the sales and marketing manager to plan schedules, arrange print and distribution of material.

The relationship between the account handler and advertiser in this case is often a healthy one. For a start, both parties are aware of the importance of the other; the client must maintain other sales or administrative functions and so welcomes the support afforded by an agency. He or she is able to give a clear brief often supported with valuable market research data and will also have realistic expectations about the potential success of campaigns. The agency welcomes the client's understanding of its industry and knowledge of the general costs and deadlines associated with advertising and associated projects.

For example, the marketing manager of a commemorative plate making business understands the rationale behind paying several thousand pounds for a full page advert to appear in a Sunday colour supplement.

To the uninitiated, these costs can seem daunting, particularly when one is responsible for many thousands of pounds to be spent wisely on advertising. Often the fear of spending is what results in failure, the less experienced advertisers opting time and time again for 'cheap deals' that neither fulfil their advertising objectives nor create the level of sales desired. So the sales and marketing manager has an appreciation of 'value': an understanding of consumer attitudes; an understanding of the means to communicate; an understanding of what it is they want their advertising to achieve.

4.2   The value of the brief

The aforementioned decision-maker profiles are, of course, generalisations based on my personal experiences. Advertisers all share one common aim: a belief in and willingness to advertise. Whether through press advertisements, shop window displays, bus backs, leaflet drops, TV campaigns or websites – ultimately they all want the same thing. Advertising in its simplest form, as already mentioned, is 'making someone want to do something'.

Earlier in this chapter I alluded to how surprised I was at the times when advertisers do not take their responsibility seriously. Let me be more specific. You would be amazed how often I am met with a blank face when I ask the question: 'What do you want your advertising to achieve?'

'More sales.'
'Of what – a specific product line?'

'*Yes.*'

'How many more sales?'

'*A 20% increase.*'

'Is that achievable? Is the product affected by seasonal buying trends? Has it proved to be a big seller in the past? Are we going to look at a price-led campaign? What information do we have to support our offer? Do demographics affect the potential sales of the product?'

You get where I'm going with this don't you?

The point is that advertisers have a responsibility to themselves and (if they use one) their agency to try and formulate a brief – simplistically – the rationale behind what they want to achieve and why.

An advertising agency appreciates the value of a detailed brief and is able to provide much better researched and ultimately effective campaigns by tailoring advertising to meet customer expectations. It can also seek to amend advertiser expectations if they are unrealistic, thereby avoiding unnecessary expense and disappointment. The better the brief from the advertiser, whether to themselves, a designer, printer, newspaper representative or agency – the better the advertising campaign.

4.3   Why use an agency?

I have tried to avoid this chapter becoming a flag-waving exercise for advertising agencies but I want to briefly consider what advertisers have to gain from working with agencies.

- They buy-in experience – agencies frequently work across a variety of market sectors. This experience allows them to evaluate what has worked for other clients in other areas and apply many of those strategies to other clients' campaigns. An agency is able to think beyond the parameters of individuals who are often too close to their own business to 'see the wood from the trees' and therefore offer creative, innovative marketing solutions.
- Credibility – an agency can make a one-man-band operation look like a multi-million pound corporation. A multi-million pound corporation can make itself look like a one-man-band without the right design advice and production.

  Consider the Internet – a fantastic global advertisement that offers the sole trader the same potential audience as Mickey Mouse or James Bond. Some modest investment in website design can give the little guy huge advantages in the worldwide marketplace. Image, while not being everything, is important. Professionally produced advertisements, posters, websites and vehicle livery create a sense of confidence with consumers. People want to deal with successful businesses and a company that exhibits its dynamic and appealing face to customers is more likely to succeed than one that remains shrouded in a cloak of mediocrity.

- Value – like the mortgage broker or independent financial adviser, an agency is able to use its knowledge of the products and services available in the marketplace. This means it is ideally positioned to ensure that the advertiser benefits from its increased buying power while maintaining the levels of quality required.

4.4   So how should an advertiser choose an agency?

Well, for a start, he or she could do worse than to look at how the agency advertises its own services! Look at the advert in Yellow Pages, ask for a company brochure and visit the website. It may be wise for the advertiser to ask to see samples of the agency's work prior to arranging a meeting. Also to establish the types and sizes of clients the agency deals with. An agency dealing primarily with blue chip corporations may not be able to offer a small business the same time, creativity or value for money as an agency with a more modest client base, often purely because it is staffed and structured around specific accounts with specific needs and budgets.

The advertiser should also try and establish at the outset the charges or fee structure the agency operates to avoid souring a potential relationship due to a misunderstanding about costs. Does the agency work to agreed project costs or will it always charge on an hourly basis? Is there a service charge? What does it entail? Are meetings and general consultancy work charged for?

Overall though, like buying a new house, car or pair of shoes, I would advise advertisers to go with their instinct. If the initial meeting between client and agency 'feels right', then the chances are it usually is. Ultimately, trust, mutual respect, honesty and a relationship that encourages ideas and enthusiasm will benefit both advertiser and agency.

Symbiosis is the key to successful long-term partnerships but the advertiser should also be wary of agencies slipping into a 'comfort zone' and not be afraid to challenge their ideas, costs or working practices if it is ever felt that some of the spark has gone!

See Section 12.4 for more ideas on choosing an advertising agency.

4.5   So what of the responsibility of the advertiser?

Well, from the agency's point of view, he or she needs to offer clear, meaningful briefs, develop an understanding of the likely costs associated with the project and respect the deadlines imposed by any proposed advertising campaign.

Beyond that, however, the advertiser (and agency if one is employed) have to respect and obey any legislation that applies to what they can or cannot say in an advertisement (whatever its form). See Chapter 21 – Advertising, Self-regulation and the Law. Advertising codes of practice require advertisements to be 'legal, decent, honest and truthful' – that means not making false claims about a product or service. The advert should not be misleading, it should respect the particular laws of that land (you will notice throughout the world how the same advert can be 'doctored' to ensure its suitability for that particular culture – the middle eastern countries being a good example where the amounts of flesh that can be exposed in advertisements is restricted in accordance with religious beliefs) and also the boundaries of good taste. What constitutes good taste, however, is a matter of some conjecture as people's attitudes as to what is and is not acceptable change rapidly just like hairstyles or fashion.

Advertisers who employ shock tactics just for the sake of it (remember the Beneton adverts in the late 1980s?) sometimes push the boundaries of taste to enhance their brand recognition (on the basis that controversy has always come with the added benefits of high media exposure – just ask Madonna!) Yet, peculiarly, we have recently seen Barnardo's rapped across the knuckles by the Advertising Standards Authority for portraying images considered too shocking for public consumption. The irony is that here is a charity that genuinely needs that 'shock value' to get its point across and I, for one, am sometimes disappointed by the inconsistencies that exist within our self-imposed industry censorship guidelines.

4.6 Why thank advertisers?

Let us never forget that without the advertiser, books like this would not exist. They are the foundation that multi-billion pound global industries are built upon. Advertisers means advertising. Advertising means sales and sales generate employment, wealth and the structure of an economy.

Advertising has existed in nature since the dawn of time; the courtship rituals of tropical birds of paradise give credence to that! It is mankind that has expanded the focus of advertising to such an extent that it is now able to change what we eat, what we wear, what we drive – even how we think.

And think we must – because advertising without thought is not really advertising at all.

4.7 Summary

In this chapter:

- We saw how the market is made up of many different types of advertiser from sole traders through to major international organisations.
- It was made clear that advertiser clients have a wide perspective on how they view advertising from the very simplistic to the complex.

- We discovered how the variety of advertiser clients go about buying advertising and the way they take decisions has implications for advertising agencies.
- We had an outline introduction to how advertisers might go about selecting an advertising agency and confirmed that the advertiser has the responsibility to provide a clear brief to the agency.

5 The Advertising Agency

Richard Mayer

Learning outcomes

By the end of this chapter you will:

- Understand the nature and role of the advertising agency.
- Appreciate the importance of client and agency relationships.
- Understand the structure of a modern advertising agency.
- Develop an awareness of the key factors impacting upon the advertising agency business.

5.1 Introduction

Few major organisations design their own adverts. Most rely upon the services of an agency. The services provided by an advertising agency include market research, message development, advertising copy and creativity, media planning and scheduling and production. The range of services provided is dependent upon the size of the agency and its level of expertise in each area. Many agencies will provide a 'full service' that will incorporate alongside advertising other promotional areas such as direct marketing, sales promotion and public relations. Others will specialise in specific aspects of advertising such as creativity, production or copy writing. Most marketers choose to enlist the services of an advertising agency. The agency will provide creative and business services to clients in planning, preparing and placing advertisements. The agency offers a professional service with specialised talents, expertise and experience that in most cases cannot be matched by in-house employees.

5.2 The origin of the advertising agency

Early advertising agents were exactly that: they were selling agents for newspapers, receiving commission from those newspapers on the amount of advertising space they could sell to advertisers. Often they would act as media brokers by buying space in quantity and then retailing it to advertisers in smaller portions: the main point to grasp is that their income came from the media, much as it does today – despite the number of changes that have occurred within the industry.

These early agents soon discovered that it was easier to sell the space if they offered to show the advertiser how the space could be filled, that is, to design the advertisement and to write the copy. This rapidly grew to a stage in which the agent from being a one-man all-rounder, started to employ specialist writers, designers and, at a later stage, media buyers and production executives.

As the early agencies built up their client lists, clients became more important than the media. Thus, although the income of agencies continued to be derived from the media, it was the advertiser that guaranteed their continued use of any particular medium and, therefore, the commission from it.

The first acknowledged advertising agency was William Taylor, in 1786. The name of Jem White, who started up in Fleet Street in 1800, existed until the late 1980s in the context of White Bull Holmes, a well-known recruitment-advertising agency in London.

As advertising developed during the 1920s and 1930s some famous advertising themes emerged: they became famous for two reasons; first originality, and second the fact that they were used consistently for a long period of time. The examples which even today may be remembered are 'Guinness is good for you', 'What we want is Watneys', 'Virol for growing babies', 'Bovril prevents that sinking feeling', 'Players please', 'Craven A does not affect the throat' and many others.

It is interesting to observe that some of these famous slogans would not be admitted today under the series of laws and self-imposed controls, which now exist. This former freedom of advertising is particularly noticeable in some of the medical advertisements, which ran in the earlier part of the century, making outrageous claims to cure a whole assortment of afflictions. (See Chapter 21 – Advertising: Self-regulation and the Law.)

5.3   The evolution of the advertising agency

The period between the 1920s and 1940 was largely one of creative advertising, an era in which flamboyant personalities who ran their agencies in an autocratic manner, generated campaigns of great originality, style, panache and memorability. In this sense they were right for their times. The advertising agency business has always been one in which individuals have been able to strike out and start up new companies. But more significant developments were under way in the 1950s with the emergence of larger agencies, heavily influenced by America. There was a general move towards research in assessment of tasks to be done and measuring advertising performance. Big agencies like Young and Rubicam, The London Press Exchange, J Walter Thompson, McCann Erickson, Erwin Wasey and others built up substantial marketing and research departments (the forerunners of today's planning departments). These departments not only conducted research into what the advertising task was, but also started to become closely involved with clients' own plans for developing and marketing new products. Side by side with this development was the growth of research companies and more sophisticated measurement systems. During the 1950s companies like A C Nielson, Attwoods and – a little later on – AGB were able to provide highly detailed pictures of consumers' daily activities in purchasing goods, and in the effect advertising had in influencing their choice.

In the same period, colour in magazine production gradually improved. It was not at that stage a dominant force on a large scale, apart from a small number of mass-circulation magazines. The newspaper world was comparatively untouched. Nevertheless, printing techniques were improving all the time, leading to the skills of production buying becoming much more accepted in advertising agencies. Production departments gradually assumed an importance far beyond that which had applied in the 1920s and 1930s, and began to be consulted at the campaign planning stage.

Then in 1955, on 22 September, came an event which was to change the face of advertising – and therefore of agencies. This was the launch of commercial television, largely in black and white in the early days. Until that time, most large-scale campaigns had sought to begin with a half-page in the old broadsheet *Daily Express*, (the leading circulation newspaper at that time). Now campaigns were launched with mass television coverage, and the exploitation of this to the appropriate trade distributors of the product concerned. Advertising began to permeate the life of the nation and helped to lead to the acceptance of advertising as a commercial weapon. More and more, it became an essential part of the market planning of large manufacturers.

Equally, advertising began to attract a more critical eye from the nation. Such was the mushrooming of the advertising industry that the law was amended on a number of occasions to cope with new situations as they arose. One of the most significant measures was the Merchandise Marks Act of 1956, later replaced by the Trade Descriptions Act of 1968, providing a strong legal framework in which advertising has been required to operate.

Side by side with the strengthening of the law, a voluntary code emerged, sponsored and supported by the Advertising Association, the body that represents all sides of the advertising business. The Code of Advertising Practice was formed originally in 1961, and was followed in 1963 by the Advertising Standards Authority, which carried the status of a semi-official body. This provided a source through which consumers could complain about advertisements: details of complaints were published, with not only the name of the advertiser, but also the name of the agency concerned.

Thus, the agency had over the course of 20 or 30 years become a more professional organisation, relying more on professional research and marketing techniques, carrying a greater sense of ethical and moral responsibility, but at the same time almost exploding with new bursts of creativity as the new medium of television changed the whole scene. Radio advertising started to offer commercial opportunities but its real progress was to come later in the 1980s. Cinema advertising also provided agencies with immense creative opportunities during the 1950s but its audiences were rapidly affected by the advent of television. But however much cinema audiences changed, creativity in the cinema remained of a very high standard, and does to this day. In fact, the late 1980s saw a considerable revival of this important medium.

As the 1960s drew to a close, a fresh spark of creativity seemed to light up the London agency scene. What many regarded as the deadening hand of marketing and research techniques was lifted by a new generation of young creative advertising people seeking more exciting ways of communicating in a very competitive world; companies like Saatchi & Saatchi and Kirkwoods were formed.

In the late 1970s, this rebirth of the creative influence found an important new way of giving expression to itself, through the development of 'Media Brokers' (companies who performed all the media planning, buying and checking work previously done by an advertising agency). This enabled bright young creative people to start their own agencies more easily. The media buying responsibilities and financial risks were passed to media brokers, who received part of the commission. The fledgling agency was able to concentrate its energies on the true and final product of any advertising agency – the advertisements themselves. Many agencies started on this basis – companies like WCRS, Gold Greenless Trott, Bartle Bogle and Hegarty, and many others.

The introduction of the media independent was born as a result of the frustration many media specialists felt: that their discipline was under regarded, poorly resourced and poorly rewarded within the traditional advertising agency structure. Initially, they were greeted with hostility and suspicion, seen as an attack on the commission system and threatening the industry's status quo. The growth of the creative agencies alongside the growing complexity of media provided the media independents with a platform for growth. Within a few years the leading media specialists were pitching for work alongside top advertising agencies. Now, media specialists in Europe have over 85 per cent of the market with many of the top advertising agencies deciding to set up their own media independents managing an ever more complex media planning and buying process.

With the competitive business atmosphere emerging everywhere during the early 1980s, a number of monopoly procedures were broken down. Among these was the rigid commission system, by which advertising agencies were not allowed to pass back any commission received from the media to their clients. Once this practice was officially deregulated, deals between agencies and clients became common. Gradually, it emerged that 15 per cent of the billing represented a good starting point for negotiation. In some cases, an additional fee supplemented this since even a full 15 per cent commission did not cover the amount of work an agency did. On other occasions the agency was satisfied with a commission below the 15 per cent norm: a typical example would be a multimillion pound campaign using three or four television commercials repeated over the year. An industrial advertising campaign involving dozens of low unit cost trade or technical publications is a very different kettle of fish.

The 1990s saw the development of the international 'full service' agency, providing a one-stop solution to global clients' communication needs. The increased attention given by clients to integrated marketing communications and international communications led to the development of global communication companies. Many were built through the process of acquiring smaller specialist agencies. The largest agency of its kind is the WPP group. The world's top 10 advertising organisations now command over a third of the world's advertising revenues. Within these larger agencies faster growth and higher profit margins are found in non-advertising-based services such as public relations and direct marketing, than from income derived from traditional mainstream advertising.

Alongside this growth in large international agencies new specialist agencies have successfully evolved, offering services in the Internet and interactive communication. At the same time new independent communication agencies have successfully positioned themselves in specialist niches within the market offering new ways of thinking on marketing issues. Agencies such as Circus, Foundation and The Fourth Room, combine management consultancy skills with advertising, providing strategic advice, knowledge of the business, brand development as well as expertise in communication. These agencies offer their clients a multi-disciplinary strategic planning and communications service, which is not wedded to traditional advertising agency disciplines and solutions.

The Fourth Room*

Pier Schmidt, one of the founders of the Fourth Room, has a neat way of describing what his agency is all about. He calls it 'corporate homeopath'; the place clients should come if they are seeking some alternative medicine to more conventional agencies. With an office based in a Georgian terraced house in Bloomsbury, the working environment lives up to this promise.

Scmidt says the Fourth Room aims to marry analytical skills with 'strategic skills' to help companies grow. He argues that many clients have recently been so preoccupied with cost cutting exercises or growth through acquisition that they have not focused sufficiently on how their markets are changing and developing.

The agency established in July 1998 has a small team of staff who utilise a range of creative working practices on client projects. Illumination teams are used to dramatise findings occasionally even acting out scenarios. For client BP Amoco, for instance, the agency mocked up a Fortune magazine supposedly from the year 2010, which carried a 'case study' of how the client had successfully integrated its brands over the previous 10 years.

The Fourth Room* *(Continued)*

Another Fourth Room innovation is systematised networking with regular breakfasts for its clients to exchange ideas. Clients are also encouraged to drop in to the agency's offices.

Clients include furniture retailer MFI, whose marketing and strategy director stated; 'I find them very creative and inspiring. They don't always do what you ask them to do – they do what's right, which is really what you want from an agency. There's good chemistry between the founders and they've allowed us to do research that's leading edge for a retailer.'

* Adapted from *Marketing*, 17 February 2000, p. 29.

This structural upheaval is taking place at an unprecedented rate and at the same time as a revolution is unfolding in advertising itself. Consumers are now bombarded with a greater number of fragmented messages and the digital age has enabled dialogue and interactivity rather than a simple monologue. Marketing communications budgets are being increasingly scrutinised and budgets diverted from advertising spend is moving into direct marketing and other promotional disciplines.

Changing Times*

Twenty years ago, maybe 20 advertising agencies handled nearly 80 per cent of the business in the UK, provided the strategic thinking and bought the media. Even within this group there were perhaps an elite five or six who appeared on most clients' wish lists. Agencies were more similar than they were different. Today, everything has been unbundled. Media has been separated, not once but sometimes twice, with specialist planning agencies being set up alongside buying shops.

There are now big differences between agencies, not only in terms of their size, but also their cultures and approaches, and the variety of different communications products they deliver. There are advertising agencies that produce direct marketing, direct marketing agencies that produce advertising, design agencies that provide strategic consultancy, strategic consultancies that provide design – and so it goes on.

* Martin Jones, A.A.R. – *Admap*, May 2001.

5.4   Types of advertising agency

Within the communications industry a variety of organisations will provide a range of services for the client. A company such as Kellogg's will utilise different agencies to provide advertising, sales promotions, public relations and point of purchase materials. Media scheduling and buying will be outsourced to a media specialist. (See Figure 5.1.)

Advertising agencies:

- Full-service agencies
- Creative boutiques
- Media-buying services
- E-commerce agencies
- In-house agencies

Agency services:

- Account services
- Marketing research
- Creative and production
- Media planning and research
- Media buying

Promotion agencies:

- Direct marketing and database agencies
- E-commerce agencies
- Event planning
- Design firms
- Public relations firms
- Field marketing agencies
- Point of purchase agencies

Figure 5.1 *Agency organisations*

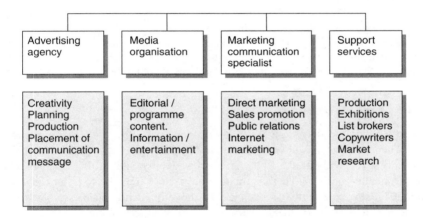

Figure 5.2 *Full-service agency*

5.4.1 Full-service agencies

The largest advertising agencies provide additional services such as direct marketing and public relations. These agencies most commonly began life as advertising agencies and over time have grown through acquiring smaller specialist agencies. A typical full service agency will provide a client with the facility to purchase all of their marketing communication requirements from a single source (Figure 5.2.)

The full-service agency offers its clients a 'one-stop shop' for all of their marketing communication requirements. The largest agencies such as J Walter Thompson and Saatchi & Saatchi grew their agencies through the acquisition of small specialist agencies. Smaller agencies also broadened the range of services on offer away from just advertising to provide services such as production, media, sales promotion and direct marketing. Full-service agencies argue that grouping together all of the clients' communication needs under the umbrella of one organisation leads to synergy gains between the various departments, the provision of more integrated marketing communication solutions and a single point of contact for the client when working with and monitoring agency performance.

Experience has shown that not all clients want all of their communications activity managed by one agency preferring to shop around and utilise the service of selected independent agencies. The notion that clients would get the best quality and best value for money from a single agency was not necessarily achieved. Clients began to question the quality of service that they were receiving. There was no guarantee that they could obtain the best creative, media, production and marketing solutions from a single provider. Clients preferred to engage specialists in different organisations. Issues also arise with regard to the internal structure and relationships within the full-service agency. In an ideal situation each department would have an equal degree of influence, as part of an integrated proposition to the client. In reality, internal conflicts occur between the specialist departments regarding roles, respective importance, influence and sometimes exclusion from the planning and implementation process.

5.4.2   Creative boutiques

Creative boutiques have long been an important part of the advertising industry. Their strength has always been the ability to turn out inventive creative work quickly without the constraints imposed by agency bureaucracy or departmental conflicts. They commonly have more freedom to be unconventional, a key competitive advantage in the advertising business. Creative boutiques focus only on the delivery of creative solutions to clients' communication problems. Clients will often use creative boutiques alongside a full-service agency to provide fresh ideas and novel approaches. Boutiques cannot compete against full-service agencies in providing integrated communication strategies. Their work is often short-term project based. A key benefit to the client is that they can often get more attention and better access to creative talent than they would at a larger agency.

5.4.3   Media independents

A combination of the growth of television sales houses, the increasing fragmentation and complexity of the media market and the clients' desire to control media costs led to the development and growth of media independents. For anyone entering the media profession now it is hard to imagine the days when media was the Cinderella of advertising: unsophisticated, unappreciated and unfashionable. Today's media specialists are used to working with companies dedicated to the business of media planning and buying, whose media staff are the lifeblood of the agency and whose culture is to champion the media profession. Media independents provide specialist media services in the planning, buying and monitoring of clients' media schedules, particularly in television and radio. Agencies and clients will determine their media requirements and then pass these to the media independents that negotiate and purchase advertising time. The media independents employ media specialists who have detailed knowledge of the media industry and particular skills in analysis, planning and negotiating. Traditionally, this role was carried out as part of an advertising agencies service. Media independents such as Carat now purchase large amounts of media and, therefore, arguably can negotiate larger discounts on behalf of their clients. As mentioned previously, many of the major advertising organisations have now formed their own dependent media companies in response to the rapid growth of this sector.

The birth of the media specialist*

We believe that for agencies and advertisers, the first decade of the twenty-first century will be the decade of the media. Media are playing an increasingly crucial role – there is no point in producing fantastic creative if the consumer does not see it. Also, traditional 'media planning' as we know it is changing, as new forms and formats become available and opportunities to integrate media with other forms of communications grow. As 'total communications' becomes the norm, the job of setting communications objectives grows in importance; and, along with that, the role of media agencies.

The separation of traditional media planning and buying allowed media to fight for its own position alongside creative experts at the top table within client companies. At the same time, the evolving media map and the arrival of the first marketing-literate consumer generation forced media companies to think smarter, broaden their skill base and move upstream. For lucky clients working with the more enlightened media agencies, the unveiling of media has revealed deep understanding of consumers, the role of media in their lives and their relationship with media brands. For the media team, as guardians of the bridges that link consumers to brand messages, the opportunity to chart the contact map for communications strategy is ours to own.

* Denise Gardner and Marie Oldham, Media Planning Group, *Admap*, October 2001, p. 35.

Over the past three decades the media planning and buying industry has proved itself the most dynamic, progressive and forward thinking of all the communications disciplines. It has moved from the backroom of the agency business to the front of the clients' communication needs.

5.4.4   Interactive and e-commerce agencies

The age of new media has led to the growth of agencies that specialise in interactive media and the Internet. Interactive agencies prepare communications and promotions using new technology such as CD-Rom, interactive TV, mobile phones communication and interactive shopping booths. E-commerce agencies handle activities related to using electronic commerce. This can range from creating websites, web page design, online promotions and e-mail campaigns, to developing banner advertising. These agencies provide specialist knowledge and expertise in the new media that have enabled marketers to explore and exploit new methods of reaching and interacting with their target audience.

5.4.5   In-house agencies

These operate within an organisation's own departmental structure. They take responsibility for planning, developing and implementing the organisation's own marketing communications activities. While some benefits can be identified for keeping the agency function in-house it is not a common occurrence. As a client you have better access and more control over agency personnel and activities if the agency personnel are employed by the organisation. Agency personnel will also have a good understanding of the products, services and markets in which the organisation operates. The agency can also generate its own income from the commission it receives from the media. However, such an in-house operation can also be a considerable overhead burden to the organisation. Such departments incur considerable costs and it is often cheaper and more efficient to outsource such services. As a client, being tied to an agency negates the opportunity to evaluate alternative agency approaches and utilise other services. Finally, there may be a lack of objectivity due to over-familiarity between the in-house agency and the marketing department. While the in-house agency is not a common occurrence, many marketing departments will look at doing some work in-house where they have the necessary resource and expertise.

5.5   The structure of a modern advertising agency

5.5.1   Account handling

Today's advertising agency is a complete service organisation. The point of contact for a client is the account handler, ranging from the board director in charge of an account to account supervisors, account managers and account executives. It is the job of the account handler to maintain contact with the client, building up a full understanding of that client's marketing and advertising situation, so that he or she may brief the agency on what needs to be done. The account handler then, as part of the agency team, assists in analysing the advertising problem and devising the appropriate solutions. The account handler has the task of presenting the agency solution in a clear and articulate manner to client personnel, who could range from middle management level, right up to the chairman of the board. Finally, once the client has approved a campaign, the account handler is responsible for ensuring that it is implemented. This means supervising the whole process of producing press and poster advertisements in their final form, preparing artwork, proofs, etc., making television films and ensuring that the whole programme of printing and production is completed on time.

Account handlers, therefore, have to be a 'jack of all trades'. They need to be good all-rounders, who understand all facets of the business, they must be clear thinkers who can get to the nub of the situation and brief the account team accordingly, and they need the skills to present work to a client. Finally, they have to be a highly efficient manager to ensure that all parts of the process are working effectively including making sure that the agency gets paid properly and punctually for its work!

To perform this task, the account handler relies on a number of departments within the agency.

5.5.2 Creative department

Marketers generally turn to advertising agencies to develop, prepare and implement their creative strategy since these agencies are specialists in the creative function of advertising. For some, the creative department is the most important department since it produces the product for which an advertising agency exists. The creative specialist or team is responsible for developing an effective way to communicate the marketers' message to the customer. This usually consists of combining the roles and skills of an art director and a copywriter. The art director is responsible for producing the visual ideas while the copywriter will produce the words. Other individuals on both the client and agency side work with the creative specialists to develop the creative strategy, implement it and evaluate its effectiveness. (See also Chapter 7 – Creativity.)

Those who work on the creative side of advertising often face a real challenge. They must take all the research, the creative briefs, strategy statements, communications objectives and other input and transform them into an advertising message. Their job is to write copy, design layouts and illustrations or produce commercials that effectively communicate the central theme on which the campaign is based. Rather than simply stating the features and benefits of a product or service, they must put the advertising message into a form that will engage the audience's interest, make the advertisements memorable and achieve the client's communications objectives.

Many clients are afraid to take creative risks, preferring to follow proven approaches to advertising rather than try something different. This can often lead to frustration between the creative team and the client. The creative team is encouraged to follow these proven formulas to produce safe advertising whereas they would prefer the client to take more risk. The clarity of understanding and degree of trust between the client and agency are, therefore, crucial to avoid time wasting for both parties.

Creativity in advertising is a process of several stages. Creative strategy development is guided by the client's specific objectives and is based on a number of factors, including the target audience, the basic problem the advertising must address, what the message seeks to accomplish and the major selling idea or key benefit the advertiser wants to communicate.

Initially, the creative team needs to build an understanding of the key issues gathering raw information through background research and immersing themselves in the product, service or issue. Various sources of information are available to help the creative specialists determine the best campaign theme, appeal and execution style. The creative team will normally sit in on the original briefing with the client or be briefed by the account handling team. The creative team will engage in a process of gathering facts and information from background research such as focus groups, interviews and observation, reading, listening to people and using the product or service.

Taking this information, the creative team will spend time evaluating the information, working it over and wrestling with it in the mind. At this stage, the creative team is involved in making sense of the data, unravelling the complex strands of information, thoughts and key issues that arise. Issue clarification is the key at this stage with a clear identification of the communication problem and task.

The next phase is to arrive at a creative solution. The challenge facing the creative team is to come up with fresh, unique and appropriate ideas that can be used as solutions to communications problems. Creative teams will 'interrogate' the brand to try and find new insights that can be used as the foundation upon which the creative idea is developed. Brainstorming sessions provide a wide-ranging and long list of ideas that can be organised into creative themes or issues on which creative strategy could be based. Techniques such as problem detection involve asking consumers familiar with the product or service to list the things that bother them or identify problems they encounter when using the product or service. Creative teams will try and put the problems out of the conscious mind, get away and let ideas develop.

David Bernstein on the enduring paradox that is creativity*

The central core of our activities is creative. The basic decisions are judgemental. The results of our work depend on human behaviour. Thus, advertising can never be a science.

But if you are in advertising and accept our working definition, if you believe in advertising's role in the economy, if at the end of the day you want to feel that you have helped the man that pays your salary (i.e. the client) by at least pointing him in the right direction . . . then you'll have to make it a science.

* Bernstein, David, *Creative Advertising*, Longman, 1974.

The final phase is the evaluation of ideas generated. Ideas that show potential are refined and polished. Others are rejected. Creative concepts are developed and tested through focus groups and viewer reactions. Concepts and copy at this stage are rough layouts or storyboards and are used to test what meanings are taken from adverts, what consumers think about the adverts and how they react to a slogan or a theme. A storyboard is a series of drawings used to present the visual layout of a proposed commercial. It contains a series of sketches or key frames or scenes along with the copy and audio portion of each scene. At this stage of the process the creative team is attempting to find the best creative approach or execution style before moving ahead with the campaign themes and going into actual production of the advertisement. The process may include more formal, extensive pre-testing of the advertisement before final production.

The creative team can be regarded as the engine that drives an agency's performance. If the creative team is dysfunctional, or unable to come up with winning creative concepts, no business will be generated and existing clients will look for new suppliers.

Collaborating with creatives*

Until recently it was the norm for clients to have little, if any, direct exposure to an agency creative team. The stereotype of creatives as troublesome types with artistic temperaments was fed by account handler's apparent fear of what their more casually dressed and individualistic colleagues might say or do in the presence of the client. They consequently went to great lengths to make sure contact was kept to a minimum.

Depending upon the philosophy of the agency, creatives could be elevated to the pinnacle of existence, the raison d'etre of the agency par excellence, in which case account men were just required to 'sell the ad' and told not to come back until they had. If clients would not accept an advertising execution or idea without changes being made to it, then the agency would respond by doing a completely new campaign. Neither account men nor clients were allowed to touch the advertisements.

'When we were at Lowes we never met clients', says Seyoan Vela, formerly at Lowes and now creative director at St Luke's. 'I only met a client once while I was there and that was only because I was wheeled out as a secret weapon when they were about to dump the agency.' At St Lukes the culture is completely different. Clients are encouraged to work together. This, he says, avoids misunderstandings. In the more traditional agency structure, he feels, account handlers can sometimes be over-protective, which can lead to problems when a client has concerns about an element in an advertising execution.

Account handlers may not be entirely sure which parts of the advertising creatives may be happy to change and which they consider sacrosanct. At worst, they risk killing off what may otherwise be a brilliant ad. Ongoing dialogue between clients and creatives avoids such a scenario. Creatives can benefit from continual exposure to the in-depth knowledge clients have of their brands and target audience.

* Adapted from *Marketing*, 23 August 2001, p. 23.

5.5.3   Planning department

In most agencies, the task of deciding what strategy should be followed in developing an advertising campaign is basically that of an account executive working together with the creative team. Larger agencies, however, usually have a specialist function (that of account planner) to perform the major part of this task. As planners do not write advertisements, the purpose of planning and advertising research is to help the people that do. The man widely credited with inventing planning, and giving advertising a way to articulate strategy, was Stanley Pollitt of Boase Massimi Pollitt. BMP set up its planning department in 1968 around the time that J.Walter Thompson was launching a similar operation. Pollitt believed that agencies were continuing to produce advertising without a clear understanding of how their output was affecting the consumer. He advocated the need for a new breed of advertising professional whose primary responsibility was consumer insight. For Pollitt, the voice of the consumer was paramount. He saw consumer research as vital to the development of intelligent strategy and creative communication.

The first requirement of planners is that they are experienced marketing people with expertise in market analysis. They must have knowledge of what information exists; understand consumer motivation, the creative development process, brand management, media planning and marketing measurement and evaluation techniques. The planner's job is to assemble all the available information about the client's products, service and its market, obtained from the client's brief, from published information sources and from market research commissioned by the client and/or the agency. This information is analysed and translated into a campaign strategy, which provides the basis on which the creative team will work in devising advertising.

The account planner role is complex and varied. An effective planner is required to work closely with the creative team on the interpretation of the client's brief, to identify gaps in the picture of the market and to suggest further research, establish clarity in consumer insight to convey the consumer's present and intended perception of the product/service to the creative people. It is the planner's job to provide creative guidance, guidance on brand positioning and client understanding of what advertising can contribute to building and maintaining brand equity. Finally, the planner will be involved in testing different creative executions and evaluating advertising effectiveness against communication objectives before, during, and after the campaign.

The role and the value of the account planning function is widely debated in the industry and in recent years the planning function has increasingly had to justify its place in the agency by their value to the agency and its clients. The reason why this type of job has arisen in agencies is complex and reflects issues in agency staffing and structure and the client's ability to brief their agency in the right way. On the agency side, the account executives rarely have the time or depth of market research know-how and experience to conduct and interpret market research. Similarly, on the client side, some agencies have found that the client's marketing management, especially at brand manager level, has a limited ability to use and interpret market research and to interpret it in a way that is appropriate for agencies to use. This has been exacerbated by a continuing tendency for clients to reduce the size of their marketing departments.

However, key trends are undermining the planning function. These include account planning functions being outsourced to external market research organisations, clients reverting to mechanistic sales-based advertising as opposed to longer-term brand building campaigns and the rapid growth of marketing consultancies offering guidance and support in strategic marketing and brand planning. Many advertising agencies were keen to spread the word when they set up dedicated planning departments. They were equally keen to keep a lid on it when these departments were slimmed down a few years later as a cost cutting measure. The danger for advertising agencies is the loss of a valuable source of income from market and advertising research and a widening gap between themselves and the client on strategic and brand management issues, thus leaving the advertising agency simply with the task of advertising strategy and execution.

Planning and creativity – help or hindrance*

Relevant creativity

By relevance I mean marketing relevance – the advertisement will help the client to sell more. This may seem to have nothing to do with creativity, but there is a connection, albeit indirect.

A problem with having planning done by account handlers and creatives is that they are not trained researchers. This can lead to inappropriate strategies. There is an example in why JWT introduced account planners. The agency was presenting its advertising recommendations to the Managing Director of Cutex nail varnish. At some point in the proceedings, the MD asked what share Cutex had of the market – the answer was about 80 per cent. He then asked what percentage of women used nail varnish – the answer was about 40 per cent. He received this information with considerable interest and then asked why in the light of these facts, had our advertising concentrated on claiming that Cutex was better than other brands. 'Would it not be more sensible, he asked, to spend his money trying to persuade more women to use nail varnish?' This had not occurred to the account group and the meeting dissolved into grisly silence.

A lesson might be that unless the strategy makes marketing sense, all the creative craft skills in the world will not save the agency come the next review.

* Adapted from 'Planning and Creativity – Help or Hindrance,' Tim Broadbent, *Admap*, July/August 2001, p. 18.

5.5.4   Media

The department in an agency that effectively spends the advertising budget is the media department. This department is responsible for being totally familiar with all available advertising media, with particular reference to the changing patterns of individual readership or viewing trends, the changing media landscape and media costs. The increasing sophistication and fragmentation of the media scene alongside the growth of independent media selling and buying houses has led to this function increasingly being outsourced by agencies.

Media departments consist of media researchers, media planners and media buyers. An immense amount of thought and planning goes into determining the correct media strategy, which has to be established in tandem with the planning and creative departments. Once media strategy is established, the media department is responsible for drawing up schedules indicating which media will be used, the cost of such media and recommended dates, size and length of advertising space or time. This will often involve considerable discussion and negotiation with media owners or sellers to get the best position for an advert and the best possible price/discount. The proliferation of media and the growth of new media such as cable, satellite, interactive television and the Internet offer some significant challenges to the media department. Increasingly, they are being encouraged to be more creative and innovative in the use of media.

Ultimately, the media department is responsible for the buying and scheduling of advertisements in media. They will be guided and measured by their success in achieving media objectives (i.e. coverage, opportunities to see/hear, etc.). Media commission is a traditional source of agency income and the growth of media specialists has had a crucial impact on their function and on both agency income and client costs.

5.5.5   Production

The production department is responsible for taking agreed advertising designs and turning them into material ready to be used in the selected media. The production department will work closely with the creative department, to establish the type of artwork, typeface, photography, etc. required and then commission outside suppliers to carry out the work. Clearly, the nature of the task will determine the degree to which external suppliers are outsourced. For television work, specialist production units, producers, directors, actors and studios are required. For other media work, it may be that just the print requirements are outsourced. The production department is responsible for negotiating fees, progress chasing and signing off the work that is produced by outside suppliers. They will also work closely with the account handler in getting the work signed off by the client. The skills required in this function are the ability to handle multi-tasking, project planning and handling a mass of detail with speed. Coupled with this, the individual will require personal characteristics of assertiveness, empathy and good teamwork. Fundamentally, production is the department responsible for getting the job completed on time and to the complete satisfaction of the client.

5.5.6 Selecting an agency

Agency selection can be likened to the personnel recruitment process. There is no single best practice, a range of methods and techniques can be adopted, but in the same way a person is short listed and interviewed to determine their suitability for employment, there is an agency selection process, the outcome of which an agency will be contracted to carry out the promotional work. The agency business is very competitive and at any moment in time there are only a small percentage of organisations looking for a new agency. Some agencies, in their determination to attract new clients, will use fairly direct techniques to get an opportunity to speak to clients. While business development and finding new clients is an important part of an agency's operations, clients generally frown upon such direct agency approaches as they hint at desperation. Many good agencies obtain their work from client referrals or their reputation in a specific market or promotional discipline. (For more information, see Chapter 12.)

5.6 The client brief

The brief is the most important piece of information issued by a client to an agency. A clearly communicated brief provides a point of reference that can be agreed at the outset between the client and the agency and to some extent forms part of the contract between both parties. It is from the brief that the agency can understand the client's markets, brand position, marketing objectives and critical issues. From this understanding, the agency can work with more clarity in developing recommendations and creative solutions to the client's problems. The better the brief, the better and more accurate the results – and less wastefulness in both time and money for both client and agency. Many agencies are critical of the quality of the client brief and perceive clients to lack understanding of the importance the briefing document has both on the creative process and its role in instilling a discipline on the agency team about what the client objectives and expected outcomes are.

A good brief will provide clarity of thinking and objectivity leaving the agency with an understanding of what is expected. The business problem should be clearly defined and the brands situation and key issues highlighted. Objectives should be clearly outlined and where possible quantified as these can form part of the effectiveness criteria and evaluation of campaign performance.

The IPA has published formal guidelines on briefing the agency in an attempt to improve both client and agency understanding of the process. While such a formal process does not have to be adopted, such guidelines do assist in helping clients and agencies. (See also Chapter 7 – Creativity, and Section 12.6.)

5.7   Agency remuneration

The traditional method of compensating agencies is through a commission system; where the agency receives a specified commission from the media company (usually 15 per cent of the media spend on any advertising time or space that it has purchased on behalf of its client). This method provides a simple method of determining payments, as it is transparent and easily understood by both client and agency. For every £100 of media spend, the agency will earn £15.00 in commission. If a client maintains strict control of its budgets, it will know precisely the cost of utilising the advertising agent's services against its advertising spend. While the commission system is still applied there are disadvantages and some difficulties with this approach.

Critics argue that the commission system encourages agencies to recommend high cost media rather than use lower cost media more creatively and efficiently. At a time of increasing focus on budgets and evaluation, clients find it increasingly difficult to justify such high cost media. A second concern is that the commission system does not take into account the amount of work carried out by the agency. Where an advertising campaign is repeated, sometimes over a period of several years, the agency will still earn its commission even though the work carried out is minimal. Equally, the agency may well have committed considerable time and resource into planning and developing a campaign, but the campaign only earns a small commission, which does not cover its true costs. Defenders of the commission system argue that it takes price competition out of the process and allows the agency and client to focus on the quality of the advertising produced. They also argue that it is the largest clients who have the largest spend and, therefore, require more of the agency's time and attention. The commission system remains a hotly debated topic. It is still a common method of remuneration adopted by agencies although the proportion of agency income derived just from commission is declining.

As a result of concerns over the commission system, alternative remuneration systems have developed. The opposite of a pure commission system is a fee arrangement. Under this arrangement, every item of an agency's time and services is itemised and charged for. In principle, this is the same system as that adopted by a solicitor when charging for their services. Under this system, the agency must carefully calculate the cost of serving the client and ensure that what is being charged for is clearly laid out. The client must agree on these charges up front to ensure that no disagreements arise throughout the contract. Many clients prefer this arrangement to the pure commission system, as they receive a detailed breakdown of costs attributed to agency activity. The fee system does add more complexity to the remuneration system and some agencies argue that it reduces their flexibility due to the constraints it imposes. It is increasingly likely to see a combination of both fee and commission payment adopted. It is agreed at the outset of the contract what services should be charged for and which are covered by the commission payment.

A more recent development of remuneration adopted by agencies and clients is payment by results (PBR). As part of the drive for more accountability demanded by clients, agencies are being paid based on performance. The agency's ultimate fee is determined by the extent to which it meets predetermined performance goals. These goals will include objective measures such as sales, market share and brand awareness, as well as more subjective measures such as the quality of the agencies creative work and how well the agency performed to deadline. Three key criteria frequently used for measurement are, performance of the agency, performance of the advertiser and performance of the advertising itself. Before the advertising gets under way, how each of these three elements is weighed against the other two, and the measurement techniques to be used, need to be agreed upon. One set of criteria involves an assessment of the agency itself, such as the quality of service, backup and delivery times, and the quality of the imaginative thought and ideas that come from the agency team. The second set of criteria assesses what the advertising itself has achieved with such elements as awareness and recall. The third set is based on actual business performance such as the client's sales performance, share price and market share. These three elements represent a potentially powerful combination for rewarding agency performance.

Orange

In January 2001, Orange announced that they were launching a PBR agreement with their agency Lowe Lintas. The criteria to be used would include the contribution of advertising to the company's overall performance and share price, as well as awareness of the brand and the agency's level of service. Performance of Lowe Lintas would be measured against the agreed criteria every 6 months and the agency could stand to earn up to 50 per cent on top of the agreed fee.

Payment by results

Anecdotal evidence of enormous riches being made out of PBR abound. Such as the one about the president of Sony Computers Entertainment Europe walking into his agency with a suitcase stuffed with £250,000 in cash just after the launch of PlayStation in 1995.

For many, payment by results seemed a good solution. Issues arise as to the level of control the agency has over other aspects of the client's marketing activity, which can impact on performance and determine the success or failure of the campaign. Selecting appropriate performance measures is also critical. The measures must be relevant, measurable and provide incentive, while at the same time ensuring that the agency is appropriately rewarded for delivering to the client's goals.

Today, remuneration methods are more diverse than ever, there is no simple standard (Figure 5.3). While many agencies still use commission on media spend as a basis for charging for their services, such commission charges are 'negotiated' at the outset. Fees now account for the highest proportion of agency agreements. These provide agencies with safer returns than the vagaries of the commission system even if at lower profit margins but have proved to be more cumbersome and inflexible. Many agencies combine commission and fee-based systems to balance some of the problems that each inherently has. Increasingly, agencies are adopting at least in part an element of payment by results. Agency remuneration is linked to agency performance, most commonly agency service delivery and achievement of advertising objectives. The difficulty of PBR is in agreeing on the performance criteria and determining the most appropriate methods as to how this should be measured.

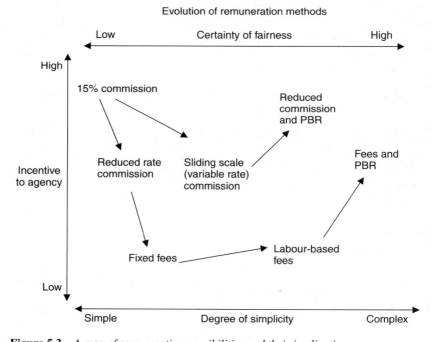

Figure 5.3   *A map of remuneration possibilities and their implications*

Source – Jonathon Lace, 'Agency Remuneration: Time for a New Paradigm,' *Admap*, October 1998, p. 28.

5.8   Managing client/agency relationships

Regular reviews of agency performance are essential to ensure that the client/
agency relationship is managed in a professional rather than ad hoc manner.
Agencies can be evaluated against financial measures, operational measures
and communication performance measures. Financial measures aim to verify
costs and expenses incurred to ensure that both parties are not being over- or
under-charged. Operational measures include factors such as meeting deadlines, the quality of the service received, and the level of professionalism of
agency personnel. Communication measures cover the extent to which the promotional campaign is meeting promotional objectives. The evaluation process
provides valuable feedback to both client and agency. The information can
assist in improving the agency's performance and the quality of the agency
client relationship. Issues can be identified early and dealt with rather than
trying to resolve problems after the event.

There are many reasons why clients retain or switch agencies. Many agencies work with their clients for several years, but long-term relationships are
becoming less common. Large agency account changes commonly make headline news. Reasons why clients do not remain with agencies include the agency
performance not meeting (clients') expectations or requirements, clients putting unrealistic demands on agencies particularly with regard to payment for
services, change of key personnel or personality conflicts between agency and
client staff, conflicts of interest where an agency takes on the work of a competitor's brand, and at times simply the client wanting fresh ideas and insight or
a new approach. Some of these factors are out of the agencies control while
others are potentially avoidable.

Surf*

Lever Faberge has handed its £8m European ad account for *Surf* to Bartle
Bogle Hegarty without a pitch. Lowe has held the business for the past 8 years.
The latest £4m TV ads, which star comedians Adam and Joe, debuted in
October. BBH was given the business on the basis of its work for Lever Faberge's
Lynx.

Simon Clift, divisional marketing director at Unilever, said, 'This is part of our
continuing plan to make BBH a key strategic partner, along-side Lowe, which
remains our agency partner for the majority of Unilevers's Home and Personal
care division's global brands.'

In April, Lowe retained the Surf business in a re-pitch against Mother. The
agency had a long-standing relationship with the brand, which was first won by
Ammirati Puris Lintas in 1995.

* *Marketing*, 4 December 2003, p. 2.

Lastminute.com*

Lastminute.com's advertising agency Quiet Storm has resigned the Internet-based late-deals specialist account after just 6 months. Quiet Storm was appointed in to work for the brand on a project basis, following a creative pitch. But the agency claims it disagreed with lastminute.com over remuneration. According to Quiet Storm, discussions between agency and client over the past few weeks centred on Quiet Storm's requests to be paid more for its work.

The agency also says it was interested in developing a long-term commitment from lastminute.com, to which the company would not agree.

Lastminute.com's UK managing director Helen Webb confirmed the split. 'Each project has its own requirements, so we didn't want to pick one agency for all our projects,' she said.

* *Marketing*, 11 December 2003, p. 3.

Kellogg*

Leo Burnett and Kellogg celebrated 50 years together in 2000. They claim that common values from their roots in the US Mid West have helped them stay together, as well as a mutual dependency, which is rare in a relationship of this kind. In the UK they have worked together since 1977, having created icons such as Tony the Tiger and the Rice Krispies characters. Leo Burnett has had a huge influence on the Kellogg brand. Likewise, as one of the world's top 10 advertisers, Kellogg's has done a lot to shape the fortunes of Leo Burnett.

Ed Christie, marketing director for convenience foods at Kellogg, says, 'We depend on Leo Burnett's service and it depends on our revenue. It is totally integral, to the point that it is a semi-outsourced marketing department. We have quite a lean team as a result.'

The launch of NutriGrain was a crucial test for the relationship, as it took Kellogg into unchartered snack-food territory. With 90 per cent of its advertising traditionally using TV, the agency persuaded Kellogg's to adopt a UK launch strategy based almost entirely around ambient media. Christie says, 'We were very resistant about not using TV, but Leo Burnett was a driving force in persuading us. A newer agency wouldn't have done that – it would have been more reluctant to challenge us.'

Leo Burnett's European account director for Kellogg, John Sheehy, adds that continuity of people working on the business helps cement the relationship. He has been on the account for 10 years. 'The agency immerses people in the account, but also moves them around the world, which keeps things fresh. If you run out of ideas for a brand as strong as this then you're in trouble.'

* James Curtis, *Marketing*, 17 August 2000, p. 23.

5.9   Summary

In this chapter:

- We reviewed the advertising industry's considerable evolution from its early days when it simply acted as a media broker.

- Key trends impacting upon the agency business were outlined and the key developments that have emerged particularly in the structure of the advertising industry with the growth of the major full service agencies, the development of the media specialists and more recently the growth of specialist agencies.
- Different agency functions were outlined and the importance of the relationships that exist both internally and with the client were discussed, in particular:
  - (i) The importance of greater openness and transparency from the agency towards the client.
  - (ii) Improved teamwork within the agency.
  - (iii) Better briefing and ongoing communication from the client.
- The key issues surrounding agency selection were introduced, in particular, the importance of a good client brief. The importance of good communication was highlighted in this section alongside a structured and planned approach from both client and agency.
- We considered the difficult issue of agency remuneration and evaluation. The advantages and disadvantages of the commission system, the fee-based system and the more recent 'payment by results' method were outlined.
- Methods for evaluating agency performance were also outlined looking in particular at agency performance, advertising performance and the communications impact on the client's overall business performance.

Further reading

www.IPA.co.uk (currently available to guests).
   The Client Brief: A best practice guide to briefing communication agencies.
   The Guide: Twenty-eight section document that sets out the key components of best practice, including guidelines on the process of search and selecting agencies and managing client/agency relationships.
Cooper, A. *How to Plan Advertising*, 2nd Ed. Cassell.
Ward, J. *Using and Choosing an Advertising Agency*. WARC.
Feldwick, P. (ed), *Pollitt on Planning*. ADMAP Publication.

6   Media

Sangeet Kaur Chana

Learning outcomes

By the end of this chapter you will:

- Review recent developments in television taking particular note of legislative changes and review both terrestrial and satellite media.
- Discover how the printed media (press) have developed over recent years and learn how the UK press is organised.
- See how commercial radio has developed as an advertising medium and see how much is spent in this medium.
- Review cinema advertising and know how airtime is purchased.
- Uncover the breadth of outdoor advertising, which will include an expanding raft of non-standard outdoor media such as airships, postcards and shopping trolleys, etc.
- Note how the Internet has developed in recent years as an advertising medium and consider the impact of Broadband.

6.1   Setting the scene

Over recent years the media scene has undergone a dramatic change. Evolution of the sector continues at such speed that by the time this book is published, much of this chapter will inevitably be out of date. Not only have we seen changes to the regulatory regime, the various media players have also undergone transformation with significant consolidation having taken place. Following innovation in technology, there has also been a surge in the development of interactive media, not to mention the influx of new entrants in existing media. With the choices of media now available to the advertiser being much greater than ever before, competition for a slice of the advertising cake has been fierce. This has been fuelled by the difficulties experienced by the advertising market in 2001 and 2002, when poor performances were recorded, largely due to economic conditions triggered by the events of 11 September 2001. Figure 6.1 illustrates how the revenues of various media players were affected

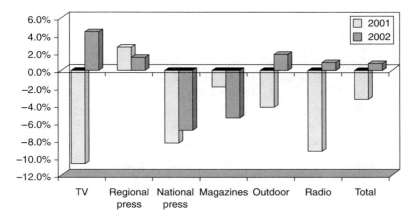

Figure 6.1   *UK media % change of total advertising revenue share (year on year)*

Source: Advertising Association's Advertising Statistics Yearbook 2003, published by WARC/newspaper Society Intelligence Unit, June 2003.

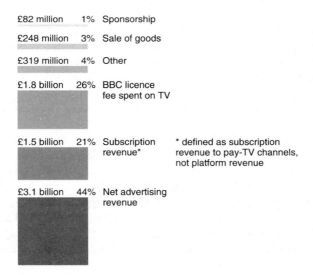

Figure 6.2   *Components of television revenue in 2002 (12 months to end September)*
Source: ITC.

during 2001 and 2002. The concern of the commercial media sector at the downturn in spend is understandable when we consider the percentage of total revenue derived from advertising. Figure 6.2 provides a breakdown of the components of television revenue in 2002 and is evidence of the crucial part advertising revenue plays in television production. In fact, independent television would not exist at all were it not for advertising income. Fortunately, commercial television has clawed its way out of recession although national newspapers continue to suffer from the backlash.

The most groundbreaking piece of legislation to affect the UK media sector in recent times is the Communications Act 2003 (CA 2003) which received Royal Assent on 17 July 2003. As a result of changes introduced by the Act:

- The scope for cross media mergers has increased;
- Ownership of UK television and radio by non-EEA companies is now allowed;
- A new super regulator, the Office of Communications (Ofcom) has been introduced;
- Rules preventing ownership of Channel 5 by newspapers have now been lifted;
- Rules restricting merger of ITV companies have been lifted; and
- The scope for radio mergers has increased significantly.

A few minimum guarantees of plurality remain. For instance, any company holding an ITV regional licence cannot merge with a company owning more than 20 per cent of the newspapers of that region. Nor can a company holding a national ITV licence merge with a company owning more than 20 per cent of the national newspaper market. Safeguards ensuring that no merger denies consumers two sources of local radio in addition to BBC radio have also been implemented.

Ofcom has acquired regulatory powers covering broadcasting and telecommunications networks and the services delivered on them. It has inherited the duties of the five existing regulators it replaces: the Broadcasting Standards Commission, the Independent Television Commission (ITC), Oftel, the Radio Authority and the Radiocommunications Agency, and also fulfils additional duties enacted in the provisions laid down in the CA 2003. Ofcom assumed its powers on 29 December 2003.

It should be noted that the CA 2003 is not a carte blanche for media mergers. The Secretary of State has the power to intervene in mergers if public interest considerations so require. Following such intervention, Ofcom would review the details of the proposed merger. Competition law will continue to be applied in situations where regulation has been eased.

Figure 6.3 compares the UK advertising shares of the different media in 2002. We can see that in the UK, the main media for advertising continue to be the press and television. We shall now look at the key developments and trends of each media in the advertising market and the development and impact of new technology.

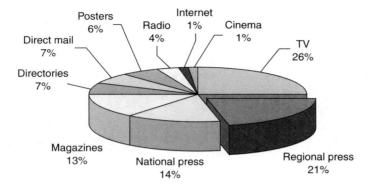

Figure 6.3 *UK media advertising revenue share 2002*

Source: Advertising Associations Advertising Statistics Yearbook 2003, published by WARC/Newspaper Society Intelligence Unit, June 2003.

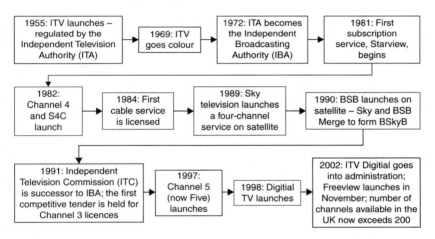

Figure 6.4 *Key milestones in the history of commercial television*

Source: ITC.

6.2 Television

On 29 December 2003, Ofcom took over from the ITC in licensing commercial television services in the UK whether delivered by analogue or digital means, terrestrially or by cable and satellite, public teletext and certain other text and data services.

Figure 6.4 highlights some of the major milestones in the history of television since the launch of ITV in 1955. The sector has undergone unprecedented

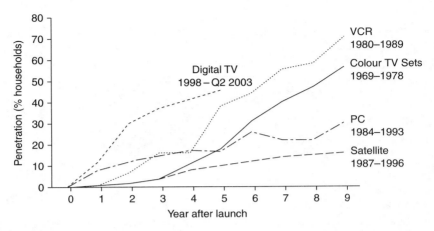

Figure 6.5   *Take-up of digital television compared with other home technologies*
Digital TV's strong initial growth is, in part, a result of the move to switch existing
subscribers from analogue to digital packages – by 1998 analogue multi-channel TV
had already achieved penetration of some 25 per cent of households.

Source: ITC.

transformation in the last few years. The take-up of digital television has been
significant and there has been rapid growth in the number of digital channels
including free to air channels. The graph at Figure 6.5 charts the take-up of
digital television compared with other home technologies. Benefits to viewers
of digital TV over normal analogue TV include a larger selection of channels,
higher standards of picture and sound quality, widescreen pictures, electronic
guides which tell the viewer what programmes are on next and interactive
services including digital text and games. Digital TV can be received in three
ways: through a normal television aerial, through satellite and through cable.

6.2.1   Recent developments

The total number of channels now available in the UK exceeds 200. This has had
a significant effect on analogue viewing patterns with ITV1 being one of the
most hard hit. ITV saw its market share and revenues plummet in 2002. Not only
has it had to contend with a tough market place but it has also faced competition
from the BBC, which many think has adopted a commercial approach to competing for audiences. In this context, the Competition Commission was asked to
consider the potential effects on competition of a merger between the two major
ITV companies, Carlton and Granada. The companies announced their plans to
merge towards the end of 2002 with a vision that this would lead to a stronger
united ITV empowered to deliver better programmes. As outlined above, the
CA 2003 removed some of the obstacles blocking the merger. In particular it
removed the upper limit of 15 per cent on the share of the TV audience that any

one company may control and removed the rule preventing joint ownership of the two London ITV licences.

One of the main focuses of the Competition Commission was on the selling of Carlton and Granada's airtime, currently sold separately by their respective sales houses, Carlton Media Sales and Granada Enterprises. Advertisers were concerned that the merger would result in a substantial reduction of competition in the television advertising sales market given that a combined ITV would have more than 50 per cent of the market. This is well in excess of the usual 25–30 per cent market share limit the Competition Commission tends to enforce. The advertising sector's main concern has been a rise in airtime prices given that there will no longer be direct competition between Carlton and Granada for revenue. However, the Commission was satisfied that the TV advertising market exhibited a greater degree of substitutability at the time of review than when they last examined the market in July 2000 and accordingly there was now stronger competition. However, the Commission felt that certain mechanisms should be put in place to offer advertisers some degree of protection. The Commissions' recommendations were accepted by the government with OFT, ITC and Ofcom then negotiating the detail of the Contracts Rights Renewal (CRR) remedy with Granada and Carlton in consultation with the advertising industry. Under CRR, advertisers are able to renew their current deals with no increase in the share of their spend that they commit to ITV and no reduction of any discounts they receive. The remedy also gives advertisers the right to automatically reduce the proportion of the spend they give to ITV if the merged Company's audience shrinks. Additionally, advertisers are able to take contractual disputes to a newly formed 'adjudicator'. CRR also sets out a number of additional advertiser rights including:

– The rights of the advertiser to move between media buyers;
– How advertisers who previously held contracts with ITV should be treated;
– How new advertisers should be treated; and
– What happens when advertisers or media buyers merge.

It would appear that the path is now clear for the merger that Granada and Carlton hope to complete early in 2004.

More recently, on 1 December 2003, the ITC and Ofcom announced their decision to withdraw the ITC's rules on joint selling of airtime (governing airtime sales in the UK television advertising market) altogether. The decision has immediate effect and means that other larger licensees with a national advertising revenue share exceeding 5 per cent (i.e. Channel 4, Five and Sky) who could not previously combine their sales operations can now do so subject to the provisions of the Competition Act. This has angered advertisers who fear that further consolidation in the TV sales market following the ITV merger will have a devastating effect on competition. The ITC and Ofcom believe the robust provisions of the Competition Act and the increasing body of competition case law provide sufficient mechanisms to prevent distortions of competition in the joint selling of airtime. Following implementation of the provisions of the CA 2003, Ofcom now has concurrent competition powers with the Office of Fair Trading. Any joint selling by sales houses will be considered under Chapter 1 of the Competition Act.

6.2.2   Television as an advertising medium

Television continues to be one of the most popular, powerful and effective forms of advertising media. The general perception that no advertising campaign is complete without the inclusion of TV advertising continues to exist. This is not surprising when we consider its mass appeal. According to figures in the Public View 2002, in an average week 85 per cent of the UK population watch TV every day of the week. Current figures suggest that on average, viewers watch 3.6 hours of television per day. Table 6.1 compares this figure to consumption of some other forms of media. The Broadcasters Audience Research Board (BARB), a non-profit-making limited company funded by the major players in the industry, is the primary provider of television audience measurement in the UK and covers all channels broadcasting across all platforms – terrestrial, satellite and cable in both analogue and digital.

Television has proved over the years that it can play a significant role in building large and successful brands. There is no other medium that can create a brand image as dramatically and arguably, sell as persuasively be it through visual images, music, emotion, celebrities or humour. If we take the Halifax as an example, we saw the former building society re-invent itself as an aggressive competitor to the major banks within the space of 1 year. According to CIM data, over 50 per cent of the Halifax's total advertising spend was invested in the TV medium with television being instrumental in establishing the new brand personality. The TV advertising helped generate audience awareness and led to large amounts of positive press coverage. See also Section 16.3.

Table 6.1   *Average weekly hours of media consumption*

TV	●●●●●●●●●●●●●●◀	*27*
Radio	●●●●●●●●●●●	22
Newspapers	●●◀	5
Magazines	●	2

Source: Granada Enterprises.

It should be noted that the amount of advertising time sold and the use made of it are strictly controlled by Ofcom. One of the most important rules is that viewers must be able to tell programmes and commercials apart. Any product placement within programmes is strictly prohibited, a stark contrast to the position in the USA.

Before considering satellite and cable TV, let us consider the three terrestrial commercial channels: Channel 3 (ITV1), Channel 4 and Channel 5 (Five).

6.2.3   Terrestrial channels

ITV1 continues to lead in the commercial television sector, attracting considerably more viewers than both Channel 4 and Five combined. Table 6.2 sets out the performance of the terrestrial channels and their subsidiaries and Table 6.3 compares the advertising revenue of the three commercial terrestrial channels and other platform channels.

The regional basis for airtime sales on terrestrial commercial television allows the advertiser to use the medium tactically by putting across its message nationally or in a number of chosen regions. The advertiser can target regions where impact will be highest thereby minimising potential wastage outside a key catchment area. Table 6.4 highlights the flexibility with which advertisers can use the medium. TV allows the advertiser to target a specific audience by advertising its

Table 6.2   *Performance of the terrestrial channels and their subsidiaries*

Channel	Logo	Owner	Share[1](%)	'Subsidiary' channels (share[1])
BBC1	BBC ONE	BBC	24.5	BBC3 (0.7%); BBC4 (0.2%); CBBC (0.6%); Cbeebies (1.2%); BBC News 24 (0.6)%; BBC Parliament (n.a.)
ITV1	itv 1	See Figure 6.6	22.9	ITV2 (1.8%); ITV News (0.2%)
BBC2	BBC TWO	BBC	11.5	See BBC1
Channel 4	4	Channel 4	9.7	E4 (0.7%); FilmFour (0.1%)
Five	five	RTL (65%); UBM (35%)	6.3	n.a.

[1]Share figures for terrestrial channels are for all homes in August 2003; figures for the subsidiary channels are for multi-channel homes in August 2003 and are only available for those channels with 0.1 per cent share and above.

Source: With thanks to ITC and BARB.

Table 6.3   *UK Net advertising revenue by channel*

Channel	NAR 2002
ITV1	£1,727m
Channel 4 (Inc S4C)	£623m
Five	£221m
Cable, satellite and other	£575m

Source: ITC.

Table 6.4   *Relatively low budget TV campaigns*

Advertiser/brand	Channels/regions	Estimated TV spend (MMS data) (£)
Panasonic Batteries	National C4 / E4	289,000
Expedia.co.uk	ITV, C4 and Five	281,000
John Frieda 'Frizz Ease'	ITV and C4 (Midlands and North only)	222,000
Robert Dyas	ITV (South East) and C4 (London only)	217,000
University of Lincoln	C4 (Midlands and North) and national E4	199,000
Bourjois 'Rouge Connection' Lipstick	National C4 and E4	170,000
Page and Moy Holidays	C4 (South, Midlands and North)	144,000
Milton Keynes Shopping Centre	ITV (Anglia West)	128,000
Marton's Pedigree bitter	ITV (Midlands)	122,000
West Quay Shopping Centre	ITV (South)	89,000
Rubicon Exotic Juice Drinks	National C4 (with London and Midland Region upweights)	65,000
Paignton Zoo	ITV (South West)	63,000
Clarks Village Factory Shopping	ITV (West only)	42,000
University of East London	C4 (London only) and national E4	22,000

Source: Chartered Institute of Marketing.

Table 6.5   *A comparison of average spot costs across Granda Group TV Regions by time of day*

Area	11.00 (e.g. Trisha)	18.15 (e.g. Local News)	Centre break in Coronation Street	21.20 (e.g. ITV drama)	300 TVR's based on average delivery
LWT	2,976	9,522	33,328	17,259	357,087
Granada	708	2,265	7,927	4,105	84,933
Border	51	162	567	294	6,079
Yorkshire	575	1,840	6,440	3,335	68,997
Tyne Tees	284	906	3,177	1,645	34,044
Meridian	1,202	3,845	13,459	6,970	144,200
Anglia	764	2,444	8,552	4,429	91,633
Ulster	172	550	1,926	997	20,636
ITV Network	8,592	27,495	96,234	49,835	1,031,076

Source: Granada Enterprise Estimates, average spot costs (adults) March 2002–February 2003.

product in a slot within a programme or at a time when its target audience is likely to be watching. Since television advertising is a commodity, the number of advertisers wishing to purchase airtime at any one time will affect cost. Easter, November and the first 2 weeks of December are usually the most expensive times to buy a campaign. Prices are related to demand as supply is fixed at an average of 7 minutes commercial airtime per hour. Variations in advertising cost also occur depending upon the time of day, viewing figures, number of advertisers in the same product field, the length of the slot and, in some instances, average earnings of the population in a region/regions. In reality, advertising airtime is sold in packages and generally includes a production subsidy to contribute to the cost of making a television commercial. For instance, the regional licence holder Yorkshire Television sells various regional packages, examples of which include a 'Bronze' package comprising 10 slots, three in peak time and seven in off-peak time and a more expensive 'Platinum' package comprising 25 spots, 9 in peak time and 16 in off-peak time. Table 6.5 compares costs of advertising in separate Granada regions and the whole ITV1 network.

6.2.4   ITV1

ITV1 comprises 15 regional licensees and the national breakfast time licensee (GMTV). ITV1 services are broadcast both on analogue frequencies and on the digital terrestrial multiplex and are financed mainly by the sale of advertising time. In 2002, the net advertising revenue of the regional licensees reached £1,686m. Figure 6.6 sets out the ITV1 licensees' current ownership structure.

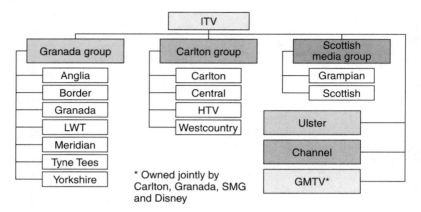

Figure 6.6   *The ITV licensees – ownership structure*
Source: ITC.

The networking arrangements for ITV set out in the 1990 Broadcasting Act were designed to enable its regional services taken as a whole to operate as a nation-wide system while ensuring that each met their regional commitments. However, the Act does not specify the form that the networking arrangements should take and as a result the channel's licensees developed a system of arrangements, the purpose of which was to provide a national schedule for ITV1 and to commission programmes centrally on behalf of all regional licensees. The licensees cannot modify the arrangements without the approval of Ofcom. The ITV Network Centre carries out the day-to-day functions of the ITV Network under the Network Agreement, an agreement between the ITV Network and the 15 regional licensees. The ITV Network Centre acquires and commissions programme proposals, negotiates terms with licensees and independent producers for the acquisition of rights to completed programmes based on such proposals and drafts the network schedule. Figure 6.7 sets out the organisation of the ITV Network. Once Carlton and Granada have merged, the merged entity would have over 90 per cent of the votes of the ITV Network Council and would, therefore, be able to pass any resolution of the Network Council.

The ITV1 network offers the advertiser most regional options with some of the ITV1 regions being broken down further into 'micro-areas', which is an effective and cost efficient option for advertisers. Conversely, advertising over the entire ITV1 network delivers huge audiences unrivalled by any other commercial channel. To reach the same number of viewers through cable and satellite would involve the lengthy and time-consuming process of booking airtime over a vast number of channels.

Over the last decade there has been a significant consolidation of the various advertising sales houses for ITV with only two sales houses remaining: Granada Enterprises and Carlton Media Sales. The map in Figure 6.8 shows

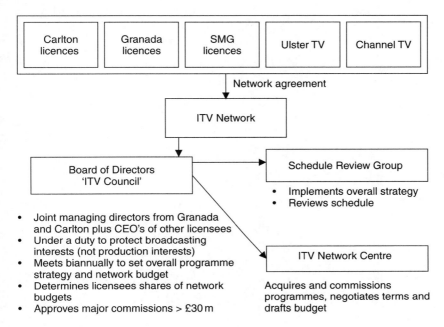

Figure 6.7 *Organisation of ITV network*

Source: Competition Commission.

the various regions. Granada Enterprises sales house is responsible for sales of television advertising airtime and programme sponsorship on behalf of the majority of ITV's licences including Anglia, Border, Granada, LWT, Meridian, Tyne Tees and Yorkshire. It also sells airtime for UTV and Welsh terrestrial channel S4C. Carlton sells airtime and sponsorship on behalf of Carlton, Central, HTV and Westcountry. Granada and Carlton jointly sell airtime for GMTV, Channel and SMG.

6.2.5 Channel 4

Channel 4, created by Act of Parliament in 1982, transmits across the whole of the UK, except some parts of Wales, which are covered by the Welsh language channel S4C. It is available on all digital platforms as well as through conventional analogue transmission. It is a publicly owned corporation but unlike the BBC, receives no public funding and is funded solely by its own commercial activities. Under the CA 2003 it is required to:

– demonstrate innovation, experimentation and creativity
– appeal to the tastes and interests of a culturally diverse society
– include programmes of an educational nature
– exhibit a distinctive character.

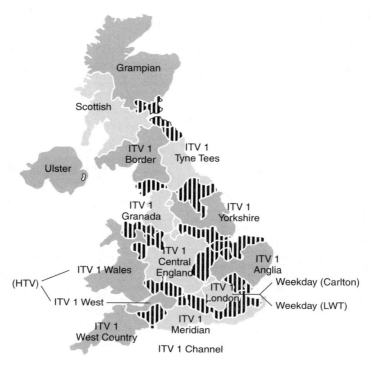

Figure 6.8   *ITV1 regions*

Unlike ITV1, Channel 4 does not produce its own programmes but commissions them from more than 300 independent production companies across the UK. Advertising airtime is sold by its own dedicated sales force and generally at a smaller entry cost than ITV1. This is due to the lower audience share and the general trend that its audiences tend to be light watchers of television. However, the channel has enjoyed considerable success over recent years with huge hits such as Big Brother and Wife Swap.

6.2.6   Channel 5 ('Five')

The Broadcasting Act of 1990 required the ITC to establish a fifth terrestrial channel in the UK. In 1995, the ITC awarded the Channel 5 licence to Channel 5 Broadcasting Limited for a 10-year period. The Channel launched on 30 March 1997 with the main teletext service beginning on 15 October 1997.

The Channel has experienced troubles, not least because of its former image as the downmarket alternative to its terrestrial rivals. It was rebranded as 'Five' last year following a multimillion pound relaunch in an attempt to stimulate viewers' reappraisal of its programmes and brand that it hoped would lead to higher audience ratings and increased advertising income. The move also saw a stark change in the programme schedule with the acquisition of rights to terrestrial premieres of box office hit movies and the recruitment of big television celebrities for its programmes. Recent figures suggest that Five's share of advertising revenue has shown a modest but steady increase year on year over the past 2 years. Like Channel 4, Five has its own dedicated sales force.

6.2.7   Satellite and cable

One third of UK households have already switched to digital television and more are signing up everyday. By 30 June 2003, multi-channel and digital TV penetration was estimated to have reached 49.8 and 45.5 per cent of UK households, respectively. In the 2003 run-up to Easter, multi-channel TV pushed the BBC and ITV into second place for the first time in history despite the fact that less than 50 per cent of all households had access to digital channels through satellite, cable or Freeview.

The growth of the Satellite sector over recent years has been phenomenal and has increasingly posed a threat to terrestrial broadcasters' advertising revenue share. Figure 6.9 sets out the share of multi-channel television homes by platform. The dominant platform is clearly satellite with over a 59 per cent share of multi-channel homes. In 1999, Sky had 1m subscribers which increased five-fold by 2000, when the figure hit 5m. At the end of the June 2003, subscriber figures reached 6,845,000 in the UK and Ireland. The number of channels available via satellite has risen sharply in the last 10 years. According to figures from Company Literature (30 September 2003), 187 channels (including free to air) are now available through Sky alone.

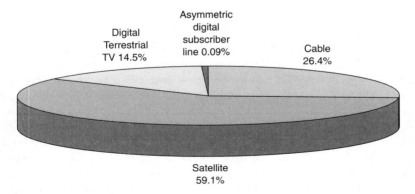

Figure 6.9   *Share of multi-channel homes across platforms*

The share of total multi – channel homes across platforms (both pay and free to air) at the end of Quarter 2 2003 is as shown.

Source: ITC Multi-channel Quarterly.

Although Sky has virtually monopolised the sector, other broadcasters are now 'upping the ante'. Certain terrestrial broadcasters have clearly reviewed their multi-channel strategies having realised the value of the platform. This has led to increasing investment in the multi-channel platform. For instance, ITV2, one of the strongest channels on the platform and now the seventh most popular television channel overall, is certainly giving Sky a run for its money.

Earlier this year, Sky announced its plans to create TV adverts in-house for its clients in an effort to bring more brands onto television. This could help it seal even more deals with advertisers in the future. Sky is also well known for offering brands cross-media solutions including interactive and print options in addition to traditional broadcast spots.

The cable industry has seen more limited success. It has undergone consider-able consolidation in the last decade or so, starting with 29 companies in 1992 which has been whittled down to only two major operators today: NTL and Telewest Broadband. Over 100 channels (including free to air) are available through each of these operators. According to the ITC multi-channel quar-terly review for April–June 2003, cable saw a decline in share in the second quarter of 2003 for multi-channel, pay and digital channel homes, and the number of subscribers to cable fell during that quarter although digital cable saw an increase in subscriber numbers of 1.8 per cent.

Through the huge number of digital satellite and cable channels available, it is possible for the advertiser to reach various audience segments in a highly cost efficient way. The various satellite and cable channels also offer a variety of relatively low cost sponsorship opportunities for brands.

There are a number of multi-channel sales houses through which airtime, sponsorship and other options can be purchased.

6.2.8   Broadcast sponsorship

In October 2000, the ITC changed the rules of sponsorship. Sponsors can now directly show products on screen in the sponsorship credits and place a phone number or website URLS on credits. These simple changes turn credits into direct response marketing opportunities and make sponsorship credits an increasingly effective tool. Table 6.6 provides examples of brand sponsorship of programmes. Sponsorship can help increase awareness of the brand and build its personality, benefiting through the association with the programme and broadcast environment. O_2's multi-million pound sponsorship of Channel 4's Big Brother in 2002 helped launch its new brand identity in the highly competitive mobile phone communications sector. The final result was a fully integrated cross-platform communication. Through sponsorship of chosen areas of the Big Brother website in addition to the aired programme, O_2 was able to reach viewers representing the key segment for mobile phone purchases.

Again, local advertisers have the added choice of sponsoring regional programmes helping to reinforce the brand with a strong local identity.

Table 6.6 *Examples of programme sponsorship 2002/2003*

Sponsor	Programme	Channel
Nestle	Pop Idol	ITV
Cadbury	Coronation Street	ITV
Heinz Salad Cream	Emmerdale	ITV
Stella Artois	Contemporary Films	C4
Assertahome.com	Location, Location, Location	C4
Kenco Rapport	Bo Selecta	C4
Air Wick	Family Affairs	Five
Skittles	Buffy the Vampire	Sky One
Taylor Made	World of Golf	Sky Sports

Cheaper options such as sponsorship of regional weather forecasts may also present opportunities for advertisers working to a restricted budget but who would value a form of television presence.

In summary, though television advertising airtime may appear expensive compared to other media, when the benefits are set against the investment, it is clear that TV proves its value as an advertising medium. Quite often, broadcasters offer incentives with advertising packages to provide an attractive entry cost to new and regional advertisers.

Although for many types of products and services television is the leading medium, very few advertising campaigns are confined to TV alone. The amount of information that can be given in a TV commercial even if it lasts for 30 seconds or more is limited. Therefore, it is generally used in conjunction with other forms of media.

6.3   The press

In the UK, the press, which includes newspapers, magazines and periodicals, is the most widely used advertising medium, accounting for around 50 per cent of all advertising expenditure. One explanation for this is the diversity of the press, which includes national dailies, national Sundays, regional dailies and weeklies, local free distribution newspapers, general and special interest magazines, trade, technical and professional magazines, house magazines, yearbooks and reference journals. In total, there are well over 11,000 publications to choose from in the UK. Therefore, advertisers have a vast selection to choose from and are able to target specific audiences with a particular interest in their business. The high circulation (in total over 12 million a day for national newspapers), wide coverage and ability to target demographically and by region makes it an attractive option. Advertisements can be purchased and designed at very short notice. Often, last minute changes can be incorporated, thereby ensuring topicality. It is possible to use colour, illustrations or photographs to enhance the message and in the daily press there is even the option of relating an advertisement to a current news story. Advertisements can also be booked to appear in a specific issue or in a given position at a premium. The alternatives are Run of Week (meaning it is up to the publishing paper which day in a given week the advert is published) and Run of Paper (position of advert will be at the discretion of the paper). In cases where response coupons or telephone hotlines are used within the advert, the response to the advert can be measured allowing the advertiser to assess the success of an advertising campaign. The National Readership Survey is the source for readership figures in the national press and some other titles and for free newspapers, Verified Free Distribution is a source of such information. See Chapter 13 for more on Media Research.

The newspaper sector has transformed over the last 8 years. Since 1996 there have been a series of mergers, buyouts and restructures. The provisions of the CA 2003 further open up the possibilities for consolidation across media.

British people are among the most avid newspaper readers in the world. According to the National Readership Survey, over half the population reads a national newspaper every day. However, it is the regional press that has strengthened its market share in the last 3 years. Almost 85 per cent of all British adults (40 million people) read a regional newspaper compared with 70.5 per cent who read a national newspaper. Since 2000, regional press coverage has grown by 2.3 per cent and total readership has increased by 883,000 readers. According to the Newspaper Society database as at 1 July 2003, there are 1286 regional and local newspapers in the UK including 24 mornings (18 paid for and 6 free), 75 evenings, 21 Sundays, 524 paid for weeklies and 642 free weeklies. However, the national press appears to have suffered over recent year with national press coverage falling by 4.3 per cent since 2000 (a decline of 1,489,000 readers) (source BMRB/TGI 2003). This has affected the sector in various ways including price wars between national papers, one such war taking place last year between The Mirror and The Sun.

Magazine advertising revenues have also suffered with the Advertising Association predicting that UK magazines will take some time to recover with no sign of significant upturn until 2006.

Various measures have been taken to turn the tide, including the setting up of the Newspaper Marketing Agency (NMA) in January 2003. There are hopes that it will have as positive an effect on the popularity of the national press as its equivalent for the regional press, the Newspaper Society, had on the regional market. A number of problems have been identified with the national press:

–   working with newspapers is not viewed as a sophisticated or exciting activity for advertising agency creatives;
–   national newspapers are renowned for not delivering what the advertisers want;
–   The National Press' complacent attitude to advertising; and

– The tug of war over space between the editorial and commercial parts of the business with journalists being known to view advertising as a hindrance in their efforts to inform the reader.

The NMA has also urged the Fleet Street players to forget the intense competition with each other long enough to co-operate on research in a drive to impress advertisers. It holds the view that price wars only serve to reduce the perceived value of the newspapers in consumers' minds. The NMA also plans to look at sections of newspapers that are currently advertisement free zones and review the quality of advertisements by driving up the standard of creative work in newspaper advertising. The benefits of the NMA remain to be seen as most of what the NMA has the potential to achieve will take a few years.

The press has also invested huge sums in new technology and electronic systems. There has been a growth in strategic alliances and a surge in the number of newspaper websites (particularly in the regional press).

There are a large number of sales houses, national and regional, which deal with the sale of advertising space. Table 6.7 sets out the national representation of regional and local newspapers by sales houses. Costs of advertising in the press vary from paper to paper and a comparison of the cost of advertising in

Table 6.7   *National representation – January 2004*

Sales house	Titles	Weekly circulation	Market share (%)
AMRA	261	15,882,630	23.3
Mediaforce London	386	11,435,601	16.8
Newsquest Media Sales	217	10,620,940	15.6
Northcliffe Newspapers Group Ltd	110	9,108,571	13.4
Associated Newspapers	7	6,415,350	9.4
Clacksons	195	5,824,853	8.5
Scottish Daily Record & Sunday Mail Ltd	2	3,705,721	5.4
D C Thomson & Co Ltd	3	1,243,894	1.8
Scotsman Media Sales	6	1,149,880	1.7
Belfast Telegraph Newspapers Ltd	6	877,451	1.3
Regional Advertising Company	19	748,709	1.1
Kent Messenger Group – London	20	639,132	0.9
No sales house	59	523,265	0.8
Jackson Rudd & Associates Ltd	4	n/a	n/a
The Media House	3	n/a	n/a
Maple Media	2	n/a	n/a
Total	1,300	68,175,997	100

Source: NS database, 1 January 2004.

Table 6.8 *The cost of advertising in four national newspapers, plus circulation and readership figures*

	The Daily Mirror	Daily Star	The Times	The Independent
Price	32 p (Monday–Friday)	30 p (Monday–Friday)	45 p (Monday–Friday)	60 p (Monday–Friday)
Circulation (number of sold, reduced price and free copies of the title distributed on the average day) over 29 September 2003 to 26 October 2003	1,943,382	908,101	631,109	240,326
Readership (average number of people reading the title on an average day) over January 2003 to June 2003	5,444,000	2,007,000	1,894,000	568,000
Cost of full page advert (£)				
Colour	36,800	15,925	41,000	22,000
Mono	29,000	–	26,750	15,000
Per single centimetre column (£)				
Colour	142	–	108[1]	53
Mono	112	48.50[1]	66[1]	35

Source of data: NRS/ABC.

[1] These figures are for publication of the advertisement on a firm day.

four national newspapers in conjunction with circulation and readership figures is included in Table 6.8.

6.4   Radio

There are now over 240 commercial radio stations that are currently licensed and regulated by Ofcom. Such national, regional and local stations pay for themselves with revenue received through advertising. Unlike television, commercial radio stations are no longer limited as to how much advertising they can broadcast per hour. However, to avoid putting listeners off, the general limit of 9 minutes is adhered to. As with television, radio advertising is sold on a spot basis although peak audience times differ from those of television, with the largest radio audiences tuning-in during the breakfast period and the evening rush hour. Radio sponsorship is also a growing method of communication on radio although the regulations are more relaxed than those applicable to TV sponsorship. Commercial radio covers virtually the whole of the UK. In areas of larger population density there are multiple commercial options. For instance, in London there are 30 different services available, both BBC and commercial. The use of radio depends very much upon the overall objectives of the advertising campaign. Radio is an excellent medium for those wishing to build familiarity, accessibility and involvement with a product or service.

Commercial radio is available to advertisers on a local and national basis through the network of national and local sales houses. According to figures published by the Advertising Association, in any 4-week period, over 80 per cent of 15–44-year-olds listen to commercial radio. Most radio listeners have a very small number of stations within their personal repertoire with listeners relating to their favourite programmes and presenters. Commercial radio has been extremely successful in attracting advertisers and has recorded substantial growth in revenue over 2003. Radio Advertising Bureau revenue data for the third quarter of 2003 show a 6.4 per cent increase in spend from national advertisers with total advertising spend reaching £149.5 million across July–September 2003. Advertising Association forecasts predict that commercial radio share of total advertising expenditure is set to reach 6 per cent by the end of 2003 (excluding radio sponsorship and promotions). Table 6.9 provides examples of commercial radio advertising spend by various brands. It is a very popular medium, largely due to its flexibility (a radio portable can be listened to anywhere while doing other things) and the fact that it is a relatively inexpensive option. The cost of writing and recording advertisements is usually relatively low and stations will often incorporate this with their package deals. However, with no visual support for the message, creativity is essential to capture the listener's attention.

Growth is expected to continue boosted by increased audience sizes from digital radio. Audience figures are published by Radio Joint Audience

Table 6.9   *Top radio spending brands in October 2003*

Brand spend

Sainsbury's Product Range – £1,185,000
118 212 Directory Enquiries – £677,000
Shell Optimax – £548,000
DHL Worldwide Express – £507,000
Carphone Warehouse Product Range – £495,000
Carphone Warehouse TalkTalk – £400,000
Specsavers Opticians Range – £391,000
Virgin Trains – £379,000
Camelot Group Daily Play – £360,000
Times Daily Newspaper – £338,000

Source: Nielsen Media Research.

Research Limited (RAJAR) which was established in 1992 to operate a single audience measurement system for the radio industry.

6.5   Cinema

There are currently over 3000 cinema screens in the UK. The majority of single screen cinemas have closed and instead, larger multi-screen complexes have opened. Since 1985, there has been a steady growth in cinema admissions (rising by 70 per cent from 1992 to 2002) and the trend is continuing. There are various advantages to using cinema advertising. The audience is captive and the attention levels are generally unrivalled. The use of vision and sound is displayed to its best possible effect through the use of big screens and sophisticated sound technology. The market also has a strong grasp on the valuable 15–34 year-old market.

Cinema advertising airtime can be purchased locally, regionally or nationally. Sponsorship is again an option. The advertiser may choose to be linked to certain categories of film or even specific film titles. Such options allow the smaller local advertisers to appear on the big screen at very affordable prices. Production costs using facilities offered by the major cinema advertising contractors are surprisingly low.

Although not often an obvious option for advertisers or media buyers, the medium is becoming increasingly popular due to its ability to increase brand awareness by creating a talking point and showcasing an advertisement. The Cinema Advertising Association (CAA), the industries joint marketing body, has continued to increase awareness of the benefits of cinema advertising. The two founder companies of CAA, Carlton Screen Advertising and SMG owned Pearl & Dean, are the only sales operators in the UK cinema market and in 2002 held a 63 and 37 per cent share of UK cinema screens, respectively.

6.6   Outdoor advertising

Outdoor advertising, sometimes referred to as the 'out of home' sector, has been the subject of rapid change. The main changes to the sector over the last decade are:

–   poster sizes have settled into three main sizes being six sheets (typically 1.2 m by 1.8 m), 48 sheets (6.1 m by 3.05 m) and 96 sheets (12.19 m by 3.05 m). The latter two are commonly referred to as 'bill boards'.
–   Consolidation of outdoor media ownership into the hands of fewer companies. For instance, the number of poster companies has been slashed by well over 50 per cent.
–   The development in 1996 of a new audience measurement system, POSTAR (POSTer Audience Research) which succeeds its predecessor, OSCAR. Transportations Displays Incorporated (TDI) produces its own audience research for the London Underground and national bus media.
–   The development of ambient media which now deliver a significant chunk of the outdoor industry's total revenues.

Outdoor advertising is an extremely diverse medium. The more popular forms of outdoor advertising will now be considered in greater detail.

6.6.1   Roadside advertising

Roadside panels have polarised into the three standard sizes referred to above. The larger 48 and 96 sheets are predominantly located alongside busy roads and junctions and the smaller six sheet sizes are frequently found on bus shelters. Recently, we have seen the emergence of a number of different display sites. For instance, 48 and 96 sheet posters can now be multi-faced whereby three different subjects are displayed on revolving prismatic faces. Illumination is also playing an increasingly important role in the development of both existing and new forms of outdoor media.

6.6.2   Street furniture

Over recent years, contractors have invested huge amounts in local authority contracts for the provision of street furniture and amenities, on the sides of which advertising space can be sold. This has seen a surge in the six sheet format.

6.6.3   Point of sale

Outdoor contractors have increasingly developed relationships with retailers and shopping precinct owners, resulting in panels on or very near to retail premises. This provides an excellent trigger at or near the point of sale and can, therefore, be used for very specific announcements.

6.6.4   Transport media

This category includes poster sites located both at travel termini and on or inside public transport vehicles and, therefore, includes buses, coaches, trains, the tube, the underground stations, National Rail stations and a wide variety of panels inside and outside airports. This sector is dominated by TDI which has exclusive rights to the London Underground and national bus advertising.

6.6.5   Ambient media

This term embraces the rapidly expanding raft of non-standard outdoor media examples which include airships, postcards, bus tickets and shopping trolleys. Further examples of ambient media are set out in Table 6.10. More recent examples of ambient media include built-in digital screens playing commercials on hand driers in public toilets (launched by Washroom Media Network) and new initiatives to put advertisements on escalator handrails at airports (launched by MediaRail).

Table 6.10   *Examples of ambient media*

Non-standard poster formats	*Transport related*	*Advertising sponsorship*
Exhibition halls	Airline tickets	Airport lounges
Floor posters	Boarding passes	Golf holes and pins
Leisure centre posters	Car park tickets	Playgrounds
Litter bins	Underground/bus tickets	Train stations
Perimeter boards	Taxis – inside and out	Tube stations
Petrol pump nozzles	Lorry sides	Sports stadia
Washroom advertising	Bicycle posters	
Scaffolding advertising	Balloons/airships	**Screen advertising**
Schools advertising	Sky writing	Petrol forecourt monitors
Supermarket trolleys	Towed banners	Post-office television
Telephone box posters	Sandwich boards	Shopping mall video pub
Pub and club advertising	Liveried trains, buses,	Screens
Post boxes	trams, lorries, aeroplanes	
Packaging related		
Paper bags/carrier bags		
Milk cartons/take away lids		

Source: ISBA.

Due to the diversity and complexity of the outdoor market, media buyers and advertisers often instruct outdoor specialists. Such specialists usually have access to sophisticated computer mapping systems that are able to locate specific site requirements. These systems can also assist in planning campaigns targeted at specific audiences. Contractors tend to sell pre-selected packages with a fixed number of sights. With an array of national and regional sites to choose from, packages are generally selected on the basis of geographical spread, site location and quality of site. The remainder of sites are sold on the 'line-by-line' market with each site being selected by the buyer from a pool of non-package sites and built into the advertising campaign. As with other media, discounts connected to volume are available. New advertisers are often offered discounts as an incentive.

With such diversity, the outdoor market is a valuable tool. There are various pitfalls to be wary of. If advertisers and media planners bombard consumers with advertising messages, the medium can become intrusive, resulting in the audience switching off. Therefore, media planners need to plan such campaigns very carefully. Another disadvantage it has over some other media is that by its nature, outdoor advertising cannot be acted upon immediately as people tend to see them as they pass by. Consequently the message must be very short and easy to digest. The most effective use is, therefore, as a reminder and it is universally recognised as being a highly effective support medium, reminding the audience of other forms of advertising for the same product/service.

The future looks promising for the outdoor sector. According to figures published by the Outdoor Advertising Association, the industry's revenue for April–June 2003 is £184.5m, an increase of 6.3 per cent on the previous year.

6.7 The Internet

Clearly, the most successful form of interactive media, the Internet is the fastest growing medium of all time and has made an extraordinary impact on the advertising industry over the last 5 years. Spending on the Internet rose by a fifth in 2002 despite the general gloom in the advertising market. The Interactive Advertising Bureau (IAB) (which represents leading companies in the interactive space) and PricewaterhouseCoopers announced that internet advertising spend in 2002 reached £196.7 m. An increase in the number of professional sales teams, improved research and the growing amount of time consumers spend on the Internet have all contributed to the sharp rise. Bigger brands have started to turn to the web because they can easily track the effect of their ads. Banners continue to represent the largest component of advertising revenue although there is a real development of additional media formats such as tenancies, nested content, interstitials and sponsorship. There are an array of multi-media specialists who are able to offer valuable practical advice on the use and purchase of advertising in this medium.

Leading publishers and advertising networks continue to dominate market share as internet advertising remains concentrated in this area. There is still a considerable gap between the percentage of people's time the Web takes up (between 8 and 10 per cent) and the slice of advertising share it takes.

The Internet's potential is enormous. With the Internet market constantly seeking out fresh ways to use the technology, more advertisers are likely to be tempted by this medium. One example is the recent initiative of Melodie Mall Music which used state-of-the-art internet technology over the run-up to Christmas 2003 to deliver music and advertising through UK shopping centres allowing advertisers to re-inforce an advertising campaign at the point of sale.

With the recent introduction of broadband, the growth in use of this media by advertisers looks set to continue with the target of a 2 per cent slice of the advertising market by 2004 seeming well within reach. Alternative interactive options include telecoms and digital television.

Various other options exist for advertisers such as directories, direct marketing/ mail and leaflet distribution which provide more targeted alternatives.

6.8   Discussion points

- Will there be a flurry of mergers, acquisitions and restructures following the decision of Ofcom to withdraw rules prohibiting the joint selling of airtime in the UK? Outline the reasons for your decision.
- Do the rights granted to advertiser / media buyers under CRR provide them with adequate protection in an industry where the possibilities for future consolidation have increased substantially? What other measures which might have been effective could have been put in place?

6.9   Conclusions

Taken all together, the media now make it easier than ever before for the advertiser to reach the whole population or any part of it. With so many demands for consumers' attention, sophisticated systems for media buying in place and competition for market share intense, it would be very dangerous for any of the media players to rest on their laurels.

Following the generally weak performances of the advertising market in 2001 and 2002, 2003 is unlikely to record a significant upturn. It is thought that there has been a weakening of the link between advertising spend and key economic variables such as consumer expenditure and unexpectedly severe problems in certain media, particularly national newspapers. Both factors are due in part to a continuing shift towards international budget setting while electronic media such as the Internet remain a threat to classified advertising and print media.

With relaxation of the foreign ownership rules, there is speculation that foreign takeovers will be rife in coming years. One example is the rumours surrounding Rupert Murdoch who is thought to be circling 'Five' with a potential takeover in mind. There is no doubt; the future is uncertain and exciting.

6.10 Summary

In this chapter:

- We have considered the main types of media used in the advertising world. As we have seen, the Communications Act 2003 has brought about a major shake-up of the media sector, relaxing rules relating to cross media ownership and like media ownership subject to competition law.
- The most popular forms of media continue to be television and the press, although both sectors have faced considerable competition following the rapid development of new media.
- The national press has been the most hardly hit by the recession but has put in place various measures to kerb the declining circulation and purchase of advertising space.

Further reading

The Communications Act 2003.

7 Advertising Creativity

Roger Stotesbury

Learning outcomes

After reading this chapter you will:

- Understand how an agency creative department works.
- Be able to discuss some of the key drivers of advertising creativity.
- Appreciate the importance of a creative idea to the advertising process.
- Discover how advertisements are typically developed using a four-stage process.
- Have a checklist for judging advertising and key ideas to help you sell-in creative work.
- Know better whether you are creative enough to work in advertising.

This chapter is not just for those who personally wish to win creative awards. Everyone from clients to agency account managers has a key role to play in the search for strong advertising solutions, so it is for all those who care passionately about the creative work they and their agency will produce.

7.1 What is it?

Arthur Koestler said 'creativity is the defeat of habit by originality'. Artists, sculptors, potters and clothes' designers are all creative, and creativity is the life blood of advertising. It is what makes working in this business exciting, unpredictable and rewarding, as well as frustrating and very demanding.

So what is special about advertising creativity? It is about communicating the key thought or message your client wants to communicate. So do not seek to work in this world if you want to articulate your own agenda, whim or cause. You would be better off as a sculptor, potter or clothes' designer instead. Advertising is part of the business agenda, and it is about triggering a desire, want or action.

'When I write an advertisement', said David Ogilvy, a famous advertising guru, 'I don't want you to tell me that you find it creative. I want you to find it so interesting that you buy the product.' Yet advertising that is different and somehow out of the ordinary (in other words, that is creative) will break through the competitive clutter and grab the consumer's attention. Jazz musician Charlie Mingus said: 'Creativity is more than just being different. Anyone can play weird, that's easy. What's hard is to be simple as Bach. Making the simple complicated is commonplace. Making the complicated simple, awesomely simple, that's creativity.'

One of the realities about advertising is that everyone believes that they are able to comment on it. If you are new to this industry it is, therefore, valuable to remember a few simple home truths about creativity:

- There are great pressures to come up with new ideas.
- Everyone in an agency process can help the creative process, or hinder it.
- A clear, focused brief, with a strong consumer insight, is the best start.

7.2   The creative department

The creative department of an advertising agency exists to develop advertising campaigns aimed at specific audiences, designed to achieved specific objectives, and to do so within certain budget constraints.

Read 'e' by Matt Beaumont and you will have a pretty clear idea of what goes on within a creative department. Matt has worked in agencies as a copywriter and has based his book on real agencies, real creative people and real events – though you should take the whole thing with a sackload of salt.

What is true to life, however, are the people, the pressures and the 'playful' atmosphere.

Agencies in general, and creative departments in particular, are staffed by men and women from hugely diverse backgrounds. As well as Oxbridge graduates there will be ex-motorbike despatch riders. An ex-journalist could be working alongside an ex-schoolteacher or an ex-construction worker. Increasingly in creative departments there are people who have gone straight from a vocational advertising art or writing course into an agency job, but there are still plenty of 'ex-anything' to be found there.

What moulds them together is the pressure under which they work, continually having to create new advertising ideas, often under tight time constraints. The result, as well as many brilliant ideas, is a determination to enjoy themselves in the process. So, the only type of person you probably will not find in a creative department is the nine to five, suit and tie, conventional conformist.

The key roles in the department are as follows.

7.2.1   The creative director

Sometimes known as the Creative Head and likely to be one of the agency's most senior and highly respected people. The creative director is in charge of all creative output and is responsible for delivering the right creative environment through inspiration, cajoling and team leadership. Perhaps the greatest quality needed in a creative director is the ability to set high standards. They need to be good teachers and recruiters and have sound judgement. They need to know what to sign off and what to send back for further work without crushing the enthusiasm of the people who have put their heart and soul into it, and now have to go back and do it all again. And they must have the ability to spot a true pearl of an idea among a pile of polished pebbles. Creative directors often come with a monster ego and sometimes a monstrous temper, but it simply is no role for a shrinking violet.

7.2.2   The creative team

There are two types of creative people in an agency: art directors and copywriters, often simply known as 'the creatives'. They usually work in pairs on a brief provided by account managers and assigned by the creative director.

It was Bill Bernbach, the founder of Doyle Dane Bernbach, who first put art directors and copywriters together in teams. As they work together to create a strong advertising idea, the images versus words split increasingly becomes blurred, and the art director is as likely to think of a headline as the copywriter is to suggest a visual idea.

On some high-profile projects the decision will be taken to assign more than one creative team to the task, to add more energy and produce more options. There is nothing like competition to motivate.

7.2.3   Freelancers

Certainly one result of the recent downswing in the business is greater reliance on 'freelance' creative teams. For creative directors this offers flexibility when allocating briefs. Agency creativity has become a bit like a Champions League football team. A place for the agency on the £2m pitch shortlist is the equivalent to a place in the last 16, and stars are bought-in to make up a winning team for the Final.

7.2.4   Creative services

Of course, advertisements are not just created by copywriters and art directors working with ideas and sketches (or 'roughs' as they are usually known). Depending on the scale and culture of the agency the selected ideas ('concepts' for press and posters, or 'scripts' and 'storyboards' for TV commercials), once approved by the client, are crafted into finished advertisements by artworkers, film directors and photographers, under the supervision of the creative team and traffic (workflow) managers. Many of these roles are sub-contracted out, though some are managed in-house. Co-ordination of the whole process is carried out by a production manager.

7.3   Drivers of advertising creativity

7.3.1   Diverse agency styles

What sets one agency apart from another is not so much the creative people – who come and go – as the mindset of the agency. Every agency has its own culture, values and beliefs and it is this that catalyses their creativity. One agency might have a reputation for edgy work, another a showreel full of solid, worthy films. It is this diversity that feeds the UK's reputation for strong advertising creativity.

7.3.2   Different types of strategy

The type of creative approach adopted will often be determined by the positioning of the product or service within its marketplace. Charles F. Frazer, in his paper 'Creative Strategy: A Management Perspective' (*Journal of Advertising* 12 No. 4, 1983) summarises relatively distinct creative strategies that are responses to different marketing environments:

Characteristic of product/service and market	Creative strategy
Extreme dominance in sector	*Generic*: straight product or benefit claim
Growing or awakening market	*Pre-emptive*: general claim with assertion of authority
When point of difference cannot be matched by competitors	*Unique selling proposition (USP)*: a superiority based on unique feature or benefit
Homogeneous markets where physical differences are difficult to establish or easy to match	*Brand image*: based on psychological differentiation
Product/service attacking a market leader	*Positioning*: attempt to build specific niche
Discretionary items	*Emotional*: using humour and fun without strong selling emphasis

7.3.3   Emotional versus rational emphasis

It is sometimes useful to review where a creative solution falls on an emotional versus informational matrix (Figure 7.1).

Strong fmcg (fast moving consumer goods) brands are created and nurtured by emotion. Carlsberg, Coca Cola and Walkers are all quadrant 3, but Dell, easyJet and Argos are always found in quadrant 2. Personally I would like to see more ideas that can work in quadrant 4.

7.3.4   Media synergy

Creative thinking also requires thinking about the media. Will the ideas work best as two sequentially placed ads on different spreads? Should the TV commercial use a mix of 10-second teasers as well as longer time lengths? Does the creative idea justify the extra cost of running colour in the regional press? If media planners and the creative team work together to resolve these questions early in the process (even if they work for separate agencies), both the creative work and the media strategy can often be made more effective.

7.3.5   Integration

Reaching today's fragmented audiences often requires an integrated approach, combining different channels and techniques such as advertising, direct marketing, SMS and on-line. There is increasing potency in advertising ideas that can work across different channels in a synergistic way (making $1 + 1 = 3$) and this should be one criterion for judging advertising ideas.

7.3.6   Increased interactivity

New technology is offering exciting creative possibilities for engaging in a two-way 'conversation' with consumers. Digital TV advertisements can be direct response at a click. The interplay between press advertising and micro websites is another area to be more fully exploited by switched-on creative

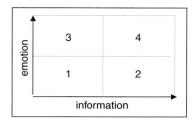

Figure 7.1   *Emotion versus information matrix*

teams. And there is growing use of text messaging as part of integrated campaigns. Creativity is increasingly tapping into these possibilities.

7.4   Creating the creative idea

Behind most good advertising is a strong creative idea which is dramatic, memorable and often emotional.

Think of Kit Kat's 'Have a break' or Carlsberg's 'Probably'. These campaigns have at their core a simple thought that is the foundation for humour, charm and entertainment. Their many different TV advertising executions over many years all have the same core thought, which has now become inextricably linked to the chocolate bar or the beer.

Great ideas like these are the result of a structured process that starts with a client's requirements and leads sequentially to the finished advertisement. The steps will vary from agency to agency but a typical four-step process (Figure 7.2), which places a focus on the search for a creative idea, might be:

Stage 1 – the creative brief and key message
Written by the account manager, with the support of the planner, and signed off by the client, this is a one or two page document that sets out what the advertising is to achieve and how it will be judged. It will usually summarise:
- – why are we advertising?
- – what are we selling?
- – who are we talking to?
- – what must we say? (known as the key message)
- – why should the consumer believe it?
- – what are the values of the brand?

It is intended to inspire advertising creative people, not only by giving them scope for their imaginations, but also by focusing their thinking and clarifying the dos and don'ts.

Stage 2 – the creative proposition
This is the start of the creative journey. It is a simple, maybe unexpected expression of the key message, which the agency believes will connect with the target audience. Developed by the planner and account director

Figure 7.2   *The four stages of the creative process*

or manager, and agreed on by the creative team, it provides a powerful launch pad for creative thinking although (or perhaps because) it can sometimes be distilled to just a single word.

Early in my career I was taken through the creative process by looking at Kellogg's All Bran. The agency translated the key message of '*All Bran is still the most effective palatable way to clear constipation*', into the simple proposition of '*All Bran is powerful*'. This led to advertising featuring snowploughs and ice-breakers as powerful visual metaphors.

Stage 3 – the creative idea
With an agreed brief and direction in the form of the proposition, the agency creative team is now able to brainstorm and develop alternative creative ideas. At this stage we are not interested in finished scripts or detailed visuals, but in the basic thinking behind what can be developed. For this reason the ideas are best reviewed by the agency team, and presented to the client, as quickly produced concept boards (usually simple line drawings or scamps with quickly scribbled headlines). Showing the idea to the client in this way helps to involve them in the process and lets them use their own imagination.

An account director from Saatchi & Saatchi turned up to an important client presentation with apparently no work to show. After the usual pleasantries, he began the formal meeting by saying: 'Well, I suppose you want to see the work', and producing from out of his suit jacket a single folded sheet of paper. It did not matter that the scamp (simple illustrative line-drawing) it contained could have been done in the pub the night before. It was a simple, relevant and great idea, and 4 weeks later rolled out nationwide on 500 poster sites.

Stage 4 – the execution
Once an idea is accepted by the client, it is developed into the actual finished advertisement, also known as the execution. This is the stage where the numerous crafts of advertising – copywriting, art direction, photography, typography, film production and so on – come into play; co-ordinated by the agency production manager.

For every creative brief, there are numerous possible propositions. For every proposition there are numerous creative ideas. For every creative idea there are numerous executions. It is the job of everyone involved with the creative process to ensure that the final execution, or series of executions, selected is the best possible creative response to the original client objective (Figure 7.3).

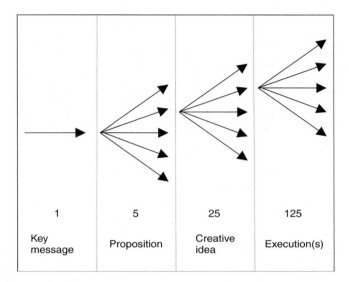

1	5	25	125
Key message	Proposition	Creative idea	Execution(s)

Figure 7.3   *The numerous routes that can emerge from one key message*

There are three advantages to the 4 stage process we have just explored:

- It is kicked-off by the creative brief. With good agencies it is the creative brief that is 'king', and it is only moved away from for very strong reasons.
- Throughout the four stages there are points of review and decision to determine the best way to go forward from the brief to the actual execution. These reviews facilitate team working between agency colleagues, and partnership with the client.
- Stage 3 provides a focus on the idea, allowing it to be judged without the embellishment of executional details. In advertising it is customer insight that sells, and it is ideas that lead to some of the best remembered and most successful ads.

7.5   How do creative teams create?

Too many in the industry underestimate the challenge of the empty layout pad.

While not as mysterious as some would like to suggest, the process by which creative people search for their ideas is an activity difficult to describe. Perhaps the key verb is 'to search'. The best ideas do not originate in isolation. Creative people need to interact with one another, and they need to immerse themselves into the world of the brief: the product or service, the audience, the triggers that will make people want to buy or use it and so on. Creativity at this stage is primarily all about investigating, asking questions and listening. The seed for an idea can come from anywhere: from talking to an assembly mechanic on the production line (as in a BMW ad), from reading internal office memos (as in the French Connection FCUK campaign) or from listening to focus group tapes (as in my agency's ads for Argos).

Even creatives themselves do not know where ideas come from. One copy-writer once described his creative process as 'moving around the office on my chair until I'm under the bit of ceiling where the ideas drop from the sky.' An old agency joke also highlights the way many creatives seem to work: 'Q. Why shouldn't a creative team stare out of the window all morning? A. Because they'd have nothing to do in the afternoon.' And despite their way with words, copywriters often find it hard to describe how they do what they do. Once, when the Duke of Edinburgh was being shown around an agency, he looked in on a creative team who were sitting, feet – and blank sheets of paper – on desks. 'What's your job, then?' asked the Duke. 'Thinking what to put', replied the copywriter.

All creative teams work in different ways as they 'think what to put', but inevitably they need space and time to develop their thinking. Creative people flourish in an environment that is open, not closed, and energetic, not judge-mental. Typically, layout pads will be filled with doodles and isolated words, random observations and thoughts, as the first stages of brainstorming get under way. The saying that 'you cannot discover new oceans until you have the courage to lose sight of the shore' is as good a description of the creative think-ing process as any.

The best creative teams not only generate many, many ideas but are also self-critical and will narrow their work down to only those that really hit the mark. With perhaps three to six sound ideas, it is time to show them to their creative director for feedback and development. Good creative directors will be looking for the opportunity to build on this first thinking, and to turn a sound idea into a great one.

At our agency, **infocus**, we have established a 'Challenge Wall' where ideas are pinned up for open discussion and debate. It is a simple way of involving the whole agency team, of bringing to life the best thinking and of setting a standard for the agency. Many other creatively led agencies practise similar improvements on the old-fashioned nervous line-up outside the creative director's office.

7.5.1   Six tips on how to think creatively

All creatives work in different ways but a few thinking techniques seem to be used by many:

1   *Lateral thinking*: A common technique used to extend the imagination, by making, often subconscious, links to alternative thoughts on a different plain.

2 *Pushing boundaries*: Come up with one idea, then brainstorm it to see where it takes you. Do not be satisfied with one idea: carry on until you have 10. The last idea may be the best, or may prove that the first one was.

3 *Think like a child*: Often children see things in a new, exciting way that cuts through conventional barriers.

4 *Swapping shoes*: Put yourself in someone else's shoes. How would Gandhi, Beethoven or Noel Gallagher interpret the brief?

5 *Out and about*: A word overheard, a moment from a movie or a sentence from a focus group can all be the stimulus for a creative idea.

6 *Edward De Bono's Six Coloured Thinking hats*: A system for getting people into doing one sort of thinking at a time; for instance, emotional, rational, judgmental.

7.6   Ten tips on how to judge creativity

Judging creativity is at the heart of the creative process. But how to judge and what are the rules?

The judgement criterion for the creative team, led by the creative director, is how the creative idea will work. For the account team it is whether the idea truly meets the brief and the client's expectations.

Given the importance of judging creativity, and indeed its subjective nature, it is sound practice to establish a yardstick for how to judge a creative idea. Here is one possibility:

1 *Does it have impact?* In the increasing clutter of TV, print and radio, the criterion of impact is of key importance. Without arresting the viewer's, reader's or listener's attention, no advertising can meet its basic objective of communication.

2 *Does it have an idea?* As discussed above, the benefit is best conveyed not just by a product message or a series of messages, but by one clear idea: a key thought, exclusive to the brand and attractive to the consumer. This idea should be arresting, original, unexpected, stimulating.

3 *Is it involving?* The consumer is not particularly interested in your message. The onus is on the advertising to arouse attention and desire. And if it is relevant, the advertising will involve the target consumer.

4 *Is it on brand?* How many times have you seen a great ad, but cannot remember what it was selling? The advertising must be about the brand, not a story to which the brand is merely an unimportant addition.

5 *Does it show simplicity?* One interesting thought about the brand – simply, attractively and single-mindedly expressed – is the essence of great advertising. Too many messages will confuse, and lose the consumer's attention.

6 *Does it demonstrate credibility?* The fundamental brand benefit must always be believable and obtainable, although the manner in which this benefit is expressed may involve exaggeration, fantasy or humour.

7   *Does it offer a distinctive promise?* A brand is 'a promise to deliver'. Advertising is, nowadays, a key way of creating 'uniqueness'. Thus, whether the benefit is unique or not, its expression must be.

8   *Is it brand building?* Each advertisement affects the consumer's perception of the brand. If any one advertisement conflicts with that perception it will cause at best a neutral, at worst a negative, feeling.

9   *Is it campaignable?* The idea should be capable of development – not just into a single advertisement but into a campaign across different media, and not just into one campaign but into a series of campaigns. This requires more than simple repetition or variations on a theme.

10   *Is it capable of media adaptability?* The effectiveness of a communication can often be strengthened by translating a good idea created for one medium into another. This is rarely achieved by mere transfer but often by intelligent adaptation. Wise clients will ask to see early mock-ups of executions across all the planned media.

7.7   Selling creativity

However good it is, all creativity needs to be sold. The creative team needs to sell their ideas to their colleagues, to the account team and then to the client.

If you are new to the industry, ask to sit in on as many sell-in sessions (usually known as presentations) as possible. In the meantime, here are six thoughts:

- Your presentation, particularly to the client, is going to be the highlight of their day. Learn the importance of creating an almost theatrical setting.
- Do your preparation so that you can relate to what your audience is looking for. Every client has a different definition of creativity.
- Before revealing the creative work, put it into context and explain what the thinking is that led up to it.
- Learn how much to say. When you show the work be silent and reverential. The work is the hero not you.
- Advertising is a hybrid of science and art, with creativity the least tangible of all the parts. So welcome reactions – after all, that is what all the work is there to provoke – but also have the passion to drive through the case.
- Never lose sight of the fact that it is the client who is paying the bill. But also never forget that the bill they are paying is for the agency's specialist skills: they are buying your expertise and will be reluctant not to accept your advice and recommendations.

When new people join our agency and work on their first project, the first question they normally ask is 'How many ideas are we going to show the client?' This is a good question, and demonstrates that they are thinking through the options.

One idea only can smack of preciousness and hardly fits within a spirit of client / agency partnership. Or, it can suggest real confidence in a brilliant idea, while presenting too many can make the agency appear indecisive and muddled. The real answer to the question is: never present poor ideas. Too many agencies seem content to pack an account manager off to see a client with one good idea and two they know to be half-hearted. It does not impress anyone and totally undermines the agency culture.

7.8   Discussion points

7.8.1   The importance of copy

Today's audiences are increasingly becoming visually rather than linguistically articulate. But the right words in the right advertisements still have an important role to play. You may not need to read 500 words before you buy a packet of breakfast cereal, but you will probably want something more than just a striking image before you invest in a pension plan.

7.8.2   The use of creative pitches

Peer recommendations, smart credential presentations and the odd business lunch may get an agency onto a shortlist. But they are usually not enough to win the work. Nothing underlines the unique role of creativity within the advertising business so much as the creative pitch.

Solicitors do not do some of their work prior to being appointed, so why is this virtually standard practice in advertising? There are perhaps three reasons:

- The creative route is central to what the client is buying, and with an increasing need for marketers to accelerate their returns, a pitch provides clients with maximum control.
- The advantages of one creative route over another will often result in a massive contribution to the bottom line.
- Clients (and let us be honest, agency people too) enjoy them. Pitches are the adrenalin-rush of an agency.

The creative pitch is the ultimate moment of theatre in a world full of drama. Key agency people take turns to present, explaining how keen the agency is to work with the client, how the agency interprets and shows great understanding of the task and how the budget might be allocated across different media. At some point, sometimes as the climax to the meeting but always as the high point, the creative director will reveal the creative thinking.

The client will often see up to five pitches over a 2- or 3-day period, which might translate into between 5 and 10 campaigns. So, the agency that stands out – perhaps through strong personal chemistry, the use of a new and arresting strapline to run through the whole campaign or the single-minded use of a personality – will edge ahead. I recall when **infocus** pitched for Unisys' European e-business account, we based everything around our line 're-thinking business', with the 'e' highlighted in Unisys red. It was a simple idea that won the day.

I have spoken about the role of scamping within the creative process. Sometimes at pitches it can work against you. After pitching to a client, an agency got a call: 'Your thinking was good, but the work was too rough – we couldn't see where it was going.' The response? 'We'll present some finished concepts to you first thing in the morning'. The creative team worked late into the night, and the next day the pitch was won.

Perhaps what this illustrates best is that there are no hard and fast rules for pitches, and maybe they are all down to luck after all. But as a famous golfer once said: 'the more I practice, the luckier I get.'

7.8.3   A role for the client?

Is there a role for the client in the creative process? The answer is a definite yes. The client's knowledge of their product and audience should be fed into the process from the beginning, but there are four key moments when a good client is absolutely at the heart of things:

• In the preparation of the brief which kicks the process off.
• In supplying and facilitating awareness of the product or service and its audience (the swimwear manufacturer who briefed their agency in the Jacuzzi of the local pool understood the difference this makes).
• In giving the agency the right amount of time and space to come up with the solution.
• In signing off the creative work at both concept and execution stages.

7.8.4   The value of creativity

Agencies were traditionally paid through a percentage on the media budget. So the more a campaign extended the more the agency could bill. Now, with the fragmentation of media buying, creative agencies are often paid specifically for their creative ideas and the associated production fees. This means creativity is now a direct revenue stream, and many agencies now agree on fees that include a performance-related element.

The implications for agency people are a focus on the value of creativity in itself, but also a need to ensure its cost structure is aligned with the agency fee structure.

7.8.5   Working in the creative world

Whether or not you intend to be a creative yourself, an advertising agency is a creative world, and it is important to understand the creatives' role and to cultivate the skills and sensitivities required to work with them, if you want to get the best out of them.

You will only be a success in advertising (and a respected creative or colleague of the creatives) if you genuinely have a passion for advertising. If you are not continually fascinated by mailshots, TV commercials, posters and so on – think again. Account managers who do not get a buzz out of seeing their ads in the national press are too tired and should move on. Creatives who do not think of new approaches to an fmcg brief after walking around a shopping centre are probably never going to make a creative director.

As already discussed, agencies have different cultures and values. Your particular approach and personal style may be better suited to some agencies than others. If you are a junior creative, find yourself an agency where you will feel part of the fabric – not where you are always battling against the 'system'. If you are an account person who is keen to have their creative viewpoint listened to, check whether you are joining a culture that welcomes your comments.

7.9   Summary

In this chapter we have seen that:

- Creativity is what makes advertising so special; it is the output which everything else in advertising should be geared up to support.
- Creative advertising will make an impression, be empathetic, be involving and memorable, and be awesomely simple.
- Strong advertising is built on a strong creative idea and powerful executions. This should be the focus of any creative process.
- A strong creative idea is the framework for increasingly integrated advertising.

Further reading

David, O. *Ogilvy on Advertising*, Prion, ISBN 1-85375-196-0.
Terence, A. S. *Advertising Promotion*, Harcourt College Publishers, ISBN 0-03-021113-1.
Arden, P. *It's Not How Good You Are, It's How Good You Want to Be*, Phaidon, ISBN 0-7148-4337-7.
Sticky Wisdom? What If!, Capstone, ISBN 1-84112-021-9.

8 Press Production

Mark Maguire

Learning outcomes

By the end of this chapter you will:

- Understand what has changed and what is expected of the press production candidate.
- Recognise the type of knowledge required of new production candidates when fulfilling their duties now and in the future.
- Investigate some real world examples of how some successful agencies have tackled press production with the objective of streamlining their production process and ultimately providing competitive pricing gained from enhanced efficiencies.

8.1 Introduction

The role of press production in any agency is a fast changing environment and requires the ability to deal with demanding situations imposed on us as clients react to their competitors' advertising with equal measure! The role has changed because over the last 5 years a constant evolution of technology has had an impact on the day-to-day production role when fulfilling an advertising campaign.

It is worth noting that we will have to generalise when describing press production working practices as it will very much depend on the size of the agency with respect to the resources available at their disposal.

The chapter is divided into categories in order to provide a clear explanation of press production and is structured as below:

- Tasks (technical breakout on pre-press and publication specifications)
- Trends (the agency model of the future)
- Trends (market pressures)
- Case study
- Summary
- Useful links

8.2 Tasks (technical breakout on pre-press and publication specifications)

By breaking down the tasks involved in getting a project from creative to print we will see how the production role is the 'glue' department to any agency and how the traditionally separated roles of Traffic and Production have started to blur. Thus, a combination of both jobs has become possible as technology and the drive to reduce cost shows an overlap of territory.

Let us now look at the components of production by listing out the steps to fulfilling a successful campaign and then we will take up each task and describe the subject in more detail.

Listed below are the areas which our production candidate will have to deal with:

1 Media booking
2 Estimating
3 Creative
4 Art buying
5 Account management
6 Traffic
7 Artwork
8 Pre-press
9 Technical breakout – including page sizes/content/colour/publication
10 Specifications & distribution
11 Approvals
12 Billing.

8.2.1 Media booking

Most of the larger agencies either own or part own a share of a media company and this is fundamental to how well a working relationship can be built upon to provide good communication with the agency.

Booking the space in any national newspaper or magazine for an advertisement is the start of the process to fulfil a campaign that may span over multiple publications and the production department needs to act on this information as soon as they receive it.

A schedule may arrive in many different formats but usually this will be in the form of an Excel spreadsheet outlining the following:

• Publication name
• Page size
• Insertion date
• Copy date
• Rotation (repeat dates).

Over the last couple of years this is where our production department problems start! These schedules can very quickly become out of date and can end up having several iterations after the first draft as the media buyers negotiate better or last minute deals with advertising managers at the publications. It is common practice to actually run a campaign even without an up-to-date schedule due to the pressure of time as a call will come into the production department asking for an ad that no one knew was actually booked (apart from the media company!). This means you have to react very quickly to ensure that the relevant material is delivered on time and the space is filled – not much pressure there, then!

8.2.2   Estimating

This is a very important aspect of the production role and, if for no other reason, demands that the schedule from the media company is accurate when quoting the number of insertions a campaign will go into.

Once you have a schedule that you are confident with it would be passed to a pre-press supplier to quote for the work based on the agency client price list. Traditionally, there has always been a close link between the agency and pre-press supplier production departments as the pricing will depend on the type of materials needed by the respective publications. The pre-press supplier will normally hold this information in an extensive database that is regularly kept up-to-date and, therefore, can quote fulfilment of the campaign accurately. However, during the cycle of the campaign situations change and additional insertions may be booked so it is important to keep records up-to-date when it comes to reconciliation (comparing the estimate to the invoice) at the end of the campaign.

8.2.3   Creative

Production is not really involved in the creative process as this communication will normally be handled by the Traffic department. If we take the example of a smaller agency with limited resources you will find that a combined role of traffic and production is commonplace and involvement in all communication is necessary.

Creative departments will come up with a concept and, once approved by the client, it is then the responsibility of Traffic to coordinate the resources to get the campaign under way.

The creative process could involve many types of materials to obtain the desired look and feel of a campaign. Traditionally, this may have involved the use of storyboards from visualisers commissioned to produce drawings and indeed, recently, creative people are turning to computer-literate designers using computer packages to project their ideas and output to a colour printer to gain approval from their client. For a fuller discussion of the creative process please see Chapter 7.

8.2.4   Art buying

The art buying department of an agency will source images and negotiate the necessary rights (copyright) for using that image. The fee paid by the agency to the artist or image library will determine the usage rights (and set an expiry date for usage) and agree on the types of media where the image will have exposure.

They will commission photographers (generally from a portfolio) to shoot a subject working to budgets as agreed with account management, which may involve hiring studios or shooting on location.

These images will come into the agency either as digital files or more traditional methods such as transparency or negative film. Further manipulation of the image may be required to meet the creative brief and this is where the production / traffic role necessitates estimating the cost of additional retouching work.

8.2.5   Account management

This is the team that represents the agency and sits directly between the client and all the processes that take place in order to get a campaign to press/TV or radio, etc. They will be intrinsically involved in managing budgets and dealing with the clients during creative and pre-press approval cycles where necessary.

8.2.6   Traffic

The Traffic department is the hub to the operation and has to liaise with all the relevant departments to ensure that the campaign runs smoothly. Its role is to support the creative department of the agency to achieve the desired results and work with art buying to find the best solution to obtaining the art director's objective. Traffic is responsible for working to budgets and obtaining estimates when sourcing a creative retouching house to enhance and manipulate an image by whatever technology possible.

When the concept and images are finished they will liaise with Production to find out how many masters, artworks and adapts are required to fulfil a campaign and then instruct the artwork studio to produce these pages.

Once the pages are constructed, Traffic will need to obtain approval from the creatives and account management before releasing the artworks to Production for reproduction at the pre-press house.

As previously mentioned, the Traffic and Production roles have overlapping areas of responsibility and, depending on the structure of the agency, may be handled by the same person.

8.2.7 Artwork

Generally speaking, most agencies have their own artworking department to create the master artworks and any adaptations that may be required for the different sized publications.

It is the job of Production to work out how many masters and adaptations will be required to meet the production schedule. This is where Production works closely with their pre-press supplier to obtain the information on page sizes and often relies on this part of the service for estimating too. Most agencies use BRAD (British Rate Card Advertising Directory), a Bible for obtaining addresses, phone numbers and page sizes for a particular publication and, indeed, there is an online version available, too. However, most agency production departments will not rely on this method as it is often out of date and does not have accurate technical specification details that a pre-press supplier database will have (explained later). The artwork department will have to create the number of artworks requested following the necessary brand guidelines and pass them through to the production department with a colour laser.

Brand guidelines are an intrinsic part of retaining the brand look and feel for any corporate client so that their products are instantly recognisable by the consumer. What the consumer does not realise when flicking though a newspaper or magazine is the level of detail these rules have to be adhered to by the artwork studio. For instance, logos have to be the correct colour across all types of media, set measured distances from the edge of a page, correct font type and size for headlines and body copy, etc.

Artwork used to be a skilled paste-up artist job of carefully placing copy on grids to follow a layout guide derived from a creative brief. This process has become completely digital and today's artworkers have to be technically conversant with working on an Apple Macintosh (PCs are starting to be used more) using a number of applications to produce a page. To facilitate laying out images and text, two main desktop publishing packages are used, Quark Xpress and Adobe Indesign.

Quark Xpress has been the industry standard for many years and is regarded as the de facto for producing pages for press advertising without ever having a serious rival. However, over the last year, Adobe has revised and improved its 'Indesign' package and now, finally, the industry has a competent alternative to the relief of many designers and artworkers!

8.2.8 Pre-press

By far the most important part of the production role is to have grounded understanding of all aspects of pre-press production, as a lack of knowledge could prove very costly indeed to their agency!

There are many areas to cover on this main topic, so, for ease, let us break down the categories and elaborate for discussion where necessary.

- *Scanning*
  The digital capture of film images (transparency or negative) on a device that uses laser beams to read an image fired through a set of optics/photocells in red, green and blue. It is common practice to scan the image to the correct size and resolution with the various media requirements in mind so that the image can be repurposed later down the line. Images that are enlarged above the conventional tolerances will degrade in quality and suffer jagged edges (that is any detail in the image with edges like car shots that will contain door shut lines, bumpers side rubbing strips, etc.) and may also appear blurred!
- *Page sizes*
  There are many different ways of describing how a page fits in a publication; the most common are:
  - *Trim size* – This is the most widely used and is the actual size of the magazine itself, a finished size.
  - *Bleed size* – This is an amount of image area bigger than the page size that allows a tolerance of error when the paper is guillotined to its desired size, otherwise, where an image may cover the whole page, white paper would be seen if the cut was inaccurate.
  - *Type area* – Very commonly used for newspapers where adverts are floated in a page area (you never see an image cover to the very edge of a newspaper).
  - *Columns* – This description is again common in newspaper publications as they divide their pages into column widths to make it easier to work out the method of fitting adverts round editorial copy (hence the structure of all newspapers working with columns to flow copy into pages simply and efficiently; if this were not the case – imagine the clutter!)
  - *Spine* – Known as the centre of the magazine, where glue or stapling takes place to hold the pages together.
  - *Perfect bound* – This is commonly used in magazines with larger pagination to describe a process where the pages are all glued to the spine evenly.
  - *Gutters* – This is used to describe an adjustment needed to the page size in order for a double page spread advert to run across the spine and allow the subject such as a car to still be seen as a full image instead of part of the car being obscured by the middle of the magazine.

  Extra image will be allowed for in the middle (by actually increasing the size of the left and right hand page in the centre direction only at the pre-press stage) and thus, when this extra area is used, the effect is given of the image coming back together in the middle perfectly.

8.2.8.1 Content/colour and brand guidelines

Once the creative element is agreed on for the look and feel of a page and we have our masters and adaptation page sizes calculated to complete the campaign, arranging the content in the page to conform to brand guidelines is essential. This is where a keen eye for detail is paramount for the production department to ensure that type is not going dangerously close to the trim and liable to be cut off or any other potential pitfalls before passing to the pre-press house for reproduction. The Production Department is there to give advice on what is or is not suitable for an advertisement in any particular publication. For instance, very dark images tend to lose detail and look muddy in newspapers, whereas in a glossy magazine these can look very effective to generate the mood required especially for fashion shots!

The colour of type is also important. Many times we read a magazine where the text is difficult to read due to black type used on a dark picture or white text on a light background subject. Sometimes, you wonder who approves these advertisements or editorial pages before going to press! It is very possible that some publications' editorial pages go to press without having a proof of the page to save cost and hence may have been approved on a monitor and thus the problem was not apparent at the time due to the inaccuracy of the colour. This is illustrated well by walking into an electrical store and seeing 30 televisions showing the same channel with no two alike for colour. This is where colour management is critical for managing this process and is mentioned later on.

When a proof is returned to Production after reproduction it is the Production Department that has the main responsibility to ensure that nothing has altered on the page and that it matches the original colour laser signed off by the respective Traffic, Creative and Account Management Departments.

One of the most important aspects of the role is to judge the quality of colour reproduction from the pre-press supplier and their ability to match back to the original image passed by the creative department. The pre-press supplier has the job of colour matching the images across multiple publications that may be utilising very different printing techniques and thus requires great skill and the use of colour management technology.

For the Production Department to gauge how well this match has been executed, the pre-press house will supply what is known as 'contract proofs' to the agency for approval. These are colour proofs made to simulate the press match usually to a given print standard set down by industry bodies.

So, what can go wrong I hear you thinking?

- *Fonts* (otherwise known as typefaces) – are critical to the look of an advertisement and it is important to know what can go wrong with fonts on a page so that you are aware what to look out for. There are thousands of fonts and all have a different name for a particular family such as Helvetica/Times/Garamond, and have different styles such as bold/italic.

  There are also different font manufactures such as Adobe/Agfa and many more and this can cause a problem – it is a bit like buying 40-W light bulbs. They may be the same wattage as the one you want to replace but the ambiance they give off is different from the others you have in the room! Thus, manufactures may call the fonts the same name but their metrics (size) are slightly different and hence things may not turn out as desired.

- *Text reflow* – This can be caused by numerous things but primarily by the pre-press house using a different font from the agency and copy can go missing by either not fitting in a box or running off the page!
- *Images* (we will go on to colour later on) – There is a possibility that the pre-press house may not as accurately put the image on the page as the artwork studio; this could be because they have a different image from the studio or have used a previous out-of-date image they hold.

So, as you can see, when a Production Department receives a proof back from a pre-press house, there is much to look out for before passing round the agency for approval by the Traffic/Creative and Account Management Departments.

8.2.8.2   *Publication specifications (technical breakout)*

This subject is one of the most intricate parts of the process and one where agency Production Departments are heavily reliant on the knowledge of pre-press houses to supply the correct materials to the publication on time!

So, what do production people have to know in order to converse with their pre-press suppliers on an equal level and be confident when using technical language?

The crucial word here is 'transition'. The printing industry as a whole has endured a transition over the last 3 years from using analogue film to image printing plates, to using digital data with computer to plate machines to produce these plates. This has meant that instead of advertising agencies and pre-press houses supplying film and cromalin to the publication it has now moved on to digital files and digital proofs.

So, let us look first at the technology to get some acronyms explained to understand the terminology and combine a look at past and present methods to see what effect the digital revolution has had on our industry.

- *Four-colour process*
  To generalise, everything we see printed in newspapers and magazines is made up of four colours, cyan blue/magenta red/yellow and black (also known as key – meaning the colour that adds detail). On a printing press these four colours are laid down separately on top of each other to the paper.
- *Litho printing*
  The most common type of printing process for magazines and direct mail is litho printing, due mainly to the speed and economy of this process. The imaged and non-imaged (blank) areas share the same surface of the plate and this differentiation has come from the image exposed on the plate by

a light source followed by a chemical process to retain only the printed image. The process relies on the fact that oil and water do not mix and the printed areas are receptive to grease and water repellent. Dampening rollers wet the non-image areas preventing ink adhering to those parts and when the ink comes into contact with the imaged areas of the plate it is transferred to an inking blanket via an impression cylinder and then to the paper.

- *Gravure*
  This process uses shrunken or depressed areas for the image area and is etched into a copper cylinder or wraparound plate. The plate cylinder is rotated in the ink bath where the recesses are filled with ink and the excess wiped off the cylinder with a blade. The ink in the recess forms the image which prints directly to the paper as it passes between the cylinder and impression cylinder. This method of printing is considered excellent for long runs at high speed while maintaining a very high quality.

- *Black-and-white*
  This is single colour only where an image is represented by shades of grey due to only black or white dots being present in the image.

- *Duotone/tri-tone*
  This is the addition of a second or third colour to a black-and-white image to provide a denser or colour bias effect such as sepia (to replicate old photos effect)

- *Halftone screen*
  A printed image is composed of dots of varying frequency (number per square inch/cm) and size. Smaller dots produce lighter images while larger dots produce darker images and, in effect, allow less paper to show through.

  High screen rulings are preferred for quality publication, anything from 120 lines per inch (LPI) upwards, while newspapers will run using low screen rulings of 85 and below.

  This relationship is quite a simple one. Keep the dots closer together to enhance the detail and colour fidelity but keep them further apart to prevent spread and hence dot gain on fast print runs if using very thin absorbent stock such as newsprint.

- *Resolution*
  A measurement of the amount of information in output, specified as dots per inch, pixels per inch, bits per pixel or lines per inch – depending on the device and application. Higher numbers have more resolution, which results in a higher level of image information.

- *Dot size/shape/gain*
  Dot shapes can have a marked effect on an image and there are several types such as round, square, elliptical, etc. Round dots are generally used in newspapers to help keep dot gain to a minimum. Dot gain is an increase in the size of dots due to many factors such as inking blankets, paper saturation, humidity and water content all of which can increase the intensity of the image.

- *Under-colour removal (UCR)*
  This is a process where black ink (key) is used in place of cyan, magenta and yellow (CMY) to prevent the build up of too much density of colour mainly in the shadow areas of an image. The theoretical combined ink weight of all four colours could equate to 400 per cent and would saturate the paper (and possibly show through the other side!) to produce a very dark muddy image. Publications are acutely aware of this and set maximum ink weight levels in their specifications in order to prevent poor colour printing.

  As a good guide, it would follow that quality magazines printed on a high grade paper limit at 300–350 UCR, whereas a newspaper printed on very thin newsprint stock will limit at 250 UCR. Usually, UCR will only affect the areas where equal or balanced amounts of CMY exist for the black to replace, keeping the colour bias of the image intact.

- *Grey component replacement (GCR)*
  This has the same principle as UCR but can affect greater areas of the image such as highlights, midtones and shadows as the process looks to substitute black for CMY in neutral areas of colour. This colour could be fleshtones, as the GCR looks to replace any combination of CMY that has some percentage of ink equivalent to grey.

  There are two main benefits to using GCR on press. The first is the potential for huge savings on ink by the reduced consumption of CMY, and secondly, mis-register is far less of a problem due to the fact the black ink provides much of the image detail.

- *Trapping*
  A pre-press technique that allows for mis-register on press by providing an overlap of colours to prevent white halos appearing around type or images that should butt together without seeing the paper beneath. This can be applied at either the pre-press house or the printers.

- *Colour management*
  This technology has revolutionised our industry and improved both the quality and the consistency of colour we all take for granted today. Bad colour reproduction has become a problem of the past while the possibilities of using colour in areas previously unheard of are all the more common. Have you noticed how local papers and Exchange & Mart, etc. have exploded with colour advertisements?

  The industry is moving towards keeping the image in the red/green/blue (RGB) colour mode for as long as possible in the workflow and converting to cyan/magenta/yellow/key (CMYK) on output. RGB has a much wider colour gamut (colour space – number of colours available) than CMYK and, therefore, when using an image for multiple media formats it makes sense to clip the image gamut to the myriad of CMYK colour spaces only when necessary.

It is now possible to mimic the behaviour of a device whether it is a printing press, digital camera or a colour monitor and wrap that information into what is known as a profile. Once a device has been profiled it is possible to simulate how it will print or display colour and hence manage the expectation of the final result. Therefore, back to viewing our editorial pages on a monitor before going to a press is possible if you colour manage (profile) the monitor and use a second profile to simulate the printing press match to see the effect. This is known as 'soft' proofing and is becoming more popular as the technology and colour management skills of the industry improve to bring us a more accurate representation of the printed page / advertisement.

- *Raster image process*
  Generally speaking, before a page can be printed by a device (ink jet printer/digital press, etc.) the page has to be interpreted by the RIP so that it translates the coordinates and elements of the page for the printing and instructs the printing engine where to put the data.
- *Image formats (pictures)*
  The principal image formats for pictures are:
  TIFF – (tagged image file format) – most common for images
  EPS – (encapsulated postscript) – embeds images and text into the file
  PDF – (portable document format) – portable format that combines images and text.
- *Digital file formats (for the supply of adverts to Publications)*
  The area of how we deliver digital files to publication has undergone much change in the last few years and will continue to evolve as standards are put forward by industry bodies representing both publishers and printers.
  Here are the four main formats for delivering an advertisement to publication as a finished file.
- *Tiff / IT8 P1 –*
  One of the earliest formats adopted and safest ways of saving an advertisement into a file format that was secure to prevent alteration of the file at the printers.
  It came into existence mainly in the Gravure market (as cylinders are very expensive to engrave if errors occurred) and is still used in this market to some degree today. It is still a popular format in the USA.
  Note – it is difficult to edit the file as the text and images are separated. Moreover, it produces very large files indeed and this alone hampers file delivery across the Internet and other networks. File resolution is set and it is very difficult to repurpose the data for another publication that uses different screen rulings.
- *Open files –*
  This was again an early method (and is still used commonly today depending on workflow requirements) to get digital files to Publications. A pre-press house would collate all the necessary files into a folder that went together to make up an advertisement and pass this to the printer/publisher.

This leaves room to make last minute changes and provides the chance to repurpose the data for other media. However, these last minute changes mean that there is a huge possibility that something may go wrong with the conversion process and your advertisement may look different from the proof signed off by the agency!

- *Encapsulated postscript (EPS)* –

This format helped build the confidence in the industry that it was possible to encompass all the elements of the page into a single file format and still remain fairly resolution independent.

The advantages are that it had the fonts built in and, therefore, overcame the issue with the legality of transferring the typefaces within the page. Moreover, it was secure and very difficult for anyone to tamper with the file.

The disadvantages are that, depending on the system producing the file, problems were common with interpretation of the file at the ripping stage and the size of the files are still quite large.

- *Portable document format (PDF)* –

It would be fair to say that this file format has evolved to such an extent that it has truly revolutionised the printing industry and accelerated the proliferation of digital file delivery. The basic promise behind the PDF format is that it is the safest and most accessible document format irrespective of the application and computer platform in use. Virtually every computer program in use will have the option to output PDF – and Adobe have produced a nice little free application called Reader, that will allow anyone to open the file and print it out!

However, there are problems. Originally, it was never intended to be a file format to support the output of press advertising and had many flaws for this type of use. To fully understand PDF would need a chapter dedicated to the subject.

To address the issue of PDF for print, Adobe and numerous other software developers came up with different flavours of the file format and flight checking applications to assure senders and receivers of the file that everything was present and verified.

These are some of the current types:

PDF/PDF X1 / PDF X1a / PDF X2 / PDF X3 / Pass4Press PDF

The Periodical Publishers Association (PPA) (see website link at the end of this chapter) in the UK set up a body to deal with the issues facing the industry for developing standards in proofing and file format. They came up with 'Pass4Press' to describe those standards which have developed and will continue to develop and will probably become one of the most commonly used file formats in the UK.

- *Flight checking*

This is an application that will check the files before sending to Publications to ensure that all the elements of the page are present and correct to prevent costly errors and missed copy deadlines due to incorrect files.

Software developers are working closely with publishers to produce specific checking procedures for their applications to compare against as set down by a particular publisher or industry body such as the PPA. This criterion is commonly referred to as 'profiles'. These profiles will look at the majority of file formats (PDF/EPS/open files) and run a report that will check the elements present in the file and report any errors.

The type of potential errors the application is looking for may be:

- Image resolution (not high enough).
- Colour space (RGB or CMYK).
- Font information embedded in the file, size and type of font that is not considered safe.
- UCR value, etc.
- *Digital file delivery mechanisms*

With the explosion of the communications industry, supply and demand have driven down the costs of bandwidth to the effect that fast, always online connections to the Internet are commonplace in the industry. Publishers, printers and agencies alike have recognised the need to have dedicated links to the Internet to enable their business to communicate with the outside world at a fixed cost.

Listed below are the most common names of services and protocols you will hear and all facilitate the ability to send a file from a producer to a receiver of advertising material (digital data):

- Compact disc (CD) – An EPS/PDF advertisement burned on to disc to be sent direct to the publisher via courier.
- File Transfer Protocol (FTP) – Internet based delivery mechanism, very cheap but has security pitfalls.
- Integrated Services Digital Network (ISDN) – Point-to-point sending of data via an address book of single or multiple files.
- Advertising Delivery System (ADS) – Embeds fonts into the EPS file for point-to-point sending via an address book, although decreasing in use due to the adoption of PDF.
- VIO (communications solutions provider) – Manages delivery service of all data in one place for ISDN/Email/FTP and has useful job ticketing information.
- Wamnet (communications solutions provider) – manages delivery service of all data in one place (as VIO) with the facility to have dedicated server space to offer access to data online.

Adfast (regional newspapers delivery service) – Provides an online database of regional publications specifications and flight checking facility before sending a file to its destination. This has diminished the need for ADS due to the speed, reliability and much smaller file sizes of the PDFs.

- *Contract proofs*

  This is a specified method of producing a colour proof that matches the press of a particular publisher or an industry standard agreed by multiple publishers such as SWOP (Specification for Web-Offset Publications). These proofs are produced by digital printers that conform to a set of parameters combining all variables such as paper substrate (including actual newspaper stock) dot gain, density values and ink type.

  To capture the characteristics of a press, a test form (a set of approximately 2000 colour patches) is run on the press and an average value calculated from several sheets of the run. This information is contained in a press profile and it can be used by pre-press suppliers to load on their colour printers to simulate how the press will translate an advert. So, it is very important for pre-press suppliers to hold the press profiles for publishers so that they can present to the agency a proof the both parties feel confident to sign off for colour accuracy.

- *Advertising material delivered to publication*

  There are three basic requirements for sending an advert to Publications:

  (a) The digital file (such as a PDF on CD)
  (b) The 'contract proof' to the correct publisher specification for colour and content
  (c) One of the most important parts is the copy instruction document or CI (as it is better known!)

  This is an instruction from the agency to tell the production department at the publishers what the advertisement is and what to do with it. The kind of information on the document would be:

  Advertising agency name / order number / advert title / headline text / insertion date / repeat insertion dates (if appropriate) and the agency contact name and telephone number.

8.2.9 Approvals

Advertising agencies have traditionally always had very regimented procedures for dealing with approvals of a project throughout the production process. As you can imagine, this is a very important aspect of agency life due the vast sums of money at risk if something was to go wrong (and there are many, as illustrated earlier in this chapter!). This process normally takes the shape of a sticker to be found on the back of the proofs (either proofs from the artworking studio for page layout and masters or contract proofs supplied back from the pre-press house) with blank checkboxes. These boxes are there ready for account handlers, creative directors and Traffic to sign and date the content to uphold the quality of the work produced and reduce the chance of error.

Once again, this is another area of the business where technology is changing the way this process is traditionally handled and now these approvals can be managed over the web, reducing the costs and time taken to obtain sign off. Application software now enables collaboration by the client and its agency (or departments within agencies) to view images and PDFs of adverts to approve or decline the content using comment boxes, all driven via email notifications. This type of functionality has enabled agencies to offer a centralised or 'hub' approach to clients to facilitate the distribution of advertising from one location and offer reduced time to market when fulfilling campaigns.

8.2.10   Billing

At the end of a campaign, Production needs to complete what is known as 'reconciliation' in order to agree costs with their pre-press supplier from the original estimate. Why would there be a change from the original estimate?

There could be several reasons;

- Extra retouching was required by the Traffic / Creative Departments that went away from the original transparency, therefore it was deemed as chargeable
- Extra publications were added to the schedule because of attractive late deals obtained by the media company
- An error may have been found in the copy (legal discrepancy / interest rate changes, etc.) and revised material had to be produced and sent to publication
- Expensive bikes / couriers were required to deliver materials from situations outlined in point 3 when a cheaper overnight delivery was quoted originally.

These are just a few examples but as stated earlier, Production have to be very organised, meticulous individuals to keep track of a campaign to ensure all costs are logged accordingly. Generally speaking, agencies have very process-orientated management information systems (MIS) to log the activities of all departments and track any transactions that have taken place both inside the agency (such as the artwork studio) and those with outside suppliers (such as pre-press houses). Agencies are strict on making sure all purchase orders, estimates, reconciliations, time sheets and invoicing are documented and entered into their respective systems accurately.

8.3   Trends (the agency model now and the future?)

Many of the larger agencies are seeing the value of installing pre-press and creative retouching services on site in order to improve efficiency and reduce the costs of using outside suppliers. Agencies over the last few years have used different strategies to bring these services in-house depending on the nature and size of their business. The most common ways of providing such services to their clients are as follows:

- *Embark on a joint venture with a reputable pre-press supplier*
  This method has become increasingly 'in fashion' as it allows an agency to concentrate on its core business of creative strategy and faithfully rely on its partner to execute the fulfilment of pre-press and creative retouching. By tapping into years of experience built up by the pre-press partner, the agency can very quickly produce quality work, on time, using the latest workflows to gain a competitive advantage over its rivals. Depending on the relationship and structure of the partnership, the agency and pre-press partner may share the cost and financial risks associated with the business.
- *The agency makes the investment in the technology and people*
  This is not always the favoured route due to the fact that it makes financial directors nervous of adding huge capital investment to their asset registers and head count to the payroll. Most agencies run and benchmark their businesses on number of staff in relation to profit ratio and this leads to increased pressures on overheads. That is not to say that this method is uncommon or has not worked for agencies in the past; it really depends on the nature of their clients and the revenue it generates.
- *Why does it make sense for advertising agencies to add these services on site?*
  Income – Income – Income! Traditionally, agencies have invested in artworking facilities onsite to gain control of the creative and layout process and thus generate a revenue stream vital to the numerous services they provide to the client. The explosion of the Macintosh in the early 1990s enabled the agencies to invest in this technology and hire the skills required to produce the layouts. As the technology improved in hardware (speed) and software (application functionality) and the natural forces of supply and demand took hold, the cost of setting up artworking studios became less expensive.

  When an agency is in a position to offer pre-press and creative services in-house it provides an additional revenue stream and reduces the reliance on third party suppliers.
- *So, our agency has installed pre-press and creative services on site, what exactly are the benefits in addition to providing another service it can make money on?*
  Efficiency – Efficiency – Efficiency! Communication is where efficiencies are to be gained and look at how many there are when you consider how they previously traded with their pre-press and creative suppliers to produce material that was geographically apart: couriers / taxis / telephone calls / ISDN data transfers/fax/post and staff leaving the agency to visit creative and pre-press houses to brief specific work.

  It is very easy at the beginning for such 'soft costs' to go unnoticed! By removing all those methods of communication above, not only is there a

tangible financial saving to be had but more importantly, a significant gain in time! By having operators on site, the agency can provide a more efficient, reactive service with reduced lines of communication and a better understanding between departments from face-to-face discussions.

8.4   Trends (market pressures)

- *What pressures are exerted on today's agency?*
  The most obvious considering the current world economic climate is of course cost reduction or 'time value management' and the other term we all understand very well, a lower *Price!* Corporate clients are looking for ways to reduce their global media spends and look to their agencies to find ways of fulfilling worldwide advertising campaigns more economically. Centralisation of media fulfilment has been recognised by corporate clients as the way forward to reduce costs and, just as importantly, retain brand consistency across all markets.
- *So, if our agency has taken artwork / pre-press and creative retouching in-house how can it find ways of becoming more cost efficient and how does that impact on pre-press?*
  Looking at the case study below will show how the use of collaborative technology and efficient workflows can streamline the process for the clients and, ultimately, add value to the services provided.

8.5   Case study

Advertising agency Ogilvy & Mather (O&M) based in Canary Wharf (also has offices all round the world) wanted to offer its clients a more efficient service and at the same time protect its revenues. The agency felt that by bringing more services in-house it could not only control the production process to a greater degree (by not relying on third party suppliers) but, in addition, generate a new revenue stream from pre-press and creative services. Traditionally, it had used multiple prepress and creative retouching suppliers and therefore, working practices could be supplier dependent and its data (or assets such as images) were spread around those companies.

In September 2002, O&M set up a new operation at its Canary Wharf offices in London with one of its trusted suppliers TAG (The Adplates Group) and Tag@Ogilvy was born. Tag@Ogilvy has a staff of just seven people dedicated to the Ogilvy client base and in the course of 1 year demonstrated that an efficient operation not only gives the clients added confidence but also the flexibility to be more creative with ideas and time! By implementing in-house facilities O&M now had all their assets onsite (images and page layout documents) rather than spread between multiple suppliers depending on who was handling which campaign. This gave the agency the opportunity to market a centralised services approach to its clients and offer to fulfil global campaigns from the

London location. Whereas the client was previously billed by local markets (non-UK offices) for pre-press (and sometimes creative), now it had one focal point for all information relating to their media campaigns.

TAG supplied its creative technology, specifically its Tracker & Traffic applications, for O&M to market a complete online collaboration and transparent MIS service to its clients. Kimberly Clark now approves creative images or layouts using these systems and has their own web portal to store all documents and briefs in one place.

So what are the tangible benefits of this in-house operation?

- Removal of soft costs (outlined previously in this chapter)
- Dedicated staff to the client base
- Increased quality control and awareness to brand consistency
- Agency production and creative time increased with on-site facilities
- New revenue stream for agency
- All image data held within the agency and available on the network
- Agency can offer centralised (hub) services for global fulfilment to its clients
- Reduced lines of communication with face-to-face internal briefings
- Salient working practices from creative through to artwork with pre-press integration
- Online approvals technology (Tracker & Traffic applications)
- Online status of any campaign – track an ad for multiple statuses such as Booked/Planned/In production/Awaiting approval/Despatched/Charged, etc.
- Up-to-date costs for any campaign available online 24/7.

8.6 Summary

- The objective of this chapter was to give insight to the role of press production in an advertising agency and define all the tasks needed to successfully fulfil a campaign.
- The intention was to show the interaction required with the other departments in the agency such as Traffic and Account Management when the need arises and why an understanding of the overall process is vital when applying your skills to the role. The other departments need to feel confident that you not only understand your side of the process but also sympathise with their roles and when things do go wrong, that you have the know-how to still get the job out!
- Although the departments traditionally operate independently you will find that this changing environment driven by technology and cost cutting will make closer collaboration even more common in the day-to-day duties. Often production departments end up being the go-between in the agency and it needs strength of character to push for the materials needed in order to satisfy the production department of a publication chasing copy and threatening blank spaces if the advert is not there soon!

- A sound knowledge of pre-press and the ability to work well under pressure in this very demanding environment is crucial to being part of a successful team.
- One cannot stress enough the importance of training to obtain the necessary skills and current advice would be a combination of college courses and in-house (especially now that many agencies have on-site creative and pre-press facilities) schemes to really become a proficient production resource to the business. Computer literacy is virtually a given requirement for this type of role, paperless office no, but great tools to do the job, yes!
- Due to the fact that our industry is going through such a digital transition this chapter has tried to focus on the information needed currently and in the future rather than dwell too much on the past.
- I sincerely hope this chapter has been of use to you and stimulates the desire to join a very exciting industry by choosing a very challenging and rewarding role in the business.

Useful links

www.ppa.co.uk
(Periodical Publishers Association) A body split into sub committees to represent the industry in all areas of publishing from digital photography to following green polices as set down by the government and EU.

www.appa.org.uk
(Advertising and Pre-Press Association – top 20 London pre-press houses) A group of 20 plus pre-press suppliers that represent the technical body to advise publishers and manufacturers on new products and digital workflows.

www.digitaladlab.co.uk
(Industry body representing advertising agencies / publishers and printers) This group holds regular events to discuss openly the issues facing our industry and looks at ways to resolve them by inviting manufacturers/publishers and agencies to talk about the way forward.

www.lcp.linst.ac.uk
(London College of Print) This organisation has continually evolved to offer the printing industry a solid foundation of knowledge to new people and those already in the business, by running lectures and courses to improve skills.

www.tagworldwide.com
(A creative technology company with over 30 years media and production experience leading the market with the development and integration of specialised creative solutions)

www.ogilvy.co.uk
(Ogilvy & Mather worldwide advertising agency)

9 TV, Radio and Cinema Production

Nigel Foster

Learning outcomes

By the end of this chapter you will:

- See that the production process for TV production requires a high degree of planning that must go into pre-production.
- Understand the production and post-production stages along with how the distribution of the final advertisement is achieved.
- See that cinema advertisement production is similar to TV, the major difference being the format for distribution.
- Recognise that radio advertisement production is best handled by a professional radio production company.
- Note that the best advertisements are produced by a team effort between all parties involved.

9.1 TV production

The TV production department in agencies controls the creative content, timetable and budgeting from approval of script through to supplying finished client approved copy to the TV/radio station or cinema distributor. TV production spend in the UK for 2003 was £550 million, making around 7500 commercials. There are a total of 2000 directors available for TV and cinema commercials working through 600 production companies.

With this size of industry, competition and costs have to be controlled and overseen by experienced producers.

There are three main stages of production:

1 Pre-production
2 Production
3 Post-production.

9.1.1   Pre-production for TV

The producer will be allocated to a specific production for which the account executive will hand over a Broadcast Advertising Clearance Centre (BACC) approved script with a recommended airdate and budget.

9.1.1.1   Ball-park costing and timing plan

The producer will then, following discussion with the creative team, produce a ball-park (area of costing) estimate along with a timing plan. The ball-park should be an accurate indicator of costs when the script is first presented to the client. This stops the embarrassing situation where a client falls in love with the script and then 4 weeks later is told it costs £x amount, which is way beyond monies the client has allocated. It must be pointed out that it is the job of the account executive to find out the client's budget available, prior to initial briefing of creative people. All this saves time and upset.

To enable the producer to put together a ball-park figure, he or she will have had to consider its practicalities–location, studio, casting, length, weather, etc. In discussion with the creative team he or she will begin to think about the type of director, that is, visual, dialogue, beauty, action, animation, etc.

The timing schedule should be realistic and based on the practical considerations of the script, with the all-important factor of 'lead times'. The client will then be presented with the BACC-approved script, ball-park cost and production schedule. This will allow the client to judge what sort of an 'asset' his capital investment will be buying.

9.1.1.2   Research

Prior to go-ahead to production, the client may wish to research the idea. There are a number of research methods, but the most common is an animatic–combining drawn frames (possibly from the storyboard) with a voice/music/effects track, very much like a cartoon with minimal movement.

The producer should quote this operation and have a signed client estimate before starting on it. The estimate should allow for the drawings to be done, filmed and put together with a sound track. Another, less expensive form is to have key frames drawn and a separate narrative track describing the action.

9.1.1.3   Selecting the director

The producer and creative team will have been discussing the choice of director from the early stages of initial script presentation to client. This will have needed to be done early in respect of the calibre of director for ball-park costing purposes, and therefore a short-list of directors should have been arrived at.

The agency producer should have a wide knowledge and experience of the talent available in the production company market to lead and advise creative teams and clients. Utilising this, together with the values of style and technique in the script idea, his or her decision with the creative team should aim to combine these production values with the all-important cost factors and timetable availability of the director.

9.1.1.4 Production briefing specification – PBS

The shortlist of directors should comprise approximately three names. Meetings will then take place between the agency producer, creative people and the director with his or her producer to discuss the script. The PBS sets out the responsibility of costing requirements, which will eventually form the basis for the production company estimate and joint contract.

9.1.1.5 Production company estimate

Each selected director's production company will supply a full AVA quote to the agency producer. He or she will then examine this thoroughly before presenting a complete breakdown along with the agency costs to the client and cost consultant (if necessary). It must be remembered that the director/quote put forward as the agency recommendation may not be the cheapest. The right person for the job is the most important thing.

9.1.1.6 Cost consultants

Many large advertisers employ cost consultants with TV production experience to oversee and discuss final production cost on the client's behalf with the agency producer before giving the final go-ahead to production.

9.1.1.7 Actual pre-production

Upon clients' signature of the estimate and approval of the director, actual pre-production can begin. This stage is the most important factor in controlling costs, creating a team effort, getting attention to detail, and ensuring a positive result. Any problems or negative reactions that follow the showing of the final film to clients can often be traced back to a failure or omission of detail at pre-production.

This is the stage when the following elements are produced or discussed:

- Director's storyboard or shortlist
- Set designs/location
- Casting

- Wardrobe/hair styles/make-up
- Music
- Timing plan.

All these elements should be covered at an informal 'pre-pre-production meeting' approximately 2–3 weeks before the actual final pre-production meeting, so that these elements can be openly discussed and agreed upon at the early stages of pre-production.

9.1.1.8   Final pre-production meeting

This is a formal and fully detailed meeting chaired by the agency producer, with representatives from the client, production company (director and producer), agency account group, and creative team. This meeting should be scheduled far enough in advance of the shoot to incorporate any changes without incurring additional cost penalties.

The following list makes up the necessary agenda:

(1)   BACC
(2)   Script and storyboard
(3)   Set drawings
(4)   Location stills
(5)   Casting
(6)   Hands artist
(7)   Wardrobe
(8)   Director's interpretation
(9)   Computer graphics/ special effects
(10)   Special models
(11)   Test footage
(12)   Animals/veterinary supervision
(13)   Props
(14)   Product and special packs
(15)   Food and home economists
(16)   Male voice over/Female voice over
(17)   Music-original/library
(18)   Copyright
(19)   Schedule
(20)   Artwork-titles
(21)   Opticals
(22)   Cinema version
(23)   Address of studio/location
(24)   Safety
(25)   Insurance, including weather

(26)   Post-production
(27)   Artistes' overseas usage
(28)   Any other business.

This agenda can be tailored to fit the script being discussed. It is the agency producer's job to ensure that all parties present, understand and agree on each item before moving on. Within 24 hours, thorough pre-production meeting notes should be distributed to all parties present.

This meeting is the last opportunity for client / agency / director to have a discussion before committing the script to film.

9.1.2   The TV shoot

If all the correct and detailed planning has been carried out properly at the pre-production stages, then the agency producer and creative team should be free to concentrate on the practical and creative elements of TV production. It is the responsibility of the agency producer to ensure that everything that was agreed upon and contracted with the client / agency at the final pre-production meeting is filmed. This is not to say that new ideas that happen at the shoot cannot be filmed, but always subject to cost implications. For cinema commercials, it may be necessary to change the framing from a TV format to cinema format.

Every morning following a shoot-day, rushes are viewed by the production company, creative team and agency producer. This is an initial approval system for the director and agency team to approve the photography, lenses and performances before moving on to the next scenes and breaking down the used sets.

9.1.3   TV post-production stage

An editor is employed on behalf of the director to assemble a cut, which, on the director's approval, is then presented to the agency team. The editor will be in charge of the post-production element in terms of 'all the right elements in the right place'.

Nearly 99 per cent of commercials are shot on 35-mm film and then transferred to the avid system for editing purposes.

When a cut is approved by the agency and client, the original negative will be transferred to a digital tape system for grading and editing at the facility house. Here, the digital grade edit is electronically matched to the approved avid cut, with the necessary Paint box / Henry / Flame taking place, and then married to the dub sound track with visual titles.

It is important to remember that at the avid cut stage time for experimentation is reasonably cheap, but to change things or try out new ideas once on to a D1 system can cause costs to run away, with the consequent breakdown in trust and relationship between client, agency and production company. A client-approved D1 is clocked with the relevant agency /client code numbers, and a copy sent to the BACC for its clearance before airing. Once approval is obtained, the commercial is played-out down a BT digital line to each TV station on the media schedule. This is the end of a TV producer's role.

9.2   Cinema

The pre-production and production stages are exactly the same as TV production but differ in post-production. Again, the majority of originating footage is shot on 35-mm film and then the production company's edit will be done on avid. Once this has received agency/client approval, a copy negative will be made from the 35-mm original negative and cut to match the avid approved cut. An 'answer print' is then made, marrying the sound and picture, and viewed for colour and sound quality. Sometimes three or more answer prints can be seen and rejected before a final answer print is approved.

From this approved answer print, cinema 'bulks' matching its quality are made and distributed to the necessary cinemas with a cinema certificate of approval.

9.3   Radio

Once a script is approved by the client, an agency can either choose to book the necessary artists / studio and direct the production itself or put the job through a professional radio production company. This can be more expensive but will add value to casting and performances, along with a higher standard of radio production by radio experts.

Once the radio production has been approved by the BACC, a satellite link will be arranged and the commercial will be sent on a digital satellite system to the relevant stations.

9.4   Conclusions

TV, cinema and radio production is essentially a team effort, with the highest degree of financial risk an agency carries. Therefore, it is essential that those involved or party to its decisions are seen to act with total professionalism and towards the same goal. A successful commercial sells clients' products.

9.5   Summary

In this chapter:

- The production process for TV production has been outlined in detail showing the high degree of planning that goes into the pre-production part of the process.

- The production and post-production stages were described along with the distribution of the final advertisement that is played-out down a BT digital line to each TV station on the media schedule.
- Cinema advertisement production was shown to be similar to TV, the major difference being the format for distribution being by 'bulk' from an 'answer print'.
- The point that radio advertisement production is best handled by a professional radio production company was made.
- It was emphasised that the best advertisements are produced by a team effort among all parties involved.

10 Printing

Leslie Claridge

Learning outcomes

By the end of this chapter you will

- Have a clear idea of the overall printing processes in use today.
- Be aware of the processes involved in image production.
- Review desk-top printing and the more popular file formats.
- Explore the current printing methodologies and understand how to get the best out of the technologies.

10.1 Introduction

Printing is often a reference to many things. Generally, it is associated with the physical process of print production and the following printing processes: offset lithography, flexography, gravure and screen imaging. These systems represent the traditional process associated with commercial printing formats and the products that are linked to those processes: brochures, newspapers, stationery, labels, posters, textiles, books, magazines and the inevitable junk mail that arrives through the front door.

The term printing is also associated with alternative methods of imaging including laser, laserjet, inkjet, bubblejet and digital printing. These processes represent techniques associated with proofing, computer-to-print and large format digital systems.

Inevitably, therefore, the term has become confused through the development of these new technologies. This has had the effect of broadly changing the natural perception of what constitutes printing. This is demonstrated most powerfully by the average domestic computer purchaser, who includes a printer as part of their system. Cheap and effective, it complements the input process and thus the term is clearly linked with the process of printing. To ensure that there is a distinction, we must distinguish between methods; we must consider: 'what is the print process?'

Printing can be characterised into sectors of activity, firstly, concept brief and specification, secondly, digital imaging and origination, thirdly, pre-press, printing and post-printing.

10.2 Production processes

The function of printing is to establish in global terms the production of the graphic form into a multi-copy format. The likelihood is that the printing will require multi-colour photo-images as well as pages of text. The process requires the creative skills of graphic designer, the constructive knowledge of the originator to interpret the design form into production reality, the printing team that prepares, prints, outputs the product and of course the finisher who completes the task.

Inevitably, the production processes and techniques are complex and different; however, the essential elements are established and the procedures well defined. The industry in the UK is a major provider of employment and uses specialised personnel from all areas of activity. Print processes are inexorably linked to methods of reproduction including the use of highly sophisticated electronic imaging systems such as desktop publishing (DTP) and specialised digital software solutions.

10.3 Original image production

The likely original is produced from different sources, either from within the company or as a constructed image produced by a graphic designer or desktop image producer. Text and images may be supplied by the client or may be developed by a design studio or independent designer. The likelihood is that the image would be produced electronically on a computer using specialised software such as Quark XPress or Adobe's InDesign or similar packages for page make-up and then saved in a form that can be transferred between computers and proofing systems, prior to being sent direct to plate or to film and subsequently exposed to plate.

The size and nature of the printed sheet is determined by the number of pages, size of page and folding and securing procedure.

10.4 Paper sizes

When designing and planning a printed product, the size of the sheet is paramount. In Europe and the UK the metric measure is the standard size for paper purchase and usage. The basic paper size is B0, 1000×1414 mm; from this the standard A0 (841×1189 mm) size sheet is produced. The subsequent process requires that the sheet be halved along the long cross, producing an A1 size which is 841×597 mm and so, revealing A2, A3 and A4, etc. This standard is the basic trimmed version of each value. Paper can be ordered in

B0 size following the same criteria as A0. The various size stocks allow for differing page and magazine sizes. Paper is also purchased by the printer with additional trim values added. For example, A2 (597 × 420 mm) has an RA2 value, which is 610 × 430 mm; this allows for basic trims to be included. In addition, there is an SRA value as there are with each independent sheet size; in the case of SRA2 the values include extra trimming for multi-imposition. SRA2 is 640 × 450 mm. Naturally, this is purchased at this size according to need, and it is a costly process to buy SRA if you only need RA.

This underpins the importance of the specification for the job being produced by an individual who understands not just the printing processes but how a job is positioned for production.

10.5   Desktop publishing

Desktop publishing involves the technical computer application of the principles of graphic design within a computer software template. DTP is the generally accepted term for this process and is, in many eyes, the image of modern printing. DTP has fundamentally changed the nature of the origination process.

Prior to this method of producing originals, all artwork was produced as copy ready, prepared for direct filming. Lithographic plates were produced directly from the film. Subsequent processes have replaced, in the main, these processes. Computer-to-plate is now an accepted technology.

Desktop imaging allows designers to use a wide range of digital systems to add to and develop images for reproduction. Software production is a primary method of providing files for reproduction. It is not unreasonable to suggest that the great majority of graphic designers use desktop publishing software and techniques to produce their origination. The files are complemented by the introduction of digital images such as scanned photo-forms and directly introduced digital camera images. These files may be produced and prepared directly for hard-copy published images or saved for use on the Internet as soft-copy additional imaging or complementary forms of media output. The files are likely produced in formatted form: TIFF (tagged information file), EPS (encapsulated postscript file), JPEG (joint photographic expert group) or as a PDF (portable development file). Alternative file formats exist and might well be used including specialised files such as Quark XPress, Adobe Photoshop, Adobe Illustrator or other well-established software formats used in the production, editing or development of files for production.

Files produced for output are inclusive of style, page construction and all the features associated with the printing of images within a product. In order to transfer these files to the pre-press or studio for development they must first be saved onto a removable media of some kind, including Iomega's zip disk, a recordable CD-R, or any memory able media. Diskettes or floppies are no longer able to provide the size for multi-page files and are not likely to be used.

Files are checked by their originator or the pre-press studio for correct style and format. Key concepts include correct use of text fonts, appropriate picture or graphic file placement and pixel support for the appropriate output resolution. The file should also include the appropriate imposition for page number correction. These procedures are often referred to as pre-flighting.

Additional aspects of this method of checking include scaling and rotating graphics, converting spot colours to process CMYK output, ensuring that RGB images are replaced with CMYK files and ensuring that halftone resolutions are embedded. See page 141 for definitions.

Once checked by the studio the file may normally be outputted to proof. Files may be digitally checked on screen or produced via digital proofing materials from such suppliers as Hewlett Packard, Epson, Cromalin and other market leaders in previewing images and pages before the files are passed on ready for film or direct to plate.

Proofing establishes that the images are showing the correct text and image credibility. Colour output is a fundamental aspect of the process; the file must demonstrate that the output will fulfil the key aspects of four-colour printing separation. Multi-colour files must contain the appropriate checks for ensuring that the output values associated with the specific printing process are embedded for the pre-press process to correctly output the plate or film.

Proofs should reflect exactly what is represented on the file or plate film; mistakes made at this stage can be costly and involve pre-prints and other avoidable problems.

The text output of desktop publishing remains an issue. Previous experience with text setters ensured that text production was perfectly formed in image and space terms but required highly sophisticated technology, which needed code driven instruction by highly skilled personnel, and was time demanding. Text production produced by desktop publishing is quick, accessible to a wide range of people and a valuable asset to the originator. However, it has had the effect of diluting standards of text production. Desktop publishing uses intelligent software capable of manipulating and controlling even the most demanding page make-up needs. The best desktop users are trained in the use of text production, which takes into account the key aspects of text-to-fit, and the importance of appropriate font usage. Typographic imagery is essential for the continued credibility of the printed word. Desktop publishing can be marginal as well as fundamental to the health of the printed form. Advertisers and users of print should always work closely with the printer to ensure that these standards are maintained and enhanced for the future health of the printed product.

10.6   Pre-press

Preparing the image for reproduction is a key element of the process. (See Chapter 8 for a detailed exploration of printing for press production.) This is often referred to as pre-press. However, recently, through the influence of digital systems, this description has started to become known as pre-media. Either seems appropariate.

Files are supported while they are dispatched to the Open Pre-press Interface (OPI). This allows the image to be checked, held in a server data to allow high-grade images to replace duplicate positionals, which allow the file to be structured prior to output.

The files are held in a Raster Image Processor (RIP), which communicates with the front-end computer and the output device, directing the needs of the file and the output qualities associated with the product. It is often referred to as the RIP drive as it informs the image production values. Spreads, chokes and bleeds (to ensure that images are trapped together), trim marks, high resolution files and instructions for working with Desktop Colour Separation (DCS) file output are clearly associated with pre-press procedures. Pre-press is a particularly independent process. File generation and support for the full colour output are essential for ensuring that the colour image generated on the screen is represented as closely as is practicable when the file prints.

Clarity of screen-to-print output is usually dependent on the individual graphic originator who, through well-rehearsed procedures, is able to construct colour output that is reflective of the original. Scanning and preparation are key to this process. Images can be produced on cheap, over-the-counter scanning solutions that produce basic reproductions. The importance of the qualities associated with a quality scan can be described in the support pixels at the first scanning stage. The amount of pixels per linear value in the scanner allows the original image to be supported for output in such a way that the image is capable of showing full colour value and tonal resolution. Originator may use sophisticated software packages that support the measure of the screens colour dexterity to ensure that the product has a relationship with the final output print.

10.7   Process printing

Multi-colour printing is produced via the four colours: cyan, magenta, yellow and black (key) output (CMYK). Matched colour may use a designated ink value such as Pantone matching systems. These colours may be integrated into the four-colour process printing procedure. Colour images or illustrations are produced by separating them into only four colours of ink: CMYK. Original images are 'separated' into cyan, magenta, yellow and black and reproduced into small structured dots. The size of these dots determines the appearance of the final printed colours. This is referred to as a halftone and ensures that the image contains tonal graduation and colour balance. These processes are fundamental to the reproduction quality of the file and generated image. Spot colours (individual colours) may also be produced to complement the separated file format.

10.8 Printing processes

Many processes come within the definition of printing, and these can be classified into groups such as:

- *Stencil printing*, where the image is cut, photo-masked or etched through a sheet of paper, card, fabric or other material in order to allow ink to pass through to the substrate. Typical examples are screen process and wax stencils.
- *Planographic printing*, where the image to be printed is formed directly on the surface of a plate or cylinder. Ink applied to the surface will be rejected by the non-image areas and accepted by the image areas for transfer to the substrate. Essentially offset lithography!
- *Recessed printing*, where the image to be printed is laser etched, cut, engraved, photo-mechanically produced into a plate or cylinder. The recessed image is then flooded with ink, the surplus removed from the surface of the plate or cylinder and an impression made. Typical examples are photogravure and intaglio.
- *Relief printing*, where the non-image areas are photo-produced, cut, etched or washed away, leaving the image to be printed in relief for inking and impressing. Typical examples are letterpress and flexography.

10.9 Traditional processes

10.9.1 Offset lithography

Offset lithography is unanimously considered the major commercial printing process. It is often described as 'offset or litho', both references to the production procedures or a shortened version of the process term, 'lithography'.

The lithographic process is also referred to as a planographic format, that is, the image is reproduced onto a plate, normally aluminium, which has a thin grease sensitive image representing the positive graphic image. Under tension, the plate is applied to a cylinder configuration, which makes contact with a rubber-covered cylinder. The image is offset onto the paper or card travelling between the rubber cylinder and a solid metal cylinder, which acts as a pressure point. The key to producing a print by the process of lithography is the presence and attraction of ink (on the image) and water (on the non-image area). The antipathy of grease to water does the rest. In principle, the plate is lightly damped by rollers covered with a linen type material or through a water- or alcohol-based solution. This is attracted to the background of the plate (non-image area) and once damp is continuously kept in this state while an alternative set of rollers transfers ink onto the image, which is grease receptive, the construction of this condition and the ability of the press and the printer to maintain the condition is paramount to the quality of the printing process. This maintenance of solution and ink is often referred to as ink and water balance.

Lithography demonstrates that if the process is maintained adequately it is capable of printing on most substances, though paper and card are more likely to be the obvious material. It also underpins the fact that the process is flexible and capable of producing any manner of product, from leaflets to high quality brochures. Lithography is widely respected as the most quality capable printing process available to the printer.

The likely screen ruling (dot value) is around 150 lines per linear inch or 28 lines per linear centimetre. Offset printing is capable of reaching values in excess of 200 lines per linear value, further demonstrating the qualities of finesse and tonal control.

Lithographic reproduction is considered to have sectors of activity. Web offset (continuous reel of paper, such as that associated with newspapers or long running brochure work), large offset, primarily 'A1' and above (597 × 840 mm), and small offset printing, 'A2' (420 × 597 mm) and below. These sectors reflect the type of work associated with the offset process and help determine the appropriate procedures and methods of working the lithographic sheet.

10.9.2   Flexography

Flexography is the most widely used packaging printing process in commercial use. Its history has not always been spectacular, tradition has it, that flexography relies on a simple relief system. The flexographic image surface consists of a raised area, known as relief printing. This raised form is inked and forced, under direct contact, onto the substrate. Non-image areas are below the printing surface and do not contact the substrate. The importance of this process is to ensure that the features that dictate the nature of the image are pressed sharply and cleanly onto the receiving surface.

Flexographic printing uses a printing plate made of rubber, plastic or some other flexible material. The plate is attached to a cylinder configuration by adhesive or as a magnetised plate.

Historically, this was known as 'aniline' printing when developed in the UK at the beginning of the last century. The first machines had hand cut flexible rubber plates mounted on the cylinders of the press with liquid ink applied directly from rollers running in a trough of ink. The essence of the system was reflected in the limited quality of reproduction, which confined the process to basic line work on items such as paper bags and wrappers.

Flexographic inks are by nature, fast-drying, ideal for printing on materials like plastics and foils. This makes flexography the primary method used for printing plastic and flexible bags, wrappers and similar forms of packaging including wallpaper, printed tissues, corrugated board and materials such as highly coloured festive foils. Inks used in flexography are usually either water- or solvent-based.

Ink control is supplied by the use of a monitoring roller referred to as anilox cylinder with an etched or engraved cell pattern of specified area and depth that applies a positive film of known thickness to the printing plate. 'Doctoring' of the anilox cylinder by means of a blade to shear off surplus ink ensures that the ink film remains constant. Anilox roll technology has gone hand-in-hand with higher quality print output. Ultra-sound and other quality processes have helped ensure that flexography is a dynamic and valuable addition to the print system. The finesse of the halftone screen remains at a basic 120 lines per linear inch, but the strengths of the process are the strong solid colours associated with packaged materials.

Most flexographic presses are reel-fed and will vary in their construction, depending on the nature of the required end product. For printing on paper, film or foil wrappers, the roll-to-roll press will be used, with all units printing on the same side of the web of material. Publication presses will require a different construction for printing on both sides of the web plus additional provision for folding and cutting the finished sections. For close register work, the printing cylinders may be grouped around a common impression cylinder to minimise the possibility of slip or stretch between one colour and the next, while printing on impervious stock such as plastics and metal foils will require special drying facilities.

10.9.3 Gravure

As the name implies, gravure developed from the cutting or engraving of an image into a metal, sometimes steel but more often copper. The engraved image was flooded with ink, the surplus wiped from the surface, paper or card applied and an impression made. The terms 'copperplate writing' and 'engraved image' have entered the English language as a result.

A feature of early engravings and 'etchings' – where the image was etched away by an acid – was the ability to reproduce fine detail. A problem, however, was the inability to print large solids as the wiping action would remove ink from such areas. The technique of ' cross hatching' was developed, whereby 'solid' areas were represented by a pattern of finely cut channels or cells. Another problem was the difficulty of matching and registering several colours.

The photogravure process, developed in the latter part of the nineteenth century, solved the problem of solid area printing and close registering by dividing the whole area of the printing plate or cylinder into a fine grid of very small cells that were individually etched in depth according to the needs of the image.

As a result, gravure was able to achieve a high degree of local control of ink film thickness to a precision not attainable by other processes. This of course was of particular importance for reproducing colour artwork and, combined with gravure's long run capability, enabled the process to predominate in certain areas of catalogue, magazine and packaging printing.

One minor fault resulting from the adoption of the photogravure process was that even the text matter had to be reproduced via the gravure cell pattern. This meant that the screen pattern could be detected around the edges of the letters, and this could be particularly noticeable on small typefaces and those requiring very fine lines.

Moving into the electronic age, gravure cylinders are now produced by laser generated scans working from computerised information. This has the twin advantages of speedier production of the individual cylinders and more flexible control of colour balance. Although the cost of cylinders is still expensive when compared with other processes, gravure's advantages of long life, high speed, consistency and the ability to print good quality colour on a variety of substrates, from newsprint to plastic film, continues to keep gravure as one or the major printing processes.

Gravure presses are almost invariably reel-fed and fall into two main categories – publications and packaging.

- Publication presses will be designed to handle wide webs at high speeds, printing four colours or more, often on both sides of the web. Ancillary operations will include slitting, trimming, folding and delivery as sections or complete magazines.
- Packaging presses will vary in construction according to the substrate and the end product. Film and foil presses will require sophisticated drying systems to ensure that surplus solvents and vapours are extracted safely, leaving the residual ink to key firmly on the material. Roll to roll presses are quite common when printing wrappers and bags, while carton production will require appropriate finishing equipment to be incorporated.

Specialised gravure presses may also be designed for printing stamps, labels, tickets and textiles.

Intaglio printing, in which cylinders are directly hand-engraved or mechanically engraved, is still practised for some specialised areas such as security work and fine art printing. The fine detail that can be reproduced by this method is difficult to achieve by other processes, while the characteristic individuality of intaglio printing makes forgery more difficult.

10.9.4   Screen process

Stencil printing, from which screen process derives, claims to out date the letterpress process, citing evidence from prehistoric cave paintings in which colouring material appeared to be dabbed around or through basic patterns.

Be that as it may, stencilling did not become a major printing process until the early part of this century, when the practice of mounting stencils on a fabric mesh or screen was developed. This technique allowed the stencil to remain intact, while ink could still pass freely through the screen. Screen printing also avoided the need to make 'ties' to hold various parts of the stencil together and enabled a considerable improvement in quality to be accomplished.

Originally known as 'silk' screen, due to the nature of the fabrics used, the process received an added impetus with the development of the photostencil, which improved its versatility and quality even further.

Among the advantages of screen process are simplicity, low initial cost and the ability to print on almost any material from papers and boards to metals, glass, fabrics and plastics, as well as printing directly on to irregular shaped objects such as bottles, cans, ceramics and T-shirts. One of the great strengths of screen imaging is the ability to work with textiles which offers uniqueness among the primary print processes.

The simplest screen presses comprise a rectangular frame hinged to a base-board. The screen mesh is stretched taut across the frame and the stencil attached. The material to be printed upon is placed between the screen and the baseboard, a supply of ink placed at one end of the frame and ink forced through the mesh by a rubber or plastic 'squeegee' blade.

Variations of the basic technique are employed to enable printing on non-flat items. For wallpaper and textile printing the screen and stencil are mounted around a cylinder with the ink and squeegee blade inside the cylinder to enable a continuous design to be printed as the cylinder revolves in contact with the material.

Screen inks are more likely to be water-based as opposed to the solvent dependent materials of the past. Ecological standards have helped move this process on and ensured that the creative qualities associated with screen are retained.

10.9.5 Letterpress

Like flexography, letterpress uses a plate with a raised image on a metal or plastic plate, some example of wood images are still used but are restricted to unique presses which are predominantly aimed at specialised or traditional markets. Letterpress printing may be delivered as flatbed cylinder, platen output or, as is still commercially available, web-fed rotary letterpress as applied to stationery printing or label production. Letterpress is essentially a non-process, its influence as a major printing method is no longer a key issue, yet it retains its sense of tradition and closeness to the typographic form. It offers antiquity, typographic excellence and the opportunity to print cheap stationery.

10.9.6   Digital printing

Printing is still clearly associated with traditional ink and paper processes. While they remain the primary printing formats for commercial use, the development of a digital solution to meet the needs of the modern print consumer is crucial. The developing processes associated with digital solutions have provided an alternative, flexible, individual solution to a variety of publishing and general print requirements. The ability of a digital process to integrate data from storage into output means that individual printing sheets can be achieved. Advertising and marketing solutions are now more achievable by the introduction of a digital format.

This concept of a digital printing allows for on-demand printing with the added advantage of reducing the burden of full print costs, while allowing the opportunity for marketers to access customers, one-to-one. The process is especially appropriate for short run, multi-colour, multi-page brochures and catalogues which require only hundreds of copies.

Where is the break-even point for short print runs? Well, it can be anything from a dozen copies of a 48-page A5 report to a couple of hundred copies of an A4 brochure. Generally speaking, though, it is any print run of less than 2500/3000 copies. The development of mainstream commercial digital printers such as the Indigo's UltraStream 4000, capable of 4000 four colour sheets per hour, the ChromaPress DCP, roll to Sheet, 4-Color, 600 DPI, Dry Toner Electrophotographic Imaging press and the Heidelberg QMDI, 4-Color 12″ × 18″ Format, Direct Imaging Press are examples of how the digital market has progressed.

10.9.7   Colour printing

The essence of colour printing is that it reflects life! Customers are more than likely attracted to the idea of a coloured image or advert than they are to monocolour. Printed images should, in principal, be the same as those displayed on a computer screen. After all, that is what the designers wants, images brought to life. The problem is, can we replicate the same values in a restricted colour form as generated by a light form?

You start with a white sheet of paper, which reflects all the light that falls upon it. The ink laid upon the paper selectively absorbs light so that only certain wavelengths are reflected, which we then call colour. When no light is reflected at all, we observe black. With computer screens, the reverse situation occurs. Starting with the absence of light, proportions of red, green and blue light are added in order to achieve the desired colour. These facts must be quantitatively understood if desktop information is to be converted to coloured printed images. Red, green and blue represent light rather than coloured forms; thus, when the computer transmits an image, it is looking to mimic the original, bright and garish colours included. Printing inks do not possess the ability to display the same bright and garish colours; the printing press has to simulate those colours from the plates provided or the inks selected. Printing inks vary considerably in their physical and chemical structures as well as colour, but we can start by classifying them as either opaque or transparent.

- *Opaque* inks are essential where the substrate is coloured or where one ink has to overprint another without its colour being affected. It is important to be specific when referring to colours – grass green, sky blue and salmon pink will not do! Attaching a sample of coloured material may also be unsatisfactory, as inks often vary in their apparent colour on different substrates.

There are a number of colour specification systems available but the best known and most widely used is the Pantone matching system, which is now adopted as an international standard world wide. Pantone issue reference books containing swatches of more than 1000 colours printed on different stocks. Most ink makers can supply Pantone matching inks and most art and design materials and supplies can be obtained in Pantone colours to ensure fidelity with the final copy. Each colour has a reference number, which can be used in the artwork or specification to identify it accurately. The Pantone standard also provides electronic colour values and tint values. By this means it is even possible to give precise colour instructions through the specification, e-mail, etc.

- *Transparent* inks are used where overlapping ink films are required to produce a range of colours. Transparent red over yellow, for instance, will produce orange, while the same red over blue will produce purple.
- *Process* inks are used for colour halftone work to simulate the range of toner and colours in photographic origination. Early attempts at colour reproduction used only three inks, yellow, red and blue, all three of which had to be overprinted in order to achieve black. It was soon discovered that the most effective, efficient and economical way to print black was to use a black ink, so the colours settled down to the now familiar four – yellow, cyan, magenta and black, which is usually referred to as the key, partly to avoid confusion when initials only are used and abbreviated to CMYK.
- *Colour halftone* printing requires the continuous tone dye-based image of a photograph or transparency to be converted to a dot pattern. The dots will vary in size and colour according to the appearance of the original. A white image, for instance, will have no dots at all, whereas a neutral grey may have dots of each colour. In practice, colour scanners are programmed to use as few dots as possible and as little ink as practicable. For instance, there is little point in printing solid colours, yellow, magenta and cyan, and

then overprinting these with a solid black. The scanner will therefore remove colours where there is a solid black (under-colour removal or UCR), replace neutral greys with a reduced percentages of black and reproduce any given colour or tint with the most efficient and effective pattern of dots.

Dots are formed by breaking the original down into dots of various sizes, within a grid space of standard space. The stronger the colour value the bigger the dot, small dots, perhaps of 3 or 4 per cent of a solid reflect a lighter or high-lighted area. The essence of a halftone is that each aspect of the image should be represented by a dot. Pictures that have no highlight dot are often described as 'bleached', while darker areas need to demonstrate a dot, albeit, a strong dot, to ensure that it does not 'fill-in'. Tonal balance is an essential aspect of quality printing, it should demonstrate grey values across the image; the alternative is highly contrasted pictures and the loss of gradation, a feature that printers call 'saturated'.

If all the dots in the four different colours were arranged at the same angle, these would result in unnecessary overprinting of the smaller dots and also the visual problem of screen clash or 'moire' patterning. This is avoided by arranging the four images at different angles so that the dots print as cleanly and unobtrusively as possible. Similarly, moire patterning can also occur if printed halftone pictures are used for original artwork and double screening occurs as a result. Current digital technology removes the likelihood of patterns occurring, for manual users it still represents a challenge.

- *Control patches* and strips are often included at the origination and planning stage to measure and monitor the progress of the work. The simplest device is a cross located on each plate, which shows that the four colours are in precise register. The crosses can be scanned visually or electronically to check quickly the accuracy of fit. Scanning devices on presses can be linked to the register control system which automatically adjusts the register in the event of the slightest movement.

More ambitious colour control strips will also include patches to measure colour values, ink film density, overprinting (trapping) quality and any changes in dot size. As the run progresses and the press warms up, ink values may change, blankets and rollers may swell or shrink, wear may take place and all of these factors could affect the detail of a colour halftone print. Constant measuring and monitoring of the control strips will enable corrective action to take place as soon as a variation is detected.

10.10   Post-press activities

Once a job has been printed there are numerous activities that the product might require. These might include a matt varnish to reduce handling deficiencies, spot lamination to enhance the image with a gloss cover layer, die-cut shapes for image removal, thermographic image enhancement, print or blind embossing for stationery or foil blocking to optimise the image.

All of these features are add-ons and give the advertiser and marketers the opportunity to 'value add' to the printing experience.

The structure and the function of the printed product is an essential component of the product. Print finishing techniques allow for fabrication to occur: folding multiple pages or specific styles, pre-cutting and post-trimming, blocking and stamping, stapling and securing.

Emphasis on print finishing is essential for the final product to be seen in the best light. Post-press operations are sometimes seen as nondescript, whereas in reality they inform the strength and functionality of the product.

The key to a well-organised production cycle is to ensure that the appropriate values are in place to assist. Below is a list of some of the principal factors that influence production. Feel free to add your own!

10.11   Checklist for production issues

- File formats are correct.
- Original images are included for output.
- Appropriate computer platforms supported.
- Fonts supplied / indicated and available for postscript production.
- Indication of proof requirements.
- Spot colours indicated by measure (pantone).
- Specific technical requirements indicated.
- Trapping values indicated.
- Imposition schemes understood.
- Securing methods described.
- Add-on features marked up such as spot laminating.
- Visual / dummy supplied as appropriate.
- Colour / ink density values for reprints.
- Lead and delivery times / dates indicated.
- Indication of contact person.

10.12   Summary

In this chapter:

- The overall printing processes in use today were overviewed with many of the key terms described – this included a summary of the many paper sizes available.
- The processes involved in image production were outlined with mention made of specialised software.

- Desk-top printing and the more popular file formats including TIFF (tagged information file), EPS (encapsulated postscript file), JPEG (joint photographic expert group), PDF (portable development file), as well as specialised files such as Quark XPress, Adobe Photoshop and Adobe Illustrator.
- Current printing methodologies were described from traditional processes such as offset lithography, flexography and gravure to more modern processes.
- The chapter finished with a useful checklist to ensure that you get the most from your processes.

11 Advertising Planning and Budgeting

Martyn P. Davis

Learning outcomes

By the end of this chapter you will:

- Understand the importance of a thorough situation assessment – gathering information on which to base your advertising plan.
- Discover how to set specific objectives – which your advertising should seek to achieve.
- Get guidance on determining the advertising budget – deciding how much to spend on achieving these objectives.
- See how to prepare proposals – to achieve these specific objectives.
- Recognise the importance of putting the plan into effect – where we look at campaign execution and ways that it might be improved.
- Note the importance of evaluating results – only by measurement and evaluation can we be sure to improve over the next cycle.

A full planning sequence extends to campaign approval, execution and evaluation, thus becoming a 'closed loop' operation with the results of previous advertising providing valuable data on which to base future campaigns.

These principles apply equally to both consumer and business-to-business advertising, although their practical implementation differs considerably according to circumstances. Various specialist applications are covered in separate chapters of this book.

11.1 Situation assessment

Advertising planning must be based on information. There are as many briefing methods as there are people, but the approach outlined here has one thing in its favour – it is probably the shortest ever written! Rather than an extensive list of questions, it comprises nine 'trigger' topics – each of which brings to mind innumerable questions on important points of detail. Although some information may be discarded later (when deciding the strategy on which to base your advertising), it is important to explore every avenue – far better to have some irrelevant facts than perhaps overlook a key attribute on which your campaign could be based.

11.1.1 Your firm

For many consumers, the company that makes the products they purchase is a major consideration, and the 'sourcing' of industrial products is of equal importance. In consequence, many advertising messages reassure potential purchasers in this respect. Organisational structure is also important – does your firm function in self-contained operating divisions, and are its products marketed individually or under the company's 'family' brand? Ideally, campaigns mounted for any one product or division should benefit the others.

11.1.2 Your product or service

Full details of the product or service to be advertised play an important part in determining advertising messages and media. Price, packaging, colour and design, ingredients, method of manufacture, quality control, guarantees and/or after-sales service can all be important. One consideration often (surprisingly!) overlooked is 'What does your product actually do?' Sales of multi-function products can be increased by campaigns that convey its multiple applications, whereas the advertising of single-use products may be targeted at persuading existing users to use more, or at persuading purchasers of rival products to switch brands.

11.1.3 Your market

A major consideration in media planning is the 'demographics' of your potential purchasers, who may be defined in terms of age, sex and socio-economic groupings. Manufacturers of business-to-business products, on the other hand, define their targets differently, in terms of occupation and industrial classifications. Other important considerations for both types of campaign are frequency and value of purchase, and geographic location, which influence both messages and media. In cases where target market characteristics are unknown, as with a revolutionary new product, this could lead to a campaign aimed at getting potential purchasers to identify themselves, with advertising thus serving a market research function. For effective creative planning, it is equally important to consider 'psychographics' and target market behaviour. Unless you understand potential purchasers' lifestyles, thought processes and purchasing patterns, how can you create effective advertising messages?

Many advertising planners find it helpful to divide all markets into two categories, one of which then sub-divides. Some campaigns may target non-users, for example, while others aim at users, who may in turn be classified as light, medium or heavy. Each category could call for creation of differing advertising messages, delivered through different media.

11.1.4   Your marketing policy

With products/services and the people who might buy them clearly established, the next consideration is the 'mechanics' of purchase and sale. Where your product is actually available can call for detailed messages listing outlets at which potential purchasers can buy your products, or for media that cover specified sales areas. Companies engaged in direct selling, on the other hand, may seek advertising campaigns that generate sales leads.

11.1.5   Previous activity

Previous activity must be carefully investigated. What advertising has been mounted in the past, in terms of media and messages? More important, which types of advertising proved effective, and what lessons can be learned for future planning? You should also investigate other promotional activities that influence buyer behaviour, to ensure that your advertising is synergistic with public relations and below-the-line activity.

When a new product with no previous promotional activity is due to be launched, a useful preliminary step is to study 'candidate media': those it seems likely you may use and will later analyse in depth, once you have completed the next planning stage. That is deciding your specific campaign objective, as discussed below.

11.1.6   Restraints

Restraints that might restrict advertising planning can be internal or external. Internal restraints could arise under any of the five headings just considered, when a 'warning bell' should signal their implications. Your firm, for example, may have financial constraints that directly restrict the amount to be spent on advertising. Unavoidable delays in product delivery will influence the content of advertising messages. Some market segments may be permanent non-users, or completely brand-loyal to rival products – there are better uses for your advertising budget than targeting either group. Marketing policy can be equally important, calling for selection of media that target particular areas and/or can invite direct response.

External restraints such as the various Codes of Advertising Practice affect all categories of advertiser equally. Others, such as The Financial Services Act, are specific to certain product areas. Chapter 21 discusses these legal and self-regulatory systems.

11.1.7   Competition

The competition you face must be reviewed under each heading so far considered. With which firms are you competing? What products do they produce, and how do they compare with your own? Who are the purchasers of rival products? How are these products marketed? What advertising campaigns do your competitors mount? Finally, what restraints do your competitors face – external restraints such as the Advertising Codes affect all equally, but competitors' internal problems may give you a competitive edge in the market place.

11.1.8   PEST

This acronym reflects the fact that you and your competitors do not operate in isolation, but against a background influenced by Political, Economic, Sociological and Technological factors, and are all-important considerations in planning effective advertising.

11.1.9   SWOT

This second acronym also assists the planning process, drawing attention to both Strengths and Weaknesses *internal* to your organisation, its products or services, as well as Opportunities and Threats present in the *external* market place.

Although listed as your first step in the advertising planning process, situation assessment must be treated as an on-going exercise – this morning's papers might well contain vital new information.

11.2   Setting your specific campaign objectives

With situation analysis complete, you can now start more positive planning. Before creating messages or selecting media, however, it is vital to establish a clear purpose for your advertising. There is an extensive range of possible reasons for mounting a campaign, but those most frequently encountered include – not in any order of priority – the following:

- Remind previous purchasers
- Reassure existing users
- Counter the natural decline inherent in any market
- Inform the constant flow of new customers

- Inform the market of changes
- Overcome resistance
- Launch a new product or service
- Extend distribution
- Stimulate existing distribution
- Provide leads for sales representatives
- Persuade unknown potential purchasers to identify themselves
- Build up a mailing list
- Level out variations in the sales graph
- Strengthen individual product promotions with an 'umbrella' campaign covering your full range
- Improve your company's image
- Fight declining sales
- Increase sales

11.2.1   Dangers to avoid

There are various dangers to avoid when setting your objectives.

11.2.1.1   Being imprecise

The objectives listed are in outline only, and must be made specific. Take the last three, as examples. To 'improve your company's image', you need answers to very basic questions. Whose opinions concern you? What opinions do these target groups hold now? What opinions do you wish them to hold? Without answers to these questions, the so-called aim of 'an improved image' has no real meaning.

The same imprecise thinking must be avoided with general objectives such as 'Increase sales' or 'Fight declining sales'. If sales are falling, why is this? If because of the natural decline inherent in any market – which Lord Keynes once illustrated by pointing out that 'In the long term we're all dead!' – the solution lies in targeting the constant flow of new potential purchasers. Alternatively, are sales falling because existing users are switching to rival brands? If so, there are clear implications for both creative strategy and media selection. If, however, the reason is that your product has reached the end of its life cycle, do not expect advertising to work miracles! To counter declining sales, you must first identify why they are falling and then plan your advertising accordingly.

A similar analysis should apply to the so-called aim of 'increased sales'. Where is this increase to come from – getting existing purchasers to use more, attracting new users or persuading buyers of rival products to switch brands? These three routes to increased sales each call for different advertising messages, and different media to deliver them.

If your objective is to be measurable, this precision should also extend to numbers and dates – an X per cent shift within Y months. One temptation to avoid is thus the too easy solution of an imprecise objective.

11.2.1.2 *Being too greedy*

Another danger is too many objectives. Throw someone a tennis ball and most people will catch it. A few individuals may catch two tennis balls, but as for three or more? Some advertising campaigns do indeed achieve more than one objective, but this is achieved by careful planning rather than luck!

11.2.1.3 *Being too ambitious*

Deciding how much to spend is the next stage in the planning process but, however generous the budget, there is never enough money!

Campaign objectives must be realistic – to make *everybody* think well of your company *all the time* is neither achievable nor affordable.

11.2.1.4 *Creative confusion*

Campaign objectives must not be confused with *communication* objectives, which concern a later stage in the planning process: preparation of proposals. Should your campaign objective be to increase sales by brand-switch means, this raises the quite distinct communications question of 'What should you say to persuade people to switch brands?' And what media schedule can best deliver this message to the selected target groups? Failure to distinguish between campaign and communication objectives results in ineffective advertising. Both categories of objective must be clear if the creative and media elements of your campaign are to achieve the results you seek.

11.3   Determining your advertising budget

The next planning stage is deciding how much to spend on achieving your specified objective. This is an important step, since, without such a discipline, money may be frittered away. It is equally necessary to clarify two possible misunderstandings. One is your budget's coverage. How can you prepare a meaningful plan without knowing exactly what your budget must cover and, just as important, which costs should be carried by *other* departments? An equally practical consideration is your budget period – how can you prepare a plan without knowing the length of time in question, and when the planning period starts and finishes?

Your advertising budget serves as an effective management tool, focusing attention on how, when and where to best spend the money. It equally helps control expenditure. Although there are numerous ways of establishing the advertising budget, they can be grouped into four main approaches.

11.3.1 How much shall we *spend*?

Various methods approach budgeting as a percentage costing exercise based on past or anticipated sales, or on production costings that indicate a given percentage for each unit produced.

11.3.2 How much *extra* shall we spend?

An alternative approach is the marginal or zero-based method. Rather than establish a budget and then decide how to spend it, the marginal method adopts a more pragmatic approach. Those applying it decide their expenditure 'layer by layer', with each advertisement paying its way. Needless to say, not all advertisers can adopt this method: only the fortunate few able to evaluate results directly, in terms of actual sales.

11.3.3 How much are *they* spending?

Some advertisers adopt a competitive parity approach, to ensure that they are not outspent by competitors. Some compare actual expenditure figures, while others consider 'share of voice': is their share of total advertising expenditure the same as their sales market share?

11.3.4 How much will it *cost*?

The target sum or objective-and-task method approaches the problem in a different way, by establishing how much it will cost to do the job. The desired campaign is planned and its cost calculated. In short, this approach reverses the two planning stages of deciding the budget and then devising the campaign. Many PR budgets are decided this way, and the same approach can be applied to advertising.

Whatever the sequence, the planning stages of specifying objectives, setting budgets and preparing proposals should always be interlinked. This linkage raises the important matter of priorities, as the planning process may not always proceed smoothly. If the desired campaign is unaffordable, then planners must reconsider. Can the campaign be achieved at lower cost by better media planning? If not, then either the budget must be increased, or objectives reduced to a more realistic level. Reality impinges!

With full background information, a specific objective and a clear budget, you are now in a position to plan your advertising. Before starting on any detail, however, you will find it is sound practice to consider a contingency reserve. Rather than plan expenditure to the last penny, most advertisers find it advisable to keep some funds in reserve. This 'spare cash' can serve two purposes. On the negative side, it allows for unexpected expenditure, which, without such a reserve, would weaken your carefully planned campaign. On the positive side, reserves allow you to take advantages of unexpected opportunities. In establishing your contingency reserve, you are in fact trying to predict the unpredictable! Trial and error over the years can provide valuable guidance as to a suitable size reserve for your own company.

11.4   The advertising brief

As already stated, there are as many briefing methods as there are people. Most, however, comprise the three planning stages so far considered: situation assessment, objective and budget. These summarise the problem, which must be distinguished from possible solutions.

Preparation of proposals is a quite distinct stage in the planning process, and should not be pre-empted by statements such as 'I await your proposals for delivering message A, with full-colour illustration B, through double-page spreads in media C, D and E!'

It is equally important to avoid 'non-instructions' such as: 'What I really want is an eye-catching, attractive, interesting and memorable campaign'. Who in their right mind ever seeks to produce unnoticeable, unattractive, dull and forgettable advertisements?

First define the problem – *then* turn to the next stage in the planning process: preparation of creative and media proposals to achieve your objective, within the constraints of the budget.

11.4.1   Preparation of campaign proposals

Preparation of campaign proposals comprises two inter-related elements – messages and media – and clear objectives are vital for both. Creative staff must convert campaign objectives into communication objectives, applying stringent creative discipline to the task of selecting – from the mass of information gathered at the earlier assessment stage – the unique selling proposition (USP) on which to base their proposals. Some practitioners refer to the essential benefit or promise, brand image, positioning or key I attribute rather than USP. Whatever the *terminology*, the selected copy platform must also be made 'to come alive' in compelling fashion. *'What you say'* and *'How you say it'* are *both* important, but neither sufficient on its own. Chapter 7 discusses creativity in detail, whereas this chapter focuses on media's contribution to effective advertising. This, in its turn, also comprises two elements – media selection and media planning.

11.4.2 Media selection

Before commencing any detailed planning, you must study the media likely to feature in your campaign and compare their relative strengths and weaknesses. Chapter 13 discusses the wealth of both qualitative and quantitative media research data available. It is important to look beyond the statistics, however, and know individual media in depth. Which editorial features appear regularly, and what opportunities exist for suitable positioning of your advertisements? Average issue readership figures, valuable though they may be, are only a guide. Should a newspaper carry, for example, a regular gardening feature on a given day each week, readership by gardeners will increase on that particular day. Furthermore, by placing your advertisement on the gardening page, you not only select out of the total readership those with an interest in gardening but, equally important, reach them in receptive frames of mind. Hence, the vital importance of an in-depth knowledge, constantly updated.

11.4.3 Media planning

In addition to the three main components of any advertising brief (situation analysis, objective and budget), media staff now need additional input – creative requirements. Although creative and media proposals are prepared separately, they must be in accord on two inter-related creative/media decisions.

11.4.3.1 The planning unit

The decision to book, say, colour pages in women's magazines is two decisions in one. It is a creative decision to prepare full-page colour advertisements to appear in the women's press. It is equally a media decision, to plan a schedule whereby colour pages will be booked in selected women's magazines. Creative staff must accept that this planning unit and media choice gives them full scope to convey your product's benefits persuasively, and media staff accept them as the basis for effective scheduling.

In this joint decision, creative or media considerations may be dominant – and sometimes in conflict. When preparing advertisements for a product that benefits from demonstration, creative staff may press for media such as TV or cinema, which offer colour, sound and movement. Media staff may, however, point out that other media provide far more effective market coverage. Some element of conflict is often unavoidable, but the two sides must nevertheless reach an agreement. There is little point in creative staff preparing advertisements for media that do not reach the market, nor media planners preparing schedules giving insufficient creative scope. Similarly, it is pointless for creative staff to demand large sizes when media planners explain that budget limitations rule these out.

11.4.3.2   Attracting attention

Creative and media staff must also agree on another important point of principle – how to attract attention. It is insufficient to create effective advertisements and then simply place them in suitable media (however persuasive or efficient either campaign element may be) in the hope that people will see them. Positive action must ensure that your advertisements not only appear but are actually seen.

There are various ways to attract attention, by both creative and media means. Media methods include front-page or solus advertisements, or positions facing the editorial. Other routes to attention are purely creative, including persuasive headlines and eye-catching illustrations. Some attention devices have implications for both creative and media staff, who will equally welcome the use of colour and large sizes – but for different reasons. Whatever means of attracting attention is selected, there must be creative and media agreement. This need applies equally to all media groups likely to feature in the final schedule.

11.4.4   Overall media planning

In addition to creative requirements and media research data, two important considerations affect the media planning process:

11.4.4.1   Media allocations

General planning involves allocating money to different media groups such as press or television. This decision is sometimes known as the 'media split', After funds have provisionally been allocated on an inter-media basis – so much for television, so much for press and so much for other media – preliminary schedules are costed and considered for each media group. All going well, these initial allocations will be sufficient to finance effective schedules in all desired media. On the other hand, these preliminary costings may reveal that the sum allocated to television, for example, is insufficient. If the sum allocated to press advertising leaves some latitude, however, the media split will be adjusted accordingly, with funds transferred from one allocation to another. The ideal media split is rarely achieved at first attempt.

With agreed allocations for each media group, another general planning consideration concerns how the budget should be divided between different target groups or sales areas.

11.4.4.2   Market weighting and case-rate spending

A parallel aspect of allocating money concerns marketing data. Irrespective of media used, this underlying consideration influences both where and when to target your advertising budget. Many planners follow the 'case-rate' spending principle (the name originating from the number of cases of the product sold) whereby money is allocated according to market weights or values – which could be by area, by market segment, by month or by product. If a given area accounts for 30 per cent of sales, it seems logical to spend 30 per cent of your budget on media that stimulate that area.

Similarly, if 20 per cent of sales occur in a given month, 20 per cent of media expenditure would target that same month. The same logic applies to market segments, and to expenditure by product. Frequently, case-rate calculations allow for a number of factors simultaneously, so that a suitable proportion of the total budget is allocated to a particular product, expenditure on which is then divided among target groups according to their levels of expenditure. These sums are then further allocated to individual sales areas, and then month by month within these areas, in accordance with sales figures.

Hence, the importance of a thorough situation analysis, to provide media planners with statistical information as to product sales by month and area, and purchasing figures by market segment: all essential data if the advertising budget is to be targeted accordingly.

The basic principle behind case-rate spending is to spend money when and where sales figures indicate it should be spent. High sales call for high expenditure to gain maximum benefit from this potential, whereas less money is spent on those products, market segments, areas and times of year where sales figures indicate the market is not in a buying mood.

Although media planners may later challenge the underlying assumption of case-rate spending, the method nevertheless provides a sound initial basis for schedules directly linking media expenditure to marketing data.

11.4.5   Detailed media planning

Before deciding in any detail how best to spend the various allocations, it is wise to recall an unwelcome home truth – there is never enough money! This being the case, the media planning process necessarily involves – as with deciding the media split – constructing, costing and comparing numerous alternatives, and then reviewing these to select the best.

11.4.5.1   *The basic variables*

With advertisement unit (and attention factor) agreed with creative staff, media staff can now plan how best to spend the sum allocated to each media group. A first step is to relate, in expenditure terms, the agreed advertisement unit, the length of your campaign, how frequently the advertisements should appear, and in which individual media. The four basic variables are thus advertisement unit, frequency, duration and media list.

This preliminary costing will, more often than not, spend too much money – rarely the other way round, alas! It is always possible to ask for more money, but this is rarely a wise move, as the advertising budget was decided after careful consideration at an earlier planning stage.

It is equally possible to return to the media-split stage, and release spare funds from one allocation to increase another, but what if *all* are over budget? Another possible solution is to reconsider the basic variables, but three have implications extending beyond media.

Creative staff are now hard at work on the basis agreed. Any move to reduce the advertisement unit will be most unwelcome, quite apart from the waste of time, effort and money that scrapping their proposals would involve.

Two other basic variables – frequency and duration – also have wider implications. Marketing staff will view with considerable mistrust any campaign proposal that gives the target groups too infrequent a stimulus, or leaves the market uncovered for any significant period of time.

The only basic variable media planners can adjust directly, without affecting others, is the media list – must your advertisements indeed appear within publications A, B, C and D? If planners are, however, convinced that all four titles (or media groups) are essential to achieve full market coverage, it appears that the planning process is at an impasse. There are, however, other possibilities to consider.

11.4.5.2   Other variables

*   *Multiple-size campaigns*
    When financial limitations do not permit regular full pages every week, some campaigns are based on two advertisement sizes – a full page followed by three half-page advertisements, in a monthly repeating sequence. Multiple-size campaigns give the best of both worlds: impact and repetition. The same principle applies to other media, with TV campaigns featuring both 60- and 30-second commercials. If they are well executed, viewers will, on seeing the shorter of the two, recall the 60-second version! Exploring this solution when creative work is already at the execution stage is unnecessarily expensive, so ideally this possibility would be considered earlier, when reaching initial agreement with the creative staff.
*   *Market weighting reconsidered*
    Case-rate spending, whereby media expenditure matches sales figures, might be a chicken-and-egg situation – the reason target group A or area B accounts for only 10 per cent of sales is that it receives only 10 per cent of the total stimulus. Together with marketing staff, media planners therefore review matters in terms of *potential* rather than actual sales.

    One alternative is to increase expenditure beyond that suggested by case-rate figures. If sales in a particular area were considered elastic, spending more money could be a good investment, in the belief that any additional expenditure will pay for itself in terms of increased sales. You may rightly think this makes matters worse rather than better: you were already over-spent, and here you are spending even more money! Where are the additional funds to come from?

The alternative to spending more money is of course to spend less. If demand in certain market segments or areas is inelastic, then, even if media expenditure were reduced, sales will remain at a stable level. This could be for either negative or positive reasons.

One target group may simply have no spare cash at a particular time of year, so there is little point in trying to stimulate them to buy more. There may, however, be a minimum expenditure level they have little choice but to maintain, even if advertising stimulus were reduced. On a positive note, some regular purchasers may be more brand-loyal than others, with therefore less call to remind them as frequently.

A minimum level of reminder advertising is necessary for both groups, but the frequency of stimulus – and thus the level of expenditure – could be reduced in the belief that demand levels are inelastic.

- *Drip versus burst*

A 'drip' campaign comprises regular advertising, in the belief that, constant dripping wears away a stone'. Advocates of the 'burst' approach, however, argue that some drip campaigns are too small to be noticed, and that increased impact would be more effective.

Burst campaigns achieve this by a combination of both the multiple-size and increased/decreased expenditure approaches, the difference being that one multiple size is zero! Advertising is omitted in certain weeks to boost impact in others, with periods of no market stimulus alternating with bursts of heavy advertising.

- *Multi-media campaigns*

Few if any advertising schedules rely on a single medium – to achieve complete market coverage, most campaigns feature two or more. One primary medium may cover a considerable proportion of your market, and a 'penetration' figure of 50 per cent means in simple terms that half your potential customers have the opportunity to see your campaign. How best to reach the other half?

Here, the difference between 'duplication' and 'net extra coverage' becomes important. Two supplementary media may be under consideration, but if the readership of one overlaps that of your primary medium, this duplication means that, rather than reaching new readers, you have unknowingly changed one of the four basic variables: frequency. Readers seeing both publications have two opportunities (rather than one) to see each insertion and, in such circumstances, you would select an alternative candidate publication that provides net extra coverage, with minimum duplication.

The two publications together give a 'cumulative coverage' figure. Should this still represent insufficient market penetration, the solution is to seek additional media providing even more net extra coverage, thus taking cumulative coverage even higher. This 'building bricks' approach may continue until budget restraints indicate that it is uneconomic to cover the small proportion of potential purchasers not yet reached. Economists refer to 'The Law of Diminishing Returns' and the same principle applies to media planning.

To illustrate the practical outcome of this overlap process as simply as possible, let us consider a campaign based on two publications, A and B, with title B providing some duplicated readership with, at the same time, a significant element of net extra coverage. Those who read only title A have one opportunity-to-see (OTS) your advertisement and the same argument applies equally to those who read only publication B. Those who read both publications clearly have two OTS. Most campaigns call for significantly more insertions, and a 'frequency distribution' summarises the number of opportunities each different target group has to set: your advertisements should reflect desired frequencies and actual (or potential) market weightings.

- *Synergism*

  The cumulative coverage and frequency distribution approach applies across media groups as well as individual publications – using one medium to supplement (or rectify any weaknesses in) the coverage of another. Here the concept of 'synergism' becomes important. One media-planner explained this as making two plus two add up to five rather than four! All media overlap in that people read newspapers and magazines, watch TV, listen to the radio and see posters. Some media groupings are more synergistic than others, however, as when people hearing a radio commercial recreate in their mind's eye the visual aspects of a parallel TV campaign. With some other media groupings, by way of contrast, creative and media staff must work far harder to achieve synergism.

11.4.5.3   The final schedule

Numerous options are open to the media-planner. All must be explored, different approaches developed and the best selected. Effective media schedules are rarely (if ever) achieved at first attempt but only after costing and comparing many alternatives.

As there is never enough money, all media schedules necessarily represent a compromise. Planners must decide which is the more important – impact, frequency, campaign duration or the range of media. Increases in any one element can be achieved only at the expense of others.

While some element of compromise is inherent in any advertising campaign, it is important to avoid a weak schedule. Should media-planners fall into the trap of trying to please everybody by meeting all requests, the outcome is likely to be an ineffective schedule, with small infrequent advertisements spread over too wide a range of media. One established media planning axiom is 'Concentration – Domination – Repetition', which results in effective campaigns concentrating on a limited number of media in such a way that your advertisements have impact, and appear regularly throughout the campaign period.

11.4.5.4   Other media

This chapter has concentrated on advertising planning. For maximum effect, however, advertising should be supported by and synergistic with other forms of promotion – press relations to achieve editorial coverage, and below-the-line activities such as merchandising and sales promotion – thereby multiplying the media effect. Any company failing to utilise all communication channels cannot achieve maximum market coverage. If it does utilise all channels, but delivers different (or even conflicting) messages, it will confuse potential purchasers. Marketing communications should also be synergistic over time, with each new campaign building on preceding ones, and contributing to future success. Chapter 3 deals in greater depth with this integrated approach.

11.4.6   Approval of proposals

While media staff were planning the schedule, creative staff took parallel action to develop their proposals. The next step is to ensure that both campaign components – messages and media – are as effective as possible, interlock with each other and are complemented by and synergistic with other forms of marketing communications. The total campaign must be fully integrated, and care taken that all these efforts interlock with marketing activity – there is little point in stimulating the market if your products are not available for people to buy. You will not win any medals for stimulating competitors' sales rather than your own!

11.5   Putting the plan into effect

Having devised a strong campaign and ensured that it is the most effective possible, you must next to put your plan into effect. There are various stages:

11.5.1   Campaign execution

Your plan so far exists only on paper. Putting it into practice entails a great deal of detailed work – individual orders must be sent to all media included in the schedule. Similarly, creative proposals must be converted in actual advertisements appearing in all selected media on the due dates. In short, your campaign must actually run. The necessary administrative work is a major operation that should not be underestimated.

11.5.2　On-going improvement

Execution should not be simply 'carrying out orders' but a positive process. Television advertising provides an extreme example, as campaigns are planned in outline only, before future programming is known. Most television spots are shifted repeatedly as new viewing figures are released or new programmes announced. Alterations are less frequent with other media but rate changes, new circulation or readership figures or a newspaper or magazine launch, all mean that media schedules must be reviewed in the light of new circumstances, and changes made accordingly. It is true to say that if a media schedule is executed exactly as originally planned, someone must be asleep on the job!

11.5.3　Buying versus planning

Quite apart from allowing for new media research data, on-going improvement can bring valuable financial benefits. A media-planner with expert knowledge of the media market place can make a positive contribution to the advertising budget, by buying premium positions at standard rates or negotiating valuable discounts on rate card costs.

Some practioners separate out the planning and buying processes, in the belief that the abilities called for in implementing media schedules differ markedly from those called for at the earlier planning stage, which, by comparison, seems a dull arithmetical exercise.

11.5.4　On-going control

While executing, and improving, your media schedule, you must keep expenditure under tight control. Running totals of expenditure month by month against schedule, by media-split allocations, together with incursions into (and availability of) contingency reserves, and savings achieved by expert buying, all combine to form a vital tool of control.

11.6　Evaluation of results

The final stage in advertising planning is measurement and evaluation. Did you achieve your campaign objective? Did your schedule achieve the expected television ratings? How were your press advertisements positioned in the selected publications? Did you fare better or worse than competitors? Which campaign elements proved effective in terms of results, whether measured in actual sales or changes in attitude? And why? Most important of all, what lessons can be learned for the future – what leads should be followed up, and which weaknesses eliminated? This final planning stage thus 'completes the circle', with this year's results contributing to future effectiveness – just as last year's results contributed to your current advertising.

As 'Previous Activity' was a trigger topic in 'Situation Assessment', a salutary thought on which to finish is that if you say, 'The brief is the same as last year', then you should either resign or fire the agency, since it appears that all the time, effort and money devoted to your advertising had no effect whatsoever!

11.7   Summary

In this chapter:

- We have seen the importance of a thorough situation assessment from a number of perspectives about the business, its markets and the interaction between them.
- How to set specific objectives which your advertising should seek to achieve has been reviewed and a selection of dangers has been identified.
- Guidance on determining the advertising budget has been given looking at how much to spend in the light of a number of variables – not least on competitive activity.
- In order achieve these specific objectives, we have looked at a wide range of issues with respect to media selection and planning.
- We looked at campaign execution and ways that it might be improved.
- Finally, the point was made that we need to evaluate results to be sure we have captured our experience to improve over the next cycle.

Further reading

Davis, M. P. and Zerdin, D. *The Effective Use of Advertising Media*, 5th Ed., Century Business, 1996.

Davis, M. P. *Successful Advertising: Key Alternative Approaches*, Cassell, 1997.

12 Getting the Best from Advertising Agencies and Other Outside Suppliers

Adrian R. Mackay

Learning outcomes

By the end of this chapter you will:

- Recognise the place that service suppliers have in assisting you with your marketing communications.
- Review some key thoughts on how to find and appoint your advertising agency.
- Discover some checklists on how best to brief an agency.
- Explore how to evaluate an agency's work.
- Know what to consider to ensure that you get best value from your suppliers and how to control expenditure.
- Learn about best practice in managing the relationship with your agency and discover 10 smart things to do.

12.1 Introduction

When you consider the many thousands of transactions that your business is engaged in every year from buying capital equipment, purchasing raw materials to buying next week's staplers, it is hardly surprising that there are well-defined procedures laid down. Purchasing and supply is a profession in its own right. Even more modest organisations will support purchases with purchase orders, counter-signatories, and accounts departments to check and authorise the inevitable invoices. Many computerise the whole process. Whatever organisation, and whatever system it employs, as the customer it remains in full control and knows what to expect.

However, when it comes to buying services that support the marketing communications mix the organisation engages in, much of the basic commercial discipline is by-passed or short-circuited. Why is this when British industry can be spending over a billion pounds a year on marketing communications?

Perhaps it is because an organisation engages an agency to undertake a broad canvas to 'do the marketing'. That said, there may be a form of agreement – or just a letter of intent – that aims to cover the hoped for relationship. But it is the day-to-day activities that form the minutiae of the business that collectively can amount to a considerable sum of money.

Advertising agencies are, in general, relatively small businesses in terms of income but they are entrusted with large amounts of money by advertisers. How they make their money has implications on the relationship too. The commission system has traditionally been a cause of some confusion making the financial relationships with advertisers less transparent than they perhaps should be. In the early stages of an agency/advertiser relationship, the agency may invest a considerable amount of 'unpaid' time on the account and income from the advertiser may be non-existent. Later, as an advertising campaign unfolds, the income starts coming in automatically as long as the media campaign runs, irrespective of the time that is being spent on the account. If the advertiser is obliged to cancel the campaign through unforeseen commercial pressures, the income stops. The commission system also can tend to limit the integration of marketing communications (see Chapter 3) by discouraging advertising agencies from thinking beyond the context and parameters of advertising. It is also possible that the advertising agency may be buying-in services on behalf of the advertiser that it will subsequently charge a mark-up to cover the cost of handing the transaction. While legitimate commercial practice with which few advertisers would disagree, it is often a point where many disputes would originate. (See also pages 72 and 86).

There is an old agency saying that 'accounts are won by creativity but lost by administration' and more often than not, the administrative problems have their root in money. Advertisers and agencies should constantly be looking for improved effectiveness, efficiency, and results. There are clear areas of best practice that can help the process and enable the relationship between advertiser and agency to be mutually successful. I was fortunate enough to have a client who once said to me, 'I don't want an agency working on my account that does not make a fair profit'. I replied that I wanted him to 'profit' from our working relationship, too.

This chapter is dedicated to all those clients and the many agency people that I have had the privilege to work with over the years and from whom I have gained some insight. It is designed to give you some ideas on how to get the best out of your advertising agency and other outside suppliers so that *both* may profit.

12.2   Service suppliers – their focus

It is worth pausing for a moment to consider the service suppliers' focus. Let us look at how this might vary from that of an advertiser under a number of headings:

- *Business perception*
  Any know-how business is a service business – but not all service businesses are know-how businesses. A marketing communications business sells its know-how – its creative, media buying, campaign planning, design, print, research, and marketing consultancy – all know-how advice. Its human capital may be its only significant asset; it may have a smart office or some cash in the bank yet it is essentially a people business. It may have some information management expertise – like databases – but even that is dependent on peoples' know-how to turn that data into useful information. For these services it will take a commission, work to a retainer, or charge a fee. An agency's know-how is inseparable from its people. Their business perception is all about managing their peoples' know-how and bringing that to bear on your business which may have a quite different asset base.

  Therefore, in order to get the best out of an agency or any other outside know-how providing supplier, you will need to improve your people management skills.
- *Business specialism*
  Your advertiser organisation may consider itself to be a bit special – leaders in its field; perhaps a special brand or two. However, an advertising agency will pride itself on its ability to understand your business, what makes it tick, and what will make it run faster. While some agencies may specialise in a sector like fast-moving consumer goods or health care, many have a broader client base bringing their specialism – their service offering – to a wider industry. Their best sustainable competitive advantage will be their ability to learn faster than competing agencies.
- *Customer base*
  Most advertiser organisations are aiming to broadcast their message to a wide – albeit clearly defined – audience. Many are playing a numbers game aiming to win the hearts and minds of many more customers. On the other hand, an advertising agency will not have quite so many customers; their focus will be on a handful of clients.
- *80/20 Concept*
  The seventeenth century economist, Pareto, suggested that 80 per cent of Italy's wealth was in the hands of 20 per cent of the population; the same equally applies to an advertising agency. While a food manufacturer may have 80 per cent of its income through one distributor, it is not going to have

80 per cent of its income from 20 per cent of its *consumers*. So, are you one of the 20 per cent of clients that bring in 80 per cent of your agency's income – or is it the other way round? How does this affect your relationship and service from them?

- *Service verses selling*
  Many business owners consider that their bank is more concerned with selling its products than actually serving its needs. However, what of your agency? So much depends on developing a good working relationship, particularly when it is not easy to quantify the value of much of the client service work involved. Does your agency have a myopic view of your marketing communication focusing on what it does best or advising on what your brand most needs?

- *Acquisition and retention*
  Some agencies are brilliant at winning new business and the senior people spend much of their time focusing on business acquisition. But then what happens? Is the new account left to some of the less experienced staff to 'cut their teeth'? While many agencies reward the business winning teams – and justly so as it is a competitive market place – look for the agency that rewards its successful business retention teams too!

- *Business development*
  The period of a new business pitch and the 'beauty parade' is an exciting one for the agencies involved and the adrenaline flow to meet the challenge may obscure the harsh commercial realities that await the successful agency as it begins to deliver to its promises made during the pitch.

  The advertiser's adrenaline is flowing for different reasons. While the search and selection of a new agency is a challenge, especially against a backdrop of unabated commercial pressures, there may be a gap in the support services that now needs filling quickly by the new appointee. There may be a rush to get the new agency to 'hit the floor running' and deliver to reinforce the confidence and commitment made by the new marketing team. The euphoria generated can often swamp the reality that time and energy must first be invested to agree on the foundations for a soundly structured business relationship.

  A while ago I was Marketing Manager for a hospital products division. I had been in the job for less than a month when the Divisional Director asked me where my new advertising campaign was. Given that the existing half-year campaign was launched just 6 or so weeks previously, I told him I was awaiting the first set of brand tracking studies on that new (and expensive to produce) journal media campaign before taking any 'new broom' decisions. Poor man was under pressure from the Board that just wanted to see some new advertising from the new marketing guy and he could not see my logic. Disaster!

12.3   In-house or buying-in?

For a number of marketing communications services, some organisations consider developing an in-house resource to service their needs. (See also Section 5.4.5).

An internal department will be easier to control both in terms of the activities they follow as well as the costs they incur. They will have closer involvement with the business and may also gain over their external rivals with the advantage of better technical know-how. However, they may be too close to the problem and suffer less originality coming from a narrow perspective. An internal department may not have the resources to handle a peak of activity and be surplus to requirements during troughs.

External providers can give much more objectivity and should have broader experience in terms of the type of work, their media experience, and the solutions they can provide. They are more able to provide the right amount and the right calibre of talent the work demands than their in-house cousins. With a supply of known freelance specialists, they can meet the advertisers' variable demands. Some agencies, of course, do provide the advertiser with prestige. However, they are always external and may not ever get the full picture from their briefs and may not be as attuned to the internal politics of the client.

12.4   Finding outside suppliers

Here you have to do your home work! Find out as much as possible about those service organisations around you as you can by talking to contacts, colleagues, and even competitors. Read the advertising and marketing trade press and keep an eye on promotional material in your area of interest. Consult appropriate trade associations such as ISBA[1] or the IPA.[2] Tell them your needs, objectives, and anticipated spend so they can advise you on the type or size of agency that you should be considering.

Look to various trade directories and lists of who does what – BRAD[3] publishes the Advertiser and Agency Lists, a comprehensive source of reference, and the '*Campaign*' portfolio provides an annual showcase for many of the major agencies.

There are some commercial organisations that will be happy to advise you (for a modest fee) and will arrange for you to visit to find more about the agencies they have suggested and to see examples of their work. Others will guide you in your search for a new agency and advise you on such issues as remuneration and other issues concerning your relationship – they also keep your situation totally confidential.

From this exercise you will probably have up to a dozen that seem to meet your requirements of size, type, and location. Speak to them, ask for a 'credentials' presentation to help you make a subjective assessment of their people, style, attitude, terms of business, and work. Ask to speak to a couple of existing clients. Then, you will have reduced your list to no more than four whom you can ask to respond to a brief on a specific project.

Select a project that is related to your long-term aspirations but limit the scope and give each prospect a tightly written brief. Specify if you want strategic proposals or creative work, too. If any of the contenders are not willing to undertake speculative creative work, they will advise you. I know of some advertiser organisations that will make a contribution towards creative work – it gets the business relationship on to the right footing at the outset. Make sure everyone agrees to keep the information and work undertaken confidential.

Expect that some agencies will do further market analysis but ensure that you assist their understanding by providing your own perspective on the situation. Also allow sufficient time – 4-6 weeks – and be ready to provide those who wish to improve their knowledge more opportunity for visits or further meetings. It is how an agency responds to the brief that will tell you a lot about them, their style, and their culture long before they arrive to do their pitch.

When it comes to making a final judgement, treat all contenders in the same way and score them against a checklist. Table 12.1 below is one example. If you are judging their creativity, refer to Chapter 7.

Table 12.1   *Comparing the capability of contenders (L=low score; M=medium score; H=high score)*

Selection criteria	*Importance to you*	*Contender 1 (big agency)*	*Contender 2 (big agency)*	*Contender 3 (modest agency)*
Relevant sector experience	H	H	H	H
Strategic argument	H	M	M	H
Strength in depth	L	H	M	L
International experience	L	H	M	L
Agency name	M	H	M	L
Location	H	M	M	H
Media buying	H	M	H	L
Media thinking	H	H	H	L
Added value	M	H	M	L
Cost control	M	L	M	H
Innovative	H	H	H	L
Close working relationship	M	L	H[1]	M

[1] One potential advantage in this hypothetical situation is that the account planner at this agency trained in your organisation. Therefore, she is likely to be better at developing a close working relationship because she knows your systems and is very familiar with the brand and the market sector.

Evaluate their approach to you, the way their presentation was conducted, how they responded to and interpreted the brief, and the quality of their thinking. Consider their media thinking and their approach to creativity and, most importantly, the way they propose to charge for their services. How transparent is their charging system and will you have confidence at all times that you will know what is happening to your money and will you have any nasty surprises when their invoices hit your desk?

Finally, judge them as colleagues. In the author's consultancy, we have always proposed that we function as '*contract colleagues*' to our clients. Is the chemistry right? Have you met the full team who will be working with you and are you clear on individual responsibilities? Remember, you probably also want the team that won your business to work on your account and not be fobbed-off with a trainee!

12.5   Appointing an agency[4]

Once the appropriate agency has been chosen (and you have had the courtesy to let down the losers) great care has to be paid to setting up the relationship in the right way. Not only is it important to settle on the appropriate method of payment but there are two other key aspects that are best made clear:

1   What is actually expected of each party in terms of services to be provided, information to be made available, etc.
2   The technical and legal 'nitty-gritty' of matters such as ownership of copyright, termination of contract, etc.

Both the ISBA and the IPA (representing the advertisers and the agencies, respectively) favour an actual written contract to cover these aspects that really do need to be made absolutely clear at the outset if misunderstandings are not to develop and give rise ultimately to an unnecessary and expensive breach in the relationship.

You should by now be able to make your final choice but this does not constitute an appointment. This only follows after detailed discussion and the agreement of a formal contract. Most agencies are reasonably flexible in their approach to handling their client's business, as these businesses by definition will vary considerably. It is, however, essential that a legal document exists, detailing the framework of the agreement that the client and agency have negotiated. It is particularly important that the client selects the method of remuneration best suited to his needs (e.g. commission or fee, or a combination of both).

The contract should typically cover the period of appointment (normally a year), the services the agency agrees to provide, approvals and authority, scale and method of charges, terms of payment, copyright, legal liability and agreed arbitration procedures in case of dispute. The IPA and ISBA both publish useful booklets on the technicalities of agency/client agreements. ISBA have standard agreements available for advertising agencies, be they full service, creative, or media only, and also for other types of suppliers.

Of all the headings covered in a contract (which should always be reviewed by competent legal advisers) the complex subject of copyright deserves special mention and careful attention. As a general rule copyright rests with the individual artist, designer or photographer unless otherwise assigned and by commissioning work as a client you are granted reproduction rights for a specific job. Further use of the same material in a different task could, unless otherwise agreed, be subject to further copyright charges.

Normally, an agency employed artist will assign ownership and copyright to his or her employer but this should be checked and included in the contract. The matter becomes further complicated if the agency buys in creative work from third party sources and the question of ownership and copyright in such instances should also be included in the agency/client agreement. The whole subject becomes of particular significance if at some stage the client and agency decide to go their separate ways. It is then in the client's central interest that they have a binding agreement on ownership and copyright to cover termination of an account. To neglect this facet is to court disaster, expense and acrimony.

Finally, remember that while it is the agency's responsibility to make sure that you do not contravene the various codes of practice, you will have authorised them to proceed by giving your approval. Therefore, it is essential that you are fully conversant with all the relevant guidelines published by the organisations involved. (Reading Chapter 21 is a good place to start.)

12.6 Briefing an agency

Before briefing an agency, it is worth thinking through your communications plan. There are a number of checklists that one might use but the following covers most considerations. Table 12.2 contains an alternative checklist.

12.6.1 Communications plan[5]

Thinking through the issues and actually writing your ideas under each heading helps to ensure that you know what you are doing and helps your supplier know much more about your business so they can respond appropriately.

- *What are the campaign objectives?*
  As Tweedle-Dum and Tweedle-Dee concur, 'if you don't know where you're going, you're sure to get there!' Give some careful thought to the market and where your campaign is going to take them. Review Chapter 1 to get a clear idea of where your marketing communications fit in your 7C

Table 12.2   *A checklist of information for briefing*

Background	• Strategy statement
	• Positioning strategy
	• Sales history / projections
	• Company / product / brand / service data
	• Relevant competitor data
	• Other information (trend analyses, economic forecasts, etc.)
Purpose	• What is the advertising aim?
	• How do we want to achieve this?
Specific aims	• What specific results should be aimed for?
	• How should these be measured?
Target audience and timing	• Primary, secondary (even tertiary)
	• Seasonality, key time points, critical path analysis for output
Must / must nots	• Details of any essential inclusions in campaign (e.g. logos)
	• Details of anything to be totally excluded
Output requirements	• Do you want a media proposal?
	• Do you want a creative proposal?
Budget details	• As agreed internally

model of the marketing mix, then Chapter 2 on how advertising works to clarify what you aim to achieve with your campaign.

• *Who are we talking to? (Primary and Secondary audiences)*
Very few products or services are bought by individuals without regard for other opinion. (Parents buying for children are often influenced by what the child would accept). So, define who you should be mainly directing your communications to and who is secondary.

• *What do they currently think?*
Often overlooked but where are your audiences now ...?

• *What would we like them to think?*
... And by the end of the campaign, where would we like them to be?

• *What is the single-minded message to communicate?*
As Chapter 3 confirmed, getting the messages clear and being focused means that the effect of your communications will be more substantial. Jam spread thinly does not taste as good! Being single-minded prevents dilution of your message.

• *How can we substantiate it (functionally and emotionally)?*
What can you do to substantiate your messages rationally – what technical aspects are there to your arguments? Then think about the emotional – right brain – approaches that will influence the target audiences. (See Chapter 2, Section 2.5 – Individuals' Reaction to Advertising.)

- *Creative guidelines?*
  While you do not want to compromise the creative thinking of your supplier, you will not win many friends if you do not prevent them investing time and effort into something that would not be acceptable. This is particularly useful where you have one supplier working on part of the communications mix and another on a second. If you have a lead campaign in magazines, posters, and transport media (taxis or buses) you would be courting disaster not to tell your sales promotion agency what creative execution was being run though other media!

  Be sure that you allow your agency to 'think outside the box', too. (See the examples in Chapter 5 – The Fourth Room and the Kellogg Case Studies.)
- *Tone of voice?*
  Often overlooked but it is useful to consider the tone of voice of your marketing communications. In face-to-face communications we have words, voice, and body language to put our message across. The 'tone of our voice' carries around a third of the impact of those carefully chosen words.* It is the same with marketing communications.
- *Media considerations*
  Again, not wishing to compromise creativity, what are the likely media options and what are not can save considerable time and effort by both parties.

12.6.2 The client's responsibility on briefing

As a client, there are a number of things that you can do to ensure that your agency is given every chance to do a good job. A checklist would include:

- *Set agenda* – Do not spring briefing meetings on people without agreeing on a plan for the meeting.
- *Allow time for pre-meeting work* – Having given forewarning, give time for people to respond and prepare.
- *Agree on attendees ahead of time* – Good people are busy. Make sure everyone knows who is to attend and why you want them there; then you will give them every chance to add value for you.
- *Have documentation ready (including examples)* – If you are expecting people to integrate their part of the communication mix with others, give them the right material to work with.
- *Make your needs clear* – This invariably means writing them down. While it can be hard to express what you want in the written word, it is a salutary exercise and gives you opportunity to get your thinking straight at the outset.
- *Agree on next steps and timetable* – Be clear of what you want them to do (or not do) and when you are expecting a response!

* Words are about 10 per cent, body language around 55 per cent of the impact of any given message in face-to-face situations.

- *Agree on points of contact* – There can be many people working on your account and there may also be many people in your team. So, who says what to whom will be crucial and managing the flow of information and instructions is one of the biggest challenges facing the agency/client relationship. Getting the systems right at the outset is fundamental. So is getting things written down.
- *Agree on clear output guidelines* – Again, there is a very strong case for getting your instructions written down. This is better than getting them to record your meandering thoughts in a contact report – you ought to take control and provide the necessary guide. The 'I-know-it-when-I-see-it' approach is not very professional.
- *Do not expect the answers there and then!* – I had one client who thought that if they literally stood over a creative artist, like some demonic schoolmaster, they could get the results they wanted that evening. Not so!
- *Share the culture* – The way you 'do things' and the way they 'do things' are often quite different but share your common ground and develop an appropriate chemistry.

12.6.3   The agency's responsibility on briefing

As the agency, there are a number of things that help when called to a briefing meeting.

- *Carry out pre-meeting preparation* – Given that you have been given appropriate notice, do your homework, and do not expect to 'wing it' every time.
- *Right team at meeting* – Make sure you show commitment to the client by getting the right people to the meeting and make sure that they are briefed appropriately.
- *Ask pertinent questions* – The quality of your thinking often comes from the quality of your questioning in response to your internal pre-meeting discussions.
- *Have a clear understanding of requirements* – Do not leave until you have a very clear idea of what is expected of you and your team – and by when. Remember, if you 'assume' you could make an 'ass' of 'u' and 'me'!
- *Know who the contacts will be* – With two teams working on the account – yours and the clients – there is plenty of opportunity for 'Chinese Whispers'. Make sure you manage the contacts through the right people. Working to help your client with their internal communications will pay dividends too.
- *Be on time* – Be professional!
- *Get the tools* – You need the right people, with the right information, properly equipped to do the required job. This may mean making the right investments or buying them in.

Table 12.3 *Checklists for briefing creative work and media requirements*

	Creative brief		Media brief
Campaign requirements	One off, number of treatments	Target audience	Specific details, characteristics, influences
Target audience	Details, characteristics, influences	Creative requirements	Demonstration of product, colour options
Aims	e.g. Generate awareness, reposition brand	Coverage	Cover, frequency, impact, share of voice
The proposition	USP,[1] single-minded, benefits to consumer	Regionality	Where to appear, what gaps?
Substantiation	In product – rational and emotional, service support	Seasonality	When to appear, key times?
Mandatory inclusions	e.g. Stockists, phone numbers, logos	Budget	What's for media? – do not forget production!
Desired brand image	Competitor analysis, marketplace, previous executions	Research	Own market intelligence, competitor activity, historical trends, etc.
Media	Nature of treatments required	Other activities	Timed plans for all other marketing communications
Budget	Creative budget available, what for media?		

[1] Unique selling proposition – what is it that makes your market offering unique?

Chapter 11 on advertising planning and budgeting, along with Chapter 7 on creativity, will guide you on preparing a creative and media brief. Table 12.3 provides a concise checklist to assist your thought processes.

12.7 Judging proposals

We saw in Chapter 7 ten tips on how to judge creativity. At the end of the day we want to know, did the proposed campaign take our audience further along the continuum (Chapter 2, Figure 2.1) from where they were before the campaign to where we want them to be afterwards? So, does the proposed execution:

- Attract attention?
- Provoke interest?
- Comprehend easily?
- Convince the audience?
- Induce desire?
- Spur action?
- And finally, will the media hit the target?

12.8   Controlling expenditure

There are a number of things that you can do to help your outside supplier provide the best value they can without compromising their creative flair. (See also Chapter 3.)

- *Avoid briefing one job in two halves* – There is little point in briefing them on a press advertising campaign and then telling them a few weeks later that you want to use a linked sales promotion, too.
- *Get it in writing* – When you have your needs in black and white, it is so much easier to evaluate whether your instructions have been followed.
- *Competitive quotes* – While everyone can buy cheaper, do make sure that you are comparing like with like. Look at the service you get and look beyond the print quote; it will make all the difference if something goes wrong! As I heard one agency say, 'there are two types of oats: those before the horse has eaten them and those after – it is just that one is cheaper than the other!'
- *Negotiate* – While professional buyers are seasoned negotiators, do ensure that your enthusiasm to get a few pounds knocked off the price does not mean that your supplier trims elsewhere and compromises the ship for a 'hapeth o' tar'!
- *Know the market* – This comes with experience, of course. However, remember that organisations like ISBA will guide their advertiser members on what specifically constitutes best value from agency fees to press production.
- *Do not change the brief* – One of the advantages of providing a written brief is that you have to get your thinking right at the outset. There is less temptation to let your ideas come off the top of your head in the 'heat of the moment' that you later revise in the 'cold light of day'!
- *Plan ahead* – The effort you put into planning for the long-term pays dividends in terms of the action you take today.

12.9   Managing the relationship

There are three areas that warrant further exploration in managing the business relationship with your external suppliers. When we have looked at how we might control those suppliers, we will review some personal views on how to get the best before looking at how to enable our business relationship to flourish.

12.9.1 Controlling external service providers

While we need to make sure we hold the reigns, we do not want them to lose their initiative. Finding a middle path is crucial.

- *Clarity of expectations* – Be very open and clear about what you expect from your suppliers – and what you do not. Obvious perhaps but so many business relationships falter through misunderstood assumptions.
- *Both parties in agreement* – There is no future in a negotiated position where only one of the parties agrees. Good communication and a willingness to look for options of mutual gain in a spirit of cooperation will take things forward towards an agreement.
- *Clarity of contract* – This is one area where experienced legal advisors who can make the contract work without ambiguity will pay dividends.
- *Communication* – While both parties are in a communications business, it is surprising how often individuals fail to communicate properly. Remember the old adage: 'We've two ears and one mouth – use them in the same proportion!'
- *Control* – It is the job of your external providers to give you professional advice. For this you need to trust them. If you cannot trust them, then find a new supplier that you can. That said, suppliers work best when given very clear parameters that you control – like by when and how much within a clear brief – and then given the freedom to do their job within those guides.
- *Use of meetings* – Business people waste so much time in 'meetings' that lack a clear idea of what is required to be done in preparation beforehand and what is planned to happen after the meeting. Moreover, meetings without a clear set of objectives can soak up so much time leaving the participants resentful. To improve the relationship with your suppliers, start by being professional about how you run your meetings with them.

12.9.2 A practical approach to supplier management

There are a number of fundamental things that you can do to get the best from suppliers and the following represents a few practical thoughts:

- *Right supplier for the job* – It sounds so simple but it is surprising how often one can forget what your main suppliers were contracted for. You may have started with your lead marketing communications activity – like advertising – and have recruited a good local agency. Since they are very proactive and a willing bunch, you find that they are then doing some direct mail too. Your campaign needs a bit of public relations so they do that as 'part of the service'. After a year you feel that some brand tracking studies and some customer research is required and before you know it, the agency has done this, too. But they were recruited as an advertising agency and they have now developed into a full service agency! Unless they are capable of subcontracting the extra specialism for you and you are happy with their fees (which may include a mark-up on the bought-in service) you may have to consider an alternative approach.

While your main supplier may be able to do a fine job for you in a number of different marketing areas and you may not have a large enough budget to bring in a range of specialists, do think carefully if they are the right supplier for the job. If you are good at managing suppliers, then dealing with two is no more of a headache than dealing with one that is not the right supplier for the job. See also Section 5.4.1 which looks at the role of the full service agency for larger accounts.

If you have, say, both advertising and public relations to develop in equal measure, to avoid duplicating effort on a modest budget, why not consider bringing in two specialists to work together to the same marketing communications brief. Both are specialist disciplines and there is a case for being a larger client with two smaller suppliers working in harmony than a small client in a big, full-service agency. Integrating your messages will be crucial, of course (see Chapter 3).

- *Right objectives* – Whatever supplier you chose they cannot be expected to perform if they are not working to the right objectives. Good marketing planning is vital, as is good account planning. From this basis you can begin to write good, clear objectives: SMART[†] objectives are again fundamental yet so often overlooked in practice.
- *Correct briefing* – As we saw earlier, following a comprehensive brief in a structured format ensures that your supplier has a chance of delivering what you want. This starts by being clear about what you want: if you cannot write it down then do not be surprised if you do not get quite what you had in mind – few suppliers are mind-readers!
- *Allow a fair amount of time for a job* – Creativity takes time. Be realistic. Do not shorten your time demands just to make them jump to remind them 'who is the boss'. Pushing them to have something on your desk 'by Monday' and then let it sit there for a week before your internal meeting to gain approval will just build resentment.
- *Approval procedures* – Saying that you give final approval when, in fact, a wider approval procedure is required can cause you problems. When you

[†] SMART = Specific, so there is no room for misunderstanding; Measurable, so it is easier to know whether it has been done and how well; Achievable so everyone agrees that it can be done; Results orientated, so the objective builds to the overall business objectives and is seen in that context; and finally, Time bound, so everyone knows by when it is to be achieved. Clearly, all five areas need to be congruent and work well together.

come back with technical changes that were not part of the original brief because someone internally spotted something you had not thought of may compromise time scales and have cost implications.

- *Amendment timing and implications* – Good project management will pay dividends. Experience shows that projects do not go wrong at the end – they go wrong at the beginning! Poor planning leads to last minute changes and rushed jobs; this gets the adrenaline pumping but does not necessarily make for the best use of your finite resources nor does it make for the best marketing communications.
- *Pre- and post-testing of effectiveness* – It is everyone's responsibility to ensure that the campaign is effective. So how are you going to know? Before you commit to a significant expenditure what are you going to do to test the effectiveness? Equally, what are you going to do to check the effectiveness after you have run your campaign? Table 12.4 outlines some areas

Table 12.4   *Summary of options for measuring media and creative effectiveness before, during, and after a campaign. See Section 14.6, page 234.*

Measuring creative effectiveness		*Measuring media effectiveness*	
Research before launch	• Pre-testing • Client reaction • Folder tests • Hall tests • Recall and preference	Before campaign launch	• Plans and research data • Projected levels of impact and awareness
Research during campaign	• Unprompted recall testing • Impact/identity/ preference • Prompted recall testing	During campaign	• Monitor appearance • Research awareness • Research transference factors • Unprompted and prompted recall
Research after campaign	• Effectiveness • Memorability • Recall dying out • Compare to previous/ competitors	After campaign	• Effectiveness • Value for money • Memorability • Effect on future plans • Sustaining programme needed?

for testing media and creative effectiveness. Is your agency best suited to do the research?
- *Gut feeling verses gut rot!* – it is well worth building on your factual research with a portion of gut feel; so much better than spending weeks of doubt with 'gut rot'! 'If in doubt – sort it out' (Table 12.4).

12.9.3   Managing relationships

When it comes to managing the relationship with your outside suppliers, it is worth considering it from three perspectives: getting it right from the start, developing that relationship over time, and managing problems if anything should go wrong. Let us consider each in turn. (It will also be worth reviewing Section 5.9 for further ideas.)

- *Initial relationship* – It is essential that one starts with open, clear, well-defined agreements with a fundamental clarity of expectations. Also, make it clear whether you want proactivity or reactivity from your supplier. The former seems most ideal but it will cost you more, has more risks, and you need to trust your suppliers. You will also need to let them have a little more freedom to deliver solutions to your business problems. As mentioned, the ISBA guidelines are a good place to start with your agreements.
- *Developing the relationship* – As you begin to work with a supplier, so the relationship develops, business moves forward, and the needs on both sides of the relationship change. This may mean that you need to revisit your agreement in the light of experience. Remember, too, that you are build-ing the knowledge of your team players and the agreement may need to reflect that.

  If you have in your mind that you have 'contract colleagues' when work-ing with your suppliers, depending on the closeness of those working rela-tionships, you may need to manage both social and formal settings – just as you might with your full-time employees. If you have a number of people involved in your internal approval process, why not get them to meet the agency team once in a while. It can improve mutual understanding and help the work flow.

  Finally, when developing the relationship, it is important that you keep control of the work-flow, timeliness, and cost. It is important for the endur-ing nature of the relationship that it is kept fresh, lively, and that both sides continue to profit. Make sure that you check this from time to time.
- *Managing problems* – From time to time things will go wrong but having the correct procedures in place in the first place will make life easier for both parties. It is good practice to ensure that contact reports and activity updates are managed professionally. With e-mail there is an easy audit trail and wide circulation of information possible. However, it is essential that

the quality of these communications is maintained and not compromised at the expense of quantity.

Personal matters are bound to arise from time to time and these need to be dealt with professionally and confidentially. Developing a culture of openness, transparency, and trust would seem to be the basis for resolving issues as they arise. As always, early action may be called for and one should not be frightened to explore the possibility of team changes from time to time on either side, especially if there is staleness developing in the relationship.

12.9.4   Ten smart things to do

Finally, there follows a checklist of 10 smart things to do that have been found to help get the best from agencies and other outside suppliers:

- *Meet agency specialists* – It is worth getting your team to meet their team from time to time, especially their copywriters, media buyers, designers, etc.
- *Write it down* – A fundamental discipline well worth developing.
- *Harmony meetings* – Arrange for a meeting once every 6 months or so and discuss freely how you can help your agency to work better with your team. Ask them for honesty – how you can be a better client? Do not focus on this job or that piece of work; how the way you do things can help them to do what they do better. You could be pleasantly surprised how easily you can improve things for each other. Then buy *them* lunch.
- *Set deadlines for all work* – The 'certainty of despair' is better than the 'despair of uncertainty'. If you know something is going to be late, that is better than being surprised at the last minute; you can bring in planned contingencies.
- *Go for short briefing meetings* – Good preparation makes for better meetings. Having a concise brief helps the agency know what is expected of them and they can start work immediately while your enthusiasm endures. However, giving them a headache figuring out what you meant by those hours of meandering will soon dampen their spirits for the campaign.
- *Give them a pat on the back* – Only a few feet from a kick up the backside but a world of difference! The best pat on the back is to tell someone else how good they are.
- *Keep hold of the reins* – If you do that you will not feel that you are being overcharged when the agency has tried a number of different approaches trying to help you 'know it when you see it'!
- *Specify absolute 'musts' and 'must nots'* – Before the agency gets to work.
- *Judge advertising before publication or transmission* – If your campaign backfires in the marketplace, then that is your fault for not thinking enough

about the work before it 'hit the streets'. Do pre-testing – even a little goes a long way. Moreover, ensure your organisation is on your side: just as you would not let the boss see your campaign for the first time as he or she drives to work, the same goes for other internal staff.
- *Make sure the agency profits* – Perhaps the best way of getting the best out of any external supplier I know!

12.10   Summary

In this chapter:

- We saw the place of service suppliers in assisting your organisation with marketing communications and explored the differing perspectives between the two businesses.
- Best practice on how to find and appoint your advertising agency was discussed with pointers of where to find more detailed information on drawing up agreements indicating ISBA for advertisers and IPA for agencies.
- Supplementing Chapters 6 and 7, we developed some checklists on how best to brief an agency – making the case for better planning and written briefs. We also devised checklists to help agency and advertiser prepare for the briefing meeting.
- We explored how to evaluate an agency's work and considered research possibilities before, during, and after a campaign to evaluate its effectiveness.
- We reviewed how to control expenditure on your suppliers but, at the end of the day, both organisations have to profit from the relationship.
- Best practice in managing the relationship with your agency was discussed with a checklist of 10 smart things to do.

Notes

1   The Incorporated Society of British Advertisers, 44 Hertford Street, London, W1Y 8AE, 020 7499 7502, www.isba.org.uk.
2   The Institute of Practitioners in Advertising, 44 Belgrave Square, London, SW1X 8QS, 020 7235 7020 www.pia.co.uk.
3   British Rate and Data.
4   For more information on this area, see also Wilmshurst, J. and Mackay, A. *The Fundamentals of Advertising,* 2nd Ed., Butterworth Heinemann, 1999, Chapter 6.
5   For more information on marketing planning, see also Wilmshurst, J. and Mackay, A. *The Fundamentals and Practice of Marketing*, 4th Ed., Butterworth Heinemann, 2002, Chapter 6.

13   Media Research

Mike Monkman

Learning outcomes

In this chapter you will read about:

* The reasons why media research is carried out.
* How it is used in preparing media plans and in the buying and selling of advertising time / space.
* How it is organised.
* How it is conducted for each of the main media.

13.1   The purpose of media research

Before buying space or time on any medium, the advertiser wants to know the answer to a key question: How many people are going to buy my product / service as a result of this advertisement appearing?

Regrettably, we cannot get anywhere near answering this question yet. What we could try to do, however, is to say how many people will actually *see* the advertisement. In practice, even this is too demanding a question to be answered accurately. The limitations of research are such that in the end the best we can do is to report the number of people who will have an opportunity to see (OTC) the advertisement.

This opportunity is defined in different ways for different media. As examples, for television it is defined as being in a room with a TV set switched on and tuned to the appropriate channel. For newspapers and magazines it is defined as reading the average issue of the publication carrying the advertisement.

Thus, the vast majority of media research is dedicated to counting the audience. This is, however, only the beginning of the story. By more complex analysis of the data emanating from media surveys we can evaluate a whole campaign. We can estimate the number of people who will have one, two, three, four, or more opportunities to see an advertisement that appears in many different publications, or TV time slots, etc.

We can now see the two major roles of media research in context.

- Firstly, it aids the buying and selling of space / airtime by defining a key element of its value – the number of OTCs that it offers.
- Secondly, it enables media planners to determine what particular mix of spaces / spots will achieve their desired targets of:
    (a) *coverage* – the number of people in the target audience who will have at least one OTC the campaign, and
    (b) *frequency* – the average number of OTCs those people will receive.

While it is the case that there is a great deal more to media research than simple head counting, this audience measurement element of media research is at the core of the buying / selling process, and the planning process. It is also the case that these key audience data are conducted on behalf of the whole industry, whereas much of the work that goes beyond this is carried out by individual agencies and/or media owners – sometimes in consortia – and is thus not in the public domain in the same way.

We will consider some of the approaches taken by this proprietorial research later, but first it is important to review the major audience measurement projects that are key inputs to the planning and buying of just about every campaign.

13.2   The organisation of media research

If our audience measurement is going to determine the relative value of different newspapers or magazines or television channels, (or, as is often said, to provide a 'currency' for the trading of space / time) then it has to be conducted in such a way that all the parties to the trading are happy to accept its results.

Originally, this was achieved by the setting up of 'Joint Industry Committees' to oversee these research projects. There was a committee for press, one for TV, one for radio, one for cinema, etc. These committees included representatives from both the relevant media owners and from agencies. They organised the funding, controlled the design of their survey(s), and awarded contract(s) to research agencies to conduct the research and supply the data.

This structure is still in place, except that most of the committees are now formally constituted as companies in their own right, with the various interested parties as shareholders.

The key organisations currently providing audience research data are:

TV:	BARB (Broadcasters Audience Research Board Ltd)
Press:	NRS (National Readership Surveys Ltd)
Radio:	RAJAR (Radio Joint Audience Research Ltd)
Cinema:	CAVIAR (Cinema and Video Audience Research)
Outdoor:	POSTAR (Poster Audience Research)

The importance of this type of research to the buying and selling process is such that it is felt necessary to devote very large budgets to ensuring the best possible data. For this reason, most audience research is conducted with far higher standards of survey design, sampling, etc. than the vast majority of commercial market research.

This is perhaps a suitable point to register an important point. Despite the very high standards achieved by most audience measurement projects, we must remember that the resulting data are still only a collection of estimates. Sampling theories tell us that there is a very high probability that any readership / viewing / estimate is close to the truth, but we must always be aware that we are not dealing with absolute precision.

Please note that in the following sections, which summarise the conduct of the major audience measurement projects, the processes are outlined as they are now. Much is changing in the world of media research, and there can be no guarantee that these processes will still be the same if you are reading this book some years hence. Where future plans are known, I have outlined them as far as possible, but nothing remains fixed forever.

The reader who requires a brief overview of media research can simply read the first 'Overview' section under each of the following media headings. Those who wish to develop a fuller understanding should read all sections.

13.3   Television: BARB

13.3.1   Overview

The Broadcasters' Audience Research Board Ltd (BARB) is jointly owned by the BBC, ITV, Channel Four, Channel Five, BSkyB, and the IPA.*

Its role is to commission the television audience measurement contract on behalf of all its shareholders, and to manage the delivery of that contract. Specifically, it supervises the data delivery and quality control procedures agreed under the contract. It also has responsibility for the design of the service and the continuing process of design development. The current contract started in January 2002 and is for a 5-year period.

The methodology currently employed is to recruit a representative sample of homes that agree to join a viewing panel. Currently, this panel includes over 5000 homes. Every TV set in these households, together with every VCR, satellite receiver, cable receiver, etc. is then connected to a meter, which sits on top of the set. The meter then records what all these pieces of equipment are doing continuously, and sends this information to a central storage unit in the

* The Institute of Practitioners in Advertising

panel home. All individuals aged 4 years or over in each panel home (and their guests) are asked to press a button on a handset every time they enter or leave a room with a TV set – if the set is switched on. Thus, BARB collects information about which individuals in the household are watching at any time. The information from the handsets is also passed to the central storage unit.

The storage unit then transmits all this information daily to the research contractor's base, where it is then amalgamated with the all the other homes, and the database is built up.

The household's guests are included in the data so that their viewing can be counted as a substitute for the panel household's own viewing as guests in other households. Thus BARB measures *all* domestic viewing to broadcast television channels. It does not attempt to measure any non-domestic out-of-home viewing.

We can also see that BARB defines an OTC as 'being in the same room as the TV set, with the set switched on'.

Because of the regional structure of ITV, the panel is designed as a series of smaller panels – one for each ITV region. It is also designed to allow separate analyses of the BBC regions.

13.3.2 The establishment survey

In order to make the panel as representative as possible, it is necessary to know something about the viewing population of the UK. This information is provided by the Establishment Survey, carried out under contract to BARB. It is based on a very high quality random sample of all households in the UK, and obtains information from these households about the TV viewing equipment they have, and their broad viewing habits. Currently, some 52,000 households are interviewed annually for this survey.

From this survey, we know how many households we need in our panel with various characteristics. The Establishment Survey also provides the pool of households from which panel members are recruited.

13.3.3 The panel

The use of a panel to measure TV viewing is significant in that it allows analyses of the data over periods of time. We can look at people's viewing behaviour over a period of time, and identify those with particular patterns of viewing.

Because it is a panel, the process of drawing the sample is somewhat different from most sample surveys. The reason for the difference is that panel members will, from time to time, wish to withdraw from the panel, or become ineligible. Therefore, the process of sampling is a continuous one, as replacements are needed. Given that we know a great deal about the population, from the Census and from BARB's own Establishment Survey, we can choose replacement homes by selecting those which best maintain the balance of various household types on the panel.

A great deal of effort is expended on the task of ensuring that the panel balance is maintained.

Occasionally, individual homes are withdrawn from the analysis because of a possible problem with the data being forwarded by their meter. This might be due to a technical fault in the equipment, or it might be that some or all members of the household are not complying with the button-pushing requirements. In practice, the research contractor is therefore required to maintain the panel at levels a little higher than the contractual minimum, so that there is still a panel of sufficient size left for analysis.

As noted earlier, the panel is actually many different panels, each one drawn from a different geographical area. Under the current contract, the panel sizes for each ITV area are:

	Gross target	*Net target*
London	945	850
Midlands	867	780
North West	444	400
Yorkshire	389	350
North East	222	200
Scotland	555	500
South & SE	500	450
East	444	400
South West	222	200
Ulster	333	300
Border	111	100
West	222	200
Wales	389	350
Channel Islands	22	20
Total	5665	5100

From time to time, households on the panel are telephoned, and the person answering the telephone is asked which sets in the household were on at the time when the telephone rang, and who was watching them. These answers can then be compared with that household's meter records, as a check on the accuracy of panel members' button-pushing. These data are reported regularly, and are known as the 'Coincidental Check' survey. It shows that while people cannot be expected to perform this task with 100 per cent accuracy, the errors and omissions are relatively small.

13.3.4   Analysis

The information collected by the meters in each household tells us when the set was switched on, and what channel it was tuned to, and who was watching. This information is collected continuously. Once the data have been collected from every panel household, they are amalgamated, and audience figures are produced for every single minute through the day.

These audience data are then combined with the TV companies' transmission logs, and audience estimates are then produced for every commercial transmission, for every programme, and for every quarter hour.

A great deal of processing of the raw data is necessary to produce these estimates. To find out more about this subject, consult the *BARB Reference Manual* that is available on-line to all BARB subscribers.

In a further refinement of the data collected, the meters in panel homes also have the ability to measure viewing to VCR recordings made off-air. These viewings can then be attributed to the correct day and time of broadcast. At the analysis stage, all recordings watched within 7 days of broadcast are added back to the audiences for the minutes concerned. This is known as 'consolidated' viewing (as opposed to 'live' viewing, which only counts viewing at the time of broadcast).

13.4   Press: circulation

The vast majority of newspaper and magazine publishers are members of the Audit Bureau of Circulations.

This body operates an independent audit on every member title's sales, by auditing deliveries to, and returns from, newsagents. Every issue is measured, but the data are only published as averages over a period. Circulation data for newspapers are available by month, but published every 3 months. Data for magazines are available for 6- or 12-month periods, depending on the magazine.

These data are a sound base for our understanding of the press, because they are based on an independent audit and not on any kind of sampling. However, knowing how many copies are sold does not tell us how many readers a title reaches. All publications have readers who have not bought the copy they are reading, and the number of *readers per copy* will vary from title to title. To measure readership, we need a readership survey, hence the National Readership Survey (NRS).

13.5   Press: The National Readership Survey Ltd

13.5.1   Overview

The parties represented within National Readership Surveys Ltd (NRS Ltd) are the IPA, ISBA (the Incorporated Society of British Advertisers), NPA (the Newspaper Publishers Association), and PPA (the Periodical Publishers Association).

It is the task of NRS Ltd to award and administer a contract for the provision of a readership measure, which can be used as a basis for the buying, selling, and planning of press advertising space.

The NRS measures the average issue readership (AIR) of every newspaper and magazine covered by the survey – currently over 250 titles. The AIR is defined as the readership of the average issue of a title, regardless of when or where the issue is read. As was noted earlier, the measure of an OTC a press advertisement is taken as reading or looking at the average issue of the newspaper or magazine in which it appears.

Thus, we have a measure that averages the exposure to each title over several months, unlike the television measure we have just reviewed that measures every single minute separately. This means that the data are both unresponsive to fluctuations in readership from one issue to the next, but are also some months old by the time they are published. This is not seen as a major problem since newspaper and magazine audiences are relatively stable, and nowhere near as volatile as the TV audience.

The essence of the AIR measurement is that it asks informants, title by title, when they last looked at or read a copy for at least 2 minutes. This is then coded as being either within the last issue period or not. The issue period is 7 days for a Sunday newspaper or weekly magazine, 4 weeks for a monthly magazine, etc. Reading on the day of interview is not counted, since this would be affected by the time of day of interview. Any reading is counted, regardless of where, and regardless of whether the copy looked at was current or not. In this way, reading of past issues is counted as a proxy for future reading of the current issue.

In order to alleviate the tedium of asking every single informant about every one of the 250 or so titles, there is a preliminary filter sequence, which quickly identifies which of the publications have been read or looked at for at least 2 minutes in the past 12 months. Only those publications are asked about in detail.

The NRS is a continuous survey, covering some 35,000 interviews each year. The very high quality random sample is designed to be representative of all adults aged 15 years or over in mainland Great Britain: the populations of Northern Ireland and the Scottish islands are not covered. From October 2003, all interviews are carried out using double screen computer assisted personal interviewing (DS-CAPI). This means that the interviews are conducted face-to-face, with the interviewer using a computer to control the question sequence and to record the responses, and the respondent using a 'slave' screen radio linked to the interviewer's laptop, on which appear all of the visual prompts used in the interview.

In addition to the 'recency' question that defines the AIR, respondents are also asked how frequently they read or look at each publication. These data are used as input to some probability calculations, which generate estimates of the net coverage of whole campaign schedules.

13.5.2   The survey

The readership part of the interview begins with the filter process mentioned above. Respondents are shown a series of screens, each screen showing six titles in a common typeface. Each set of six titles will typically consist of titles with some similarity to each other. The respondent first selects those screens showing *any* title he/she has read for at least 2 minutes in the last 12 months. Any rejected screens are then viewed a second time, showing the same six titles on each screen but this time showing them as 'mini mastheads' for more secure identification. Any screens which are selected at this second stage are added by the interviewer's computer to the 'have read' screens selected at the first stage. The respondent is then asked to identify which *individual* publications on each of the selected screens have been read or looked at for at least 2 minutes in the last 12 months.

The procedure is as follows. Having recorded all individual publications which the respondent claims to have read in the past 12 months, the computer shows the respondent each of these publications individually on the screen (as distinct from the earlier presentation of six publications on each screen) using the mini-masthead of each publication, and the respondent is asked, for each publication in turn, the recency and frequency questions, that is, publication A – recency, frequency; publication B – recency, frequency; publication C – recency, frequency; and so on.

Answers to the recency question are coded as:

- Yesterday
- Within past 7 days
- Within past 2 weeks (fortnightly publications only)
- Within past 4 weeks
- Within past 2 months (bi-monthly publications only)
- Within past 3 months
- Longer ago.

For daily newspapers, 'yesterday' defines the most recent issue period. (On Monday interviews, yesterday is defined as 'yesterday or Saturday.')

Answers to the frequency question, are coded as:

- Almost always (at least three issues out of four)
- Quite often (at least one issue out of four)
- Only occasionally (less than one issue out of four)
- Not in the past 12 months.

If the publication is a daily or Sunday newspaper, then the frequency question is followed by an additional screen prompt showing the range of key supplements published by that newspaper (minor or irregular supplements are not included). The respondent is then asked the same recency question for each supplement of the newspaper.

For all publications which receive a recency claim which qualifies as an AIR claim (i.e. read yesterday for a daily newspaper, read within the last 7 days for a weekly publication, etc.) two further questions are then asked, covering source of copy, and how disappointed the respondent would be if each publication ceased. These last two questions have great value, but do not contribute to the main AIR measurement.

The next section of the interview deals with exposure to other media – TV, radio, cinema, directories, and outdoor advertising. These data are of value in planning campaigns across more than one medium.

There is also a great deal of classification and other data collected from NRS respondents, allowing analysis of newspaper or magazine readerships by many different sub-groups of the population.

13.5.3   Duplicated readership and cumulative readership

From the data generated by the NRS, it is possible to count the number of people who are average issue readers of both publication A and publication B. This is duplicated readership, and can be used to tell us how many would have at least one opportunity to see an advertisement placed in both tiles.

By extension, we can identify how many would have at least one opportunity to see an advertisement placed in several titles.

We can also use some simple probability theory to tell us how many would have an OTS if an advertisement were to be placed in several issues of the *same* publication. We know that the average issue readership of, for example, *The Sun* is say 19.6 per cent of the population, but this is not the same 19.6 per cent for every single issue. Most of the readers of one issue will also be readers of a second, but not all – some new readers will come in while others will miss the second issue. To illustrate this, the Sun has an AIR of 19.6 per cent, but over several issues its readership builds up as follows:

	Cumulative readership (%)
1 issue	19.6
2 issues	24.4
3 issues	26.8
4 issues	28.6
5 issues	30.1
6 issues	31.2
7 issues	32.2
8 issues	33.0
9 issues	34.3
10 issues	35.4

In practice, calculations like this are used to provide coverage and frequency estimates for whole schedules. The mathematics behind these calculations gets very complex once we have several insertions in each of several titles, and the actual formulae are secret to the computer bureaux that devise them. Thus, it is possible to get slightly different answers depending on which bureau's software is used. However, these differences will be very small.

In addition to software, which reports the performance of schedules, there are also systems that will create an 'optimised' schedule. Given, for example, a coverage target, these systems will attempt to find the optimum (i.e. cheapest) schedule to achieve this target.

13.5.4   Future NRS developments

Early in 2004 for the first time the NRS will be releasing readership accumulation curves for all titles measured on the survey. These curves will show how quickly readership of newspapers and magazines is achieved, and will enable press schedules to be planned and evaluated with greater precision than is possible at present.

During the course of 2004, the NRS will be testing the introduction of the Personalised Media List®Ipsos in which only those types of magazines the respondent is likely to read are presented. It is estimated that this will reduce the average number of magazines about which each respondent is questioned by approximately one third, and should avoid presenting respondents with magazine categories that are irrelevant to them.

In the longer term, and now that the survey has adopted DSCAPI as its methodology, it is possible to begin development work on completely new forms of interview. DSCAPI does away with the paper-based visual prompts used in previous years, and delivers all prompts on-screen. This will enable the prompts themselves to be developed, to include colour, sound and animation if this is found to be appropriate. Just as importantly, it will enable the interview itself to be developed into new forms. Of particular interest is the possibility of putting the questionnaire onto the Web, which would allow respondents to complete an interview at their convenience and in their own time. It is likely that such a Web-based data collection method will have profound implications for the future evolution of the survey.

13.6   Press: JICREG

The NRS described above is mainly concerned with nationally distributed publications. JICREG (Joint Industry Committee for Regional Press Research) provides equivalent data for regional newspapers.

JICREG data are generated by applying a 'readers per copy' figure to a newspaper's circulation. This readers per copy figure is calculated by dividing the number of readers by the circulation. The readership data are taken in most cases from a readership survey conducted within the newspaper's circulation area, and carried out according to JICREG guidelines. The measurement processes and definitions are very much the same as for the NRS described above. The JICREG readership data, consisting of more than 1000 titles, are organised within 9000 postcode sectors and computerised mapping is provided to make the planning process easier.

In cases where there is no readership survey, the readership is modelled from other data by JICREG. Currently, around half of all regional newspapers have survey data.

13.7 Press: other surveys

While the NRS is the major source of data on readership in the UK, there are other surveys carried out on a regular basis. Most of these surveys concentrate on a particular sector of the population, such as the medical profession, computer buyers, or businessmen.

These surveys are often sponsored by a consortium of media owners with particular interests in the group being studied, and are usually (but not always) carried out using the same basic definitions and estimation processes as the NRS.

13.8 Radio RAJAR

13.8.1 Overview

Radio Joint Audience Research Ltd (RAJAR) is jointly owned by the Commercial Radio Companies Association (CRCA) and the BBC. The IPA is also represented on its board.

Like BARB and the NRS Ltd, it awards a contract to a research agency for the collection and supply of data, in this case, data on listening to radio stations – both national and local.

The research method employed by RAJAR is a 7-day diary. Some 130,000 diaries are placed annually, with a representative sample of the UK population aged 4 years and over.

Respondents are given a diary set out as a grid, which has quarter hours down the side and radio stations across the top. They are asked to record any radio listening of 5 minutes or more by ticking the appropriate station/time segment box.

The diaries are placed with respondents towards the end of each week with a fresh sample, and collected back afterwards. Each diary runs from a Monday to a Sunday.

Each radio station has defined a total survey area, and depending on the size of this area, it will have a minimum sample size that it needs to have for reporting purposes. For the larger stations, their minimum sample size will be achieved in one quarter, while other stations may need two quarters or even a full year's sample before being able to publish.

All data are published quarterly, with the smaller stations publishing data based on as many previous quarters as necessary to comply with the sample size rules.

13.8.2   The interview

The interview consists mainly of the placement of the diary together with the instructions on how to fill it in. The diary is placed with one adult and up to two children aged 4–14 years in each household sampled.

Some basic data about the household is collected for classification purposes, and then the respondent is asked about their radio listening, and in particular about their repertoire of stations. This information is used to customise each diary, so that it lists only those stations the respondent either listens to, or might perhaps listen to. This is achieved by means of stick-on labels that the interviewer adds to the diary as required. There is also a facility for the respondent to add labels for (or write in) other stations, if during the week they happen to listen to an unexpected station. On the Monday or Tuesday after the diary week, the interviewer returns, and collects all the completed diaries.

The RAJAR website (www.rajar.co.uk) contains more detail.

13.9   Cinema: CAVIAR

13.9.1   Overview

Historically, cinema audiences have always been estimated on the basis of data from the NRS survey. The NRS questionnaire includes the same kind of recency and frequency question on cinema as it does on newspapers and magazines, therefore the same kind of probability modelling used for press can be used to develop coverage and frequency estimates for cinema. These estimates were not used as they stand, but were scaled to fit known admissions data for the weeks of the campaign.

The Cinema Advertising Association (CAA) commissions the annual CAVIAR (Cinema and Video Audience Research) survey, designed to track audiences to particular films, and to monitor film audiences watching at home on video. In addition to this, the CAA also runs a quarterly *CAVIAR Film Monitor*, providing information on cinema audience on a more frequent basis.

At the time of writing, the CAA is currently in discussion to develop a new coverage and frequency calculation system, which would be based on recency and frequency questions on the annual CAVIAR survey and on the quarterly *Film Monitor*.

This will have the advantage of including the younger age groups, who are an important part of the cinema audience, but who are not covered by the NRS. The NRS only interviews those aged 15 years or over, whereas the CAA Film Monitor survey interviews those aged 7 years or over and the CAVIAR survey interviews those aged 4 years or over.

13.9.2   The CAA monitor

This is a quarterly survey of around 3000 people aged 7 years or over. The questionnaire includes the recency and frequency questions needed to generate coverage and frequency estimates. In practice, these estimates will not be derived from one quarter's survey, but from a year's interviews, together with the main annual CAVIAR survey, which provides another 5000 or so interviews with those aged 4 years and over.

The probability model used will be very similar to that used for press schedules, but its output is scaled up or down to match the known cinema attendance figures for the period of the campaign. Nielsen EDI, who conducts a continuous audit, tracking actual cinema admissions on a weekly basis, currently collects cinema admissions.

13.10   Outdoor advertising: POSTAR

13.10.1   Overview

Outdoor advertising includes not only billboards by the roadside, in shopping centres, on bus shelters, and throughout our towns, but also trackside advertising, stadium billboards, and a variety of other advertising vehicles.

The predominant source of data on the performance of outdoor campaigns is POSTAR. This is operated by a consortium of poster contractors and outdoor media agencies, and covers advertising on poster sites. At the time of writing, it does not cover transport or stadium advertising, although there are plans to extend its scope in the very near future to encompass these other forms of outdoor advertising.

The data generated by POSTAR come from a complex mathematical model based on three basic sets of data:

- Vehicular and pedestrian traffic counts for over 70 per cent of poster panels, which have been extrapolated to cover all of the 100,000 roadside billboards. This extrapolation has been carried out using the massive site database, which contains information about each site's size, angle height, road classification, etc.
- A visibility study, from which a model has been built allowing us to estimate the number of passers-by who will actually see a poster of a given

size, height, angle, distance, etc. These data are used to adjust the traffic/vehicle counts.

- A travel survey, which is used to identify the demographic profile of the poster audience, and to estimate the coverage and frequency delivered by different types of campaign.

The very nature of exposure to the outdoor medium makes it a very difficult task to research it as thoroughly as, for example, TV or press, but this amalgamation of data into mathematical models represents a very effective way of providing estimates where otherwise none would be available.

13.10.2   The model in more detail

Underpinning the whole exercise is the site database, which has to be updated continually. It contains every site's physical details, and many details about the immediate environment (e.g. nearness to bus stops, shops, stations).

These data allow assumptions to be made about those sites not covered by a vehicle or pedestrian traffic count. A computer-based process known as neural networking makes the extrapolation. As the name implies, this is an electronic attempt to mimic the working of the human brain, and it is trained to 'learn' from the data it is given, and then to make inferences about other examples. From this we have an assumed traffic count for all sites, although it is important to remember that the count is a real one rather than an assumed one in 70 per cent of cases. Also, since the 70 per cent with actual counts are mostly those on major routes, the actual percentage of the audience covered is greater than 70.

The visibility study was conducted by scanning the eye movements of people as they undertake a journey, sometimes as a driver, sometimes as a passenger, and other times as a pedestrian. By travelling through a variety of different places, it was possible to determine the effect of the main physical attributes of a site on the percentage of passers-by who will actually see it.

This is used to adjust the gross impact figure derived from traffic counts.

The travel survey asks respondents about every journey they have made in a recent period, and plots the poster sites they will have passed. This allows a coverage and frequency analysis by demographic sub-group to be carried out for different types of campaign. This can then be scaled to fit the total exposure estimate, which has already been scaled by the visibility survey.

New travel surveys are being conducted, so these data are kept up-to-date and developed as time goes on.

13.11   Internet

In the same way that ABC provides an audited circulation figure for newspapers and magazines, ABCE (ABC Electronic) audits attempts to count accesses to websites.

The whole process of measuring web audiences is in its infancy, and there is a great deal of work to be done before the industry has an agreed set of rules and definitions concerning measurement.

Another body called JICWEBS (Joint Industry Committee for Web Standards) has been set up with a view to developing standards and ensuring independent measurement of web advertising.

ABCE works closely with this organisation, and by providing an independent audit it provides some assurance that web audience figures are reliable, and to a reasonably standard set of definitions.

13.12   All media: TGI

Having reviewed the main industry research programmes, let us turn to the one survey that covers all media – and a huge amount of marketing data as well.

The Target Group Index (TGI) is a commercial venture, and not commissioned by any organised body. It is carried out by BMRB (a large and well-known research agency), and provides a unique source of data, in that it measures not only media consumption, but also purchasing/usage behaviour across an enormous number of markets – including food and groceries, financial markets, automotive markets, leisure markets, etc.

This allows media planners to choose media according to how well they reach particular sectors of their market, defined in terms of their usage. For example, TGI will report on the readership of magazines among heavy purchasers of packet tea, or frequent users of hair gel, or those who spend more than £100 a month on their credit card, or those who drive a car with an engine size bigger than 2000 cc and so on – the list is almost endless.

In order to gather data in this quantity, the questionnaire is a volume in its own right and is almost a quarter of an inch thick. This is left with respondents for them to complete themselves in their own time. Some 25,000 people complete a TGI questionnaire each year.

Inevitably, with a respondent task as onerous as this, the sample achieved is not as high in quality as, for example, the NRS, or the BARB Establishment Survey, but because of the benefits of having media data and market data form the same source, this survey is widely used.

Data in this survey on TV, radio, and cinema are only of a general nature – indicating the general level and pattern of usage. However, the data on press cover many titles. In order to avoid the confusion of different readership estimates for the general population, the TGI data are weighted to match the estimates from the NRS.

13.13   Proprietary surveys

In addition to the basic head-counting surveys mounted by the industry, there is a great deal of research carried out by media owners and by agencies into other aspects of how media perform.

Some of these surveys concentrate on the environment of the exposure and the mood of the reader / viewer / listener at the time, others concentrate on peoples' attitudes to different media, and how they react to advertisements in them.

Those surveys carried out by agencies are invariably not accessible to those outside the sponsoring company, so are not part of the general currency of research, but are often seen as valuable assets in new business pitches.

Those carried out by media owners are usually more publicly available, because it is their purpose to encourage advertisers to buy space / time in the sponsoring media. These surveys will tend to concentrate on whatever the media owner perceives as being to their advantage – often on the editorial environment.

These surveys are important because they both lift our thinking above the simple 'how many' approach, and because they provide valuable insights into how different media work, and in what circumstances they work best.

13.14   Summary

In this chapter:

*   We have seen why media research is so important to ensure that we are getting value for money from our advertising
*   The main methods by which media research is organised has been discussed and the key organisations (BARB, NRS, RAJAR, CAVIAR, POSTAR) for TV, Press, Radio, Cinema, and Outdoor media have been outlined.
*   Future trends in media research have been described and Internet research (ABCE and JICWEBS) have both been mentioned.
*   Target Group Index (TGI) have been described separately as it provides a unique set of data on both media consumption as well as purchasing and usage behaviour across many markets.

Further reading

McDonald, C. and Monkman, M. (eds). *The MRG Guide to Media Research*, Media Research Group, 1995.

This is dated 1995, and is therefore out of date in some respects but is still relevant on key principles.

International Journal of Market Research, **42** (4), Winter 2000, Market
　　Research Society.
　　Special issue – Media Research.

Useful websites

www.barb.co.uk
www.nrs.co.uk
www.rajar.co.uk
www.postar.co.uk
www.abce.org.uk

14 Consumer Research

Marilyn Baxter

Learning outcomes

By the end of this chapter you will:

- understand the basic principles and methods of consumer research.
- understand where research fits into the advertising development process.
- be familiar with the language of research and the main types of research study used in advertising.

14.1 How this chapter is organised

This chapter deals with the three main topics listed above as 'learning objectives'. After a brief general introduction, the first section explains some very general principles of how research is done. The next section briefly describes where research fits into the advertising development process. The third section describes the main research studies that are used in advertising and discusses their application. The language and terminology of research are introduced at appropriate points.

14.2 Introduction: what is consumer research and why do it?

Consumer research is the collecting and interpretation of data from consumers about what they do and why they do it, in relation to brands, products, services, advertising, and any other aspect of marketing activity. The practice of marketing requires many decisions to be taken; some of these decisions can be confidently taken on the basis of experience or judgement, but research enables decision makers (whether clients or agencies) to be better informed about what consumers do or think. Thus, decisions that are made on the basis of research tend to be more likely to succeed than those based on judgement alone.

Research will give you *objective* information about what is really going on in your market, uncontaminated by anyone's personal prejudices. In any situation, it is tempting to imagine that consumers will behave exactly as we would in the same circumstances. In truth, however, people vary widely in their needs, tastes and means, and so it pays to remember that you are only representative of people like you, not of the population as a whole, and therefore it is dangerous to extrapolate from your own experience.

This is not to say that *all* decisions (or even most decisions) should be abdicated to research. First of all, research is time-consuming and expensive, and if you were to refer every decision to research, nothing would ever get done. But also, research is not Truth – it is the researcher's best approximation to an honest picture of reality. The accuracy of that picture is limited by many things: the time the research was done, the skill of the questionnaire writer, potential sampling error in quantitative studies, the tendency of people to agree with a strong character in a group discussion, the interpretative skills of the researcher, and, not least, the inability of consumers to articulate what they really think / feel / do in relation to products and advertising to which they pay relatively little attention, or ideas that are completely new and foreign to them. In considering the accuracy and reliability of any research findings, it pays to maintain a healthy scepticism.

That said, research is used extensively in advertising throughout the advertising development process, for the simple reason that it increases our chances of making advertising that works. It would be a brave client or agency that would develop an advertising campaign entirely without the help of research.

14.3 The basic principles and methods of consumer research

There are two basic kinds of research: *quantitative* research and *qualitative* research.

Quantitative research refers to studies where large numbers of people are interviewed in order to find out how prevalent a particular attitude or behaviour is in the population at large. Since it would be impractical to interview everyone in your target market (e.g. all women or all parents or all those over 45 years), *samples* of respondents are selected using statistical techniques to be representative of the relevant population. Probability theory enables us to be confident that a properly drawn sample (even what seems like a very small one, such as 100 or 200 people) can be representative of a population of several millions and we can safely draw conclusions from the results.

The accuracy of the data and the kinds of conclusions you can safely draw are related to the number of people interviewed (not the proportion of the population). Statistical formulae enable researchers to work out the minimum sample size for any study; generally this is determined by the smallest sub-sample you want to look at separately (e.g. women aged 18–21 years, or parents with children under 5 years, or those over 45 years living in Yorkshire). As a rule of thumb, any sample smaller than 100 should be treated with caution. Since the cost of a survey is related to the sample size, trade-offs will generally have to be made between accuracy and cost.

The statistical theory that underpins the validity of quantitative research only works if you talk to the right *number* of people, if you talk to the right *kinds* of people, and if you ask the right *questions*. To illustrate this, if a car manufacturer wants to know how the public is likely to feel about a new car design, it would not be enough to talk only to men. Women purchase cars in their own right, and often children take part in the selection process, so they should be consulted too. Owners of current models of the manufacturer's products should be interviewed, and so probably should those with other makes of car, as they are potential customers. Similarly, it would be necessary to include people of different ages and parts of the country, to be sure of getting a cross-section of the population. And of course, you would need to be sure that everybody fully understands and can answer the questions, otherwise the information will be misleading or worthless.

Once a sample of respondents have been selected, they can be interviewed using a variety of methods: face-to-face in their own home or in their office/workplace, in a central location (e.g. a community hall or shopping mall), on the street, outside particular shops, at a sporting event – wherever you are likely to find the kinds of people you want to interview; on the telephone; by post; or on the Internet. Different interviewing methods are appropriate for different studies, and they all have their advantages and disadvantages in terms of speed, cost, quality, and nature of information collected; the research agency will recommend the best method for each study.

Interviews are conducted using a highly structured questionnaire. The question areas are predetermined by the client; the actual questions are written expertly by the researcher, generally on the basis of previous experience or of findings from qualitative research (see below), and are tested out in a small number of *pilot* interviews. Normally, there is little or no flexibility for the interviewer to vary the questions, though quantitative questionnaires can be designed to allow respondents to answer questions in their own words. These are called *open-ended* questions, to distinguish them from *closed-ended* or forced choice questions. There is a limit to the number of open-ended questions you can include in a quantitative survey, and so survey data generally suffer from a lack of detailed explanation about consumer behaviour and attitudes, and that is where qualitative research comes into its own.

Nowadays, a great many surveys are conducted using computer aided personal interviewing (CAPI) and computer aided telephone interviewing (CATI), instead of paper questionnaires. The interviewer's questions are prompted on a computer screen and the responses are keyed in directly to the computer. The advantage is that the analysis of the data can be produced more quickly than with paper questionnaires, where the responses have to go through another stage of being entered into the computer before analysis can begin.

Following the interviewing (*fieldwork*), the data from the questionnaires are processed and cross-analysed by demographics, attitude, and usage groups; the resulting analysis is produced in the form of tables of data and lists of open-ended responses which are subsequently organised (*coded*) into subjects. The research executive digs into the data in order to summarise it and find the conclusions that can be drawn from the study.

Most surveys are commissioned by a single client for a specific purpose; these are called *ad hoc* surveys. However, there are other more general kinds of quantitative surveys that you will encounter:

- *Syndicated studies*. These are specific to a market, but are shared between a number of clients.
- *Published surveys*. These you can buy off-the-shelf.
- *Omnibus surveys*. These are surveys covering a number of topics for different clients. The samples are usually nationally representative and composed of the general population. Omnibus surveys run on a weekly basis and you can 'buy' a number of questions, making it the most cost-effective way of asking a few questions of a large number of people. Omnibus studies are very useful at any stage of the advertising process, as they provide a 'cheap and cheerful' way to get quantitative answers to simple questions about almost anything (e.g. how many people have heard of my brand, how many people recognise a celebrity being considered for a campaign, how many people use hairspray, how many people go to rock concerts, etc). However, once you go above five or so questions it is worth considering an ad hoc study, as this might be cheaper.

Some caveats about quantitative research. Everyone has heard of the phrase 'lies, damned lies, and statistics' and it is worth pointing out that great care needs to be taken when interpreting any quantitative data. Sample sizes might be too small to be reliable, the questions might be badly worded or too leading, the data might be presented in a misleading way, or the analysis might be superficial and may not properly explain the findings. A good survey should tell a coherent story and 'make sense' in terms of what you already know. If it does not, it may be flawed. Using a reputable research agency will help avoid these problems. One way of gauging the reliability of data is to use *significance testing;* this is a simple statistical technique that can tell you how confident you can be that the results reflect reality.

Qualitative research as the name suggests, is concerned with the 'quality' rather than the 'quantity' of consumer responses to questions. It is a means of finding out not simply what people do, but why they do it. It is exploratory and diagnostic, and aims to get under the surface of consumer behaviour to find the underlying attitudes and motivations that cause them to behave the way they do. Qualitative research cannot provide numbers, but what it can do is to provide greater understanding of what people need, want, feel, and care about. It involves small samples of people who are not drawn scientifically (as with quantitative research), but who may be selected to represent particular demographic, usage, or attitude groups (e.g. students, or regular users of moisturiser, or people very clued up about financial services).

Qualitative research can be used for a number of reasons: on its own to inform the decision makers' understanding, if numbers are not required; in advance of a quantitative study, to help researchers decide what questions to ask and how to ask them; or alongside or after quantitative research, to help explain the data or to put flesh on the bones of the figures from the survey.

In qualitative research there is no structured questionnaire to be administered by an interviewer. Rather, a highly trained *moderator* conducts interviews using a flexible *topic guide*, and will probe issues that come up spontaneously during the interview as well as those predetermined by the client.

Research of this sort is almost invariably done face-to-face, and respondents are either interviewed individually or in small groups. The main types of qualitative research are:

- Individual *depth interviews* lasting an hour or more.
- *Group discussions* or *focus groups* generally with 5 to 8 respondents, lasting 1 or 2 hours, or extended groups lasting many hours.
- *Paired depth interviews*, with married couples, friendship pairs, two people with opposing views, etc.
- *Ethnography*, a recent development in qualitative research, where a moderator spends time in people's homes, living with them and observing their behaviour over several days. Although very time-consuming, this gets over the common problem in research that people are often not aware of what they do or why, and often post-rationalise their decisions.
- *Accompanied shopping*, where a respondent is accompanied by a moderator who conducts the interview while the respondent is doing her or his normal shopping.

The techniques used in qualitative research are largely drawn from those used in behavioural psychology. They are designed to elicit responses from consumers that they might normally find difficult to articulate or would normally be too polite or embarrassed to say out loud. They typically include *projective techniques* like picture interpretation, word association, sentence completion, cartoon speech bubble completion, or role-play and role reversal. *Stimulus* material is generally used to elicit (stimulate) responses – like picture boards, mood boards, colours, textures, sounds, and so on. The advertising agency will often be involved in preparing such material.

Respondents for qualitative research are *recruited* in advance by specialist agencies according to criteria laid down by the client and research agency; respondents are typically paid to attend. Given the very small number of people involved, the quality of the recruitment is critical to the value of this kind of research. The scale of a typical qualitative study would be 10–20 individual interviews or paired depths, and a minimum of four groups but sometimes as many as 20.

It is important for the quality of the discussion for the respondents to be in a relaxed and as normal a frame of mind as possible, so most qualitative research takes place in an informal setting, either in a recruiter's home or in a specially designed location. In order not to inhibit the respondents, observers are not usually present at these interviews. However, often clients and agencies like to hear what 'real' consumers have to say directly, not filtered through the interpretation of the moderator, and so it is increasingly common for group discussions in particular to take place in a *viewing facility* with a one-way mirror behind which the clients can sit and observe the proceedings.

Most qualitative research is tape or video recorded (with the respondent's permission), and subsequently analysed in detail by the moderator who will not only take note of what was said, but also who said it, what was not said, body language, the effect of group interaction, and so on, not just taking everything at its face value. Moderating a group discussion is an extremely skilled task; the analysis stage is very important in correctly interpreting the responses, and so attempts to get moderators to give their 'verdict' immediately after a group should be resisted. Similarly, consumer views will vary from group to group, so if you only observe one group, beware of drawing general conclusions.

Some caveats about qualitative research: the appeal of qualitative research is that it lets us hear 'real people' talking in their own words about their feelings and attitudes. It can be very seductive to believe that the opinion of one person, expressed powerfully, is therefore representative of the whole audience. While it is unlikely that her views are unique to her, without quantitative research you cannot be certain how many people in your audience share her views. In the same way, it is important to bear in mind when reading a qualitative debrief, that the findings describe the views of those present, and they are not necessarily representative of the population as a whole. You can gauge the *range* of attitudes from qualitative research but not the *number* of people who hold them: that needs quantitative research. It is also important to remember that the interpretation of qualitative research is necessarily subjective. Qualitative research generally costs less in total than a quantitative survey, and it can be more flexible and yield results faster, and so it can be tempting to use it instead of quantitative research, sometimes inappropriately.

14.4   The importance of the brief

In designing a research study there are many decisions that the research agency has to make: how many people to interview, what kinds of people, where to find them, which interview method to use, what questions to ask, how accurate the information has to be, how quickly are results needed – these are just some of the things they have to decide in order to design the best and most cost-effective method. So, in order to design a research study, we first need a clear and specific brief. Time spent up front on defining the issues and in thorough briefing will pay back: first, in terms of finding out what you wanted to know at a reasonable cost, and second, in enabling the researcher to provide insightful interpretation and useful conclusions.

The most common criticism of research is not that it is done badly from a technical point of view, but that it fails to tell us what we want to know. So, a good question whenever a research study is contemplated is 'What will we do with the information? What decisions do we want to make as a result of this study?' The study is more likely to deliver useful results if the researcher is fully informed about the background, what is already known, what the current hypotheses are, and so on. Keeping researchers in the dark to 'see what they come up with' is never a good strategy.

14.5   Where research fits into the advertising process

The process of advertising development can be represented in the planning cycle:

- First, the planner has to understand the situation of the brand and the issues facing it / opportunities / threats, etc., and agree with the client on the best strategy for achieving the brand's objectives.
- From this, the planner derives the role for advertising – what is it that *advertising* (in its broadest sense) can do to help achieve the brand strategy?
- Then, through a process of generating hypotheses and testing them, the planner arrives at a synthesis and identifies *the best* advertising strategy to achieve the brand's objectives; all this work forms the basis of the creative brief.
- Next, the creative team produces the campaign that will best communicate the strategy.
- Once the campaign has run, its effectiveness is evaluated in order to learn how to improve it going forward.

At every stage in this process, client and agency teams have to make decisions; research has a role to play at each stage in helping inform those decisions.

The Planning Cycle showing where research fits in

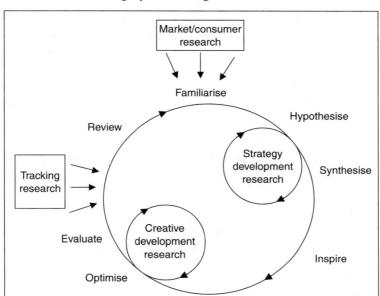

Figure 14.1 *How to plan advertising showing where research fits, adapted from M. T. Rainey*

Figure 14.1 describes the different stages of the planning cycle, and shows where research *can* play a part. It should be said that clients differ greatly in their approach to research. In some client organisations, especially the larger fmcg (fast-moving consumer goods) companies, research is deeply embedded in the culture, and is used at every point in the process. In these types of clients, the whole decision-making structure is driven by what 'research says' about a course of action, and there are protocols for which kinds of research should be done in which situation, even down to dictating which particular research companies may be used and action standards for proceeding. In other, more entrepreneurial organisations, decisions tend to be made more on the basis of experience and judgement, and research is only occasionally employed, most often to resolve a specific issue rather than as an integral part of the process. This same distinction can also be applied to advertising agencies, which can similarly be segmented by how much they value or rely on research. It is perhaps surprising, given the amounts of money involved, that much advertising is developed with little or no research input, and is run without being formally evaluated.

14.6   Types of research study used in advertising

There are many different kinds of market research study but here are the main ones you will come across in advertising. For simplicity, we have ordered them according to the stages of the advertising development process, though in practice they can, of course, overlap.

14.6.1   Familiarisation: Research that tells you about the market, your brand and its competitors, and the status of your brand in the consumer's mind

At the beginning of the advertising development process, the account team (principally the planner) does a great deal of work to familiarise themselves with the market, the brand, its competitors, and its consumers. Apart from factory or store visits, the great majority of this work relies on research – from published sources, ad hoc research done previously by the client, or research commissioned specifically for this campaign development by the client or agency. Taken together, the research and thinking done at this stage are designed to answer the question, 'Where are we now?'

The following studies are just some of the kinds of research that can be useful at this stage:

- Syndicated or published studies
- Consumer and retail panels
- Usage and attitude studies
- Segmentation studies
- Brand equity studies
- Customer satisfaction studies
- Product, packaging, promotion, and pricing studies.

Research into people's media consumption habits (what they read, how much TV they watch, etc.) is also 'consumer research' but is dealt with in detail in Chapter 13.

Most of this section describes the main types of ad hoc studies in use at this stage, but the first two – syndicated and panels – are more general types of research.

14.6.1.1   Syndicated or published studies

In many markets there are studies that are shared (or *syndicated*) between companies in the same sector, for instance, in cars and financial services. These provide useful background information on the size, shape, and trends in a market, but are less useful in examining in depth the situation of a particular brand.

There are also many *published* studies that can be purchased off-the-shelf by the client or agency that provides useful intelligence about what is going on in a market. In the retail industry, for example, Mintel publishes a whole range of studies about different retail sectors, covering the structure of companies, sales and profitability, numbers of outlets, and so on.

The published study that is perhaps most used in advertising is Target Group Index (TGI). This a survey of 25,000 households (vastly bigger than any normal research survey), which covers consumption and usage of virtually every consumer sector, full demographic and lifestyle data and media consumption habits. By cross-analysing the data, TGI shows the penetration (the percentage of people in the population who own/use it) and profile (the demographic and other characteristics of the people who own/use it) for every sector and for most large brands. A TGI analysis is always a good starting point when looking at any new market, for example, in a pitch situation when you have not had the benefit of the client's data.

14.6.1.2   *Consumer and retail panels and audits*

Panels and audits are a type of syndicated study, where the costs of data collection and analysis are shared by many clients.

> *Retail audits* measure brand sales, brand share, distribution, stock levels, and actual prices, at the individual store level and on a continuous basis. Audits are available for most fmcg brands that are sold in supermarkets and high street shops, but do not cover larger products or things that are sold through other outlets; for example: CTNs (confectioners, tobacconists, newsagents), petrol stations, and so forth.
>
> *Home audits* collect data from consumers directly, using a large representative panel of respondents who either complete a weekly diary of their purchases/consumption, or use a device to record the bar codes of their purchases. Data collected includes amount bought and price paid, from which it is possible to calculate market share. Again, these are mostly only available for fmcg brands, but there are also home audits for electrical goods, books, music – anything with a bar code on it. The data collected are linked with the demographics of the households in the panel to give a profile of the kinds of people who buy the different products and brands.
>
> *Some audit companies collect 'single source' data*; this combines the purchase/usage data with data on media consumption. Thus, direct links can be proven between advertising appearing on TV and immediate consequent purchase or consumption.

As well as the studies described above, in every market there is a great deal of other published information available, and it pays to do some thorough *desk research* to learn as much as possible before deciding to commission a new piece of consumer research.

The next studies are all specially commissioned by a single client to answer particular questions. They cover similar ground and it would be unusual to do them all.

14.6.1.3   Usage and attitude studies

Clients will commission a quantitative usage and attitude (U&A) survey either to supplement the rather 'dry' data from panels and audits, or where these are not available. A U&A will determine how many people are purchasers and users of a product sector and the brands within it. By comparing these people with the population as a whole in terms of their demographic and other characteristics, (age, social class, etc.), it is possible to construct a profile of the actual and potential market. In addition, such surveys also collect information on people's attitudes to the product and the brands in the market, how they use them, how they see them, how they differ. Given that these studies tend to be done on an ad hoc basis at a point in time, it is important to be aware of any seasonal influences in the market that might bias the results.

A U&A is usually done quantitatively, but it is also possible to get a good feel for a market using qualitative research. Using basic information from some of the other sources referred to here, a qualitative study can be designed to interview the main consumer groups about their brand usage and attitudes. Qualitative generally has the advantage of speed and cost, but you must bear in mind that it cannot tell you how many people hold the views identified – this needs quantitative research.

14.6.1.4   Segmentation studies

The consumers in any market can be segmented into sub-groups to define which of them is of interest to the brand's marketers. This can be done either by analysing data from a quantitative U&A, or by commissioning a special quantitative or qualitative segmentation study. A quantitative study surveys a large sample of buyers in a market and asks them questions about themselves – their demographic profile, the neighbourhood they live in, their lifestyle, life stage, attitudes, psychographics, needs/requirements from the product sector, their usage of and attitude towards the brands in the market, their media consumption habits, attitudes to advertising, and so on. Using statistical analysis, clusters of people who share the same characteristics are described, and those that are likely to be the best customers for the brand are identified. A qualitative segmentation study also identifies the characteristics of the segments, but the emphasis here is on providing more depth of understanding about the motivations and attitudes of particular segments, rather than their size.

14.6.1.5   Brand equity studies

This term is used to describe a range of one-off, qualitative or quantitative studies; their aim is to find out about the things that are special or unique about a brand that the brand 'owns' in the consumer's mind. Typically, these findings will be set in the context of competitors, and help to show where the best competitive advantage might lie for the brand.

The remaining two types of study are not commissioned specifically for use in advertising development, but may yield additional learning or insights about the brand's consumers.

14.6.1.6   Customer satisfaction studies

These are regular surveys of a brand's customers to find out whether they are satisfied with the product or service provided by the brand and, if not, what problems they have experienced. Information from these studies is used mostly to drive product or service improvements, but can also be used to identify real or perceived problems or misunderstandings that can be addressed through advertising.

14.6.1.7   Product, packaging, promotion, and pricing studies

Although not directly used in the development of advertising, much can be learned about the brand from studies the client has done previously on other parts of the marketing mix. Often, the issues facing the brand are more complex than can be solved by advertising alone. Learning from these studies can be invaluable in clearly identifying what it is that advertising can do.

Clearly, it is not necessary to carry out all of the studies above in order to complete this first stage of the advertising development process, and it would be unusual (though not unheard of) to have all of them on a single brand. But there must be sufficient information to enable the planner to have: a clear understanding of the issues facing the brand, the role of advertising, some thoughts on the target market, and some ideas about potential strategies, as input for the creative brief.

14.6.2   Strategy development: research that helps decide the best advertising strategy

From all the studies described above, we now have a very good grasp of our brand, its business problem, its market, its competitors, and our consumers, and we have identified how advertising can help achieve the brand's objectives. The next step is to decide what the advertising has to say or do to consumers and which consumers we should be talking to – in other words, the advertising strategy.

Arguably, the most important job of the planner is to define the advertising strategy, as it is this that forms the basis of the creative brief. There may be many possible routes to explore. Choosing between the different possibilities is a matter of judgement about which is likely to be the best way of achieving the brand's objectives. Research can aid our judgement by gauging consumer's response to the different alternatives. This is typically done using qualitative methods.

14.6.2.1   Strategy development research

The agency and client produce written expressions (*propositions*) of the various routes being investigated. These may be accompanied by pictures (*mood boards*) to try to bring the expressions to life and help consumers respond to them. They are shown to respondents, usually in group discussions. The moderator will probe for reactions to them, aiming to find out which seems to have the most potential to connect with consumers and to change their view of the brand in the desired direction.

There is also a quantitative version of this kind of research, called proposition testing. In this case, the written propositions are shown to a quantitative sample of respondents and their responses recorded in a structured questionnaire. This method is not much used nowadays, as it is regarded as too mechanistic a way of gauging response. Unless the proposition is unique or very new, a simple phrase or sentence without any creative content is rarely interesting enough to elicit a response.

14.6.3   Creative development: research that helps you develop advertising and decide which advertising to run

The art of advertising is to communicate the advertising strategy in a way that will have impact and that will create a relationship between the consumer and the brand. If someone simply faced the camera and read out your strategy, not many (any?) people would pay attention to it. What is needed is a creative idea to bring the strategy to life and carry the strategic message in a relevant and interesting way. This is easier said than done, and so a great deal of research is done on creative ideas to help develop them into successful communications.

14.6.3.1   Creative development research

This is qualitative research used to help develop advertising ideas from their very early stages of development until they are nearly finished. Rough advertising ideas are presented to relevant consumers in group discussions to gauge their potential. Various qualitative techniques are used by moderators to do this, but the most important ingredient is the skill and experience of the moderator, and how well they understand the advertising strategy, the creative ideas, and the intentions behind the creative work. Typically, these ideas will be shown to a minimum of four groups and usually more, depending on the different segments of the market to be covered.

There are many ways to present rough, unfinished advertising ideas, depending on the medium. For TV and cinema ideas:

- the moderator can simply read out the scripts, perhaps accompanied by some pictures of the setting or the celebrity to be used, etc;
- a tape recorded description of the ad with the dialogue/voice over can be played (*narrative tapes*);
- *storyboards* are put together that show the significant scenes and soundtrack of the commercial;
- an animated storyboard is filmed and played – in drawn form (*animatics*), or in photographic form (*photomatics*), or an idea of the commercial is conveyed using scenes from films or other ads (*stealomatics*).

For media other than TV or cinema, the form of presentation is simpler:

- Press advertising and posters are generally presented as rough drawing or photo mock-ups of the advertisement, with handwritten or typed copy and headline.
- Radio advertisements are presented as rough tapes, perhaps with an amateur voice-over and without the sound effects.
- Direct mail pieces are presented as concepts or mock-ups, often without the full copy.

To help consumers respond to the idea, it often helps to show it in its relevant media context, for example, in a poster shaped box, as a page in a newspaper, in a computer screen frame if it's an internet advertisement, and so on.

There is no ideal way to render an advertising idea; in order to research a range of ideas, they do not all have to be presented in the same way. The important thing is to choose the form of stimulus material that best communicates the idea that is in the creative team's mind and that best *stimulates* a response from consumers. The production of this stimulus material is the responsibility of the advertising agency.

The interpretation of consumer responses to rough advertising ideas is a highly skilled job. The moderator has to judge the strength and relevance of the consumer's response to an idea that is not yet an advertisement, but only an approximation to it. Clearly, there are some creative ideas that can be largely conveyed by a simple description (e.g. an advertisement with a simple plot and well-known characters), but there are many ideas that rely enormously on a brilliant comedy performance, a new production technique, a photographic style, a celebrity, etc. and the potential of these ideas cannot be fully assessed using rough material.

14.6.3.2 *Advertising pre-testing (also called copy testing)*

Once the advertising has been produced, clients may want to be sure that the finished advertisement conveys all the ideas and impressions intended, and will put the advertisement through a *pre-test*. Although by this stage the production money has already been spent, the media money (normally the larger part) has not, so it is still worth testing to *minimise* the risk of running an ineffective advertisement. However, the more useful research methods also aim to *maximise* effectiveness to the advertisement by understanding how it is working, diagnosing problems, and if necessary suggesting where changes might be made, even at this late stage. There are two ways of doing pre-testing: qualitative and quantitative.

> *Qualitative pre-testing* is generally done using group discussions. The practice is effectively the same as for creative development research, except that the emphasis is more on finding out whether the chosen advertisement will do its job, than on how to develop embryonic ideas to make them more effective. As with other qualitative research, the skill and experience of the moderator in interpreting consumer responses is vital to making the right decisions: after all, we are dealing with very small samples of respondents whose responses to the advertising are being 'hot-housed' in a group discussion (normal consumers do not generally discuss the merits of an ad for 2 hours with six strangers!). It is important to bear this in mind when relying on the results of qualitative pre-testing to make investment decisions.
>
> *Quantitative pre-testing* is done using a representative sample of consumers (usually 100–150). This approach is used when finished or nearly finished executions are available, and one has the advantage of providing the reassurance of numbers. Mostly the research is done in a central location (a *hall test*) and respondents are either pre-recruited or recruited off the street, though online is an increasingly used option for interviewing. In both, respondents are shown the test advertisements, disguised among others, and they are asked questions to elicit their responses.

There are many research methods favoured by different research companies to ascertain the likely effectiveness of the advertisements and there is a good deal of argument about the pros and cons of each. The ideal method is that which best meets your objectives and which best reflects your understanding of how the advertising is meant to work. Broadly, the different approaches can be summarised as follows:

- Some methods elicit responses to the advertisements then compare these with *norms* established over a large range of advertisements tested that have subsequently been deemed successful.
- Others ask purchase intention questions, show the advertisements in disguised conditions, and then ask the purchase intention again; the difference is related to the power of the advertising to 'persuade' consumers to buy the advertised brand.
- Others use two matched samples of consumers, show the advertisements to one but not to the other, and look at the difference between them.
- Others, believing that the most important job of the advertisement is to change impressions and commitment to the brand, ask brand questions before and after exposure to the advertising, as well as questions about their response to the advertising; and then use the brand shifts and diagnostics from the advertisement questions to measure the potential of the advertising.

Quantitative pre-testing is the subject of much anxiety in advertising agencies, as many of the techniques used are very mechanistic and based on historical notions of how advertising works, and so are not designed to measure contemporary creative advertising. In advertising agencies, quantitative pre-testing is regarded as a necessary evil rather than a useful tool for the development of advertising. However, in many client companies, especially the big fmcg companies, advertisements have to 'get through' a pre-test in order to get on air.

A caveat about quantitative pre-testing. An advertising pre-test is a way to test the potential of an advertisement or a campaign before it runs. Some research companies claim to be able to *predict* the success of an advertisement from a pre-test, but it is important to bear in mind that a pre-test is not real life, consumer responses to the advertisement are hot-housed in research, and so the best we can do is to evaluate its *potential* to have the desired effect.

A note about norms. When using norms derived from pre-tests, remember that these are simply measures of average performance over the cases that the research company has tested. Some context from other results is obviously useful, but care should be taken to find relevant cases for comparison.

14.6.4 Evaluation: research that tells you how well your advertising works

Once the advertisement or campaign has run, we need to evaluate the effect it has had. The client in particular will want to know if we have achieved our objectives. It is a good idea to think about how you will evaluate the campaign *before* the advertising has run, so that you can put in place the right measurement tools. One of the best ways to learn about the advertising evaluation method is to read some of the award winning case studies from the IPA Advertising Effectiveness Awards. These provide best practice models for how to measure the value of advertising.

In most markets, the ultimate measure of success will be an increase in the brand's sales or share. The consumer audits and panels referred to earlier can be used to establish this. However, this information is not always available, or there is a long time lag before it appears, or it is difficult to interpret since many things influence a brand's sales, not just advertising. Also, we not only want to know *if* we achieved our desired objectives, but *how* we achieved them, so we can learn for the future. The only way to do this is to speak directly to consumers. Consumer research is used to measure changes in the consumer's mind and in their behaviour that we think would occur if the advertising were working as intended. The most common type of research is a 'tracking study' (literally, an ongoing survey that 'tracks' people's response to the advertising over time).

14.6.4.1   *Advertising and brand tracking studies (also called campaign evaluation)*

These are quantitative surveys that measure the performance of the advertising (and that of its competitors) among its target audience. Different research companies each have their own theories about what should be measured to prove an ad's effectiveness, but the most commonly used measures are:

- how many people have seen the advertising? (*ad awareness / stand out*);
- is it correctly associated with the brand? (*branding*);
- what can they recall about the content? (*recall*);
- what messages or associations or impressions did they take out from the advertising? *(communication / take-out);*
- what was their response to the advertising – was the message believed, was it enjoyable or engaging, was it distinctive? *(ad response)* ;
- what was it about the ad that produced that response? (*diagnostics*);
- did the advertising have an effect on their beliefs or impressions about the brand *(brand response)* or their level of *commitment* to the brand, or on their *purchase intention*?
- in order to learn how well our advertising is working in the competitive context, and to disguise our interest in one particular brand from the consumer, questions are asked about competitive brands as well.

It is worth noting that, as with pre-testing, there are significant debates about some of these measures.

- *Ad awareness*: Some argue that this is a key measure of advertising effectiveness, but others think it is only one step to effectiveness and is mainly a function of the weight put behind the advertising, and the cut through of the execution.
- *Ad recall*: There is much debate in advertising research circles whether being able to recall the content of an advertisement is a relevant indicator of effectiveness, since much advertising is consumed at low levels of active consciousness. Advertising that is not recalled directly can still work.
- *Liking*: Although it can be important for some campaigns that the advertising is liked (baby products perhaps), it is not a universally applicable measure of effectiveness. For example, campaigns that aim to deter people from drink driving are seldom 'liked' but have been effective.
- *Brand measures versus advertising measures*: There are similar debates about the amount of emphasis placed in the research on brand measures; some researchers feel strongly that since the ultimate aim of the advertising is to influence people's impressions of the brand and their commitment to it, then it is essential to measure these brand effects if we are to judge its effectiveness. Advertising measures alone are not sufficient – people may enjoy our advertising, but take nothing of value out of it about our brand.

The frequency of tracking studies varies according to what is needed or can be afforded. They can be *continuous* (interviews are done every week throughout the year, so as to capture all the advertising activity, for both our brand and competitors); *semi-continuous* (interviewing every week during periods of heavy advertising activity, but less frequently during the rest of the year); or done immediately before and after (*pre-and-post*) a particular burst of advertising.

Generally speaking, tracking studies (because they are expensive to run) tend to focus on the major advertising media like TV, radio, press, and posters, but with the growth in multi-media schedules, techniques have been developed also to measure the effectiveness of sales promotion, direct marketing, sponsorship, and public relations.

14.6.4.2   *Direct response measurement*

Many advertisements contain some form of direct response mechanism – a telephone number, a website address, or a postal address – that is designed to encourage the consumer to contact the client company (e.g., to request further information or a brochure, to register for a special offer, to arrange a visit).

One way of assessing the success of this kind of advertising is to count the number of contacts made by consumers. Although, strictly speaking, this is not 'consumer research', it is nevertheless a way to evaluate this kind of advertising. If we wanted to learn more about *how* the advertising achieved its effects, we would need to use quantitative or qualitative research to talk directly to consumers who did and did not respond.

14.6.4.3　*Econometric modelling*

Strictly speaking, this is not consumer research but an advanced statistical analysis technique that describes the relationship between a complex series of variables. To build a model, the analyst collects a huge amount of historical data, and builds up a picture of the different variables that make up the total sales of the brand (distribution, price, economic growth, population trends, the weather, advertising spend, brand commitment, promotions, etc. – everything that is likely to affect the brand's sales). Econometric techniques are then used to disentangle all the different influences on sales.

Its use in advertising is, typically, to quantify the contribution of advertising to sales in the short and longer term, and to estimate whether the amount spent on advertising paid back in profits. Although it is the best possible tool with which to evaluate advertising's contribution, it is used less often than it might be as it relies on the existence of very detailed data over a period of 2–3 years, about all the variables in the model, and this is often not available.

14.7　Summary of consumer research methods and their application to advertising

Type of research	Quantitative	Qualitative	What does it tell you
1. Familiarisation			
Syndicated and published studies	✓	✓	General background information on the market, brands, and consumers
Consumer and retail panels	✓		Brand sales and share, distribution, prices, who buys what and how much
Usage and attitude studies	✓	✓	Consumer profiles, segmentation, product and brand usage and attitudes
Segmentation studies	✓	✓	How the market segments into sub-groups and their characteristics
Brand equity studies	✓	✓	What is special or unique about the brands in the market
2. Strategy Development			
Strategy development research	✓	✓	Which strategic route will be the best strategy for the brand

3. Creative Development

Creative development research	✓		How different creative ideas work Which idea will work best How to maximise its effectiveness
Advertising pre-Testing	✓	✓	Whether the chosen ad will work How to maximise its effectiveness

4. Evaluation

Advertising and brand tracking	✓	✓	Whether and how the advertising is achieving its objectives
Econometric modeling	✓		Quantifies the contribution of advertising to sales Disentangles all the variables that affect sales

14.8   Summary

In this chapter:

- We saw that marketing practice requires many decisions to be taken and we can reduce the risk in these decisions by adding to our body of knowledge through research.
- Qualitative research was described that looks into attitudes and behaviours of the population at large through researching samples from a target market. Syndicated studies, published surveys, and omnibus surveys were described.
- Qualitative research was described as being concerned with the 'quality' of consumer responses – finding out why people do what they do. In-depth interviews, focus groups, accompanied shopping, and the recently developed ethnography were discussed.
- A wide range of different types of consumer research were outlined looking at the place of those studies in the development, testing, and evaluation of advertising.

Further reading

Cassell, A.P.G. *How to Plan Advertising*, 1997.
The Research Buyers Guide, Market Research Society, published annually.
Admap Ad-tracking Buyers Guide, published annually.
Admap Pre-testing Buyers Guide, published annually.
Advertising Works, Volumes 1–12, the collected IPA Ad Effectiveness Awards papers, published by WARC.

15 Business-to-Business Advertising

Richard Jeans and Gareth Richards

Learning outcomes

By the end of this chapter you will:

- Recognise that there are major differences between consumer and business marketing.
- See that the action / reaction time scales to business marketing communications are such that direct sales rarely come from the activity.
- Understand the complexity of business-to-business markets and see the importance of both technology and face-to-face dialogue.
- Consider a model to illustrate business marketing communications and review some of its shortcomings.

15.1 A note on nomenclature

The title of this book is *The Practice of Advertising*, and it is still common to refer to 'business-to-business advertising' as distinct from the 'consumer' equivalent. Indeed, most business-to-business agencies would still refer to themselves as advertising agencies. But over the last few years, several factors have combined to diminish the role of pure above-the-line business-to-business advertising. Business marketers have widely adopted database-based marketing. They recognise the importance of an integrated through-the-line approach and the key role of the Internet.

It is still significant, of course, but its role is now played very much as part of a marketing communications mix (see Section 15.7 below). Most of this chapter, therefore, will talk about business-to-business 'marketing communications' or, for convenience, business marcoms. Similarly, when we do want to talk about above-the-line advertising, we shall call it just business advertising.

15.2   Why business marcoms is different

Table 15.1 includes enough examples to make it clear that business marcoms is different, and these differences are the key to the way a business marcoms strategy is arrived at.

However, as with any area of marcoms, the boundaries around business marcoms are somewhat blurred. Corporate marcoms may overlap with it. The role of corporate marcoms is often to influence financial commentators, business opinion formers, or potential employees rather than to sell products. But undoubtedly such brand-building activity will also generate awareness and reassurance among potential customers.

'Channels' marcoms – marcoms to companies at various levels in the distribution chain – certainly overlaps. Indeed, for a long time business marcoms

Table 15.1   *The significant differences between business and consumer marcoms*

Consumer marketing	Business marketing
Buying decisions often taken by single person (child, mother, head of household)	Buying decisions typically involve a complex decision-making unit
Buyer is spending own money	Buyer is spending corporate money
Comparatively small sums involved (one house or car usually largest)	Sums may be astronomical (Concorde, aircraft carrier)
Markets are typically comparatively large, and to a degree homogeneous, buying products in large numbers (tubes of toothpaste)	Markets may be small, highly segmented, and buying in small numbers (corporate computer solution, fork-lift trucks)
Comparatively short buying cycles – often instant, or 'impulse'	Buying cycles may be months or years (telephone exchange)
Brand and immediate / fashion appeal are very important; risks in getting a purchase wrong are not crushing	Model is 'considered purchase' – though brand-based and emotional decisions are common in real life; results of selecting wrong solution potentially catastrophic (railway signalling, air traffic control)
Products are typically fairly simple (soap, food)	Products are typically complex or even dauntingly high-tech (weapons system, ASICs)
Marcoms may be almost information-free; humour and emotion may be appropriate	Successful marcoms typically information-rich
Broadcast and mass media suitable	Specialist media usually more cost-effective
Face-to-face sales comparatively unusual	Initial sale typically face-to-face

was referred to as 'trade' or 'trade and technical advertising'. (The 'technical' side eventually split off to generate 'industrial' advertising'.)

In some cases business marketers may even set out to talk directly to consumers as part of their strategy, using consumer advertising techniques, even though these consumers are not direct customers of the company's products. This may occur when the company is manufacturing 'ingredient' products that are then incorporated into other products that are finally sold on to the consumer (such as a PC processor or a waterproof fabric). The objective is usually to generate consumer preference (consumer 'pull') for the ingredient brand, and so persuade manufacturers (the company's real customers) to include it in their products in favour of rival ingredients. The outcome may be consumer tolerance of a price premium for products that contain the company's branded ingredient.

15.3   Business marcoms seldom sets out to generate a sale directly

However, exceptions immediately spring to mind. In recent years, there have been several successful campaigns to sell computers and office equipment 'off the page', for example – though even these campaigns have often included database marketing, comprehensive catalogue production, and the other 'through-the-line' or 'integrated' activities typical of business marcoms.

But in general, business marcoms is still based, usually rightly, on the assumption that at least the initial sale is made by some sort of face-to-face contact between supplier and buyer.

There are several reasons for this. Business products are often of high capital value, in a way that only houses and cars regularly are in the consumer world (and few of us would buy a house or car without some face-to-face contact). Business products frequently incorporate high or complex technology, which needs explanation, discussion, and demonstration. Increasingly, business products are 'systems' – packages of functionality which can or must be customised to match a customer's applications. Business products above a certain level of cost (which may be quite low) tend to be bought by committees – project groups representing the financial, technological, and business interests of the buying organisation combined in a 'decision-making unit'.

The role of marcoms in these circumstances is naturally different from its role in selling low-cost, low-tech, mass-produced goods to individuals with the power, inclination, and budget to make their own buying decisions. Impulse buying is far from unknown in business purchasing, but it is usually regarded as unprofessional.

In these circumstances, the role of business marcoms is inextricably linked with the role of the salesman. A salesman's time, and the support he needs, are very expensive. Anything that can be done to reduce the number of 'calls' or increase the cost-effectiveness of each call should be done. Business marcoms can usually do most.

The role of business marcoms may be regarded as not to generate a sale, but to reduce the cost of a sale.

15.4 Information is needed for a rational market

The traditional model for the business market is that it buys rationally. Many advertisers feel that their prospects are resistant to any attempt to persuade, rather than simply inform. But as recession has driven consumer agencies to hunt business of any kind, they have made overtures to the business market. Similarly, when the scale of business in areas such as IT and telecoms has grown dramatically, companies in those sectors have sought agencies with the size and multinational presence to support them – typically consumer agencies.

Their traditional stock-in-trade being creativity as a tool in persuasion, consumer agencies have suggested that the rationality of the market has been greatly over-rated, and that 'people are all the same, really'; that individuals in their role as business buyers respond to brands in the same way as they do in their consumer role.

Business marcoms has become one of the great battlegrounds in the war over the relative importance of facts and feelings – the role of the 'business brand'. It is a phoney war.

Probably the worst sin business marcoms can commit is to be confusing. To transmit and support propositions with absolute clarity is a prerequisite.

The next in line as a sin is dullness. Marcoms is boring if it is irrelevant (however brilliant). The question, of course, is what does the business market find dull? This is not always an easy question to answer. In a mature market packed with 'me-too' products, the returns on information are low. In a fast-changing market, receptive to product innovation, the returns on information about a valuable new product are high – but times to market are now so short and technological leapfrog so rapid that building a business on product differentiation is often risky.

As rival products are increasingly variants of each other, emotion plays a higher part in business buying decisions – and is often the decider when a buyer has to make a final choice from a short list. The brand may swing the decision – but so may the personality of the salesman (which can be regarded as a component of the brand).

Nevertheless, in general, it is probably still true that in business marcoms relevant information has the edge over entertainment. Certainly, this will be the case as we get closer and closer to the decision-making point. The entertainment content of the bid documents for a telephone exchange or an oil rig contract should be minimal, whereas in the choice of a hamburger joint to visit – or even of a car – entertainment will play a part through to the decision, and beyond.

*It is always wise to assume that business buyers are looking for information –
though their decisions may not be based on it exclusively.*

15.5   The technology can be a nightmare

Before information can be transmitted, it has to be absorbed and understood.
This is a very special difficulty for business marcoms people.

It takes years to learn how to communicate with force and clarity. It also
often takes an 'arts' education.

However, it can also take years to understand the technologies of business
products – the high-tech products of the communications age, or the medium-
tech products of oil rigs, building components, or industrial gases.

There are traps even at the low-tech end. (When your copier jams, for example, it is probably the fault of the paper you are using, not the copier: its
'runnability', which may, or may not, be related to 'clumping' in its fibre
structure.)

It is possible for a communicator to bluff, for a while – to form incompre-
hensible words into sentences which mean something to someone who actually
does understand the words. But such communication is hollow at its heart.
It may have a spurious clarity, but in the end, it will lack force.

*The search for people who understand temperature and communicate warmth
is never-ending.*

15.6   In business marcoms, lunch is a medium

Business marcoms is differentiated from consumer advertising as much by its
media as anything else. Consumer media are not closed to it: TV, radio,
posters, and the national press are all used extensively.

The business press is a natural medium for it – particularly for the umbrella
brand and corporate campaigns.

It also has available a range of targeted journals (known as 'trade' or 'specialist' press) which consumer publications simply cannot match: some genuinely refined segmentation can be achieved in some product areas. Most of
these target specific industries such as agriculture, telecoms, manufacturing
equipment, and so on, but some focus on individual job functions across industries such as financial directors or facilities managers.

Most of these journals are available by subscription or controlled-circulation,
and most publishers will make available subscriber lists for direct mail or database-based marcoms. Again, the refinement of these lists is considerable, and it
is often possible to buy lists very close to the profile of a particular target market. Journals' lists can often be supplemented by well-documented lists from
brokers.

However, it is worth noting that these specialist journals have been badly hit by the rise in the use of the Web, which now carries the sort of product information for which the specialist press used to be the natural home. Also, the ability to directly generate sales leads has always been a major strength of the specialist press and this has declined as response generation has moved online. As marketers have seen response figures fall, they have questioned the value of specialist press advertising and reduced spend in this area. The effect has been a consolidation of journals, with the emergence of clear leaders in many sectors. These are well read with strong circulations and high-quality editorials.

Online advertising also has a place in many business marcoms programmes. Most national press, business press, and many specialist press publishers offer online websites alongside their offline publications and these can be effective channels for business advertisers. They are supplemented by purely online business websites, although these suffered badly with the dotcom crash of the early 2000s. Search engine sites are another valuable medium.

The mainstay of online advertising has been the 'banner ad' or variations of it. But as click-through rates for banner ads have fallen, targeting has become more sophisticated through techniques such as sponsorship of search engine keywords (where specific advertisements are served according to the keywords entered into the search engine). There is also greater interest in the broader sponsorship and branding of relevant sections of websites.

Exhibitions have waxed and waned in popularity, and seem to be waxing in the early 2000s as marketers particularly value opportunities to get in front of customers during economic downturns. They have changed their profile: big block-buster shows still happen in many sectors, but one of the areas of success is the smaller, more closely targeted show, where the capital costs of exhibiting are lower, and the quality and relevance of the audience potentially much greater.

There has been a huge growth in the conferences and seminars business, sometimes associated with exhibitions, sometimes not. Though they come and go, and some are of very doubtful value, conferences and seminars are certainly a medium, and should be budgeted for in any marcoms plan.

Electronic media have perhaps made more headway in business marcoms than in consumer, in two areas – database-based marketing and the Internet.

Database-based marketing is a natural for business advertisers: the target audiences are limited in number, the individuals are often known to sales forces or can be built up by desk research or responses to other communication, and the hunger for relevant information on business products is unquenchable. Setting up and managing a database is difficult and time-consuming (and consequently not cheap), but no activity is so immediately rewarding. Increasingly, business prospects and customers expect to be on the supplier's database, and they will continue to force the growth of the medium.

The database can be used to build relationships with customers and prospects through direct mail, telemarketing, or e-mail. And the more that is known about the targets, the better the relationship that can be built. Information can be added to the contact data about the target company itself; its size, the nature of its business, what products and services it uses, the life cycle of its installed equipment, and so on. By adding to the data, the communication can be increasingly personalised – what is said, how it is said, what offers are made and when.

With increasing tailoring and segmentation comes increasing complexity that can only really be managed by the use of computer software known as CRM (customer relationship management) systems.

The data can also be used for profiling. By profiling a customer database across different parameters marketers can hunt for similar profiles in a database of non-customers. These may represent the most likely future prospects. And if it is known what messages have produced the best results with an existing customer profile, maybe that message will be the most relevant to a similar profile of non-customers. Similar work can be done to cross-sell and up-sell products to existing customers, or to win back lapsed ones.

The Internet has become central to business marketing in sectors where internet penetration is high (and there are very few where it is not). Few companies are without websites giving information about their products and services, but this is the tip of the iceberg. Enlightened business marketers offer fully interactive sites which make available value-added information and services to prospects and customers in exchange for registering their details. This can be used for prospect profiling and to start building a relationship. Visitors may give permission for regular e-mail communication that can be highly tailored at very low cost.

There can be elaborate restricted-access areas (extranets) for certain users. Companies can use them to manage relationships with partners or supply chains. Existing customers can use them to download documentation, software upgrades, directly purchase renewables (printing ink, spare parts, etc.), and so on.

All marcoms can drive responses to the website to provide access to further information and (hopefully) the start of a dialogue. Prospects can now download response literature which was previously sent to them by mail. Apart from the speed of response and ease of management, fulfilment costs are dramatically reduced. And by monitoring the sources of the responses, marketers can make sure that all marcoms activities are truly accountable.

For a time it was predicted that the availability of literature online would soon remove the requirement for printed material, but this has not been the case. Printed product brochures, application brochures, case histories, specification sheets, and so on are still seen as an important component in nurturing a prospect through to a sale. Similarly, customer magazines published by advertisers continue to proliferate and in many cases also carry advertising from unrelated and non-competitive companies.

And just as material is needed to communicate with prospects and customers, so material must be produced to communicate with the sales channel itself: instructional pieces that explain sales strategies and key sales messages, and motivational pieces that announce the arrival of new products and marketing initiatives. These sit alongside sales tools themselves: sales aids and presentations that support the face-to-face sale.

Today, all of these activities are likely to be bound together by a 'corporate identity programme' implemented on everything from factory overalls through signage to letterheads and advertisements.

And then there's lunch. Wise companies increasingly recognise that lunch (or something like it) is a medium, particularly for business marcoms, and control the messages communicated at it, by comprehensive internal briefings (or even scripts).

Lunch may seem a long way from advertising, but its inclusion dramatises the very point that in the business environment advertising, paid above-the-line advertising, is not, and cannot be seen as, some stand-alone activity.

The best results come when any medium is seen as just one element in a through-the-line, or integrated, set of activities.

15.7   A model for the business marcoms mix

It is probably fair to say that the through-the-line concept was established earlier, and is more strongly rooted, in business marketing than in consumer advertising. (See Chapter 3)

The model is a mix, not a mess. Each medium on the menu has its own role, and supports or is supported by other media (see Chart 15.1).

Chart 15.1 tracks what is planned as an inexorable progress towards a successful face-to-face sales presentation for, say, the supply of a dozen container lift trucks to an international distribution hub – a big order!

The model takes the members of the decision-making unit gently from unawareness to awareness, from awareness to acceptance, from acceptance to preference, and then insistence, and finally to reassurance after purchase – and a predisposition to re-order.

The campaign starts with business press advertising, to establish the company as reputable, solid, well financed, here to stay – and most of all, to 'get the name across'. (This is the oldest of advertising objectives, sometimes expressed as 'keeping the name in front of the public', and sounds naive today. Oddly enough, it is not: people do not buy from a company they have never heard of.)

At the same time (why not?) the products themselves are 'exposed' in the specialist press, and their features and benefits are spelled out. Online advertising runs alongside the offline campaign.

Chart 15.1 *The role of each medium progressing towards a successful sale*

	Unawareness	Awareness	Acceptance	Preference	Insistence	Reassurance
Business Press ads		➤				▷
Trade Press ads		➤				▷
Online ads		➤	➤			➤
PR/editorials		➤	➤			➤
Website		⇨	➤	⇨		▷
DBM¹/CRM²lit offers		⇨	➤	⇨		▷
DBM/CRM journals		⇨	➤	➤		➤
DBM/CRM cases			➤	➤	⇨	➤
Literature			➤	➤	⇨	▷
Exhibitions		⇨	➤	➤		▷
Seminars		⇨	➤	➤	⇨	➤
Face-to-face		⇨	➤	➤	⇨	➤
Offers				➤	➤	
Sales Promotion		⇨	⇨	⇨		
	Attention	Interest	Desire	Conviction	Action	Repeat

➤ Strong contribution   ⇨ Support contribution

[1] Database Marketing
[2] Customer Relationship Management

Press and public relations support the advertising and, because of the credibility of editorial coverage, nudge the products towards acceptance.

So far the attack has been a broadside – very general in the business press, and fairly general in the specialist press and online. We must hope that the advertiser has been assiduously collecting, qualifying, and recording enquiries for information, so that the right names can be added to the database of prospects. Some will have added themselves, by visiting the website and registering their information.

The move to the database-based activities dramatically sharpens the aim of the campaign. Now, only people who have shown interest and have been qualified as fit and proper to have that interest satisfied are targets. The dialogue may be online or offline or a mixture of both. Literature offers build up their acceptance of the trucks. Newsletters which can explore the design principles and performance of the trucks, handle case histories, and reinforce the strength of the company and the brand can maintain and enhance the market's perception at regular intervals. Case histories can be reprinted and widely distributed.

Effective as all this activity may be, nothing, of course, is as good as seeing and driving a truck. Exhibitions allow some hands-on experience (and gather more database names), and seminars – open days on the test track, say – allow not only greater familiarity but opportunities to discuss customisation, pricing, delivery, and so on.

And then there is lunch (called face-to-face on the model). Throughout this phase, the objective is to build preference – to pre-sell the trucks as far as possible.

The outcome, of course, when the offer finally goes in, can be nothing but insistence: an order. And then, assuming that activities continue, reassurance that the right buying decision has been made, and frequent and lucrative re-orders.

Both the model and the commentary are to some extent naive. There are other media which are not included – most notably, sponsorship and telemarketing. And such an orderly sequence of events may be difficult to arrange. Furthermore, in marketing capital goods at least, the time scales may be very long – years, perhaps, for a new telephone network, not months or quarters – and given the current project, rather than campaign, thinking, such a complete programme might now call for superhuman patience and control.

Nevertheless, the model helps to show the individual roles of particular media as activities, and it offers a logic for picking a particular route through the network of paths on offer. It shows that advertising, in its narrowest definition, can only do part of the job of business marketing communications – the buying decisions on battleships are not based on reading advertisements. And some such model does underlie much of the planning of such campaigns as there are.

Unawareness. Awareness. Acceptance. Preference. Insistence. Reassurance.

An illustration

Many areas of the UK, formerly prosperous with heavy smoke-stack industry, are trying to reinvent themselves in the new UK environment of service industries and skilled assembly.

In one such area in the North, five small boroughs decided to collaborate and pool some modest funds to pay for a small marketing team and a marcoms campaign to attract inward investment from other areas of the UK. The team employed an outside marcoms consultancy.

The consultancy recommended and implemented:

- qualitative and quantitative research into awareness of the area by hypothesised typical target companies, into criteria (e.g. range, size, cost, condition of sites; logistics; workforce availability and quality; financial incentives available; etc.) that might induce them to move, and into the general propensity to move
- SWOT research in the area itself, to identify its competitive strengths
- analysis to match strengths against criteria, and segment the market by type of business and relevant strengths
- comprehensive reports built on market research
- targeted direct marketing to DMU members in one segment at a time, with faxback response mechanism and using bought-in databases to build lists, highlighting relevant strengths and offering relevant reports
- development of internal database of intermediaries (estate agencies, consultancies, developers, etc.)
- simultaneous direct marketing to intermediaries every time targeted direct marketing sent out
- support PR (often built on the results of the market research).

Web presence including interactive site search for registered visitors.

Targeting was very rigorous – a typical shot might include several different letters highlighting different benefits to, for example, plant managers, financial directors, and marketing managers, identified as relevant DMU members.

Repeated over several years, highlighting different strengths and targeted at different industries and businesses, a total marcoms expenditure of around £850,000 generated £270 m of inward investment, and brought in over 100 projects creating some 10,000 jobs. Overall awareness in the relevant markets of this formerly almost unknown area is now very high – it is usually quoted in the top two or three of areas seeking inward investment.

Research + Product knowledge + Detailed segmentation and identification of markets + Persistence = High return on investment.

15.8   Some threats to the model

15.8.1   Project management is replacing campaign planning

Substantial FMCG advertisers have for a long time planned campaigns with a duration of many months, or even years. With so large a market to address, so many sales to make, such comparatively small returns on each unit sale, long-term thinking is essential. The importance of the brand has also tended to support extended campaign planning.

Retailers have also tended to think long term, and recently, of course, retailers have themselves attached great importance to their companies' brands, and to own-branding of products.

Mail-order off-the-page advertisers have tended to think differently. Though they run long-life campaigns for products that continue to sell, they are used to the idea that they may have to change products frequently, scrap ads for products which do not sell, and test and measure very accurately and rapidly. The company brand has some importance, but product branding has been generally unimportant.

Business advertisers used to align themselves to a degree with the FMCG approach. Central advertising departments were inclined to combine individual product campaigns into one overall year-by-year advertising campaign. This was not particularly to support or protect a brand: it was usually an attempt to rationalise expenditure, and make sure that each product or product line got its fair share of the year's budget.

Two things have combined to break up this pattern. The first is the rise of the product or project unit; and the second is the recessions of the early 1990s and 2000s. The business unit tends to be achieving short-term targets: its task is to get sales now. Any long-term marcoms is reserved for an umbrella corporate (brand) campaign. The business unit is also focused on a limited product range or market sector. As a result, it will tend to think in terms of a set of finite activities with an immediate pay-off – a set of projects, rather than a campaign.

Recession has made this sort of thinking even more necessary. This year's survival may literally depend on this quarter's sales.

So far, so understandable (if frequently short-sighted). What is less fortunate has been the rise of 'procurement'. Partly driven by the imposition of management consultancy analyses, the 'supply' of marcoms has often become aligned with the supply of any other goods and services. Purchase orders have replaced contracts, as projects have replaced campaigns, and the traditional marketing partnership relationship has been replaced by a buyer–seller relationship. Accountancy logic has replaced marcoms logic. It does no harm for marcoms to be subjected to ROI criteria, but procurement managers are often not equipped to understand the organic and collaborative nature of marcoms, and the result is disillusion – on both sides.

As a result, the traditional campaign-planning approach has been replaced by a series of discrete projects, often running concurrently.

In many companies, coordinating and integrating these projects has become a major problem.

15.8.2   In absolute terms, business marcoms budgets are smaller

Whether or not they should be, they generally are. Smaller than what? Smaller than consumer advertising budgets to do jobs of similar size or importance to the advertiser – a fact that largely reflects the size of the market, and the return on the marcoms investment. The budget for a national TV campaign is necessarily large – but probably wasted if the market consists of a few thousand machine-tool buyers.

It sharpens the need for accountability: when budgets are small, nothing can be wasted. At the same time, it may simply not allow for anything other than the simplest formal measurement techniques. Sadly, it may also inhibit experiment and innovation: small budgets cannot support 'take-a-chance' activities.

This naturally has an impact on the information / entertainment discussion – but in fact affects every part of business marcoms. In recruiting, for example, it means that businesses or agencies may be looking for special sorts of people. There will be an emphasis on productivity, flexibility, resourcefulness, negotiating ability, intellectual speed, literacy, and numeracy.

The difference between consumer and business budgets is not simply one of scale. It becomes one of kind. Business marcoms people learn to operate within these restrictions as a permanent condition.

15.8.3   The business advertiser / agency relationship

If business marcoms is different in its substance, its subjects, and its structure, there is a fair chance that it is going to be different in its suppliers and relationships.

Certainly, at first glance it seems unlikely that you can take the whole can of worms, with its complex technology, small budget, multiple purchasing-decision teams, and progressive through-the-line campaign structures, and simply dump it on the desk in a consumer advertising agency.

Surely, the argument runs (and has run for years), you need a rather specialised communications consultancy to handle it all properly. In fact, it is not as simple as that. Agencies vary greatly in their capability, and advertisers in their needs.

One of the attractive things about business advertising is that the rational nature of much of its communications and the international commonality of features and benefits of many of the products make a single regional or global approach – and consequently a regional or global budget – appropriate.

A large global company with a large global market, such as an airline, may be targeting business customers – but may be targeting millions of them, worldwide. Its messages are not particularly technological, and its budget may be attractive to a big, global consumer agency.

Such a business has very little in common with a high-tech garage start-up – yet both are clearly in the business of business-to-business advertising.

In other words, the differences described above are not evenly distributed. Some businesses exhibit more of them, some fewer. Companies at one end of the spectrum will need very different marcoms suppliers from companies at the other.

Large businesses are often collections of smaller businesses, some of which may be business-to-business businesses. There may be a need for agencies and consultancies at every level. In fact, it is probably true that provided enough budget is left in any fragment to be able to attract high-quality suppliers, and provided the fragment has enough skills to select and manage wisely (or enough sense to get help elsewhere in the organisation), and provided there is a central resource within the advertiser strong enough to safeguard the brand, fragmentation is almost an objective. There is no reason why segmentation should apply to markets, and not to suppliers. The economies of purchasing scale made by centralising will probably not outweigh the added value of specialist attention achievable by fragmentation. And there is yet another factor to complicate the process. In the information age, both information and information technology are widely distributed. In information-orientated marcoms – business marcoms – there is a strong temptation for advertisers to take up do-it-yourself. This trend, too, has been driven by recession: it is cheaper to buy a desktop publishing system or some web-design software than to hire an agency.

Almost certainly, this is a trend to disaster. Every company's second business may be publishing, but that doesn't mean that every company should become a publisher. Information may be widely distributed, but the skills to distribute it are not. Literacy is in notoriously short supply. Some marketing communications activities can sensibly be handled internally, and will probably become a natural part of many companies' marcoms activities. But very few companies can or should maintain in-house, full-time, fully-qualified, communications planners and implementers in the numbers and depth required to handle all their communications needs.

15.9   A golden age for business advertising

Business advertising has always been differentiated and highly competent.

The developments of the last decade have sharpened the skills, focused the minds, and expanded the range of techniques of business advertisers. The unquestioned practices of half a century have disappeared and choice has become wider and more refined. Advertisers can find a wide range of eager specialists to work for (and increasingly with) them. Practitioners can target their skills more and more precisely, and find qualified, professional buyers among advertisers.

And as database-based techniques and interactive communications continue to play a central role in marcoms programmes, the business buyer is at last finding his rightful place as an equal third member of the marketing communications triangle.

15.10   Summary

In this chapter:

• We have seen stark contrasts between consumer advertising and business-to-business advertising and that in business markets a thorough integrated marketing communications (marcoms) plan is often considered rather than advertising on its own.

- We have also seen that few, if any, business marcoms activities lead to a direct sale further reinforcing the need for integrated marketing.
- It has been made clear that the complexity of business-to-business markets means that the importance of both technology and face-to-face dialogue is paramount.
- A model to illustrate business marketing communications has been put forward and some of its shortcomings have been reviewed including the fact that project management is replacing campaign planning, budgets are less, and that there is a differing advertiser/agency relationship.

16   Services Advertising

Richard K. Warren

Learning outcomes

By the end of this chapter you will:

- See that advertising services are closely linked to the people in the organisation that provides those services.
- Note that as with all other advertising, it will follow the same precepts as other advertising. However, the advertising of services must be consistent with customers' experience of using those services.
- Review the changes at the Halifax Bank that illustrate the key facets of successful service advertising.

16.1   Introduction

The defining characteristic of any services company is that it involves 'people providing service(s) to other people'. Whether it is financial services, retail, airlines, utilities, telephony, government or healthcare, the key component is people. The critical implication for advertising is that it must work in conjunction with this people factor. Either the experience of the brand via interaction with people will negate the advertising message, or it will positively combine with the advertising message. Either way, the people dynamic is an inherently unstable, ever-changing and inconsistent factor, the presence of which makes for a very complex climate in which advertising has to operate. Contrast this with a packaged goods environment where price, packaging, product and distribution tend to be reasonably fixed variables, creating a consistent, predictable environment in which advertising can be rooted.

This chapter will set out considerations for successful service advertising and then use a case study to illustrate. As with the previous edition, we will look at the Halifax advertising campaign, not only as an example of a financial services advertiser but also as a company that used retailer advertising as a blueprint.

16.2   Successful services advertising

The first criteria for successful services advertising are the same as for any advertising, namely cut-through (the advertising should be noticed), branding (the advertiser should be recalled), communication (the key message should be understood and recalled), relevance (the message should be motivating) and differentiation (the message should be competitively differentiated from other advertisers in the sector). See: How Advertising Works, Chapter 2.

In addition to this, there is a specific requirement on services advertising: that it be consistent with the actual experience of the service. As this experience is, as noted above, invariably a 'people' experience, it should be consistent with this human interface. Clearly, the most productive way in which it can be consistent with this human interface is if it actually empowers the interface itself. It is this that is the secret of successful services advertising. It must go beyond simple consistency and actually seek to encapsulate, define and empower precisely what each service stands for. Tesco are not content with mere consistency with their retail experience – their advertising ('Every little helps') actually looks to drive external expectations and internal standards to help create and sustain the experience. British Gas by featuring their engineers in their advertising are actually saying externally, judge us by our people and internally, you are our brand. Virgin Atlantic position themselves as a more maverick, fun, enjoyable way to fly – something that is reflected in passengers' expectation on a Virgin flight, and the flight attendants' attitude on board.

Contrast this with Virgin Trains, where the way advertising can work is exceptionally difficult to define. Given how exposed Virgin Trains is to the vagaries of Railtrack, the weather, and indeed their own engineers, makes the construction of any substantial, credible and motivating services proposition very tricky. The focus on price and new trains as effectively the only unchanging and consistent variables is, perhaps, understandable. Current advertising for the London Underground is equally limited in its ambition, merely promoting the locations of its stations! The rationale for this is obvious. Readers will recall the debacle that befell Barclays when while simultaneously declaring the benefits of 'bigness' in their advertising, they embarked on a significant branch closure programme. British Rail famously claimed 'We're getting there', when they so clearly were not.

The other requirement of successful services advertising is that it must make the people in the organisation proud. Sainsbury's suffered a set-back with their ill-fated, 'Value to shout about' campaign, starring John Cleese, as it was patronising and demeaning to the staff. The more recent Jamie Oliver campaign, however, gives a very definite and empowering stance for Sainsbury's – making good food better, younger and more accessible.

The essence of successful and effective services advertising then, is a very critical and honest assessment of how, in the first instance, advertising can be as credible and consistent as possible with the actual service experience and in the second instance, how advertising might actually go further and actually positively engender and empower the service experience.

To demonstrate the detail of this argument, we will now consider a case in detail.

16.3   Halifax plc

In 1997 Halifax demutualised and became a bank, competing directly with the big four banks. In its first 3 years as a bank, Halifax, while holding share in mortgages and savings, actually lost share in banking. This failure to grow as a business led to considerable city pressure to merge with one of the big four banks. Lord Stevenson and James Crosby, the Chairman and Chief Executive, respectively refused to accept that a take-over was the only way forward and, instead, launched an aggressive quest to grow organically, by stealing share from the big four.

The focus was particularly on getting people to switch their current account from the big four, but also on holding and growing share in the heartland areas of mortgages and savings.

Given that 80 per cent of Halifax's sales come from via the branch network, and 53 per cent of Halifax staff are customer facing, it was realised immediately that the advertising idea, as detailed above, must not only be consistent with the branch experience but actually go further and empower the service experience.

16.3.1   The Halifax service experience

What emerged in qualitative research among colleagues was a pride in being 'people not bankers'.

'It's important to be the same person at work as you are outside it.'

'The more yourself you are the better the job you do for your customers.'

And this more 'human' approach to banking was consistent too with consumers' existing perception of Halifax.

'Halifax people are people like us.'

Focusing on Halifax as a human organisation was a powerful platform. It was true and motivating to colleagues alike. Halifax's brand proposition became simply a combination of 'human' and 'value' (the key motivator in switching products), or as it became branded 'Extra friendly, extra value'. (Also see Section 1.8 – The Modern Marketing Mix). Not only was this proposition true to the service experience, and motivating to consumers, but it was also differentiated from the more corporate, image-based competition. (See Figure 16.1.)

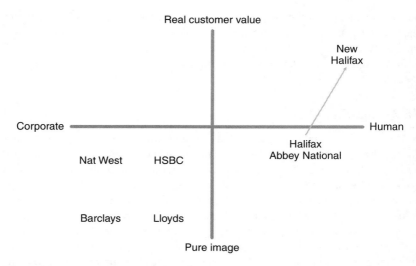

Figure 16.1   *A brand map showing how the 'Big Four' were conceived and how Halifax aimed to differentiate itself from Abbey National by adding more customer value through a more human face*

16.3.2   The communications idea

It was realised at the outset that it would take more than an advertising idea to transform a 35,000 person organisation. A communications idea was needed that had the potential to permeate and inform everything that Halifax did, both internally and externally.

The creative solution was to use real Halifax staff. The big difference was that they would be singing in their own pop video. The communications idea, which was called 'Staff as Stars', precisely reflected the importance that the 35,000 colleagues had in achieving the business strategy.

The campaign started working internally far before it was launched externally. It was launched internally on Halifax TV by Jonathon Ross. It was a request to come forward and star in the new Halifax advertising campaign. A total of 1169 people applied, and were auditioned in eight regional castings, and 20 appeared in a national final in London. The campaign was launched externally on Boxing Day 2000 with Howard Brown, from the Sheldon branch, singing Extra to the tune of 'Sex Bomb'.

At the time of writing the campaign has now run for 3 years. It has been used in TV, posters, press and radio; in direct marketing, on the website, in digital marketing, in all in-store posters and literature, in all customer communications, in all internal communications, in recruitment advertising and even on the cover of the Annual Report.

The campaign, created by the agency in which the author is a partner, Delaney Lund Knox Warren, has been the most successful financial services campaign of the last 10 years. It achieves phenomenal cut-through, branding and communication, and enjoys stand-out and likeability other bank campaigns can only dream about.

Crucially, in the context of Services Advertising, we can see from Figures 16.2 and 16.3 that it actually engenders a very positive and differentiated perception of service versus the main clearing banks amongst non-customers.

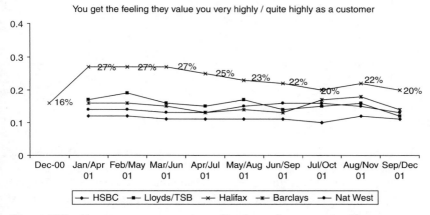

Figure 16.2 *Non-customers perceptions of banks – value customers. (Base non-customers of each bank)*

Source: Hall & Partners

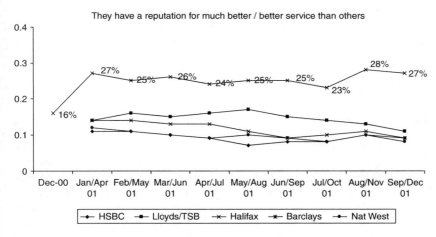

Figure 16.3 *Non-customers perceptions of banks – reputation for better service. (Base non-customers of each bank)*

Source: Hall & Partners

Table 16.1   *Showing branch staff reaction by internal e-mail survey to the new advertising campaign*

	% Agree	% Neither agree nor disagree	% Disagree
The campaign represents colleagues in a positive way	76	10	14
The campaign has given Halifax real momentum	84	6	10
The campaign has made Halifax a real competitor to the other high street banks	78	18	4

Base: 150 branch colleagues.

Internally, as Table 16.1 demonstrates, the campaign has had a very positive effect on staff.

In fact, the most exhilarating effect of the communications idea has been the internal effect. Galvanising large organisations in a very short space of time is extremely hard.

Advertising can play a very important role in achieving this. As Lord Stevenson wrote in the Chairman's Statement in the Annual Report the year after the campaign was launched,

'... nothing emphasizes the importance of the contribution made by our front line colleagues better than the television advert featuring Howard Brown from our Sheldon branch. In a way that corporate language cannot convey, Howard epitomizes the enthusiasm our people have for what they are doing. Growth and enhanced shareholder value cannot become a reality until people like Howard, Halifax people, make it happen.'

16.4   Conclusions

The rules for successful advertising should now be clear. At base level, the advertising must be consistent with, not at odds with, people's personal experience of the organisation. But beyond that, advertising has a unique role to play in actually empowering the service experience. As the case for Halifax has generated, advertising was not merely consistent with the service experience, it actually went much further giving consumers externally, and colleagues internally, a real vision of the service experience that Halifax stood for.

16.5 Summary

In this chapter:

- We have seen that the service advertising must be closely linked to the 'deliverables' of that service, that is, the people delivering the service must reinforce the advertising proposition.
- The Halifax Bank was given as a leading example of how the reinforcement of the advertising message by the staff leads to success. Indeed, we saw that the Bank staff became the message.
- We saw that advertising has a unique role to play in actually empowering the service experience.

17 Recruitment Advertising

Sarah Asprey

Learning outcomes

By the end of this chapter you will:

- Recognise that recruitment advertising is more complex than it first appears.
- Understand that the choice of media that carries the advertising is particularly important and that, since this is a rapidly changing environment, specialist advice is particularly important.
- See that the role of the recruitment agency is more than just 'placing an advertisement'.
- Explore the structure, range of services and specialism of a recruitment agency.
- Take a look into the future of recruitment advertising and recruitment advertising agencies and see what is required for long-term success.

17.1 Introduction

Recruitment advertising has always been seen as the poor relation to 'mainstream' advertising. This is reflected in the availability of reading sources about recruitment advertising – only a handful of books are available to buy which are even vaguely related to recruitment advertising, and nothing new has been published since 1994. But times are changing and the world of recruitment communications has become a more diverse, multimedia and creative world than ever before. It now shares more with 'mainstream' advertising than ever, and while it may be seen to lag behind in its thinking and status, it has begun to do some serious catching up, and in some areas has actually led the field, such as in Internet advertising.

Although it does share much of the theories and techniques of product and corporate advertising, recruitment advertising is still a very specialist area, which demands specialist skills and knowledge. As an industry, recruitment advertising is worth over £700 million[1] and recruitment advertising agencies in the UK employ thousands of people. The general status and profile of the industry is beginning to grow to reflect its size and worth. But one of the industry's biggest challenges is to raise awareness of its existence among young people choosing their careers, and hence attract the best quality of people to work in the industry. It is still the case that most people arrive in the industry by accident, rather than because they have always had a burning desire to work in recruitment advertising.

Most recruitment advertising in the UK is undertaken by dedicated, specialist recruitment advertising agencies – there are over 80 of these in the UK. These range from the smallest agencies, employing just a handful of people in a single office and turning over a few hundred thousand pounds a year, through to the largest agencies who employ over 100 people across a network of regional offices and turning over up to £200 million a year. Over the last 15 years there have been considerable changes in the agency marketplace. In the 1980s and early 1990s, the market was dominated by a handful of very large players. Then, there was a surge of smaller agencies setting up with the aim of offering a more personalised, customer-focused service. In recent years, with the difficult economic climate, many agencies have merged or been bought by larger concerns. Some of the larger agencies are part of international groups, which have agency offices in countries across the world.

The range of clients that a recruitment advertising agency might work with is vast. With the exception of very small companies, nearly all SMEs and large businesses require the services of a recruitment advertising agency at some point. Clients span the commercial / private sector as well as the public sector, including central and local government, charities, health services, armed forces and other not-for-profit organisations. The work undertaken for these clients varies from one-off black and white 'house style' or 'border' advertisements in the press (which is a simple corporate template with at the most some limited design) through to substantial ongoing national or even international creative campaigns, spanning the full range of media from press through to TV and everything in between.

17.2   How is recruitment advertising different?

As we have already noted, recruitment advertising does share much with its mainstream counterpart, but it is also very different. Where product advertising has to sell a product to a consumer audience, recruitment advertising has to sell a career opportunity to a potential candidate audience.

Recruitment advertising has a serious job to do, as it is not just about persuading someone who is already looking for a job to apply for this particular job. A good recruitment advertisement needs to reach out to people who may not be thinking of changing jobs at all, to rethink their career and really want to work for this company, doing this job. Unlike choosing a new soap powder, or even a new car, changing jobs is a real 'life choice' – it is one of the most important decisions any of us ever makes, and along with divorce, moving house, etc., is one of the most stressful. Enticing someone to consider changing jobs, when they may not have already been thinking about it, is a serious business.

The choice of media is vital. If an advertisement appears in the wrong publication, then not enough of the right kind of candidates will see the advertisement and a low quality, low volume response will ensue. Reaching the right audience is not only about choosing the right publication, but choosing the right media overall – a printed advertisement is only one of many options available today.

As is the choice of messages; 'How can we persuade THIS person, to choose THIS job, with THIS company, at THIS time?' is the question every advertisement must answer. Recruitment advertisements do not seek to attract just any people – they need to attract the right people for the company and the role. They have to have the right fit. Advertisements have to persuade someone that of all the jobs they have seen, this job and this company are offering something unique and special. And they must encourage action – they must make people want to apply now.

Measurability is a key aspect of recruitment advertising. Whereas much mainstream advertising is about branding and product awareness, but does not necessarily demand or expect a large response, every recruitment advertisement must not only generate a response – it must generate the right response, from which a client can produce a short list of candidates and eventually recruit the right person to their organisation. That is quite a responsibility – if it does not work, the thousands of pounds the client has spent is completely wasted – and the advertisement has to run again. The success (or otherwise) of a recruitment advertisement is known very clearly and very quickly.

One of the biggest differences between recruitment and non-recruitment advertising is budget – both in terms of the size of budget available, and the source of the budget. A recruitment advertising agency's contact within a company is not within the Marketing Department as you would expect with other forms of advertising. Contact is with the HR or Personnel Department. The budget for recruitment does not come from a marketing budget, but from a recruitment budget, which is often worked out on a 'per head' basis. Every single penny of the budget has to be demonstrated as working hard and delivering a successful outcome. Hence, the advice from the agency on how that money is spent is crucial.

In addition to the spend on individual vacancy advertising, some companies do have a budget for wider recruitment marketing activities. This is usually what we call 'employer branding' work, where communications activities are undertaken with a view to raising the profile of the employer and creating perceptions in specific marketplaces of the company as an 'employer of choice'. This work is usually more creative, and is more similar to the kind of work a non-recruitment advertising agency would undertake.

One of the main differentiators between product and recruitment advertising is still that of speed. Because of the nature of the activity which it supports – that is, recruitment – time scales are usually extremely tight. Media deadlines for each publication day (most newspapers have a recruitment day each week) are strict, and from taking instruction from a client, including writing new copy and typesetting an ad, to providing an advertisement to the publication, the time scale could be as little as 24 hours or less. Even new creative work has to be turned around in a matter of days, which would give most product advertising agencies a heart attack.

But quality cannot be compromised to speed. Accuracy is vital in any form of advertising, but even more so in recruitment advertising. Because of the fast turnaround times involved, and the nature and amount of text seen in many recruitment advertisements, attention to detail is crucial. Under the pressure of deadlines it would be easy to compromise. Most agencies have in-house proof-readers, and rigorous checking procedures to ensure that mistakes do not get through the system. Advertising space in the recruitment pages of newspapers is substantially more expensive than 'run of paper' advertising (anything from 25–140 per cent more expensive), so mistakes can not only cost dearly with client relationships, but can also prove very costly. As an illustration, a quarter page mono advertisement in the *Sunday Times* costs £20,655 (2003 rates).

The majority of companies do now use a recruitment advertising agency to place their recruitment advertisements – but it is still possible to look through any newspaper and spot those who have chosen to 'go it alone'. These usually fall into one of two categories: the first looks like little or no effort has been taken in its creation, with poorly written copy which provides no real insight into the company or the opportunity; the second is an over-indulgent, over-descriptive creation which goes into great detail about the company, and sometimes the job, but is actually entirely unrealistic, presenting a view of the company which no employee would recognise.

17.3   The changing role of the recruitment advertising agency

In the past, recruitment advertising agencies used to provide a very simple, reactive service to clients, which consisted of typesetting an advertisement with copy provided by the client, and booking space in a media requested by the client.

This is still a service that some clients want, but the role of the recruitment advertising agency has transformed in the last 10 years, to the point that many agencies will no longer describe themselves as 'recruitment advertising agencies', as this is a very limiting description. Phrases such as 'recruitment communications', 'recruitment marketing' or 'HR communications' are more commonly used, as they more accurately reflect the range of services now expected of an agency, and the role they now perform for clients.

Agencies no longer just place advertisements – they provide solutions. Clients come to recruitment advertising agencies for advice. They want to know how to attract the best talent for any given role within their company. Of course, in some cases, the solution may be to place a recruitment advertisement in the press. But what kind of advertisement? What style of copy? In which media? And equally, the solution may comprise a whole range of media and methods – an advertisement might not be the answer at all.

Agencies have also moved from just supporting their clients' recruitment activities, to supporting the wider personnel / HR function. Agencies have to help their clients to think about recruitment in the broadest possible sense and tackle all of the related issues. For example, consider staff retention. If a company is able to keep more of its best people, then they will need to recruit less new people. How can we help clients retain staff? We look at how the company is perceived as an employer – 'employer branding'. This can be ascertained through research, which agencies help their clients to undertake, analyse and then action. Employee communications and relations are another major area into which agencies have moved with their clients. These are just examples – more detail on typical service areas is provided later.

This is what has made the recruitment advertising a more exciting industry in which to work than ever before – and also the fast pace, the variety of work and the nature of the relationship with clients is ever changing, offering a rewarding and stimulating career environment.

In addition to working with HR contacts within companies, a large percentage of recruitment advertising placed is for recruitment consultancies. For many agencies, this income is very important to their business, as spend levels with the key national (high value) media are substantial. In some cases, consultancy advertising can account for 50 per cent or more of an agency's total media income. As clients, consultancies are different animals, and they expect a different kind of service. They are usually quite demanding, as they rely on the agency for advice and information which they will then pass on to their client as their own. Any mistakes or delays reflect very badly on them.

17.4   The Internet

The arrival of the Internet has transformed everybody's lives over the last 10 years, and as it has become widely used, so it has also transformed the way job seeking and recruitment are carried out. Recruitment has been one of the biggest drivers behind the growth of the Internet, and some of the major recruitment websites, or 'jobs boards', are now among the most successful websites in existence. The job-seeking public has embraced online job hunting with open arms, and while in the early days it was only IT staff who considered finding a new job on the web, this has extended to almost every sector of the job-seeking population, with the possible exceptions of blue collar workers (who have limited access to computers at work) and very senior executives (who expect to be headhunted). Most people now have PCs in their own home, if only at first for their children to do their homework – but the parents now go online to browse career opportunities. Online jobseeking is now used by over 11.1 million people in the UK – that is, 30 per cent of the working population – and 98 per cent of graduates now look for jobs online.[2]

And so, the role of the recruitment advertising agency has also been completely transformed.

A whole new world of media has opened up, in addition to the thousands of printed media available for recruitment. There are now over 700 recruitment websites online in the UK,[2] and agencies have to be able to recommend these with the same confidence as they would any other media.

And advertising online is not just about placing job postings (text listings, the most popular web entry) on recruitment websites. Banners and buttons, profile pages, keyword sponsorship (and so on) can be used on both recruitment and non recruitment websites to drive candidates to either job postings or back to clients' own recruitment websites. This is about online recruitment marketing. Many companies who have never ventured online for product or corporate advertising purposes are happily using online advertising for recruitment.

And so who builds companies' online recruitment sections? This is another area of great opportunity for agencies, which some have embraced more quickly and thoroughly than others. By helping clients to create functional recruitment sections, which allow key activities such as online applications (including online pre-screening) and candidate registration (like you would do if visiting a website such as Amazon), agencies can help their clients not only to save valuable time on the administration of recruitment, but also to build databases of 'warm' candidates and undertake CRM (in this recruitment context, candidate relationship management) to keep them interested. So when they need to recruit for any particular role, clients can first view candidates on their own database, and often recruit them directly without the usual costs of recruitment consultancies or placing advertisements.

This may seem like agencies 'shooting themselves in the foot', helping clients to minimise their advertising activities – but agencies cannot afford to bury their heads in the sand and ignore the fact that recruitment is changing. Their entire business structure needs to adapt to meet changing needs (and to help their clients to get the most out of new technologies) and it is better they are earning income by building those websites, rather than missing out altogether. An agency's role has come full circle, and a successful agency must now be seen to help its clients recruit in the most effective way possible, which includes being as cost-effective as possible, through implementing integrated, effective strategies and solutions.

This is a long way from just placing advertisements in the local paper.

17.5   Service levels and expertise

So what is it that clients expect from their recruitment advertising agency partner? What are they paying for?

Like most agencies, advertising and otherwise, the reason clients choose to work with recruitment advertising agencies is because of the specialist knowledge and experience they offer.

Agencies must demonstrate a sound understanding of how to attract people to work for them – through effective advertising design and copywriting, and through the choice of media and method.

Just consider for a moment the breadth of 'recruitment' as a specialist area. Think about the range of recruitment that exists – from recruiting nurses to NHS Trusts, to customer service agents for call centres, to marketing managers for manufacturing companies, to computer programmers, to the managing director of an FTSE 100 company. A recruitment advertising agency – and specifically, the account manager working with a client – must have a broad-based understanding of all kinds of recruitment and methods to be able to provide a value-added service.

At the heart of this is an in-depth understanding of the media and what works for different roles. An agency must be able to demonstrate up-to-date knowledge of which media are performing in which markets, and what methods can be used for even the most unusual of roles. This changes regularly – where one media may be the best for certain roles at one time, another may improve its performance and become the better solution at another time. This applies particularly in the fast-changing world of online recruitment websites – while the market has steadied in recent years, there are still new websites popping up all the time, and websites disappearing without a trace. It is quite a job to keep tabs on them all.

This knowledge, much of which is in the account handler's head, must be backed up by reliable, up-to-the-minute tools and resources. Numerous media tools are available to help agencies make informed choices on which publication to use. For example, *British Rates and Data* (BRAD), which is the directory (which now also exists in online form) of media used typically by product agencies, can be a useful source at times for recruitment advertising agencies – but it has the disadvantage of not being specific to recruitment, so there is no indication of (for example) how many pages of recruitment advertisements each media carries, or even a contact in recruitment advertising. A more tailored tool is WhatMedia, which is an online media database established by publishers Reed Business Information (RBI) in conjunction with some of the UK's leading recruitment advertising agencies. It is recruitment-specific and contains relevant information such as the kind of job titles commonly advertised, and is kept up-to-date by a dedicated team of researchers. Other tools are available, and different agencies rely on different systems. These comprehensive research tools, along with the agency's own in-house media database system, are essential in backing up the account management team's own expertise.

In addition to press and websites, account handlers must also be competent in working with the full range of other available media, including radio, TV, cinema, direct mail, bus advertising, bus stop advertising, sponsorship, PR and so on.

The account handling staff must also have a good insight into the jobs that their client contacts do – understand a little about recruitment in a broader context (for example what the recruitment process is after an advertisement has been placed) and how it fits into an HR professional's job.

Producing copy and creative work for recruitment – whether advertising, brochures, posters or exhibition stands – also demands specialist skills and experience. It is not an easy job to adapt from product or corporate work to recruitment, and mainstream agencies who do this are not always successful. Aside from the challenge of producing an effective recruitment advertisement (we outlined earlier in this chapter the serious job a recruitment advertisement must perform), the biggest challenge is again speed – time scales are always extremely tight and good quality creative work is difficult to achieve on a deadline!

17.6　Agency structures

The way an agency is structured varies quite substantially depending on the size of the agency.

Every agency, whatever the size, will have some kind of account management function. This is often called 'client services' in reflection of the evolved nature of agencies as we have already discussed. In very small agencies, this could consist of or include the agency directors themselves; in large agencies, this is a multi-tiered, multi-teamed department.

The key role of the account management team is to be the interface between the agency and the client. They speak to the client day to day, visit them for meetings, take briefs, and feed back research, creative work, campaign planning and strategy to the client, even if other parts of the agency have been involved behind the scenes. They are the 'gateway' to the agencies full range of services.

Roles with an account management team are similar to those within a product agency, with account directors, account managers and account executives. Sometimes there is an additional layer of account administrators. Typically, account directors are responsible for a number of account managers / executives, with overall responsibility for budget and performance, and they will be involved at a high level in strategy and account development. An account manager is responsible for most face-to-face contact with the client, and for making sure that the day-to-day work is executed to time, to budget, and to quality standards, overseeing other members of the team who may actually carry out the work. Account executives are usually office-based, ensuring that the client can always speak to someone who knows about their account, even if the account manager is on the road visiting clients. Executives must be extremely well organised, with excellent attention to detail and the ability to stay calm even under the most intense pressure – they are the real workhorses of the office-based operation, making sure the advertisements are processed through the agency accurately and on time.

Most agencies have their own in-house studio and creative resource, although very small agencies (and larger agencies when times are hard) may use freelance, external creative resources. Larger agencies will typically house a creative studio in their head office, which is then accessed by its satellite offices remotely. Like most advertising agencies, a creative team consists of creative/art directors, designers, artworkers and typesetters, in varying numbers. Each individual will have a different specialist skill or style so that the agency as a whole can offer clients a full variety of creative approaches and techniques.

Copywriters, if employed in-house, are often positioned half-way between the studio and the account management team – for straightforward recruitment advertisements, they would liaise exclusively with an account handler, but for more creative projects they would work as an integral part of the creative team.

A production and print buying unit will often form part of the studio, responsible for traffic management (managing the flow of work through the studio – which, with recruitment, can consist of tens, if not hundreds, of advertisements in any one day), job costing and print quoting and buying.

Agencies vary in how they manage media research and buying. For larger agencies, there is often a separate department dedicated to keeping up-to-date information on the key media and researching rates and data for account handlers. This has an advantage as it means that media advice for clients does not take time out of an account handler's already hectic day.

However, the disadvantage is that clients only have contact with their account management team – and these people, if not involved daily in media research and buying, are not able to provide off-the-cuff advice or discussion about media when clients require it. Hence, in many smaller and medium-sized agencies, the account management team will undertake media research, advice and buying as part of their everyday jobs.

Again, depending on the size of the agency, there may be a separate research department which holds information on salaries and benefits, and other information relevant to recruitment such as economic and social trends in different regions and employment markets. They may also carry out specific research projects, which have been recommended to clients by account handlers, such as surveys of employees' or potential employees' views on a company, or regional polls of people's views on working in a particular job type. This information helps agencies to focus recruitment communications activities more accurately, and tailor messages to appeal to the right people, to combat, for example, pre-conceptions, and to target the right audience through the right media.

17.7   Services

The range of services now offered by agencies to their clients is vast. Different agencies choose to offer a different selection of these services, and only the larger agencies will typically be able to provide each and every one of these services. But this illustrates how much has changed from the days of just 'placing advertisements'. Agencies have responded to clients' changing needs, and to the changing nature of recruitment. They have realised that stay competitive, and to retain their profit margins, they have to capitalise on every opportunity that their client relationship offers, and provide services that would otherwise be sourced from other suppliers (see Table 17.1).

As you will see, recruitment and selection is a service that some agencies choose to offer to clients. This can be an advantage when working with companies who see it as a benefit to deal with one supplier for both recruitment advertising and recruitment. However, other agencies have chosen to specialise purely in the advertising and communications side of things – which can also be a selling point for some clients. This is particularly so when working with the important client group, mentioned earlier, that is recruitment consultancies. Frequently, recruitment consultancies do not wish to work with an advertising agency if they have a recruitment section of their own, as they may actually find themselves pitching against that agency's recruitment arm for business – a very bizarre and undesirable situation!

17.8   Sources of income and costing models

Media commission is still the main source of revenue for recruitment advertising agencies, but this emphasis is steadily shifting towards other sources of income such as web and consultancy work.

Table 17.1   *The range of services that may be offered from recruitment agencies*

Advertising creative and production	Employee communications
Media planning and buying	Event management
Website design	Recruitment PR
Website hosting and support	Client training
Response handling	Graduate recruitment communications
Assessment and selection services	Employer branding services
Research	Diversity consulting
Recruitment literature and support materials	Recruitment software
Employee opinion surveys	

The commission earned varies from publication to publication – typically 15 per cent for national and quality regional papers, and 10 per cent for trade and technical and smaller local papers. Overseas media bookings can earn anything from 0 to 2 per cent up to 15 per cent depending on the country and media type. Online bookings also vary widely – some websites offer no agency commission at all, some 10 per cent, others 15 per cent. Some of the recruitment websites have chosen to go directly to the clients and choose not to build relationships with agencies – and deliberately cut them out.

Agencies cannot rely solely on media commission for income. For a start, the margins on online media bookings are slimmer simply because the average value per booking is lower. With increased use of the Internet, overall media billings are lower than they have been in the past.

In addition, for certain client types, many agencies must budget on returning a percentage of their agency commission to the client – something unheard of in mainstream advertising. This will typically be for larger-volume clients and for consultancies who are effectively 'agents' for the advertising agency, handling bookings on behalf of clients.

Creative work is another key source of income. Clients are charged for creative advertising and other creative work such as brochures, direct mail or exhibition stands. This is usually calculated based on hourly rates for art direction, design, artworking and so on. Photography and image hire costs are usually marked up to create a small income. In times of economic slowdown, as we have seen since mid-2001 and particularly since 11 September 2001, clients are less able to spend money on expensive creative work so this source of income is curbed. Clients err towards less elaborate creative advertising or, in some cases, abandon it altogether in favour of simple house style advertising.

Production costs are also a source of income – this is simply the cost charged by the agency on each advertisement to cover the cost of producing the advertisement in studio. Production costs refer to existing advertisement styles or templates, and normally encompass resizing, typesetting new text or making amends and providing artwork to the publication via Integrated Services Digital Network, Advertising Delivery System or a bespoke media artwork system. Production costs are either a fixed cost per advertisement regardless of size, or they are based on the number of single column centimetres of the advertisement, that is, its size, so a bigger advertisement will carry a higher production cost.

In many cases, depending on the client and the industry sector, agencies have had to reduce their production costs to remain competitive and retain clients. In some cases, production costs are waived altogether, and a monthly advertisement management fee charged to the client to cover production costs of an agreed volume of advertisements – this might be for a local authority client placing hundreds of advertisements each month. In some (rarer) cases, this monthly fee structure may also involve the agency returning 100 per cent of its agency commission to the client in exchange for a higher monthly cost – this offers the agency a source of regular, fixed monthly income which, in the reactive and unpredictable world of recruitment, is a rare treat.

As we have already discussed, the Internet has brought a whole array of new income opportunities for recruitment advertising agencies. From charging clients to manage the uploading of vacancies onto jobs boards, to building and hosting full recruitment websites, this area has been one of the biggest income growth areas for agencies across the board.

As the table of available services illustrates (Table 17.1), many of the services that agencies provide to their clients are not related to advertising per se. More agencies are moving into the field of providing consultancy work, which often offers higher margins than recruitment advertising, especially where tight production costings and media commission rebates have been agreed on with clients. Consulting work can be anything from employee relations to HR strategy, diversity consulting to employer branding. The aim is to add value to the relationship and also to support the positioning of the agency as an expert in the recruitment / HR field.

17.9　The future challenge

The biggest challenge, as it always is for any business at any time of change, is to adapt and remain competitive, not only in terms of remaining profitable, but in terms of providing clients with the level and quality of service they demand.

Technology brings the biggest change to the recruitment industry. The Internet has revolutionised the world of recruitment – and many thought that it heralded the end of recruitment advertising as we know it. But then, the same was said when radio advertising was first used for recruitment. However, press advertising has not died – it still forms a vital element of the overall recruitment communications mix. But it has had to change. Press advertising costs have typically come down, and some advertisements are now more about employer branding than selling vacancies, with candidates being directed to a website for more information. This allows advertisements to feature less text, which often means they can be smaller.

All this means that income streams are being squeezed – which is compounded by the new media not operating in the same agency-friendly manner as their 'traditional' counterparts. They do not always give agency commission. They often bypass agencies altogether. Their prices are low – a job posting can cost as little as £100, and 10 per cent of that will hardly cover the cost to administrate the job!

Clients, too, have become more demanding. They expect more from their agencies, demanding – as we have said – integrated, intelligent solutions to recruitment challenges. And they want it quicker, cheaper, better.

So, agencies have had to get wise, quickly. They have had to adapt their service to meet the needs of their clients. They have had to embrace new media and work out how to make it pay. They have had to move into service areas they never needed to consider before, to ensure that they are maximising the potential of every client.

Not all have been successful, and some have been quicker than others to really get to grips with new media. And of course, there are still clients who only think about agencies as a way to place advertisements in the papers – so there are still agencies who provide only that service.

But in a fast changing, unforgiving industry, only the fittest will survive. Those that shape up to the challenge will be offering dynamic, varied, integrated solutions to clients – and an exciting and stimulating working environment for staff, that will rival any mainstream advertising agency.

Watch this space!

17.10   Summary

In this chapter:

- The complexity of recruitment advertising has been explored drawing comparisons with mainstream advertising.
- The case for specialist recruitment advertising agencies has been made, explained away by the rapidly changing market place. It was noted that not only have the needs of recruitment clients changed, the changes in the recruitment media have been noted, with particular emphasis on the Internet.
- We have seen that with recruitment advertising, as with their markets, the ability to learn faster than the competition is fast becoming the only sustainable competitive advantage.

Notes

1   RBI (Reed Business Information) / Business Economics Ltd.
2   David Hurst, publisher of Online Recruitment and onrec.com, 2003.

18 Directory Advertising

Robert Love and Jackie Hewitt

Learning outcomes

By the end of this chapter you will:

- Understand the nature of directories and see where they fit in the range of advertising media.
- Recognise how the medium has grown in recent years and note some of the particular characteristics of directories.
- Explore how to choose a directory and how to develop advertising for this medium.
- Review particular regulation pertaining to directories.
- Know how to measure the success of directory advertising.

18.1 Introduction

When discussing advertising media, directories are often overlooked and undervalued. Many people do not really understand how directory advertising works and yet it accounts for nearly 6 per cent of all advertising expenditure in the UK and is a vital part of the marketing mix to many companies, large and small. There are a large number of directories published in the UK and they are used by just about everyone, in the home and the workplace.

18.2 The nature of directories

Directories are variable by nature but could probably be categorised in three ways. Firstly, there are mass market directories, such as the Thomson Local, the Yellow Pages, and the BT Phone Book. These directories are distributed for free (though extra copies are charged for), and the revenue streams come from companies advertising their services. Then, there will be a number of smaller directory publishers whose directories carry advertising. Some of these will be consumer directories such as the Hull Colour Pages, and some of which will be business-to-business publications. Thirdly, there are a number of specialist directories, usually business to business, which often carry little in the way of advertising. These directories will often be charged for rather than distributed free.

Below are some of the different types of directory published in the UK:

- Consumer directories such as the Thomson Local and the Yellow Pages
- Directories for participants of particular activities or interests
- Directories produced by the local government or trade bodies
- Public authorities' directories of services
- Trade associations listing their members
- Specialist trade or professional directories.

This variability means an exact definition of a directory is hard to pin down, but essentially a directory is a *retained or constantly available reference source*. Traditionally, directories have been in print format, but in recent years directories have appeared on CD ROM and online. Printed directories and CD ROMs are retained and online directories are constantly available.

Many directories are classified into headings or business types and others are alphabetical listings. The Thomson Local and Yellow Pages are good examples of classified directories, having several hundred or even thousand headings from Accountants to Zoos. Some directories will have both: a classified section printed on yellow paper and an alphabetical list on white paper. This deliberate use of colour relates to two different 'search terms': know the name and not the number – go to an alphabetical listing (white pages search), but know the business type but not the name – go to a classified directory (yellow pages search). (*Note*: The term 'yellow pages' is a generic term used worldwide to describe a classified directory; however, the name 'Yellow Pages' in the UK is a registered trademark owned by Yell.)

All types and sizes of companies can use directories to help put them in touch with potential buyers of their goods and services. The particular directory or directories a company chooses will depend on the scope of the publication, its distribution, readership and overall fit with a company's advertising objectives. For the advertiser, there will be a large number of directories in which to advertise, and the Advertising Association estimates this market was worth £990 million in 2002, with the two big classified directories, the Thomson Local and the Yellow Pages, making up around 70 per cent of that figure. The print versions of these directories are updated once a year and are permanent fixtures in millions of homes and businesses across the UK. They also have online companions called www.thomsonlocal.com and www.yell.com.

18.3   Growth of directories

According to *The Advertising Statistics Yearbook*, the growth of directory advertising in the past three decades has been phenomenal, growing from

£11 million in 1970 to £990 million in 2002, a growth rate of 8900 per cent! Indeed, directory advertising revenue doubled between 1990 and 2002. This tremendous growth has helped to drive directory advertising's 'share' of total advertising, which grew from 2 per cent in 1970 to 5.9 per cent in 2002. In such a rapidly growing market this is a huge achievement for directories. Furthermore, directory advertising revenues outstripped radio, cinema, and the Internet *combined* in 2002.

	1970	*1975*	*1980*	*1985*	*1990*	*1995*	*2000*	*2002*
Directories (£m)	11	20	82	209	492	639	868	990
Total advertising (£m)	554	976	2864	5052	8925	11,026	16,988	16,734
Directories share of total advertising(%)	2.0	2.0	2.9	4.1	5.5	5.8	5.1	5.9

This growth has in part been due to a number of new directories appearing over the years, both large and small. In 1981, the Thomson Local was launched, which added a significant amount of revenue and made the classified directory market more competitive. Directories' saliency increased rapidly during the 1980's as Thomson Directories and Yellow Pages launched hugely popular national TV advertising campaigns. Nowadays, both companies are major operations with large sales forces selling over the telephone and face-to-face.

Over the years, directory owners have also become more imaginative at driving revenues by offering premium advertisement positions and colour advertising, for example. More recently, online directories have started to increase revenues. Furthermore, the potential for advertising revenues is still great. It is estimated that only around one in four businesses in the UK advertise in the Thomson Local and / or the Yellow Pages; in the USA and many other countries a greater proportion of businesses are directory advertisers, so there is plenty of scope for growth in the UK.

18.4 Directories as a medium

As a medium, directories have two unique properties.

1 Many other media are much more transient than directories: TV advertisements come and go, posters change, newspapers go in the recycling bin after a few days and so on. But users keep directories, and often next to the telephone, such is the frequency of their use.

2   Being a retained reference source ensures that users refer to directories when they need to; in other words, they are actively looking for a supplier. Users of directories are in the frame of mind to make a purchase when they look at them. No one browses through a directory in the same way that they would a magazine. They have a defined need and want a supplier that can satisfy that demand. Research shows that 8 out of 10 people who use a directory have made a decision to buy.

All this essentially means that directories *connect buyers with sellers*. In this way, they are key to many businesses because they make the telephone ring or they encourage customer visits. Some companies will rely heavily on classified directories to bring them new business. Although word of mouth can be a major driver of business, advertising in classified directories will help make their telephone ring – no other medium will do this so well. For example, a tradesman's only paid for advertising may only be in a classified directory. When people have a building job that needs doing they will probably turn to a directory – they know there will be plenty of choice and the directory is always handy as it is kept by the telephone.

Users will often look at a variety of directories for their information needs as they could be local, regional, national, professional or specialist. While an advertiser's goods and services might be relevant to more than one directory, they may not advertise in all of them; this could be due to budget or preference. Therefore, by looking in a variety of directories, users may feel that they have more choice.

While directory advertising alone cannot achieve a variety of advertising objectives it can:

- Communicate information and reasons for buying from a supplier,
- Remind consumers to consider a supplier, and most importantly,
- Generate enquiries.

Often, directory advertising can work with other media, helping support the generation of enquiries when other advertisements are no longer front of mind with the consumer.

Consider the example of insurance companies. They know how important it is to get people to call them and ask for a quote. Television advertising raises awareness and can drive a favourable brand image. They may well put their telephone number at the end of the advertisement, but how many people watch TV advertisements with a notebook and pencil at the ready? This is why directories are so important to insurance companies. They know that when people want a quote they will probably pick up the Thomson Local or the Yellow Pages and work their way through the Insurance heading. Users will only make a finite number of calls so all the main players are in there trying to grab the attention of the directory user – insurance companies not in there will miss out.

To ensure that potential customers can find the right number, many insurance companies will carry a 'tagline' which is a visual reference (usually on TV or press advertising) that tells the consumer which directory to look in.

Some of the bigger directory publishers will provide advertisers with stickers, signage and logos that they can use on their premises, on vehicles or adverts, which tell potential customers where to find their contact details.

Connecting buyers and sellers and generating enquiries is the raison d'etre of directories with paid for advertising. They are not relied on to drive brand awareness or communicate sophisticated messages intended to enhance the brand image and create meaning in the minds of consumers. Directories need to be cost-effective, environmentally friendly and often have hundreds of pages, so the paper is usually thin and the advertisements have fairly low production values. For this reason you will not see image reliant goods such as perfumes advertised in directories; marketers in these companies currently prefer to advertise in glossy magazines and on TV.

18.5   Publishing directories

Today, directory publishers are pioneering the use of technology, driven by the need to mass produce titles in the most efficient and effective way possible. There are few publications that print as many copies as BT's Phone Book, the Yellow Pages or The Thomson Local; each of these titles alone will have between 20 and 30 million copies printed each year. Directories that are published in these quantities will have various editions, typically by region, and will have a rolling publication schedule throughout the year.

To produce a directory, a database of relevant, organised listings is digitally combined with a database of adverts. This creates a digital file which is then digitally proofed and finally printed. Having a database of advertisements can help reduce holding multiple copies of common logos or designs and allows the same advertisement to be used in multiple media such as print and online.

Distribution of high circulation directories is done through third-party companies who will recruit people regionally to distribute the books. Directories with a much smaller distribution are usually paid for titles and will be distributed by post or courier.

Directory circulation for both free and paid for titles can be independently audited. The Audit Bureau of Circulation (ABC) will independently verify circulation and distribution, which is a valuable tool for directory publishers to attract advertisers. Freely distributed directories are audited by Verified Free Distribution (VFD) which is a division of ABC.

In the UK, the main trade body representing directories is the Directory and Database Publishers Association (DPA). It seeks to 'promote directories and databases as advertising media and as sources of information'. The DPA also maintains and applies a Code of Professional Practice, which 'exists to safeguard the interests of legitimate directory publishers and the public alike'.

18.6   Development of directories as a medium

Over the last few years, many directory publishers have introduced online companions to their directories. With over 20 million people online in the UK, the area of online directories is proving to be a growing revenue stream that can only get bigger. For the online user, some of these directories are freely accessible to use such as ThomsonLocal.com. and Yell.com. With specialist directories, in the same way that many of these are paid for, their online counterparts often require a subscription to enable access.

Online directories will often have distinct criteria that users enter such as 'what?', 'who?' and 'where?'. Using search terms in this way means the results list is more focused, unlike using search engines when sometimes the user is presented with hundreds of thousands of results, many of which are not relevant. Online directories can offer features not available from their printed counterparts, such as:

- The content can be updated more frequently as an online directory will not rely on publishing cycles.
- Searches can usually be performed nationally or in any geographic area.
- Users can define the way results are viewed, for example by sorting the results in order of distance from the user's postcode.
- Potential for distribution with other sites increases the target audience (some search engines use content provided by directory publishers to provide better quality information for users).
- More dynamic content such as maps, links to websites, email, virtual tours, movies, local events or other timely information.
- With Internet access more common in a work environment it enables workers to have more information at their fingertips rather than hunt around the office for a single copy of a directory.

18.6.1   Pay-per-click

A new development in online directories has been the emergence of the 'pay-per-click' market. This is a very simple and effective concept which allows an advertiser to pay only for the enquiries they receive from their online advertising. Advertisers 'bid' to be associated with relevant keywords that users are searching for. The more they bid the higher up the list of results they will be. If a user clicks on their link, the advertiser is charged, at a cost per click. Advertisers interested in this model will find that Espotting, Overture and

Thomson Directories all offer this service. A number of search engines, such as Lycos, Netscape, Freeserve, Altavista, Ask Jeeves and the WebFinder internet search section on Thomsonlocal.com utilise this model.

Example: The hypothetical company 'Super Supplements' sell nutritional supplements online. They have bid for over 200 different keywords and combinations of words including 'Vitamins', 'Supplements', 'Minerals', 'Cod liver oil', etc. They have bid £1 for 'Vitamins' which is a very popular search term but only 10p for 'Psyllium husks fibre' as it is a very specific term. Other advertisers in this field would also be bidding for similar keywords. When a user enters a search term, all the advertisers who have bid for that keyword will be listed before suppliers that simply match the criteria – in order of their bid price for that word. The advertiser who bid the most will be listed at the top. If a user clicks on an advertiser's link, the advertiser will then be charged the cost of their bid. Using the 'Vitamins' keyword example, Super Supplements have bid £1, which is currently the top price. If a user enters 'Vitamins' as a search criteria, 'Super Supplements' name, link and some relevant information would be at the top of the results. If a user clicks on this, Super Supplements will be charged £1. The user will see nothing of the bidding process, only a list of advertisers in a particular order (Figure 18.1).

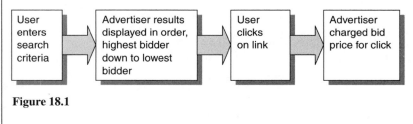

Figure 18.1

Advantages to the advertiser of pay-per-click:

- Control of advertising budget by setting their own limits on bids, in terms of value or number.
- Control of the number of incoming leads by making keywords active or inactive which helps prevent the danger of too much business and too little resource to fulfil it.
- Customers are highly targeted as they are searching for keywords that translate into very desirable enquiries for the advertiser.
- Seasonal goods or services can be promoted through choice of keywords at certain times of the year. For example, a garden centre may only use 'bulbs' in winter, 'seeds' in spring, 'lawn sprinklers' in summer and 'garden vacuums' in autumn. But they may well have other keywords such as 'compost' that they keep throughout the year.

18.6.2   Other developments

More recently, mobile phone users have been able to access classified directories such as the Thomson Local and Yellow Pages from their mobile phone. Some directory websites can send a text message to a mobile phone with the number of the supplier selected. Digital television has also been embraced as a means for views to access directory information via their TV.

The deregulation in 2003 of the Directory Enquiries service has led to many new suppliers offering directory services via the telephone. Now known as 'Directory Assistance', these numbers all have the prefix '118'. The nature of these calls is mainly 'white pages' enquiries, where callers know the name but not the number. Callers from mobile phones can receive the number by SMS on their mobile phone. Some directory publishers have their own directory assistance numbers and compete in this marketplace, others may not operate a service but will licence their vast database to Directory Assistance providers.

18.7   Choosing a directory

Evidently, with so much choice, care must be taken when choosing in which directory to advertise. When deciding on which directory or directories to advertise in there are a number of considerations to bear in mind.

18.7.1   Coverage

One of the key ways in which directories differ is in their coverage. All media reach a certain number of people, and one of the benefits of directories is that they often get delivered to a specified number of people at specified addresses. Some directories will go to a small number of people, some will go to localities and some will have a wider distribution. This means that advertisers can advertise in directories that cover the areas where they want to get their customers from. For example, a driving instructor may choose a local directory as they do not want to drive long distances to get their customers; however, vintage car dealers may want a wider catchment area as this is a more specialised market and customers will come from further afield.

Advertising with national companies like Thomson Directories and Yell gives a further benefit of advertising in multiple directories. So, regional companies can advertise in all the books in the South West for example, or national companies can advertise in all the books. Retailers can match directories to their retail footprint and so on. Moreover, customer segmentation can be carried out so directories that reach certain individuals could be chosen, for instance, directories covering Kingston-upon-Thames might be a good choice for companies selling luxury goods to affluent people.

The growth of online directories adds flexibility to the user. Using Thomsonlocal.com or Yell.com essentially means users can search in any Thomson Local area or any Yellow Pages area, or indeed the whole country. A presence on these sites gives advertisers a further opportunity for referrals.

18.7.2   Distribution

It is important for advertisers to check the distribution of the directories they are considering. Does the directory go to residential addresses, business addresses or both? Does the directory go to all addresses or just some? Is it distributed free or is it paid for? Is there some sort of proof of distribution (e.g. Verified Free Distribution)?

18.7.3   Usage

Another important consideration is the usage of a directory. The right distribution is important but the directory needs to be well used by those who receive the directory, otherwise advertisements will not generate the desired responses. Many directory publishers will carry out market research and use other methods to demonstrate the usage of their directory. This can be illustrated as penetration and frequency, that is, the number of people using the directory and how often. The Thomson Local and the Yellow Pages are measured by the National Readership Surveys, which are carried out on a nationwide basis to show readership of printed media.

Market research along these lines also allows potential advertisers to see what sort of person uses a directory. The users can be broken down in terms of age, social grade, gender, region and so on. There should be a 'fit' between the customer and the directory user, that is, a youth brand may want to ensure that sufficient usage among younger age groups is occurring with a potential directory advertising option. Here, some form of market research will need to be used. (See Chapter 13.)

18.7.4   Advertising options

Directories will offer different types of advertisement in terms of size, position and colour. Advertisement sizes can range from a single line listing through to a full page, with a number of sizes in between, such as in-column advertisements, quarter page advertisements, half pages and so on.

There are also prominent positions such as the front and back covers (inside and outside). These positions can be advantageous for businesses trying to drive brand awareness and generate calls. Publishers may also offer other special positions such as spines, tabs, bookmarks, loose inserts or sponsorship of specific sections. Some directories do not offer this type of position and, of course, availability in these prime locations is going to be a consideration.

Some directories will have the option of highlighting an advertisement in a different colour, such as using 'white knockout' on a yellow page, and sometimes allowing spot colour. Full colour is often available too, which allows corporate colours to be reproduced, and can maintain consistency of brand identity.

18.7.5   Classification

Classified directories will put businesses in a classification or 'heading'. Different directories have different headings. Specialist businesses may find that there is not a relevant heading to their business; if this is the case, some directory publishers will agree to create one. However, many businesses could be classified into multiple headings, which can be a very effective way of generating enquiries. For example, a plumbing company might advertise under Central Heating, Plumbers, and Drain and Sewer Clearance. Directory publishers often have lists of their headings and how they relate to one another. Consideration should be given to how potential users might classify a supplier. Security companies might find that most consumers look under Burglar Alarms but people looking for burglar alarms for their company might look under Security Equipment, so by advertising under both headings security companies can reach both audiences.

Some directories have specialised sections where headings are grouped together. For example, the Yellow Pages have a Wedding Section where Photographers, Cake Makers, Car Hire Companies and so on can all be found. The Thomson Local has a section called LocalPlus which has headings for companies that might not be found in the local area. These headings include Places To Go, Shopping, Computing and Games, Transport, Travel and Motoring. So, airlines and leisure parks, for example, would be found in this section.

18.7.6   Production and print quality

Potential advertisers should check the quality of a directory, bearing in mind the quality will ultimately reflect on their business. Robustness, legibility and so on should be checked.

18.7.7   Online options

Some directories will have an online directory with varying options. In some cases, the print advertisement will be reproduced, but there will often be additional options such as linking to the advertiser's website, maps and e-mail links.

18.7.8 Rates

Clearly, rates are of vital importance. Directories are normally priced according to advertisement size and the directory coverage. So, a bold line entry in one directory for a carpenter might only cost £150, but a financial services company advertising with a full page in every Thomson Local or Yellow Pages can cost several hundreds of thousands of pounds.

Sometimes rates will vary according to number of directories advertised in as well, that is, discounts may be applied for advertising in multiple books. Similarly, advertising under more than one heading offers a similar benefit. Directory publishers may sometimes offer incentives to first-time advertisers, or they may give rewards to multiple year advertisers.

Advertisers should be aware that users tend to call the largest advertisements on the page so they should check to see how many competitors there are in the relevant section. If there are a number of competitors, increased spend might be necessary to increase share of voice and ensure a decent return on investment.

18.8 Designing a directory advertisement

The classic Attention-Interest-Desire-Action model (Figure 18.2) is one that seems wholly appropriate to directory advertising, and advertisers should bear this in mind when designing their advertisement. (See Chapter 2 for more information on how advertising works.) An advertisement should grab the attention of the directory user and have sufficient information to create the interest and desire. One of the main strengths of directories is the fact that the interest and desire are to an extent already present, that is, the user is usually looking to buy. The key thing for the directory advertiser is to make the user call their advertisement (i.e. the action), often in the face of stiff competition bearing in mind there will often be many similar companies advertising in the same section. (Compare this with most other display advertising – broadcast, print, etc. – where brands in the same category may not be competing in the same advertising break or on the same page of a magazine, but the consumer will probably not be in a frame of mind to buy at that moment.)

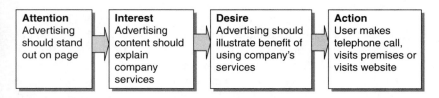

Figure 18.2

There are a number of considerations to bear in mind when designing an advertisement in order to generate the best response possible:

- One of the best ways of making an advertisement stand out is to buy a large one! A bigger-sized advertisement can sometimes make potential customers feel that the supplier is more attractive, reliable or robust. People will make very quick value judgements based on their perception of the advertisement. Occasionally, some people will avoid larger advertisements, perceiving the advertisers to be more expensive, but the market research shows that larger advertisements stand out on the page and will generate more calls than smaller ones.
- Some directories will offer colour advertising, and the use of colour is another way of making an advertisement stand out on a page. Colour advertisements will generate more calls than mono because of the way they stand out. Colour is obviously charged at a premium rate, but there are other ways of achieving stand out such as 'white knockout' (a white advertisement background on yellow paper), which are usually less expensive than colour.
- Illustrations can make an advertisement more attractive and distinctive. Company logos are usually used as trade association symbols, but sometimes advertisers will add illustrations, such as a builder laying bricks, specific car models or a washing machine for example. Some directory publishers will have their own artwork library so advertisers can choose appropriate illustrations. The salesperson should also be able to give guidelines on what to include. If the advertiser is unsure, directory publishers sometimes have in-house 'visualisers' who can design the final advertisement before sending a proof to the customer.
- Often users will be calling companies that they are not familiar with, so they need some reassurance that the advertiser is suitable for their needs. Essentially, this means that users call advertisers who provide more information about their business. Information typically provided includes: location, maps, parking details, delivery / response times, product ranges / brands, free estimates, free call out charges, payment methods, discounts, trading hours, qualification association membership, expert services / specialities / unique selling propositions and website addresses. Research shows that women tend to be more price-sensitive and men tend to want to see membership of trade associations and brand names, so advertisements can be geared according to the target audience.
- Advertisement clarity is essential. The provision of information should be counter-balanced with the size of the advertisement, that is, if the advertiser chooses a small advertisement it should not be overloaded with information at the expense of clarity. Too much information will make the font size too small for legibility or simply make the advertisement look poorly designed. Smaller advertisements should just have the most important information.

It should also be borne in mind that directory paper (especially in freely distributed titles) is, in a similar way to newspapers, relatively thin, often less than 40 gsm. This means complex and photographic images may not reproduce well, especially in small adverts. The guidelines on advertisement clarity also apply to online directories, where screen resolution means some small advertisements will be almost illegible if poorly designed.

• Of course, the contact details are the most important details for a directory advertiser so these should be prominent. Freefone numbers can be very attractive to users, especially if they are likely to call lots of companies for comparative quotes.

There is clearly a lot to consider when taking out directory advertising, and looking at the competition is a good starting point so the typical advertisement size and style can be seen. Choosing a small advertisement when the competitors are using half-pages is probably going to restrict the number of calls generated. However, to a large extent, the budget available is going to dictate the decision on what sort of advertisement to buy.

Once an advertisement has been designed advertisers should ensure that they have a proof if it is offered to them. Once received, this proof should be checked very carefully, since once the advertisement is published it cannot be undone and the advertiser will have to wait for the next edition to replace it.

18.9   Regulations

Like other media, directory advertisements are governed by legal constraints, and the Advertising Standards Authority (see Chapter 21). Directory publishers will often rely on trading standards for advice and consultation to help ensure that the content of their advertising is compliant. Advertisers in directories may be bound by both legal requirements and those of any trade association they belong to.

Example: If a plumber advertises that he can work on gas appliances of any description, he must be CORGI* registered and display the CORGI logo in his advertisement. The CORGI registration is a legal requirement and the display of the CORGI logo is a requirement of CORGI itself.

18.10   Co-operative campaigns

Some trade organisations will arrange discounted advertising on behalf of their members with a directory publisher or number of publishers who

---

* CORGI – Council of Registered Gas Installers.

they consider to be relevant to their members. This is common with trade associations, professional bodies, brands with franchisees and brands with multiple premises.

Typically, the advertisement will include a branded 'box' which contains listings of members, outlets, practitioners, etc. relevant to that directory. For example, in a local telephone directory a car manufacturer may list all their local dealers within one branded advert.

18.11   Measuring the success of directory advertisements

For the majority of advertisers the ultimate aim of directory advertising is to make the telephone ring or drive people to advertisers' websites or business addresses. In some ways, this means the advertising effectiveness can be measured more reliably than across many other media.

If advertisers use one or more mechanisms to measure response then the success of the advertisement, or the return on investment (ROI) can be measured. For example, a building company might get one call a month from an advertisement, which may not sound like much but if they only convert one of them into a job worth say £5,000 then effectively an advertisement costing just a few hundred pounds will pay for itself easily. It is clearly very important for advertisers to ask where users got their telephone number to measure effectiveness properly.

National companies will talk about cost per thousand (CPT); this can then be compared with other media. However, the real measure of success is the level of business that is a direct result of the advertisement. These companies sometimes put a unique code in their advertisement that the customer has to quote when ringing in for an insurance quote, for example. In this way they can see a number of things: how many calls the advertisement generates, where the calls are coming from, how many calls are converted into sales, what sort of people are ringing and the average value of that customer (built up over time).

Another mechanism is to use a 'metered phone', which is a unique 0800 telephone number provided by some directory companies. The number of times this number is dialled can be measured, again providing a 'true' measure of usage. Some companies might have their own free number, which is used in a specific directory.

The online arena can also provide some accurate data. For example, click through rates to websites can be measured. The cost per click model provides a direct link between the amount an advertiser pays and the number of times a potential customer comes to their website.

Essentially when it comes to renewing directory adverts, advertisers should look for a decent ROI. However, care must be taken to get as accurate a read as possible. If the response has been disappointing there are a number of options open. Of course, one option is to drop out of the directory, but another option would be to try and understand why the response might have been disappointing. Was the advertisement too small? Could the advertisement design have been better? Should the advertisement have been under different headings? Directory companies sometimes share their metered phone results and testimonials so you could see whether another company has had success with a bigger advertisement, for example. A slightly larger investment may reap better returns the following year – but clearly there is an element of risk as there is with most business decisions.

18.12   Conclusions

The fundamental purpose of a directory with paid for advertising is to connect buyers with sellers. In the mind of the advertiser, 'We're looking for customers who are looking for us' is the manifestation of this principal. Advertisers use directory advertising because it generates enquiries and can give a great ROI.

What has and will continue to change is the way in which people search for information. From the single choice of a book, through online directories and now business finders on mobile phones and digital TV, the number of information sources is increasing. Even with increased choice, people often use new technology hand-in-hand with traditional printed books depending on their circumstances or needs. It may be easier to look in a book than turn on a PC and connect to the Internet, likewise they might use their mobile phone when away from home or the office. Paper directories now have to live alongside other choices that exist on different platforms. Successful directory publishers have already embraced this and acknowledge that they are not in the business of printing phone books, they are in the business of connecting buyers and sellers.

18.13   Summary

In this chapter:

- We saw the nature of directories and saw where they fit in the range of advertising media.
- The rapid growth of the medium in recent years was outlined showing that they currently account for almost 6 per cent of advertising revenues.
- A view of how to develop advertising for this medium was described drawing on the unique way that the medium is use by potential customers.

- It was noted that directory advertising needs to follow the same regulations as other media.
- Key issues on how to measure the success of directory advertising were outlined.

Further reading

The Advertising Association, *Advertising Statistics Yearbook 2003*, World Advertising Research Centre, 2003.

19 International Advertising

David J. Hanger

Learning outcomes

By the end of this chapter you will:

- Gain a clear understanding of the international advertising scene and be more aware of what constitutes 'international', 'global', and 'multinational' advertising.
- Cover the differences that apply to 'doing it internationally' and uncover cautions and advice. The main differences covered are: organisation, planning, audience definition, research and measurement, media and creative.

19.1 Introduction

International advertising used to be the concern of a limited number of companies using the specialist sections of an even smaller number of advertising agencies. All limited even further by a lack of international / pan-frontier developed media markets. Today, the growing number of avaricious wealthier consumers, developing international businesses and the increasing globalisation of brands means that thinking and acting internationally have become a necessity. Today, international advertising is now a mainstream item in many companies and advertising agencies around the world.

There is no doubt that the development of 'trading blocs / free trade areas' and the potential economies of scale that drive product and packaging commonality have encouraged companies to look at regions as a whole and not just country by country, but the growing homogeneity of consumer groups across borders is proving an equal if not greater influence. Country borders were once seen as the main determinant of differences in consumption patterns, with subsequent differences in promotion, product and even manufacturing approaches. With some remaining exceptions, languages being one, country borders are rarely the lead determinant for differentiation any more.

Despite disappointing results from World Trade Organisations (WTO) meetings, the globalisation of manufacturing, markets, products and promotions will continue. Much of the activity of international and common platform multinational advertising is governed by the same practice and guidance given in the other chapters of this book as they relate to national advertising or advertising in general. As such, this chapter will not repeat those guidelines but attempt to build on them and point out the differences of approach, the 'why's and wherefores', the 'do's and don'ts' of *advertising internationally*

19.2   What is international advertising?

Historically, international advertising simply meant advertising beyond a company's home market, with a common message to a definable international audience. It was accepted that invariably within the 'home' market, a company's depth of market penetration was greater than abroad, its local market was broader, its sales message more detailed and its advertising created to match actual or perceived local nuances. 'International' did not mean the same Colgate toothpaste campaign appearing in Spain, Sweden or Hong Kong, though some markets might have had a translated version of the same copy line. These campaigns were seen as attacking a 'local' market. With all but a few exceptions, international advertising was initially limited to products and services that were not just common across borders, but often associated with the frequent traveller, examples being cigarettes, upmarket drinks, expensive luxury goods, hotels and, inevitably, airlines. However, other accepted international advertising categories have developed progressively, such as corporate image advertising from the large multinationals, as companies and their brands have moved to conquer the global market. The industry that overtook even airlines in its internationalism was banking and its related round-the-clock global services. All of these relied historically, and still do, upon the existence of international media, which was, and still is, predominantly, though not exclusively, the published word, and in English or English / American, aided by the strengthening of English as the global business language.

The traditional international advertisers are still there, but even more companies from many diverse sectors of business now think and act internationally. The most common campaigns are pan-regional, pan-Europe and pan-Asia being the strongest areas, but more and more campaigns are using the same message globally and appearing on a worldwide basis. The categories have moved on from cigarettes and alcohol and are replaced by the large IT companies, IBM, Oracle, HP, advisers such as Accenture and the mobile telecom producers and network providers. Banking, the travel industry and corporate tend to dip in and out of the lead dependent on the vagaries of their industries. Fashion and luxury items, particularly watches, are also a growing sector. So 'international' advertising continues to broaden its base not just by sector but also by geographic source as Asia, particularly Korean, and Middle Eastern brands are created and join the list of American, European and Japanese players.

The pan-frontier media opportunities continue to grow, still mainly *press* but also *broadcast* in Europe, the Middle East and Asia. The Internet, telephony, PDAs and PDFs all are providing further opportunities to test the creativeness of marketers. The globe has become smaller thanks to improved communications, both physical and tele-communications, round-the-clock computer links, email, Internet and facsimile transmission. The world views news, sports, current affairs, opinions from afar and even the occasional common soap opera within roughly the same time frame. It is no wonder that people in general, but businessmen in particular, are finding that their interests, tastes and needs are converging at an alarming pace.

Being an 'international person' is no longer the prerogative of the few elite, frequent-travelling, businessmen, but now a much wider audience thinks and behaves in a like-minded way. More and more executives have regular international contacts either within their own multinational company or with their clients in other countries (52 per cent in Europe, according to the European Business Readership Survey, and 53 per cent in Asia, according to the Asian Businessman Readership Survey). Advanced marketers recognise that national boundaries are not the only, nor necessarily the best, descriptives of a market. Indeed, there may be more differences between Manhattan and the Bronx than between mid-town Manhattan, Knightsbridge in London, and the 7th Arrondissement in Paris and Ginza in Tokyo. It is now accepted that 'consumer convergence' is here. Remember, the travelling elite were once just that, a small elite not always there in the large numbers that now exist nor were they readily definable. Now, though they are an important sizeable market in their own right, they are only a part of that larger market across the world that thinks, acts, works, plays, purchases and consumes in a similar manner. It is surprising that some marketers still insist that 'consumer convergence' behaviour and purchasing patterns are myths that can only be applied to the, now accepted, elite of this world and never to the broader audience.

Is there commonality in the media sense? Print media, whether specialist, general or gender-orientated is being launched from country to country and television programming is universal across the spectrum of news / current affairs, educational, travel, 'soaps', documentaries, drama and sport galore.

What is the drive behind this change? Well, is it all simply the technological advancement of improved communication and growing international media? No, it is also the economics of commerce that has been and still is the real force.

Commerce has become global; no longer can a company concentrate solely on a single market and feel safe behind a national frontier. Multinational business is entering every market and virtually every segment. The economies of large scale international production have moved the advantage irreversibly in favour of the global producer, though the drive behind globalisation has not been just production but also marketing and distribution. Even the soap manufacturers have reduced their number of production centres for regions such as

Europe to just two sites. The consequence is that the packaging plants have similarly been reduced so we now see the same product, packaged in exactly the same way, with language being the only difference; but even that may not last forever. The global producer needs the size of a global market, and the more common the basic product requirements the better. So believe not yesterday's fashionable adage 'think global, act local', the successful companies of today both think and act globally – even in advertising and marketing terms.

Is *international advertising* synonymous with *'global'*?

By definition:

- Global implies a universal way of thinking, of acting, a common product, a common image, a common promise.
- Multinational suggests an approach to many markets, but probably a different approach, and certainly in different languages, though the product may differ little.
- As we have seen, international means attacking markets beyond your home market and has traditionally meant a common message, often a single language. International and global are converging.

So where are the lines to be drawn and does the reason for growth in international advertising lie partly in a movement between and within these definitions? Fewer and fewer companies attempt to retain a different image in their home market versus their international markets. Global branding pushes them ever closer to the common message. Convergence means that even multinational advertising, that preserver of 'not invented here', is producing more single / global creative executions. Not unsurprisingly as packaging and product commonality ignore the existence of borders with companies measuring and organising themselves globally, international advertising and multinational advertising have moved and are now embraced by the global approach.

So, why not always totally global in action at first? Companies cannot always cope with such pressure for organisational reasons. The internal organisation of many companies often struggles with arranging itself to produce and market globally. Also, it does take longer to build an internationally uniform image. It is also the case that companies often grow internationally by acquiring other companies and other brands. Creating and organising these into a common culture, product and brand does take considerable planning. As, however, prescribed regions become more definable, so we shall see more pan-frontier activity within definable regions – South East Asia and Europe being the two recognised powerhouses and the best developed beyond the USA / NAFTA.

Where does local advertising and marketing fit into the ever shrinking world? Well, the certainty is it will continue, not just because there will always be some products and services that are only sold not just nationally but even just locally within a country. But the pressure must be that where a pan-regional or global image is being promoted, then the local activity must, in look, feel and message, support the global brand. This applies not just to advertising but all promotions whether they simply are 'shelf talkers' or direct marketing. All must support the overall brand message.

19.3 The practical side of international advertising

Under the following 6 headings, this chapter will cover the differences that apply to 'doing it internationally' and offer cautions and advice. They are: organization, planning, audience definition, research and measurement, media and creative.

19.3.1 Organisation

It may sound unlikely but not all companies have the structure that allows for a common advertising message across a region or around the globe. Many so-called international advertising agency groupings are also not as capable of working as a single international adviser / creator as they would have clients believe.

The largest single problem is that most companies operate with single country profit centres offering considerable local autonomy. There may be a regional layer across such single country units and cutting across all, there may be differing product category measures, but national influences still have a strong bearing on many organizations.

The start point for the international advisor must, therefore, be to establish lines of responsibility and control. The large FMCG companies have for some time been well organized to allow local action but within strict guidelines laid down by HQ and have employed only one or two advertising agencies to handle the account across the world, which in turn are managed by 'global' and 'regional' controllers. A good business example would be IBM, which in 1994 found itself with nearly 80 agencies around the world and around 200 interpretations of its brand. The then President, Lou Gerstner, aided by his newly appointed VP Marketing reduced the agency list to one, O&M, and laid down strict guidelines on brand projection. Such organisational and marketing changes not only aid the message externally but also help to pull a company together internally. An agreed common image is both a marketing and a business advantage.

Hewlett Packard, which had vacillated between product- and country-driven messages, moved in 2002 also to adopt a more singular global approach with the immediate benefit of removing any internal or external confusion and adding the full weight of the brand to all advertising messages. The Milan-based Armani allows local input as they open new shops around the world but with close involvement and guidance from the centre. Most international banks, airlines and hotel groupings are also well organised to act internationally.

So there are many good, working, blue chip examples of how to organize a company to manage international advertising. This is the first vital step in these days where it is the 'global brand' that wins.

If a company is not organized with such clear guidelines and decision processes then the dangers are such that:

– The budget will not materialise because local units will fight to keep control.
– Every disparate local unit calls for input / control resulting either in a bland, committee-created advertising campaign or disarray as the 'not invented here' syndrome takes hold.
– Even if a campaign starts, without solid lines of control, agreed and fully supported from the top, there is a danger that it will die after the first or second year as local pressures work to weaken the resolve. As the planning section will emphasize it takes longer to establish a foothold internationally, so a long-term resolve is essential.

Advertising agency organisation is equally important, and whether creating a regional or global campaign, it is vital to agree with the agency just how they will organize themselves to handle the account. Try to use a single agency grouping and within that decide which unit acts as the lead. If you need input and involvement from units in other countries / regions then agree from the outset the lines of control and remuneration.

Much of what is written here about organisation may seem obvious but the certainty is that lines of control and communication over all aspects of an international / global advertising campaign must be agreed in advance if it is to succeed.

19.3.2   Planning

Organisation was the start point, and once that is in place and fully supported as the way forward by a strong headquarters, then much of the rest of the planning process follows the same disciplines as found in other chapters.

The three main points to remember are:

• Never forget you are going to work across borders with the resultant differences both real and claimed in culture, understanding and position of the product / service – so check for obvious pitfalls without over cramping your style.
• Simply because you are doing it across a larger area and larger grouping both externally and internally it will take longer, so allow enough time.

Remember the investment may be a significant new cost so may need to be rolled out around the world over more than six months.

- When you have established the goals and the measures and have created the good campaign, even with involvement of all throughout the process, it is vital to take it 'on tour' and sell it successfully internally and not simply impose it from on high.

Setting out to introduce, build or strengthen a product or brand internationally is to work on creating one of the most valuable assets a company owns. So do not expect to get from start to finish in 3 months. The steps from concept through organisation, planning, appointing agencies, creating the campaign, selling it internally, buying the media and launch can take up to twelve months and often more in a large complicated organisation.

Be sure that there is commitment to continue. Three-year commitments to an investment in an international advertising / brand campaign should be the minimum accepted time frame.

19.3.3   Audience definition

This chapter has already touched on audience / customer and therein lays the start-point for the successful international advertisement.

Agreeing the audience definitions is even more important when operating internationally, so establish the target audience *demographically* or by *interest group*, or *service/product usage*, then, and only then, worry about the geographic limitations. Clearly, the reality of organisation and market realities will influence the geography. Having established a tight definition of the target audience, assess whether they can be treated as a single cross-border group who would react not just to the product or service in a similar manner but also to a single unchanged message. Inevitably, it is possible to push the boundaries. It is common to run an international campaign but 'top up' the reach with additional advertising in main markets, particularly where it is felt that local language translations would be an advantage.

We mentioned earlier in the chapter some of the industries, products and services that regularly use an international approach. As our exposure to international communication and media continues to increase, so it is certain that the possibilities of treating various demographic, activity or interest groups as one across the world will grow. So, any outline or limit mentioned in this chapter should not be seen as permanent. Do push the boundaries. Often the most limiting factor is the lack of either market or media research.

International business to business advertising ranges across all aspects of industry and although banking, technology and communications may lead, all sectors are represented targeting the boardrooms and senior management decision-makers across the globe. Once a company operates internationally then it should treat this powerful audience as a single unit with a common message. Much the same applies to the upper end of the consumer market. In addition to the business world, the most common internationally targeted consumer groups are frequent travellers, international purchasers of expensive fashion items and luxury goods, and early adopters of new products. Because these groups are of limited size in most single country markets, it is not just more efficient to treat them as an 'international group' but also more likely to succeed because of their common interests and their transient nature.

But can these international consumers of business and personal products and services be identified?

19.3.4   Research and measurement

Most developed markets already have reliable, independent audience and media research. However, methodologies do differ and it is not always easy to combine these researches or apply the same parameters. Clearly, the large US market does have single pieces of research. Pan-European and pan-Asian research has existed for more than a decade and is now updated more frequently.

International research is limited to the relevant universes and, mainly due to cost, has limited, though acceptable overall, sample sizes, but check each research for confidence limits and methodology and do not expect to be able to micro dissect all audiences. The largest universe researches are not necessarily the most reliable. Inevitably most are 'up market', or 'business person' universes though there are some specialist researches in the areas of finance and travel.

The main pan-European researches are:

* European Business Readership Survey (universe 423,034, sample 9029 EBRS 2002),
* Europe 2003 (universe 10.4m, sample 10,573),
* European Opinion Leaders Survey (universe 31,241, sample 2641 EOLS 2003).

The main pan Asian researches are:

* PAX (universe 8,246,000, sample 14,300 PAX 2003),
* Asian Target Market Survey (universe 3,582,000, sample 6706 ATMS 2000),
* Asian Businessman Readership Survey (universe 239,156, sample 6302 ABRS 2001).

Most cover demographics, job description, purchasing habits, both personal and business, holiday and travel patterns.

To add the USA into the international mix, then inevitably there are a number of researches, but the best options, to run alongside the pan regional researches already mentioned, would be subsets of:

- MRI (universe 210m, sample 25,511 MRI Fall 2003),
- Mendelsohn Survey of Adults and Markets of Affluence (universe 52m, sample 12,997 Mendelsohn Survey 2003).

Having used the broad-based researches as a guide, there may be a need for more specific product or market research.

Research is an important start point for international advertising. Do not always believe a company's own explanation of how well known they are in foreign markets. There are too many examples of companies that are household names or well recognised in business circles within their home country or region but are not recognised at all in more distant markets. Indeed, it is often said that it is the Japanese belief and understanding that no-one could possibly have heard of their brands which resulted in them marketing their brands so thoroughly and successfully outside of Japan.

The rule is: research the market, and remember if you wish to post-test, then you need to pre-test.

Is there any difference when conducting research internationally? As the cost of the marketing / advertising investment is likely to be high and continuous, a full investment appraisal may be required. A good econometric model needs data from the beginning if a provable result is to be obtained.

Be sure to employ a research company or a group of associates who are used to working in different countries.

The simple rules are:

- Allow more time.
- Be sure the questions 'work', translated or not; if translated, be sure the translation works; job titles and definitions change – varying tax regimes mean that people talk about salary in a different way, etc.
- In some countries, people open doors / answer mail-shots more readily than in others. So be prepared to work harder to achieve good response rates.
- Personal questions are seen as more intrusive in some cultures than others and, therefore, upset response.
- Research companies have different ideas as to what represents an acceptable standard.
- If it is the first time, pilot test the questionnaire, response, and understanding in a limited selection of the countries to be surveyed. Pick those that you expect to present the most problems plus the home base as a guide.
- Be certain that having responded to the need for minor variations across borders you can still create a common statistic where required.

19.3.5   Media

Many of the guidelines in the chapter on media will also apply to international advertising, the questions vary little – what is the company trying to achieve, what is the message, who is the audience, and what is the budget?

19.3.5.1   *What is the company trying to achieve?*

An obvious question, but it is important, for it will influence creative, media and timing of both the length of the campaign and the start-point. Is the company trying to enter a market and create a brand image which will affect market share or price, or both? What position versus the competition are they aiming for in the market? By when do they hope to reach various levels on the way to their ultimate goal? The new entrant invariably needs heavy up-front expenditure to create an immediate impact, but the message must then be sustained.

15.3.5.2   *The media opportunities*

Theoretically, every medium in the world falls within the remit of the international media planner to be dictated only by the audience definition. CDE socioeconomic groups across the countries of the European common market would, however, mean mass market press or television in each country. Mass markets can in most instances only be reached by national media and as such are more often the prerogative of the local planner. This may well change as companies and agencies treat regional markets as one and look more and more at costs, objectives and markets as a single opportunity. However, bringing all advertising thinking together, for many national and international campaigns, is still more likely to happen in detail at the buying stage rather than the planning stage. This may change as more satellite television channels begin to cut across borders, reaching not just a specified elite but lower down the demographic ladder into the television-viewing public, with news and sport programming leading the way. To date, however, these penetrations are limited and vary enormously from country to country. As such, pan-frontier satellite television in most instances still falls within the bounds of the international planner's responsibilities.

Within the broadest descriptions laid out in this chapter, common message, brand, image, relevance to audience, definable audience, and international media planning is at present limited to:

- The top end of the consumer market, with the AB socio-economic groupings across a region being the loosest definition. This, of course, is often too loose even within most national markets, so similarly it is also a loose definition when thinking globally or pan-regionally. Look for tighter clarifications.

- Businessmen form another common area of potential international influence, but even here, most companies would and should have a tighter target audience definition within that, just as they would nationally, i.e. what type of businessmen, which interest group, which job definition, which business, or are they businesswomen, too?
- Then there are the international interest groups, the consumer of luxury products, top end cars, etc.
- The international travellers who are the most obvious within this sector.

So what of the media? Well, it is impossible to list them all here, but they include, in pan-frontier terms:

- Satellite television, with its varying limitations.
- Life-style magazines, *National Geographic*, *Asiaweek*, *Asia Magazine*, *Time*, *Newsweek*, etc.
- Newspapers such as the various editions of the *Wall Street Journal*, the *International Herald Tribune*, and to a lesser extent, the *Financial Times*.
- Current affairs and business, such as *The Economist*, *Far East Economic Review*, and, out of the USA, *BusinessWeek* and *Fortune*.
- and the growing list of specialist category media.

Does the planner stop there? Not necessarily, and again, it will depend on message, objective and budget, but most would also consider specific 'national' additions to a schedule. Not just because most pan-frontier media are in English, for in the business arena that has become the *lingua franca*, but a company may need to penetrate deeper into specific sectors in some of its larger markets.

So, what to look for in international media? Consider the following first:

- Does it cover the audience?
- Is it cost-efficient?
- Is the environment right?
- What is its editorial content and stance?
- Does it write about subjects that would interest your defined global audience?
- Is it respected within its field?
- Is it truly an international, or is it simply an overspill publication with most of its circulation in its country of origin and an insignificant amount outside?
- How does the reader perceive the medium?
- Is it, as we have demanded of the advertising message, relevant?
- Are any additional national or specialist media needed to achieve the media planning objective?

Most international budgets are stretched, so with frequency and penetration at a premium it is vital that the campaign is as visible as possible. To this end, it is often worth sacrificing a few percentage points of the budget to ensure premium positions achieving maximum impact.

The main pieces of research have already been listed but there are other narrower pieces available bringing the total to 16 separate international media research studies. Access to these researches is available through the lead international media and advertising agencies.

What of the future? It seems certain that as the world becomes more like-minded, so international pan-frontier media, with common editorial across borders, will continue to expand.

19.3.6 Creative

All that is written in the earlier chapter on creative applies here but there is more. Pause and reflect on the brief for although we expect that the audience, though stretched across differing countries and nationalities, will have common interests in the product or service and enjoy some general homogeneity, they are certain to be living or operating in different environments. Any message will also be seen by more than just the targeted core customers and as such will reflect on the brand amongst a wider audience. Brands are not just the ephemeral view of core customers who are already 'members of the club' but are strengthened by knowledge and opinions of those who can only but aspire to join or wear the badge.

Although the audience definition and good media selection should guarantee the immediate environment, it does mean that in creating a message it is important to bear in mind the broader environment and the nuances of that environment in which the message will be received.

It is impossible to list every pitfall for every country here but the obvious ones are colours; 'incorrect' use of women in advertisements, and this one stretches in both directions; race, colour and creed. If you are talking internationally, then be sure to include differing elements of your audience; seasons and seasonal activities inevitably vary; and use of sport or personalities, be sure the subject is one to which your audience will relate wherever they are. Bearing all of these points and many more in mind, do research them within your own organization and test them externally in main markets and the most disparate markets.

Most of the above relate to the visual impact but language is of equal importance. Most international creative people will use English, certainly the business-to-business campaigns, but many will also have translated versions for some main markets. Good English is essential as it is more likely to be understood and leaves less scope for misinterpretation. Be very wary of colloquialisms and humour. Again, test the understanding / interpretation in other markets and be sure any local language translations are fully confirmed externally and that the original creative team are involved. Probably the most important aspect is the 'theme line', for this must resonate across all relevant markets, be relevant to the message and image the company is trying to achieve and, because succeeding internationally takes longer, the theme will need to be capable of a longer life. This is probably the greatest challenge but this is an expression of the brand statement.

Finally, despite all the warnings, be bold, be creative and beware of the multinational design committee, with its too safe, bland advertisements, and all the pressures of 'not invented here'. But remember, the creative must reflect the company, the brand, as you wish it to be seen across the world.

19.3.7   Mind your P's and Q's and beware of the law

There are many examples of successful international creative executions and quite a few that failed. There is not enough space in a single chapter to list them, but a good guide is to look at the current international campaigns, not just within your own media circle but as they appear in the other regional editions of both the international and distant pan-regional titles and broadcast stations. Observe with caution, but do observe which creative is winning the awards in different markets.

19.4   Summary

In this chapter:

- The only major aspect not covered in the previous sections of this chapter relate to the practicalities that exist beyond the advertising message. Areas such as distribution channels, local displays, local sales methods and outlets, availability of the product, local perception of the company, its services and products were mentioned. These are important, for advertising does not operate in a vacuum and is only one form of communication with the customer. So be sure you are fully briefed on all aspects of marketing activity in the varying markets before you begin.
- Remember to be more thorough with the planning, understanding the organisation and the markets, allow more time, be aware of the high cost of the investment so be ready to prove its worth, look for quality media that is genuinely engaged by your audience, beware of the pitfalls but do be creative. With a few *caveats*, good advertising works internationally as well as nationally.

Further reading

Jones, J.P. *The Ultimate Secrets of Advertising*, Sage Publications Ltd, 2001.
Anholt, S., *Brand New Justice: The Upside of Global Branding*, Butterworth-
    Heinemann, 2002.

Regular reading

M&M Europe, EMAP.
Media Asia, Haymarket Publishing.
Internationalist, International Advertising Association.

20 Sales Promotion in Marketing

Brenda Simonetti

Learning outcomes

By the end of this chapter you will:

- Have a clear understanding of what sales promotion is and its origins.
- Review best practice in delivering sales promotion that meets its objectives.
- Understand the place for sales promotion complimentary to advertising as part of an integrated marketing communications mix.

20.1 Defining sales promotion

The very nature and diversity of sales promotion has always presented a challenge in deciding how it is defined. The Institute of Sales Promotion (ISP), the trade association and professional body of the industry, has defined it as:

A consumer or business directed marketing activity that enhances product appeal by offering an extra incentive to purchase or participate.

In the simplest terms, sales promotion is all about 'adding value' and 'prompting action' in order to achieve predefined marketing objectives. The added value can be 'real' or 'perceived' but must constitute something additional to the basic brand proposition.

20.2 How it all began

Although it is claimed that the first ever sales promotion was when Adam gave Eve the apple, the discipline as we know it today dates back to the mid nineteenth century when the Co-operative Society was founded. The popularity of the dividend prompted a competitor to launch the first trading stamp, a technique that arrived in the USA towards the end of the nineteenth century. Almost a hundred years later, in 1958, the widely acclaimed Green Shield Stamp Trading Company was launched in the UK.

As early as 1890, Quaker Oats carried free-mail-in offers for bone china cereal bowls and silver plated spoons. The Victorian era also saw the first in-pack premiums ranging from cigarette cards to the packing of china plates and bowls in packets of Quaker Oats. While admiring the enterprise of these early promoters it has to be recognised that at the time there were no Codes of Practice and little legislation. In spite of the First World War, promotions flourished until the recession of the 1930s that, inevitably, led to deep price-cutting. The Second World War, with rationing and fixed prices, brought an abrupt end to entrepreneurial marketing. The big revival came in the 1950s catalysed by the end of rationing, the start of commercial television, the conversion of the major multiples to self-service, and the birth of the sales promotion consultancy. Since that time, sales promotion has grown in stature and is now a £20 billion industry recognised as one of most important tools in the marketer's armoury.

In this new millennium, the industry is responding to a consumer enjoying the benefits of new technology. Although the techniques remain the same, the Internet, short messaging service (SMS) and e-commerce are influencing the way in which they are implemented. Speed of communication and instant gratification are what the consumer expects and this is epitomised by the dramatic increase in instant win promotions at the expense of the free-mail-in and self-liquidator.

20.3   Setting the objectives

Objectives can only be set when the problems have been revealed and the opportunities identified. Conducting a market audit will reveal the current status of the brand and its performance in the context of the market in which it operates. Analysis of this audit enables the marketing team to determine the strengths and weaknesses of the brand and to put together a set of marketing objectives attacking the weaknesses and building on the strengths. See Chapter 11 on advertising planning and budgeting.

Sales promotion cannot be expected to solve all the problems. The marketer has a range of options available – advertising, sales promotion, direct marketing, sponsorship and PR.

The function of sales promotion is to *gain attention and stimulate action*, and it is most successful when its role is complementary to the advertising. The following list covers the main objectives which sales promotion can help to achieve:

Consumer and trade
- Increase penetration,
- Generate trial purchase,

- Generate traffic (retail / web / publication),
- Generate response (as opposed to purchase),
- Increase frequency of purchase,
- Increase weight of purchase,
- Increase frequency of visit (retail / web / publication),
- Reinforce above-the-line campaign,
- Create interest,
- Create awareness,
- Obscure price increase / differential,
- Gain retailer support / display.

Sales force and / or employee
- Promote call rate,
- Increase sales,
- Promote attendance / timekeeping.

The objectives state what the promotion is expected to achieve and, as such, must be quantifiable in order to measure the success and effectiveness of the promotion. They must also be attainable within the allocated budget. A common error is to expect one promotional campaign to resolve all the problems and is manifested by setting a long list of objectives. It is important to prioritise – too many objectives will reduce the chances of achieving them.

20.4   Defining the strategy

The strategy is the overall plan by which the objectives can be achieved. The results of the marketing audit are key factors to be considered when developing the strategy and identifying the options available. Some of these factors are:

- The current state of the market;
- The status of the brand within the market;
- The consumer profile and its perception of the brand / brand image;
- The trade situation and perception of the brand.

Reviewing the objectives against the market background is the route to coming up with a selection of strategies. The most advantageous of these can be isolated by considering them in the light of some of the more specific details relating to the proposed campaign. These would include:

- The budget;
- The timing and any seasonality of the brand;
- The target audience and its behaviour patterns;

- The promotional history of the brand;
- Likely competitive activity;
- Any constraints (e.g. special regulations relating to alcoholic drinks).

How this process works can be shown by the following example of the SONY Back to School promotion showcased in the 2003 ISP Awards:

Example – SONY 'Back to School' Campaign

1 *Market background*

- Sony was a late entrant into the IT market in 1998 and faced strong competition from established brands like Toshiba.
- Since 1998 their VA10 notebooks and desktop products had made significant progress and stood at number 3 in the market with 11 per cent value share.
- The market was extremely competitive with a cluttered in-store environment.

2 *Objectives*

- To boost sales of the VA10 range during the promotional period – July – September 2002 – by more than 10 per cent.
- To raise the profile of Sony IT products amongst consumers who traditionally associated Sony with Walkman and PlayStation.

3 *Strategy*

- To target school leavers, university students and their parents during the 'back to school' period.
- To incentivise purchase with an added value promotion via redemption.
- To build on the success of previous promotional activity.
- To achieve stand out in the cluttered in-store environment in an intriguing and creative way.

The technique selected was a free-mail-in offer for a premium of high-perceived value relevant to the target market. The campaign used a 'back to school theme' with striking black and white imagery (chalk on blackboard) carrying the message 'Hands up who wants a free Sony CD Walkman and VA10 Backpack'.

Customers could claim their CD Walkman and VA10 Backpack by purchasing a VA10 notebook or desktop, completing an application form and posting it to the offer address together with the original sales receipt. This was a free-mail-in technique using a premium as the mechanic. In this case, there was above-the-line support in the national press that was welcomed by the trade as was the distinctive 'black and white' point of sale material which achieved the required stand out. Evaluation of the promotion revealed a sales uplift of 35 per cent over the promotional period against the expected 10 per cent. The trade asked for the offer to be extended and the excellent sales results indicated that the campaign had enabled Sony to raise its profile as a supplier of IT products.

20.5   The budget

In most cases, the budget is set before the idea is conceived and the task is to tailor the concept to the allocated budget. This means that the objectives must be realistic in relation to the budget. An objective of doubling sales is unlikely to be achieved on a low budget. Broadly speaking, there are two types of costs to be considered:

(i)   Fixed costs
(ii) Variable costs

Fixed costs are those that will be incurred regardless of the response to the offer and would include:

* Design, artwork and photography
* Print and production
* Agency and legal fees
* List rental
* Competition / free draw prizes
* Insurance
* Sales force materials
* Distribution
* Judging and adjudication.

Variable costs are dependent on the nature of the promotion. In the case of prize promotions, which include competitions, free prize draws and instant wins, the variable element is relatively low, the prizes and judging already having been allowed for in the fixed costs. On the other hand, free-mail-ins, coupons and self-liquidating promotions have much higher variable costs. The expected level of response is the key to estimating these costs which would include:

* *Competitions and free prize draws*
  * Receipt and handling of entries
  * Data collection
  * Initial judging / sorting
  * Freepost (if applicable).
* *Free-mail-ins, self-liquidating promotions and cashbacks*
  * Receipt and handling of applications
  * Data collection
  * Cost of premiums
  * Value of cash (for cashbacks)
  * Banking / cheques

- Despatch (including envelopes, packaging, postage)
- Storage
- Complaint / query handling.
- *Coupons*
  - Face value of redeemed coupons
  - Trade handling allowance
  - Receipt and handling of coupons
  - Cheque issuing.

Estimating the level of response requires experience, judgement and an appreciation of the factors that will influence the propensity of the consumer to participate in the promotion. A good starting point is to calculate the maximum number of redemptions possible. In the case of an on-pack promotion asking for proofs of purchase from the promotional packs, this figure can be arrived at by taking the total number of promotional packs and dividing it by the number of proofs of purchase required. For example, a promotion communicated on 3,000,000 packs requiring the applicant to submit three proofs of purchase would have a maximum redemption level of 1,000,000. A leaflet-based promotion would have a maximum redemption level equal to the number of leaflets distributed. The next stage is to estimate the *likely* redemption level as, obviously, not everyone exposed to the promotion will participate. Critical to this is the examination of the results of previous similar promotions and the market conditions prevailing at the time. This process enables an experienced operator to arrive at the expected response level from which the variable costs can be calculated.

20.6   The brief

A clear, concise and detailed brief from the promoter is essential if the agency is to produce a campaign that will fulfil its objectives. It is advisable for the agency to have a set format that they ask the client to complete. In this way, account directors can ensure that they are in possession of all the relevant information before embarking on concept development. (Compare creative briefing in Chapter 7 and more general briefing ideas in Chapter 12)

The sales promotion brief should be completed under the following headings:

- Market background
- Product background – sales, distribution, market share, pricing
- Pack quantities / sizes – where relevant
- Promotion objectives
- Target audience profiles
- Consumer perception of the brand
- Budget

- Timing of activity and critical lead times
- Legal / Code of Practice issues
- Production issues
- Corporate policy and design guidelines
- Recent promotional activity and results
- Recent competitive activity
- Constraints / influencing factors

A good brief will enable the agency to become as familiar with the brand as the promoter – what is special about it, where is it sold, who buys it and who rejects it and how is it rated against competitive brands? Analysis of this information is a vital tool in helping to identify opportunities that can be exploited by the promotion.

Promoters are often nervous about divulging confidential information to their agency, but it has to be realised that the client / agency relationship can only work effectively in an environment of partnership, absolute trust and the recognition that both parties are striving to achieve the same goals.

20.7   Techniques and mechanics

The range of basic techniques available to the promoter has not changed very much over the years (Chart 20.1). The changes and evolution of promotional activity are reflected in the mechanics used to implement the techniques. For example, at one time, prize promotions were dominated by skill-based competitions, but, when it became clear that free prize draws and instant wins could be run legally if no proof of purchase was requested, the skill competition became a rarity. The Heinz promotion in the 1980s whereby a car a day could be won by sending in a label or a plain sheet of paper with name and address details was one of the first of these ground-breaking promotions. Trial promotions, previously dominated by sampling, were radically transformed when the creativity of agencies gave us the 'try me free' and 'full price refund' mechanics.

It is not possible to provide a detailed analysis of all the techniques and mechanics within a single chapter. However, we can look at them in terms of the proposition they make to the target audience which can be summarised under four basic headings:

(i)   Save (price and self-liquidating promotions),
(ii)   Free, (gift and free- mail-in),
(iii)   Win (prize promotion), and
(iv)   Give (donation).

Those offering an immediate reward include price, free item, free draws and instant wins. With other mechanics the reward or benefit is delayed with the

Chart 20.1   *A range of techniques linked to the mechanics and corresponding proposition*

Technique	Mechanics	Proposition
Price promotion	Coupons Discounts Extra free Buy-one-get-one-free	Save
Self-liquidating promotions	Premium Non-premium	Save
Free-mail-in	Premium Cash Discount offer Staff incentive	Free
Free item	In / on pack Banded pack With purchase Sample Digital reward Collection scheme Reward or task	Free
Prize promotions	Free draws Instant wins Competitions	Win
Cause-related promotions	Donation Sponsorship	Give

target audience probably having to mail-in to obtain it. The trend, with today's requirement for 'instant gratification', is for consumer response to be heavily weighted towards the 'immediate reward' techniques and mechanics. This trend has contributed to the increasing popularity of 'instant wins' and 'free draws' with major promoters.

Selecting the promotional technique is part of the strategic planning and flows from the objectives that must be precise and measurable. More than one technique can be used to achieve the objectives. For example, a promotion with a trial objective may well use both couponing and sampling. One with a loyalty objective may use a collectable free gift with purchase as well as a free prize draw. The advantages and disadvantages of any particular technique will vary according to the circumstances and, of course, the budget available. It is sensible to consider all the viable techniques in relation to the objectives and the profile of the target audience before making a final selection. Chart 20.2 gives

	Price			Special label pack	Free mail-in (pop = proof-of-purchase)		Free item		Competition	Free draw	Instant win on-pack	Charity
	Coupon on-pack	Coupon off-pack	Discount		One pop	Multi-pop	Sample	Goods with pack tf collectable				
Trial												
Generate trial purchase	L	H	H	M	H	L	H	H	L	M	M	L
Generate traffic (retail/web/publication)	L	H	H	L	L	L	H	H	M	M	L	H
Generate response (as opposed to purchase)	L	L	L	L	L	L	M	L	M	H	H	H
Loyalty												
Increase frequency of of purchase	H	M	L	M	L	H	L	L (H)	L	L	M	M
Increase weight of purchase	H	M	H	M	L	H	L	L (H)	L	L	M	M
Increase frequency visit (retail/web/publication)	H	L	M	L	L	L	L	L (H)	L	L	M	H
Awareness												
Reinforce above-the-line campaign	L	L	L	H	L	H	M	M	H	M	M	H
Create interest	L	M	L	M	H	L	M	M	M	H	H	H
Create awareness	L	M	L	L	L	L	M	M	M	M	M	M
Tactical												
Obscure price increase/differential	H	H	H	L	H	M	L	H	L	M	M	M
Gain retailer support/display	M	M	H	L	H	M	M	H	L	H	M	M

a broad outline of the major techniques and their strengths and weaknesses in achieving a range of objectives.

There are three main target audiences for promotions:

- Consumers
- Retailers / dealers (trade promotions)
- Company employees.

20.7.1   Consumer promotions

These are the promotions we all see in the market place on a day-to-day basis. They are a major tool in the marketing activity of the brand or service being promoted and, as such, need careful planning and execution. The promotion needs to be an integral part of the marketing plan and should not attempt to achieve objectives more suited to other elements of the marketing mix. Brand owners and agencies need to ensure that the promotion reflects the brand image and its advertising and that the offer or reward is consistent with the profile and behaviour patterns of the target audience. Best results are obtained from promotions with clear, concise copy and straightforward instructions for participation.

Chart 20.2 indicates the effectiveness of the most common techniques in achieving specific objectives – H = High, M = Medium, and L = Low.

20.7.2   Trade promotions

Historically, trade promotions have been recognised as those directed by the promoter at retailers and dealers to obtain additional support. With the huge expansion of sales promotion into every sector of industry they now encompass business-to-business promotions where the target audience is not a retailer or dealership. It could be, for example, a media company targeting media buyers in agencies or an automotive company targeting fleet buyers. Trade incentives to the staff of retailers and dealers reached their peak of popularity in the early 1970s until companies realised that there was little control and that in some cases they amounted to bribery. Today, many leading companies have banned third party promotions that benefit individual employees and will only accept those where the benefits offered are corporate.

20.7.3   Employee promotions

These are often described as staff incentive programmes and can make a significant contribution in helping a brand or service to achieve its overall objectives. They are designed to motivate staff either individually or as a team to perform to the very best of their ability and are often run in conjunction with a consumer promotion to gain commitment and involvement from the workforce. Typical objectives of this type of scheme are:

- To reward good performance,
- To increase sales performance,
- To improve customer service,
- To improve product knowledge,
- To reduce absenteeism.

A good example is BP's *Benefiting People*, which won a Bronze Award in the ISP Awards. The objective was to focus on key performance areas in their Express sites and motivate staff to work as a team to improve customer service. 'Mystery' motorists visited the participating sites and judged each one on its cleanliness, operational efficiency, level of service, and presentation of the staff. These results were combined with the measurement of fuel sales. Monthly reports were sent to each site with the winning sites receiving award plaques and cash bonuses. The scheme resulted in a 12 per cent sales increase versus the previous year and encouraged competitiveness across the site network.

It is important to remember that incentives offered to individuals either by their own employer or by a third party can be subject to tax and NIC liabilities and employers are obliged to declare any such schemes to the relevant authorities.

20.8   Research and evaluation

Research and evaluation go hand in hand. If the promoter has a sound evaluation programme in place then the need for research is diminished. Every promotion becomes part of the learning and research process providing an opportunity for gathering invaluable data that can be used in making decisions on future campaigns. The evaluation process starts at the planning stage when the measurement criteria are established and continues throughout the promotional period up to the time when full results, relevant audits and actual costs become available. The data generated by evaluation must be looked at in the context of the outside influences pertaining at the time the promotion was in the field. If a promotion, which was apparently extremely effective, achieving all its objectives within budget, was in the field at a time when the major competitor was suffering severe supply problems this must be added into the equation for future planning.

The data to be gathered against a promotion in order to obtain an effective evaluation would include:

- Promoted brands / services and promotion title,
- Names of agency and service companies,

- Examples of promotion materials,
- The objectives – quantifiable,
- Details of techniques and mechanics including proof of purchase requirement,
- Timing and duration of offer,
- Pricing versus competition,
- Location of offer – for example, national, regional, store specific,
- Research results,
- Budget versus actual costs,
- Level of achievement of objectives,
- Details of support material / advertising,
- Consumer panel data (AGB, TGI etc.),
- Trade distribution / deliveries,
- Retail audits (e.g. Nielsen),
- Sales force reports,
- Redemption figures,
- Competitive activity at time of promotion,
- Consumer correspondence / complaints,
- Trade and sales force feedback,
- Any unusual conditions at time of promotion (e.g. strikes, supply problems, retail price wars etc.),
- Recommendations for future activity.

Pre-promotion research provides a better understanding of the consumer and the promoted brand so contributing to a more effective campaign. In essence, it can identify the needs, preferences, desires and motivations of the consumers as well as their perceptions of the brand. Tactically, research can help in the selection of the appropriate technique, type of reward and proof of purchase requirement. Of course, what people say they will do does not always translate to their actions in the market place. Local or regional market place tests give the most reliable results, but can never replicate the conditions of the actual promotion. The best research normally uses a mixture of qualitative and quantitative approaches.

Qualitative methods include:

- Focus groups / group discussions
- Individual depth interviews
- Household depth interviews.

Quantitative methods include:

- Postal surveys
- Telephone surveys
- Hall test.

Research can also highlight any negative aspects of the offer such as unclear communication or an excessive proof of purchase requirement. Ideally, research should be an ongoing commitment to observing what is happening in the market place with specific projects being slotted in as necessary. High budget promotions should always be researched, but with a small budget the costs may be disproportionate. (See also Chapter 13 – Media Research and Chapter 14 – Consumer Research).

20.9   Creativity

Creativity is the aspirational ingredient that turns a good promotion into an exceptional one. Advances in technology such as the Internet, SMS and interactive TV have vastly increased the number of messages to which the consumer is exposed. In this highly competitive market place, brand owners are always looking for the creative twist that will give their campaign the competitive edge and will set it apart from all the others.

Accepting that sales promotion is limited to a fairly small range of techniques the creativity factor has to be delivered in the execution. An excellent example was *The 2002 Love Draw* mounted by Royal Mail. Valentine card postings were diminishing year-on-year and Royal Mail wanted to demonstrate that a Valentine card gave more pleasure than an e-card or text message. The mechanic used was simplicity itself. The sender of the Valentine card was asked to draw a large heart on the reverse of the envelope. This automatically qualified the *recipient* of the card for entry into a prize draw with prizes of Jaguar cars, weekends in Barbados and bottles of champagne. The fact that the recipient, not the sender, was the entrant prevented the promotion falling foul of lottery laws at the same time as significantly increasing the value of the card to the recipient. This promotion won a Gold Award for innovation in the ISP Awards, with judges commenting 'I wish I'd thought of that'. The results were exceptional, not only halting the decline in postings but also delivering significant incremental volume.

When looking for that creative twist it is important not to lose sight of the objectives of the promotion. If the creativity overshadows the purpose of the promotion then effectiveness is reduced. Recently, a *£1 Cash Back* loyalty offer on a meat-spread product was communicated to consumers in national press. The 'creative' headline was *Spread A Little Happiness* which many consumers took to be a charity appeal. Redemptions were well below expectations and the loyalty objective was not achieved. The same offer with the headline *£1 Cash Back* run at a later date performed well and achieved its objectives. The message is not to allow the creativity to obscure the message. Pitfalls such as this can be avoided if the briefing to the creative team addresses all the key issues and emphasises the importance of effectiveness. Trying to balance practicality with creativity is not easy but is an essential requirement when the overall objective is to stimulate action. For a comprehensive discussion of creativity, see Chapter 7.

20.10   Communication

The opportunities available for communicating a promotional offer are increasing every day and, in making the selection of which media to use, it is critical to have a good understanding of the target audience and its lifestyle. The communication media available to the promoter include:

- The pack and point of sale
- National and regional press
- Posters
- Cinema
- Radio
- Television
- Direct marketing
- Door to door
- Telephone
- Fax
- Internet
- Mobile telephones
- Field marketing
- Interactive display systems at point of sale.

The reach of the media has resulted in a much more discerning audience well able to assess the true value of any offer to which it is exposed. Bearing in mind the number of messages reaching consumers in anyone day, only those with a compelling incentive will be considered. For example, it is claimed that 50 per cent of consumers receiving unaddressed advertising leaflets take a quick look and throw them away; a further 15 per cent do not even look before discarding them. If the leaflets carry a coupon 33 per cent will keep all of them and a further 35 per cent will keep some of them.

The interactive nature of digital TV is of enormous benefit to promoters. As well as delivering a message it can be a call to action, inviting the consumer to enter competitions / prize draws or to apply for coupons, samples and brochures.

New media provides the biggest challenge and opportunity with its instant accessibility and personal relationship with the consumer. They enable precise targeting through data capture and with SMS a message can be delivered at a specific selected time, wherever the subscriber happens to be. On a cautionary note, too much of a good thing can be dangerous and the industry must ensure that it avoids public rejection through over saturation. The legal and Code of Practice aspects of new media are constantly being updated, but they are extremely complicated and specialist legal advice should always be sought in advance. (See Chapter 22 – Advertising: Self-Regulation and the Law).

20.11   Promotion administration

The promotional concept is only the beginning, and however good this is, it will only succeed if it is backed by well-resourced and well-planned administrative procedures. Administration starts on day one and continues through the promotional period to the final evaluation. The key to success lies in clear communication and the early establishment of responsibilities and accountabilities. The communication chain varies depending on the techniques and mechanics being used and could include some, if not all, of the following participants in the promotion:

- The promoter
- The agency
- The creative / design team
- The printers
- The premium supplier
- Safety testing laboratories
- The licensing company
- Road show teams
- The sales force
- The retailers
- The consumers
- The handling house
- Legal advisers
- Insurers.

Briefing the parties involved at an early stage is always beneficial giving them ample time to study the brief and time-line and to raise any questions or issues. The brief should be written and agreed between the parties before purchase orders are issued. Problems often arise when, due to the dynamic nature of promotions, changes need to be made to the original agreed brief or purchase order. If such changes are communicated by telephone, then it is essential to confirm them in writing with a request for an acknowledgement of receipt. Failure to do this can result in acrimonious disputes with the parties involved relying on printed terms and conditions, which, as we know, are written to cover any eventuality.

Tight or ridiculous deadlines can only be detrimental to a promotion and will result in errors. For example, a printer's delivery date is based on his having booked the machine time for a date following receipt of artwork. If the artwork is received two days later than agreed, then the delivery may well be 2 *weeks* later than agreed waiting for a replacement machine time slot.

Such variances must always be allowed for in the master time plan. Ideally those in charge of each promotion should plot a critical path that identifies in advance the type of problem that could arise at each stage. This is a 'What if ...' exercise and enables managers to set up contingency plans for coping with any difficulties. The management team should always check that production schedules have made allowances for any public holidays. This is especially important if merchandise is being imported from the Far East where the Chinese New Year can halt production for 3–4 weeks. Listed below are some important factors that will ensure the smooth running of a promotion:

- Involving all parties at an early stage,
- Clear written communication,
- Establishing lines of communication,
- Obtaining legal and Codes of Practice clearance,
- Obtaining signed and dated approval of proofs / samples,
- Agreeing payment terms,
- Identifying responsibilities / accountability,
- Defining budgets detailing what is included,
- Establishing time lines with allowances for unforeseen delays,
- Issuing clear and detailed purchase orders,
- Anticipating consumer queries / complaints.

Early inclusion of all parties involved in the implementation of the promotion enables them to understand the objectives of the offer and to contribute their specialist expertise thereby gaining their enthusiasm and commitment to the project.

20.12   Premium sourcing and buying

It is estimated that one in three promotions uses a piece of merchandise to incentivise its target audience. These premiums range from stickers, pens and diaries to soft toys, T-shirts, cameras and unique specially designed items. Premium buying is a specialist discipline and should not be delegated to the inexperienced. Before selecting a supplier, it must be established whether the item under consideration is suitable for the brand and the promotion mechanic. For example, in-pack premiums are subject to intensive constraints in terms of size, safety and hygiene and will need to have been tested by a laboratory for compliance with EC regulations.

There is no shortage of suppliers. The skill lies in selecting the correct one for the job in hand. The main choices available are:

- Sourcing houses
- Business gift houses
- Distributors
- Manufacturers.

Most premium buyers will have built up a list of approved suppliers with whom they work on a regular basis. When new suppliers are being considered their credentials should be thoroughly checked in terms of their trading policies on quality, safety, hygiene, factory conditions, workforce and their understanding of the promotions industry. If the supplier is a member of a recognised trade body such as the ISP or the British Promotional Merchandise Association (BPMA) it will give the added assurance that the company is committed to 'best practice' procedures.

The next most important consideration is the specification of the item to be supplied. Requesting a quotation for 50,000 T-shirts is totally inadequate. The supplier also needs to know:

- What material
- What style (e.g. V-neck, short sleeved)
- What colours
- What sizes
- Whether printed / embroidered
- If artwork will be supplied, and in what form
- If packaging will be required.

An initial estimate, which is not binding, can be given on an outline specification, but the final quotation, which *is* binding can only be given on a full and detailed specification. Hidden costs are a common pitfall and the buyer should always establish what is included in the quoted price. The following list includes most of the issues that will need to be agreed between the buyer and the supplier and confirmed in a contract signed by both parties:

- Detailed specification of item to be supplied,
- Provision and cost of samples,
- Quantity of premiums required,
- Minimum re-order quantities,
- Lead time for re-ordering,
- Length of time price can be maintained,
- 'Overs',
- Artwork and origination,
- Tooling costs,
- Production capacity,
- Quality control procedures,
- Guarantees and indemnities,
- Safety and CE marking,
- Timing,
- Packing details,
- Delivery details,

- Freight costs (if importing),
- Quotas and import documentation,
- Confidentiality,
- Exclusivity,
- Payment terms.

Quality and reliability are two critical factors when buying promotional merchandise, which means the lowest quotation is not necessarily the best. Poor quality or late deliveries will lead to consumer complaints and incur additional costs which could be higher than the savings made by accepting the lowest quotation.

Even with every possible safeguard in place progress and premium quality should be monitored on a regular basis so that any problems are identified at an early stage. Most buyers will visit the factory to gain a better understanding of the production process.

Pack insert premiums are subject to even more rigorous regulations which are beyond the scope of this chapter. However, the ISP has published guidance notes to cover this mechanic.

20.13   Europe

In the UK, we have a sophisticated promotional marketing industry fully committed to voluntary self-regulation and so free from over restrictive legislation. Unfortunately, this is not the case in many of the countries within the European Union and therefore restricts our ability to run pan-European promotions.

Since the early 1990s, there have been moves to harmonise the European promotional marketing industry and produce a level playing field that would increase the efficiency of pan-European activity and open up opportunities for the UK industry. The European Promotional Marketing Alliance (EPMA), a coalition between the ISP and the BPMA has been campaigning towards this goal since 1991. As with all European legislation progress is slow and tortuous and there are some Member States that would prefer the level playing field to be based on the restrictive legislation operating in their own countries. This is a major concern for anyone working in the UK industry regardless of whether or not they are active in Europe. When the Sales Promotion Regulation is finally agreed it will have to be applied to all UK promotions. Some of the current proposals causing concern are:

- To prevent promoters from making participation in an offer dependent on proof of purchase.
- To limit the value of goods provided as part of a promotion.
- To allow prize winners to claim cash alternatives to the goods / services offered.

- To ban pre-sale discounts.
- To allow Member States to continue to construct barriers to cross-border promotions.

The EPMA retains a lobbyist in Brussels and an MP (John Greenway) at Westminster to work on behalf of the UK to discourage any legislative initiatives that could impinge on our freedom to promote.

For those embarking on pan-European activity, proceed with extreme caution. At one time the industry published charts that indicated which techniques were permitted in each country. This has now proved to be impractical and unreliable in that legislation in any of the countries may change, and, even if a technique is allowed it may have specific constraints. The safest policy is to seek legal advice from experts versed in the legislation of the individual countries involved in the campaign.

20.14   The future

Promotional marketing is universally accepted as having a key role to play in the practice of good marketing. It permeates every industry in one form or another. Indeed, it has just been announced that the company managing London Congestion Charging is now offering performance incentives to its staff.

Although the techniques remain relatively unchanged the implementation is increasing in complexity. Practitioners will need to ensure that all their staff and the staff of the service companies they use are fully trained and competent in the understanding of sales promotion as a part of the marketing mix.

The communication of promotional offers will increasingly depend on new technology. The Internet, SMS, digital and interactive TV are ideally suited to promotional marketing and open up new opportunities for the promoter while satisfying the 'instant gratification' needs of the consumer.

Adverse European legislation is still a threat to the relative freedom enjoyed by the UK. To maintain these freedoms we must be able to demonstrate the advantages of self-regulation by strict adherence the existing laws and the British Code of Advertising, Sales Promotion and Direct Marketing. This will enable those lobbying on behalf of the industry to demonstrate that self-regulation is a viable alternative to legislation.

20.15   Summary

In this chapter:

- We have seen what sales promotion is and uncovered its origins back in the mid nineteenth century when the Co-operative Society was founded and the first trading stamp was subsequently developed by a competitor.

- Best practice in delivering sales promotion that meets its objectives was reviewed from setting the objectives, defining the strategy, budgeting, briefing and research and evaluation.
- A wide range of techniques and mechanics were reviewed with some consideration on what each does best.
- We have also seen the place for sales promotion as being complimentary to advertising as part of an integrated marketing communications mix and the need to keep a watchful eye on the detail of promotion administration.
- An overview of European sales promotion was given noting that changes are under consideration that may impact on the whole sales promotion arena.
- A look to the future was made with particular reference to new media.

21 Advertising: Self-regulation and the Law

Christopher Graham

Learning outcomes

By the end of this chapter you will:

- Have a clear idea of how the regulatory framework for advertising works.
- Gain an insight into the structure and function of the Advertising Standards Authority (ASA).
- See, through a selection of case studies, how the ASA operates.
- Understand the workings of the Code of Advertising Practice.
- Have investigated the recent changes to broadcast advertising regulation in the UK and taken a look at European regulation.

21.1 Introduction

In this chapter the reader will find a description of the framework of regulation, both voluntary and statutory, within which UK advertisers, agencies and media must operate. It is a framework that is constantly changing alongside developments in media, technology, marketing and, indeed, society itself. The growth of cross-border trade in the enlarged European Single Market is another driver of change. Over the next few pages, you will be introduced to the advertising codes and the bodies that enforce them. You will have a clearer idea of what makes marketing communications 'legal, decent, honest and truthful' and how to avoid getting into trouble with the Advertising Standards Authority (ASA), the communications regulator Ofcom or other statutory regulators such as the Office of Fair Trading (OFT).

A poster campaign for a perfume featuring a naked model (Sophie Dahl) was banned after nearly 1000 people complained to the ASA that it was offensive, yet the same image in fashion magazines was allowed. A £14 million re-branding by a leading food company had to be scrapped after the ASA ruled that health claims about the product had not been substantiated. A leading charity's fund-raising campaign backfired when the ASA found its press advertisements to be irresponsible, shocking and distressing in media likely to be seen by children. Why should these campaigns have been the business of anyone but the advertiser?

Advertising is designed to provoke a response. So, advertisements have to 'cut through' the noise of our mass communications society. Not surprisingly, everyone seems to have a view for or against particular advertisements – possibly for or against advertising itself. Whether advertisers like it or not, society has expectations.

The advertising and marketing business, made up of the advertisers of products, their agencies and the media in which their advertisements appear, has a very clear interest in playing by agreed rules. A practical concern with the ethics of advertising supports the integrity of commercial communications as a whole. After all, only if advertising is generally welcomed and believed do individual advertisements stand a chance of working. An agreed standard of what is fair makes for robust competition between products, in the interests of a free and efficient market. And more and more, ethical advertising is seen as part of corporate social responsibility generally.

The consequence of all this is that sticking to the rules and showing self-restraint is the price the advertising business has to pay for the freedom to advertise responsibly.

Commercial television came to the UK in 1955 and from the outset there were those who thought that it must be strictly controlled. Lord Reith of the BBC compared it to bubonic plague. But now the regulation of broadcast advertising may be about to adopt the self-regulatory approach that has applied to non-broadcast advertising since 1961. (See below for more information about TV and radio advertising.)

Historically, advertising regulation in the UK has developed in response to sticks as well as carrots. It was undoubtedly fear that non-broadcast advertising might be put under statutory control on the lines of the US Federal Trade Commission that galvanised the industry into establishing the Committee of Advertising Practice and the first non-broadcast advertising Code in 1961. The advertisers, agencies and media agreed to act together in support of high standards in advertising. A year later, the independent Advertising Standards Authority (ASA) was established to administer the Code. Similarly, it was a further threat to legislate by the Wilson government that, in 1975, brought forth the robust funding system that underpins the ASA and CAP today and guarantees its independence. A recommendation of the then Director General of Fair Trading in 1978 and subsequent EU legislation led in 1988 to the creation of a legal backstop for misleading advertisements in the form of referral to the OFT.

21.2   How the self regulatory system works

Non-broadcast advertising in the UK is governed by a system of self-regulation administered by the ASA. At its heart is a simple idea – that the advertisers, agencies and media will act together to maintain agreed standards. Like the best simple ideas, the actions that follow from it are impressive and far-reaching. Non-broadcast advertising is, for the most part, 'legal, decent, honest and truthful' not by Act of Parliament, but because the partners in the business have decided that it should be so.

Self-regulation, in contrast to statutory controls, has a number of significant advantages from the point of view of consumers, advertisers and policymakers. Self-regulation is a faster way of dealing with apparent breaches of the rules than going to law. It is also much more 'user friendly' being readily accessible, informal and free to the complainant. The system is able to judge in accordance with the spirit of the rules, not just the letter. Being non-statutory, self-regulation is best placed to respond flexibly to the fast-changing world of new media.

But the self-regulatory system is also part of a 'joined up' approach to consumer protection involving statutory authorities, at local, national and European levels. Some issues are best dealt with by the self-regulatory process, while others are legal matters to be dealt with by trading standards departments or national agencies such as the Financial Services Authority.

UK advertising overwhelmingly complies with the rules, but where an advertiser demonstrates inability or unwillingness to co-operate with the ASA in withdrawing misleading claims, the matter can be referred to the Office of Fair Trading (OFT) for action under the Control of Misleading Advertisements Regulations. The threat of involving the legal backstop is usually enough to secure compliance.

21.3   Advertising Standards Authority

The ASA is responsible for non-broadcast marketing communications and sales promotions in newspapers and magazines, on posters, in the cinema, direct mail, leaflets, Internet pop-ups and banner ads, commercial e-mails and short messaging service (SMS). The 'A' in ASA is much more than just conventional advertising. A single set of rules (the CAP Code) covers direct, online and mobile marketing, as well as classic 'above-the-line' advertising. Marketers who do not see themselves as part of 'advertising' could be in for a rude awakening if their marketing communications breach the Code.

The ASA's remit does not extend to classified private advertisements, packaging and labels, point of sale displays, shop windows or advertisers' own websites. Sales promotions are in remit wherever they appear. The ASA does not adjudicate on fly-posting (which is illegal anyway) or on election advertisements.

The ASA is constituted so as to be independent. The ASA Chairman, chosen by the Advertising Standards Board of Finance, has to be independent of the advertising business and serves for a fixed term. He or she appoints a 12-member Council to adjudicate on advertisements that may have breached the rules. Two-thirds of the Council members are independent are appointed following public advertisement and for limited terms of office. The one-third minority of 'industry members' bring advertising industry experience to the consideration of complaints, but do not speak for any particular interest.

In 2003, the ASA received a total of 14,277 complaints, concerning 10,754 advertisements. A total of 1,514 advertisements were changed or withdrawn as a result of ASA action. The Top Ten most complained about campaigns accounted for no fewer than 1,623 complaints – 11% of the total. 92% of complaints were from consumers, while 8% were brought by competitors. Complaints about offensiveness or social irresponsibility attracted fewer complaints than did misleading advertising. 45% of complaints were received by e-mail. What the bald statistics cannot measure is the number of misleading or offensive ads that never get published just because self-regulation is effective.

Before the ASA Council can adjudicate on whether a complaint of a Code breach should be upheld or not upheld, the staff conduct an investigation. Straightforward cases may be resolved quickly; but, if a formal investigation is necessary, the advertiser is asked to comment on the complaint and submit evidence in support of any disputed claims. The ASA can call on outside experts to help assess technical issues. The final decision rests with Council. Adjudications are published weekly on the ASA website. Where a breach of the Code has been established, the advertiser must amend or withdraw the advertisement and give a written assurance that it will not run again. Repeat offenders are challenged in the interests of consumers and also of competitors who do stick to the rules.

The effectiveness of the system depends on thorough follow-up of adjudications – to ensure that the advertiser complies with an instruction to withdraw or amend problem advertisements. Compliance action ensures that rulings are enforced across the market or sector so that advertisers are not unfairly disadvantaged. Regular monitoring of publications ensures that problem advertisements are challenged. Each week, ASA staff scan more than 4000 advertisements. Sector-by-sector and medium-by-medium, research establishes where compliance may be less than it should be.

The ASA has to be fair and thorough in its investigations, but also timely in its decision-making. There is a procedure for independent review of ASA adjudications in certain circumstances. Standards of Service set out what consumers, advertisers, and competitors can expect when dealing with the Authority. The ASA publishes information about its performance. Although some investigations can be complex and protracted, the ASA resolves the average complaint in less than 30 days.

The ASA attaches considerable importance to good communications – an informative website, good literature, and an Annual Report. ASA and CAP staff give a programme of presentations and help to train industry practitioners. The ASA's website www.asa.org.uk publishes the latest adjudications each week. These can be searched by advertiser, agency, medium, sector, subject, and Code clause. The website also contains an online version of the Annual

Report, policy briefings, news, and material for schools and colleges. The site links to a parallel website for the Committee of Advertising Practice www.cap.org.uk, which includes information for practitioners – including the Code, Help Notes, Ad Alerts, and Advice Online.

21.4 Committee of Advertising Practice

The Code is drafted, maintained and revised by the industry represented in the Committee of Advertising Practice (CAP). CAP comprises 17 organisations and trade associations, covering advertisers, agencies, media, and carriers. CAP keeps issues under review so that the Code can be kept up to date on the basis of research. CAP produces Help Notes to brief the industry in the ASA's interpretation of the Code or to alert practitioners to particular developments in highly competitive sectors. To give just a few examples, Help Notes give guidance on price comparisons (lower / lowest prices), superiority claims (better / best) and claims that require qualification (small print). Help Notes also explain permissible approaches to advertising for utilities, vacuum cleaners, air fares and mobile phone packages where competition is particularly fierce.

CAP also provides a Copy Advice service, which is free, fast and confidential from competitors. This is not the same thing as pre-clearance. CAP Copy Advice is usually not mandatory and Copy Advice does not bind the ASA Council. But many a campaign has been saved from disaster by a timely check with Copy Advice and a crucial change made, perhaps at the eleventh hour. Under certain circumstances, advertisers can be instructed to seek and follow Copy Advice (see sanctions below). Where an advertiser has not given a written assurance following a breach of the Code, an Ad Alert from CAP will warn media to check with Copy Advice before accepting further advertisements.

Copy Advice can involve submitting material to the CAP team for consideration or perhaps merely a telephone enquiry. There is a 90 per cent target for turning round written enquiries within 24 hours. The service is also used by newspaper and magazine staff who are doubtful about an advertisement that has been submitted for publication. Similarly, the Royal Mail or poster site owners might check with Copy Advice before accepting a booking for a mail shot or an outdoor campaign. Advice Online, a searchable online database of practical advice, has been introduced to assist practitioners in checking material against a deadline.

21.4.1 Panels

In addition to the full Committee, two specialist Panels provide practical advice to CAP and to the ASA in the light of developments in advertising and business. The Panels help to develop policy and identify sections of the Code that may need revision. Complex ASA investigations can also be referred to either the General Media Panel or the Sales Promotion and Direct Response Panel for a view before the ASA adjudicates. The ASA Council is not bound to accept this advice, but the view of experienced professionals on, for example, the likely meaning of claims, can be invaluable.

21.4.2   Funding the self regulatory system

One of the reasons why the system is effective is that it is properly resourced. Funding is through a levy paid by all advertisers using non-broadcast media. Media agencies collect 0.1 per cent of the space costs of all display advertising. Royal Mail collect 0.2 per cent of the delivery contract for direct mail advertising. The money is paid not to the ASA but to a funding body, the Advertising Standards Board of Finance (ASBOF). This arms length system means not only that the ASA has the resources to do a thorough job, but also, and even more importantly, the ASA's independence cannot be comprised. As a result, the ASA has 'taken on' some of the biggest multinational corporations, secure in its funding and unafraid. A similar levy system is envisaged for broadcast advertising should proposals from Ofcom for self-regulation of broadcast advertising go ahead.

Example

A claim that a children's fruit drink, Ribena ToothKind, did 'not encourage tooth decay' was found by the ASA to be misleading because the advertisers were unable to provide adequate substantiation. The stakes were high and the advertiser was a big multinational drug company. The investigation was protracted. The ASA took advice from two outside experts. Eventually, the advertisers challenged the ASA's upheld adjudication in the courts, fielding one of the country's top QCs. The ASA was able to stick to its guns because it was adequately funded and did not have to consider whether it could afford to stand up to a big advertiser. The ASA's stance was vindicated. The following year, the advertisers reported a drop in sales for the long-established Ribena brand.

21.4.3   The CAP Code

The CAP Code – or the British Code of Advertising, Sales Promotion and Direct Marketing, to give it its full title – sets the rules with which all marketing communications must comply. The current edition came into force in March 2003 and is the 11th edition in a series that began with the first code in 1961.

The requirement that advertising must be 'legal, decent, honest and truthful' stems from the original advertising code of the International Chamber of Commerce (ICC), which remains the framework text for all advertising codes. Marketing communications should be prepared with a sense of responsibility to consumers and to society, and should respect the principles of fair competition generally accepted in business. The Code is applied in the spirit as well as the letter.

The Code is made up of general provisions, applicable to all marketing communications; rules for sales promotions and direct marketing; and specific rules on various topics such as alcoholic drinks, children or environmental claims.

Many breaches of the Code are about claims that cannot be proved. The rules say that 'before distributing or submitting a marketing communication for publication, marketers must hold documentary evidence to prove all claims, whether direct or implied, that are capable of objective substantiation.' Another key provision states that 'no marketing communication should mislead, or be likely to mislead, by inaccuracy, ambiguity, exaggeration, omission or otherwise.' Testimonials alone are not sufficient.

Examples

Tetley dumped the familiar cartoon Tea Men with their flat caps and overalls for a new approach to their marketing – a big health claim about antioxidants in tea and their beneficial effect on the heart. But when the advertisers were unable to substantiate specific claims about their product, a national poster campaign had to be halted and a more generalised approach substituted.

Claims in an advertisement for the Advanced Hair Studio featuring a leading cricketer were found to be misleading. Before and after photographs of the cricket's head of hair were not accepted as adequate substantiation for the specific claims. Even testimonials and an *affidavit* were no substitute for proper scientific evidence of the effectiveness of the hair loss treatment.

Another important Code requirement is that 'marketing communications should contain nothing that is likely to cause serious or widespread offence'. The Code states 'particular care should be taken to avoid causing offence on the grounds of race, religion, sex, sexual orientation or disability. Compliance with the Code will be judged on the context, medium, audience, product and prevailing standards of decency'.

How is the ASA to judge what is offensive? The test is necessarily subjective and it does not make the ASA an arbiter of taste. Bad taste is not an offence under the Code. The ASA does not try to impose standards on society, but seeks to reflect society's view of the minimum standard that is acceptable. The ASA is not an agent of social engineering, nor does it bend to political correctness. Context is all-important. The Code requires the ASA to stop advertising that is so offensive that the advertisers forfeit their right to advertise. Clearly, offence must be widespread or keenly felt by a minority. In the end, it is for the ASA Council to strike a balance between the competing rights of advertiser and public.

Examples

Posters for comedian Ali G's 'In Da House' movie had to be taken down after the ASA ruled that the 'Tax Da Panty' would cause widespread offence. The advertisement had been refused by all but one of the poster contractors. Complainants had objected that the poster was offensive and sexist.

There are provisions relating to anti-social advertising – not causing fear and distress, safety issues, not condoning or provoking violence or anti-social behaviour, protection of privacy.

Other Code clauses govern consumer protection issues – prices, availability of products and guarantees.

Examples

Low-cost airlines have been required by the ASA to make clear the precise location of destination airports and to quote prices inclusive of VAT and other charges.

Big electrical goods retailers have been challenged to ensue adequate availability of bargains featured in their advertising. The stores also cannot claim to guarantee 'the lowest prices' when the ASA can see that the same prices have been matched by their competitors. In 1996, Dixons challenged such an ASA ruling in judicial review proceedings, and the High Court upheld the ASA ruling.

Maintaining a level playing field between advertisers is an important function of self-regulation. The Code sets the rules for comparisons with other products, and bans imitation, denigration and taking unfair advantage. In this, the Code reflects, where necessary, the requirements for permissible comparative advertising as set out in the Control of Misleading Advertisements Regulations 1988 (as amended). In particular, comparisons must be of like with like.

Rules on sales promotion apply to offers that involve a range of direct or indirect additional benefits, usually on a temporary basis, designed to make goods or services more attractive to purchasers. The Code sets rules for free offers and free trials, the suitability of promotional items, competitions and so on. Direct marketing rules cover distance selling and database practice. The ASA will help consumers get their money back when a mail order transaction goes wrong or get 'junk' mail stopped where a consumer has registered with the Mail Preference Service that they do not wish to receive advertising by direct mail.

Particular care must be exercised when advertising products in sectors that have proved sensitive on public policy grounds, such as alcohol, children, motoring or gambling. Some of the key points are summarised below, but there can be no substitute for studying the Code itself in detail and the various Help Notes that amplify it may be found on www.cap.org.uk.

Strict rules on alcohol advertising are framed to ensure that marketing communications contain nothing that is likely to lead people to adopt styles of drinking that are unwise. For example, advertisements must be socially responsible and should neither encourage excessive drinking nor suggest that drinking can overcome boredom, loneliness or other problems. Marketing communications must not be directed at people under 18 through the selection of media, style of presentation, content or context in which they appear. No medium should be used if more than 25 per cent of its audience is under 18 years of age. Advertising must not suggest that any alcoholic drink has therapeutic qualities or can enhance mental, physical or sexual capabilities, popularity, attractiveness, masculinity, femininity or sporting achievements. Marketing communications must not portray drinking alcohol as the main reason for the success of any personal relationship or social event. Drinking alcohol must not be portrayed as a challenge, nor should it be suggested that people who drink are brave, tough or daring for doing so.

Similarly, advertising to children (under 16s) is governed by clear rules. For example, marketing communications addressed to, targeted at or featuring children must contain nothing that is likely to result in their physical, mental or moral harm. Advertisers should not exploit their credulity, loyalty, vulnerability or lack of experience. They should not actively encourage them to make a nuisance of themselves to parents or others and should not undermine parental authority (so-called 'pester power' is banned). Advertisements should not actively encourage children to eat or drink at or near bedtime, to eat frequently throughout the day or to replace main meals with confectionery or snack foods.

Motoring advertisements must not be irresponsible. Marketers should not make speed or acceleration claims the predominant message of their marketing communications. Marketers should not portray speed in a way that might encourage motorists to drive irresponsibly or to break the law and should not condone irresponsible driving.

Marketing communications for betting and gaming, too, must be socially responsible and must not encourage excessive gambling.

Other areas where advertising has generated frequent complaints to the ASA include health and beauty products, therapies and 'cures', diets, business opportunities and financial products.

Health and beauty advertisements generate many complaints to the ASA. Similarly, promoters of miracle 'cures' and wonder diets are regularly challenged to substantiate their claims. Advertisers are expected to hold evidence from properly conducted scientific tests. In addition, specific rules govern the advertising of these products and promoters need to be familiar with them to avoid running into trouble with the ASA.

Complaints about business opportunities and financial products often concern exaggerated or unsubstantiated earnings claims or confusing terms and conditions in the small print.

21.4.4   Code sanctions

Compliance surveys show that non-broadcast advertising overwhelmingly complies with the Code. Recent checks showed 99 per cent compliance rates for posters while the record of other sectors stood at 91 per cent direct mail, 99 per cent for the Internet and 97 per cent for sales promotions. How is it that a non-statutory system can achieve such high levels of compliance? First of all, as we have seen, the business has an interest in maintaining the credibility of marketing communications. And the partners in self-regulation – advertisers, agencies and media – move decisively against anyone who steps out of line.

So, the ASA is working with the grain of the business when it requires compliance with its adjudications. Advertisers have to give an assurance that an advertisement that is judged to have breached the Code will be amended or withdrawn. A persistent offender may be required to follow CAP Copy Advice before advertising again. The media can be warned about a problem advertiser through an Ad Alert from CAP.

One of the ASA's most effective sanctions is the unwelcome publicity often generated by the publication of an upheld adjudication on the ASA's website. But what about those advertisers and agencies whose 'bad boy' brands relish the notoriety? A poster pre-publication vetting sanction allows CAP to send irresponsible advertisers to the sin bin, requiring them to pre-clear their poster advertising with Copy Advice. Without clearance, the poster owners will not accept future campaigns. Similarly, Royal Mail will withdraw bulk discounts that make direct mail economic where a direct marketer persistently breaches the Code. Royal Mail has refused to accept mailings from some of the worst offenders. The ASA will be seeking to negotiate similar arrangements with new entrants to the liberalised postal market. Another telling sanction for agencies involves excluding campaigns that have been banned by the ASA from eligibility for industry awards.

The legal backstop of referral of misleading advertisements or impermissible comparisons to the OFT has been described as 'the big stick in the cupboard'. Certainly, legal action under the Control of Misleading Advertisements Regulations is the sanction of last resort; but the fact that the sanction has to be invoked so rarely suggests that the deterrent effect is sufficient. Non-broadcast advertising really does regulate itself very effectively.

Examples

Posters advertising a range of underwear had to be taken down after the ASA upheld complaints that the campaign referred to masturbation and oral sex.

Magazines could only run a blank double page spread when the 'Benetton baby', bloody and screaming, was banned for offensiveness.

Royal Mail withdrew bulk discounts for a misleading prize draw mailing. The ASA also referred the marketing consultancy concerned to the OFT after repeated breaches of the Code.

21.5   New media

The impact of digital communications has introduced powerful new advertising media and challenged the regulators to keep up. Although many of the new media look like TV, they are not necessarily licensed by Ofcom.

High-quality video spots on broadband Internet. 'Television' advertisements on trains, buses and in some taxis, or on big screens at railway stations. Screens in phone boxes, on the garage forecourt or in the gym. Interactive TV ads after two clicks. None of these are licensed and so Ofcom has no means of enforcing its codes.

Even where there can be no doubt as to which regulator is responsible for new advertising media, advertising on the Internet and mobile media illustrate both the strengths and weaknesses of current regulatory arrangements. The adaptability of self-regulation has allowed the ASA to stay abreast of technological developments. But some aspects of the Internet defy effective regulation, whether statutory or non-statutory.

Self-regulation applies to Internet advertising in paid-for space – banners, pop-ups and commercial e-mails. The ASA does not apply the Code to editorial on advertisers' own websites. This is a pragmatic approach, recognising a distinction between messages that are 'pushed' at consumers and those that are 'pulled' from sites chosen by the user. In addition, since such sites have only limited third party involvement in their publication, there is no third party to enforce ASA adjudications. There is also a limit to what any regulator can do in the face of a global phenomenon. For example, the bulk of SPAM originates from outside the European Single Market.

In approaching new media, the ASA has to work with others to secure compliance. The premium rate co-regulator ICSTIS is sometimes able to act where the response channel in, for example, SMS is a premium rate phone number. The OFT is able to work with other national enforcement authorities to tackle rogue traders.

The impact of the Internet is forcing all national governments to consider how abuses can best be tackled; but it would be wrong to suggest that any approach, voluntary or statutory, has yet fully matched the ingenuity of the scammers and the spammers. The principle of 'let the buyer beware' remains the watchword for consumers online.

Examples

Advertising for a Tom Cruise movie *Minority Report* included a voice message sent to mobile phones that recipients found alarming. It was not clear from the outset that the message was an advertisement. What is more, some recipients had to pay to retrieve the advertisement from their mailbox. The ASA upheld the complaints.

The ASA rules on complaints about misleading, offensive and irresponsible commercial e-mails and SMS. The 11th edition of the Code outlawed the sending of unsolicited e-mails to consumers before the legislators did. But advertisements that have been ruled unacceptable for television have found an airing on the Internet.

21.6   Broadcast advertising

The new single regulator for telecommunications and broadcasting, Ofcom, took over from the Independent Television Commission (ITC) and the Radio Authority (RAu) at the end of 2003. Ofcom is a statutory regulator with responsibilities under the Communications Act for, among many other things, programme standards including advertising. Ofcom licenses commercial TV channels and radio stations and requires compliance with the TV and radio advertising codes.

TV and radio licensees have to pre-clear advertisements before transmission. For the most part, pre-clearance is the job of the broadcasters' own self-regulatory bodies, the Broadcast Advertising Clearance Centre (BACC) and its radio equivalent the RACC.

Ofcom also has statutory responsibilities to consider contracting out appropriate functions to effective self-regulatory bodies that are adequately resourced and sufficiently independent of the industry they supervise. The Bill also mandates Ofcom to encourage effective self-regulation where that is appropriate.

The impact of new digital media and increasing convergence have forced a re-think of the approach to the regulation of TV and radio advertisements. Multichannel and interactive television have seen the development of teleshopping channels and direct response advertising. Year 2004 saw a proposal to move to a 'co-regulatory partnership' between Ofcom and a self-regulatory system 'under the banner of the ASA'. New arrangements for the regulation of TV and radio advertisements could be in place before the end of 2004.

21.7   The law

As we have seen, all marketing communications must be legal as well as decent, honest and truthful. Legality is ultimately, of course, a matter for the courts. So what are the most relevant laws, and how can a self-regulatory system help to keep advertising legal?

Much of the law governing marketing now comes from Brussels in the form of EU Directives that have to be enacted into UK law. For example, the Television Without Frontiers Directive sets a basic framework for the regulation of broadcasting including advertisements on TV and radio. Current legislative proposals would establish a prohibition on unfair commercial practices, including in advertising, that would apply across the European Single Market. Legislation is also contemplated on nutritional claims and sales promotions. The advertising industry seeks to influence such legislation to ensure that it is workable, and ASA and CAP seek to anticipate developments.

Directives on misleading and comparative advertising are implemented in the UK in the Control of Misleading Advertisements Regulations 1988. These can ultimately be enforced by the Office of Fair Trading, but the OFT recognises the ASA as the 'established means' for applying them. So, the Code contains detailed provisions on misleading and comparative advertising, which reflect the legislative requirements.

The CAP website lists more than 200 separate pieces of legislation governing different aspects of marketing – from the Accommodation Agencies Act to the Wireless Telegraphy Act. The most important general pieces of legislation for the marketer are listed below. Compliance with the Code will frequently go a long way towards ensuring compliance with the legislation, since the Code often either anticipates or is strengthened to reflect legislative developments.

Trade Descriptions Act 1968 and Consumer Protection Act 1987

These make it a criminal offence to publish a false trade description or misleading price indication. They are enforced by local trading standards, but the ASA operates in a 'joined-up' way with them, direct or through the OFT, and many complaints which do not require or cannot be pursued in a criminal investigation are dealt with successfully by the ASA. One great advantage that the non-statutory self-regulatory system offers over the law, in terms of consumer protection, is the reversal of the burden of proof. Advertisers have to prove that their claims are true. The ASA does not have to prove a breach of the Code. In fact, inability to substantiate a claim is itself a breach of the Code. In the courts, of course, the prosecuting authorities have to establish that an offence has been committed. Note that these statutes cover labelling whereas the Code does not.

The Consumer Protection (Distance Selling) Regulations 2000 and Electronic Commerce (EC Directive) Regulations 2002

These apply to marketing where a sale may be made without the seller and consumer ever meeting, and again are enforced by trading standards.

Data Protection Act 1998 and Privacy and Electronic Communications (EC Directive) Regulations 2003

These govern how a marketer goes about gathering and using personal data. Again, the ASA and CAP maintain a regular dialogue with the statutory body, the Office of the Information Commissioner.

The Code does not seek to cover private civil law rights, such as contractual rights, or rights in intellectual property. It is essential when planning a marketing campaign for the marketer to ensure he is not going to infringe a third party's rights, for example, by misusing a trade mark, or copying someone else's artistic, literary or musical work without a licence. The Copyright Designs and Patents Act 1988 and the Trade Marks Act 1994 cover this. In the case of a hard-hitting campaign, the law of defamation may also be relevant.

Finally there is the much more detailed sector specific legislation. The following areas are particularly closely regulated:

1. Most Financial Services are regulated by the statutory Financial Services Authority or the OFT. Under the Financial Services and Markets Act 2000,

the FSA regulates marketing for investments and investment advice, banking and life insurance. This list may get longer in the course of 2004 when the FSA is expected to become responsible for the regulation of mortgage advertising as well as other insurance products. The OFT regulates other consumer loans under the Consumer Credit Act. The Government has published proposals for tighter regulation still. The CAP Code applies to financial marketing communications that are not regulated by the FSA or OFT, but all financial marketing communications are subject to Code clauses that cover "non-technical" elements of communications, e.g. serious or widespread offence, social responsibility and the truthfulness of claims that do not relate to specific characteristics of financial products.

2. Prescription-only medicines may not be advertised to the public. Health-related claims in marketing communications addressed only to the medical, dental, veterinary and allied professions are exempt from the Code. The Medicines Act 1968 and its regulations, as well as regulations implementing European Community Directive 92/28/EC, govern the advertising and promotion of medicines and the conditions of ill health that they can be offered to treat. Guidance on the legislation is available from the Medicines and Healthcare Products Regulatory Agency (MHRA), formerly the Medicines Control Agency (MCA).

3. Food advertising, where safety is also an issue, is governed by the Food Safety Act 1990, the Food Labelling Regulations 1996 and many other regulations.

4. Promoters of prize competitions need to comply with the Lotteries and Amusements Act 1976 or they could find themselves running an illegal lottery.

5. Fly-poster campaigns will be in breach of the Town and Country Planning Act's control of advertisement regulations (and, incidentally, any campaign that includes fly-posting is ineligible for industry awards).

In general the ASA operates in a 'joined-up' way with statutory authorities and in partnership with other non-statutory regulators. For example, with the premium rate regulatory body ICSTIS which has a co-regulatory relationship with Ofcom.

Where a breach of the law may have been committed, it would be wrong for an advertiser to face double jeopardy – both from the ASA and the courts. For this reason, the ASA leaves to the statutory authorities the handling of complaints about what might constitute criminal offences. There is also the pragmatic consideration that consumers' interests are best served if a single agency pursues a particular complaint. Similarly, if the parties are involved in civil litigation about the same issue there will be little point in the ASA becoming involved.

21.8   Self-regulation in Europe

In recent years, advertising regulators in the UK have had to learn to adopt a wider perspective. The UK is part of the European Single Market. Economic, political and technological developments are driving more cross-border trade. The Euro, enlargement of the EU, satellite TV and the Internet all play their part. Cross-border advertising gives the trend a further push. Direct marketing communications from one Member State can target consumers in any of 24 other countries of the Single Market. (See Chapter 19, p297).

Since 1992, it has been necessary for self-regulatory systems in any country of Europe to be able to resolve cross-border complaints on the basis of mutual recognition and the country of origin principle.

Example

UK recipients of misleading prize draw mailing complained to the ASA. But the mailing originated in the Netherlands. The ASA referred the complaint to the Dutch equivalent advertising standards body, the SRC. The SRC ruled that the mailing was misleading and instructed the advertiser to change the claim.

The European Advertising Standards Alliance (EASA) describes itself as 'the single authoritative voice of advertising self-regulation in Europe'. Self-regulatory bodies from all the Member States belong to it, including, from the UK, both the ASA and TV clearance centre, BACC. EASA has undertaken to extend the self-regulatory network to all 10 new Member States in the course of 2004. At European level, EASA is supported by industry federations representing advertisers, agencies and media.

Making self-regulation effective across the Single Market is essential to counter proposals for advertising restrictions emanating from the European Commission and the European Parliament. Policy towards sensitive sectors such as alcohol, children, and food can be quite restrictive elsewhere in the EU. Unless advertisers demonstrate effective self-restraint, the pressure for more advertising bans can only increase.

20.9   Conclusions

As a final thought, it is worth considering whether this framework of self-regulation has not paradoxically itself established a further means of promoting brands. Advertisers deliberately courting notoriety or charities seeking to draw attention to unfashionable concerns on a limited budget may gain a short-term public relations advantage from a fight with the ASA. But for every 'cool' brand or cause that relishes the disapproval of the regulator, there is an advertiser whose 'bad boy' antics bored and irritated potential customers or a campaign tamed by Ad Alerts, poster pre-vetting or compulsory Copy Advice.

Undoubtedly, the consumer is the winner from self-regulation. Misleading claims are stopped. Fair play between advertisers promotes competition. And society is protected from unacceptable and antisocial images.

Not bad for a system that most of the time relies on the mutual interest that advertisers, agencies and media share in the credibility, acceptability and reputation of marketing communications.

21.10   Summary

In this chapter:

- We have seen how self-regulation works to the advantage of both advertiser and consumer alike.
- We gained an insight into the structure and function of the advertising standards authority.
- Through a selection of case studies we saw how the ASA operates, its panels, how it is funded, and gained an insight in to its code of practice and the sanctions it places.
- Finally, we have investigated the recent changes to broadcast advertising regulation in the UK and taken a look at European regulation.

Further reading

All the adjudications mentioned in this chapter, as well as more recent adjudications, may be consulted on the ASA's website.

Useful links

Advertising Standards Authority (ASA) www.asa.org.uk
Committee of Advertising Practice (CAP) www.cap.org.uk
Office of Communications (Ofcom) www.ofcom.org.uk
Broadcast Advertising Clearance Centre (BAAC) www.bacc.org.uk
Radio Advertising Clearance Centre (RACC) www.crca.co.uk
European Advertising Standards Alliance (EASA) www.easa-alliance.org
Office of Fair Trading www.oft.gov.uk
Government consumer protection portal www.consumer.gov.uk
Trading standards portal www.tradingstandards.gov.uk
Information Commissioner www.informationcommissioner.gov.uk
Advertising Association (AA), the tripartite trade federation
     www.adassoc.org.uk
Direct Marketing Association (DMA) www.dma.org.uk
ICSTIS (premium rate services regulator) www.icstis.org.uk

Books and articles

Modern Markets: Confident Consumers, DTI Consumer White Paper, July 1999.

Alternatives to State Regulation, Better Regulation Task Force, July 2000.

Saunders, D. *Shock in Advertising*, Batsford, 1996.

Saunders, D. *Sex in Advertising*, Batsford, 1996.

The Advertising Association / WARC, *Advertising Statistics Year Book*.

Advertising Self-Regulation: The Essentials, European Advertising Standards Alliance, 2003.

Saunders, D. *20th Century Advertising*, Carlton, 1999.

Bernstein, D. *Advertising Outdoors Watch This Space*! Phaidon Press, 1997.

22 Training for a Career in Advertising

Ann Murray Chatterton

Learning outcomes

By the end of this chapter you will:

- Review the background to current training practices.
- Recognise key characteristics sought by agencies.
- Understand key skills to be learnt during a career in advertising.
- Find information sources for professional training resources.
- Review various academic options.

22.1 Introduction

Typically, people who work in advertising are drawn from a variety of educational backgrounds. While there is a slow but steady increase in the number who have studied a related degree at university (as the availability of these courses expand), it is still the norm that graduates will enter the industry with no previous training in the discipline of advertising. The industry thrives on strong teamwork, both to manage projects requiring a broad range of skills but also to come up with lateral problem-solving ideas in the first place. And teams that approach the problems from different perspectives tend to be more productive. Agencies are also much more likely to recruit on the basis of personality traits rather than knowledge acquired, as the latter can be provided by the agency through learning programmes and professional development.

22.2 Characteristics of agency practitioners

Agencies look for people who are good communicators, problem solvers, team builders and time jugglers; people with passion, curiosity and tenacity. They need people who understand that creativity and commerciality can work effectively together; and people with integrity but who also know how and when to have fun!

1. Communication skills are key as you will need to interact with many different types of people and will need to be able to understand how best to communicate effectively with each in order to achieve your end goal.
2. The practice of advertising itself is all about identifying business problems and seeking solutions that achieve defined business goals; the obvious solutions may not be the most effective, so you will need to think outside the box (incidentally, advertising as a communications tool is not always the right answer and, as a professional adviser, agencies will advise their clients if alternative solutions may be more appropriate).
3. The management of an advertising project will usually require you to work with several different agency departments, other agencies, specialist suppliers (such as photographers), media owners, clients and their internal departments – so the ability to work as part of a team, and to encourage team spirit is a key attribute.
4. The work is often very varied and, in most agencies, you will find yourself working on more than one client account; this will increase your knowledge and enable you to apply your learning from one situation to another. But it also means that you will need to be able to prioritise and juggle several projects at one time.
5. The ability to convince others of your point of view is helped enormously if you are able to communicate your degree of involvement in the idea – being passionate is very compelling!
6. Although advertising often reflects popular culture, it is vital to remember that it does so in order to achieve a commercial objective – it is not art for art's sake but creativity used as a powerful business tool. So, you will need to develop an understanding of business issues and how what you do can contribute to the financial growth of your client. Advertising is recognised by Government as a strong economic driver and, in itself, it accounts for ca. 1.6 per cent of the UK's gross national product.
7. Building trust within relationships, both within the agency and with the client, is a vital ingredient for success, so recruiters will look for evidence of integrity in potential applicants – and for people that have the personality to enjoy and get on with people.

22.3   Background to industry training

The advertising industry has grown ever more complex and sophisticated over the last 50 years, with a consequent impact on the training and developmental needs of its practitioners. In the 1950s, agencies had comparatively large numbers of staff and training was carried out on the job, under the guidance of a more senior practitioner (a process nicknamed 'sitting with Nellie'). In order to provide more formal standards, the industry developed the theory-based

Certificate of Advertising and Marketing (CAM) which became the standard qualification for advertising practitioners until the late 1970s, when – within the advertising industry – the emphasis on academic learning was switched to experiential training, delivered by the industry's trade body, the Institute of Practitioners in Advertising (IPA). Today, although most of the UK's advertising agencies are classified as (Small to medium-sized enterprises) SMEs with less than 250 employees, most now boast a designated training manager who is responsible for the training budget. Moreover, increasingly, the industry is committing itself to a new industry initiative, the IPA's Continuing Professional Development (CPD) accreditation standard, launched in 2000 to encourage continuous professional development for all staff, not just a selected few. Today, training has become a board-level matter, with agencies viewing their training plans as a key competitive tool, both in attracting top talent, in managing their human capital, and in developing and retaining client business.

22.4   The industry approach to training

As advertising as a discipline has come of age, and the business community as a whole has become more advertising literate, the industry has had to hone its skills to retain its perceived value within the business mix. Agencies typically put together comprehensive graduate training programmes which are a blend of induction programmes, practical training on the job, internal training (either using senior staff to share their knowledge or employing external, specialist trainers) and training provided by industry bodies – in particular, those provided by the IPA. The IPA's seven-stage training programme has been devised to support your career training needs from entry point, at graduate level right through to managing director, with each stage designed to provide relevant learning as you develop throughout your career: trainee, junior, manager, director, associate director, board director and senior management. Developed over the last 20 years, the IPA seven-stage training programme is mostly delivered by current leading IPA agency practitioners who are committed to giving something back to the industry in which they work so as to train its future talent (IPA courses are only open to IPA member agency staff); as such, it is unusual and is the envy of many international advertising trade bodies. The training spans craft, creative judgement, business understanding, interpersonal and agency management skills; as you develop through your career, you will develop invaluable, and eminently transferable, skills such as project management, analytical, negotiation, teamwork, financial management, people development and leadership skills, as well as the craft skills required to do your job effectively. A description of the seven stages can be found at the end of this chapter.

In addition to the annual seven-stage programme (most of which is based on week-long residential courses), the IPA develops shorter, ad hoc training courses relating to specific issues arising from the changing market place, such as digital marketing and media neutral planning. Since the introduction of its CPD accreditation programme, it now also runs weekly half-day workshops, covering a wide spectrum of topics as requested by its members to meet the learning needs of an increasingly complex and integrated marketing communications industry.

In addition to the IPA programme of ca. 50 courses, there are other industry associations that provide courses and workshops.

D&AD, British Design and Art Direction Association provides a programme of courses designed specifically for creatives* that cover craft skills, survival skills, management skills as well as purely inspirational sessions. Called 'Workout', it seeks to stretch creatives through challenge, mental exercise and stimulation.

The Advertising Association *(AA)* also has a programme of seminars and courses, the best known of which is the annual Media Business Course. Its aim is to bring together the sellers of media with the buyers and planners and it consistently attracts the support of senior executives who share their experiences and enthusiasm with those who are working on media buying and planning in media agencies and client organisations.

The Media Circle, an organisation that comprises both media agencies and media owners, also run a programme of events where experienced media practitioners share their knowledge with newcomers to the industry. Courses range from the Introductory Evening Series that runs twice a year over a period of 10 weeks and covers all disciplines within the ever-changing media world, to negotiation, presentation, sales and planning skills.

The Account Planning Group provides craft skills training in the art of planning. Courses are designed to add to the knowledge store of those involved in planning, from agencies, clients and market research suppliers. Courses include qualitative and quantitative research, creative briefing, behavioural change and creative role reversals (so that you can understand what it is like to be on the receiving end of a creative brief!).

Primarily intended for the 'client side of the business' is the programme of workshops organised by the Incorporated Society of British Advertisers (ISBA). These range from introductions to the business to advanced programmes for senior business executives: all designed to help clients increase their skills and get the maximum value from their promotional budgets.

In addition to the above, other organisations such as NABS (the industry's professional charity), the Creative Circle, Radio Advertising Bureau (RAB), the International Advertising Association (IAA) and the Publicity Club of London all provide training seminars to help the industry's workforce to operate more effectively and to learn key craft skills.

---

* Shorthand term for creative people in an advertising or design agency.

22.5   The IPA's Continuous Professional Development in Advertising Accreditation Standard

In 2000, at the behest of its members, the IPA introduced a people development accreditation standard, based on the key elements of the Government's service industry's Investors in People (IiP) standard. The impetus lay in the recognised need to raise and maintain a minimum standard of people development amongst IPA member agencies in order to attract top graduate talent and to provide clients with the most effective service.

Accredited agencies must demonstrate, on an annual basis, that they have a training plan designed to achieve key business goals, thus linking training to bottom-line performance; an induction programme for all new staff; an annual appraisal system that also reviews training needs; and the individual maintenance of a learning log recording both formal and informal developmental learning. At the time of writing, nearly half of the IPA's member agencies are either accredited or committed to achieving the IiP standard and it is the long term aim of the trade body to achieve full-scale adoption of the standard including most, if not all of the top 20 media and top 20 creative agencies amongst its members. A national IPA Excellence in CPD Awards programme is held on a biennial basis, and winning papers are available on the IPA's website.

22.6   Professional qualifications

With the continuing emphasis on mobility within the European Union, the demand for professional qualifications has grown apace. The industry provides two specific qualifications for people working in the advertising industry. However, there are also qualifications provided by other sectors of the communications industry which are useful for advertising practitioners as the boundaries between the various marketing communication disciplines continue to blur and as agencies extend the services that they offer. An overview of all the qualifications available across the industry is shown below but you will also find contact details and web URLs at the end of this chapter, should you wish to find out more.

22.6.1   IPA

While the advertising industry has embraced practical, experiential learning, the IPA has also recently launched the first in a series of planned qualifications, linked to its CPD programme. An annual IPA Foundation Certificate examination is available to staff working for IPA member agencies committed to achieving the CPD accreditation standard. It is aimed at people in their first year, or for those who are working in support functions and who wish to extend their knowledge. The Certificate tests knowledge of the brand communications process, acquired during agency CPD training programmes; it covers a syllabus comprising marketing, client service, research and evaluation, communications planning (including both media planning, creative planning and briefing), ideas and execution (including TV production, print production, media buying and legal and regulatory issues). The objective is to ensure that, no matter what type of agency you might join, you will be able to gain a base knowledge of all aspects of the industry. The Certificate is supported by an online programme, developed by current practitioners within the industry; it is available to IPA members committed to the CPD standard, and accessed via the CPD zone on the IPA website. The online programme is available free of charge and is accessible to suit the individual, both in terms of time and geographical location. It is expected that this will become part of the standard graduate recruitment training programme for IPA CPD agencies.

The Certificate will be followed in 2005 by the IPA Excellence Diploma that will encourage individuals with between 3 and 5 years' experience to explore the industry's understanding of how brand communications work in practice. Required reading will include the IPA Effectiveness Awards papers which demonstrate through careful analysis the value that advertising can contribute.

22.6.2   CAM Foundation

In 1970, a registered charity was established to oversee the examinations of the communications industry; this has now become the Communications Advertising and Marketing Education Foundation, an organisation that provides integrated marketing programmes which are taught through academic colleges throughout the UK. It provides awards at two levels: the CAM Advanced Certificates, leading to the Advanced Diploma in Communication Studies and the Higher Certificates, leading to 'Higher Diploma' qualifications. Students are usually working practitioners either in marketing or marketing communications companies and, therefore, the majority obtain their tuition at evening classes. However, other options for study include day classes, intensive courses and distance learning.

Advanced Certificates: The six areas of study are marketing, advertising, direct marketing and sales promotion, media, public relations and research / consumer behaviour. This spread of syllabus ensures that delegates gain a multidisciplinary qualification which is very useful in today's marketplace. If all six Advanced Certificates are completed successfully, the student will achieve the Advanced Diploma in Communications Studies. In addition, students can now also study an Advanced Certificate in e-marcoms (marketing communications).

Higher Certificates: The three areas of study are management and strategy, PR management, and planning, implementation and evaluation. Successful completion of the Higher Certificates (and/or the Advanced Diploma) enables entry to the Higher Diploma in Integrated Marketing Communication.

The CAM Foundation has now been incorporated into the Chartered Institute of Marketing.

22.6.3   The Chartered Institute of Marketing

Similar to the content and style of the CAM qualifications, those provided by the Chartered Institute of Marketing (CIM) are also provided through accredited academic colleges, as well as through intensive short courses and distance learning. Qualifications include the Diploma in Marketing, the Advanced Certificate in Marketing, the Certificate in Marketing, the Introductory Certificate in Marketing, Arts Marketing, Customer Relationship Management (CRM), E-marketing and Marketing within SMEs.

22.6.4   The Institute of Direct Marketing

The education body that serves the direct marketing industry provides four qualifications: the Diploma in Interactive and Direct Marketing, the Certificate in CRM, the Certificate in E-Marketing and the Certificate in Direct Marketing. The learning is developed by current practitioners and is available through seminars held by the IDM, followed by self-directed study or through distance learning.

22.6.5   The Institute of Public Relations (IPR)

The professional institute that takes a leading role in the education and training of the PR industry offers two qualifications: the Diploma in Public Relations and the Advanced Certificate in Public Relations. These are owned by the IPR and seek to provide a benchmark for the industry in terms of raising professional standards. They are cover both knowledge and practice and are delivered through accredited colleges throughout the UK as well as being available in a distance learning format.

22.6.6   The Institute of Sales Promotion

The professional institute that serves the promotional marketing industry offers two qualifications: the Diploma and the Certificate in Promotional Marketing. Both are available as correspondence courses with optional seminars and tutorials.

22.6.7   The Market Research Society

The professional institute that serves the market research community provides a number of qualifications: MA in Market Research, MSc in Market Research Management, MSc in Marketing Programme, MA Social and Market Research

Practice, Diploma in Market Research, Advanced Certificate in Market and Social Research Practice and the Introductory Certificate in Market and Social Research. Qualifications are available either through face-to-face courses, distance learning or accreditation of in-company training.

22.7   The provision of academic learning

Most of the courses and qualifications outlined above are available to practitioners already working in the industry. For those that are not (yet), there is an increasing number of full- and part-time courses provided by colleges and universities throughout the country. Available for 2004, there were 127 degree courses in advertising listed by the University & Colleges Admissions Service (UCAS) of which 10 were solus advertising and the rest combined with other, related subjects such as business, design, communications, digital, marketing, etc. On a wider basis, Art, Design, Media, Marketing and Communication Studies degree courses number each in the thousands.

Additionally, there are diploma courses in art and design and media production provided by colleges of high and further education leading to the qualifications awarded by Edexcel, the UK's awarding body that offers a range of both general and specialist qualifications including Business and Technology Education Council (BTEC's) and National Vocational Qualifications (NVQ's). Kogan Page produce a book called 'British Qualifications: a comprehensive guide to educational, technical, professional and academic qualifications in Britain' that provides details of all university awards and associated careers.

22.8   Summary

In this chapter:

- We have seen that the industry is committed to training and developing its talent.
- A variety of training courses designed for practitioners in the industry available from a range of industry bodies (as well as a plethora of bespoke training providers) have been outlined.
- We have seen that there is a range of professional qualifications available to those who wish to study further that focus on different aspects of the marketing communications industry.
- It was noted that comprehensive graduate training programmes are established in all of the larger graduate recruiting agencies and most are committed to achieving the IPA's Continuous Professional Development Accreditation standard.
- We have seen that the industry's trade body, the IPA, provides a benchmark for professional development standards (through CPD), opportunities to learn specific skills through its comprehensive Seven Stage training

programme and the ability to demonstrate knowledge and understanding reached at key stages in your career through its new programme of qualifications.

- That there are numerous related academic courses now available was noted, although it should be said that attendance at these courses does not necessarily guarantee a place on an agency's application shortlist, given the industry's search for diversity and excellence in talent and the competition that exists to get into the industry. However, they do give a good grounding in the theory behind the practice of advertising.

The IPA's seven stages

Stage 1: Evening Series for Trainees to broaden their horizons and give them insight into the advertising business as a whole.

Stage 2: Campaign Planning course to create understanding of the advertising process and how strategic planning generates effective advertising.

Stage 3: Understanding Your Client's Business to enhance understanding of how client companies operate and of the business context for advertising decisions.

Stage 4: Excellent Account Direction / Planning to equip account handlers / planners with the skills and knowledge to perform their role with confidence and expertise.

Stage 5: Advertising and Business Effectiveness to enhance understanding of business strategy and financial management through exposure to modern management and marketing techniques.

Stage 6: Four modules covering People Management, Negotiation Skills, Understanding Agency Finances and Financial Impact of Marketing designed to equip Board Directors with knowledge and understanding of key management issues.

Stage 7: Senior Agency Management Programme to provide intensive training to senior managers and leaders on how to run their organisations effectively.

Organisations

The organisations referred to in this chapter are:

- The Account Planning Group 16 Creighton Avenue, London N10 1NU
  Tel: 020 8444 3692
  www.apg.org.uk
- The Advertising Association Abford House, 15 Wilton Road, London SW1V 1NJ
  Tel: 020 7828 2771
  www.adassoc.org.uk

- The Advertising Standards Authority Brook House, 2–16 Torrington Place, London WC1E 7HW
  Tel: 020 7580 5555
  www.asa.org.uk
- Communications Advertising and Marketing Education Foundation Moor Hall, Cookham, Maidenhead, Berkshire SL6 9QH, UK
  Tel: 01628 427120
  www.camfoundation.com
- The Chartered Institute of Marketing Moor Hall, Cookham, Maidenhead, Berkshire SL6 9QH
  Tel: 01628 24922
  www.cim.co.uk
- Creative Circle 22 Poland Street, London W1F 8QQ
  Tel: 020 7734 9334
  www.creativecircle.co.uk
- D&AD 9 Graphite Square, Vauxhall Walk, London SE11 5EE
  Tel: 020 7840 1111
  www.dandad.org.uk
- Edexcel Stewart House, 32 Russell Square, London WC1B 5DN
  Tel: 0870 240 9800
  www.edexcel.org.uk
- The Incorporated Society of British Advertisers 44 Hertford Street, London W1Y 8AE
  Tel: 020 7499 7502
  www.isba.org.uk
- The Institute of Direct Marketing 1 Park Road, Teddington, Middlesex TW11 0AR
  Tel: 020 8614 0277
  www.theidm.com
- The Institute of Practitioners in Advertising 44 Belgrave Square, London SW1X 8QS
  Tel: 020 7235 7020
  www.ipa.co.uk
- The Institute of Public Relations 15 Northburgh Street, London EC1V 0PR
  Tel: 020 7253 5151
  www.ipr.org.uk
- The Institute of Sales Promotion Arena House, 66–68 Pentonville Road, London N1 9HS
  Tel: 020 7837 5340
  www.isp.org.uk
- The International Advertising Association (IAA) 12 Rickett Street, London SW6 1RU
  Tel: 020 7381 8777
  www.iaauk.com

- Kogan Page 120 Pentonville Road, London N1 9JN
  Tel: 020 7843 1934
  www.kogan-page.co.uk
- The Market Research Society 15 Northburgh Street, London EC1V 0JR
  Tel: 020 7490 4911
  www.marketresearch.org.uk
- Media Circle 44 Belgrave Square, London SW11 3LR
  Tel: 020 7235 3657
  www.mediacircle.co.uk
- NABS 91a Berwick St, London W1F 0NE
  Tel: 020 7240 6005
  www.nabs.org.uk
- The Publicity Club of London c/o Communication Solutions,
  33 St James's Street, London SW1A 1HD
  Tel: 020 7925 1132
  www.publicitycluboflondon.co.uk
- Radio Advertising Bureau (RAB) The Radiocentre, 77 Shaftesbury
  Avenue, London W1D 5DU
  Tel: 020 7306 2500
  www.rab.co.uk
- UCAS Rosehill, New Barn Lane, Cheltenham, Gloucestershire GL52 3LZ
  Tel: 01242 222444
  www.ucas.ac.uk

Index

To Jan, always

The Practic sing